PATHWAYS TO PROMINENCE
IN NEUROPSYCHOLOGY

PATHWAYS TO PROMINENCE IN NEUROPSYCHOLOGY

Reflections of Twentieth-Century Pioneers

edited by

Anthony Y. Stringer, Ph.D.

Eileen L. Cooley, Ph.D.

Anne-Lise Christensen, Ph.D.

Routledge
Taylor & Francis Group

NEW YORK AND LONDON

Psychology Press
Taylor & Francis Group
711 Third Avenue
New York, NY 10017

Psychology Press
Taylor & Francis Group
2 Park Square, Milton Park, Abingdon,
Oxfordshire OX14 4RN

Psychology Press is an imprint of the Taylor & Francis Group, an informa business
First issued in paperback 2012

Library of Congress Cataloging-in-Publication Data

Pathways to prominence in neuropsychology:
reflections of twentieth century pioneers/
[edited by] Anthony Y. Stringer, Eileen L. Cooley, Anne-Lise Christensen.
p. ; cm.
Includes bibliographical references and index.

1. Neuropsychology—History. I. Stringer, Anthony Y. II. Cooley, Eileen L.
III. Christensen, Anne-Lise.
[DNLM: 1. Neuropsychology—Biography. 2. Neuropsychology—Personal Narra-
tives. 3. Neuropsychology—trends. 4. History of Medicine, 20th Cent. WZ
112.5.N4 P297 2002]
QP360.P365 2002
612.8'09—dc21   2002017807

ISBN13: 978-0-415-65074-8 (Paperback)
ISBN13: 978-0-863-77686-1 (Hardback)

Oscar A. Parsons and Laird S. Cermak passed away shortly after completing their chapters for this book. They were an inspiration to the end. We dedicate this book to their lasting legacy.

Contents

III. PATHWAYS IMAGINED

Contributors

Martin L. Albert
Boston University School of Medicine
Boston, MA, USA

Dirk J. Bakker
Free University
Amsterdam, Netherlands

Russell M. Bauer
University of Florida
Gainesville, FL, USA

Dmitri Bougakov
Institute of Neuropsychology
    and Cognitive Performance
New York, NY, USA

Meryl A. Butters
University of Pittsburgh
    School of Medicine
Pittsburgh, PA, USA

Nelson M. Butters
(1937–1995)

Laird S. Cermak
(1942–1999)

Anne-Lise Christensen
Gentofte, Denmark

Eileen L. Cooley
Agnes Scott College
Decatur, GA, USA

Philip DeFina
The Fielding Graduate Institute
Santa Barbara, CA, USA

Elkhonon Goldberg
Institute of Neuropsychology and Cog-
    nitive Performance
New York, NY, USA

Kenneth M. Heilman
University of Florida
Gainesville, FL

Edith Kaplan
Boston University School of Medicine
Boston, MA, USA

Manfred J. Meier
Bruce, WI, USA

Lena Moskovich
Brookline, MA, USA

Mary Brown Parlee
Massachusetts Institute of Technology
Cambridge, MA, USA

Oscar A. Parsons
(1920–2000)

Karl H. Pribram
Radford University
Radford, VA, USA

Antonio E. Puente
University of North Carolina
    at Wilmington
Wilmington, NC, USA

Ralph M. Reitan
Reitan Neuropsychology Lab
Tucson, AZ, USA

Byron P. Rourke
University of Windsor
Windsor, Ontario, Canada

Otfried Spreen
University of Victoria
Victoria, British Columbia, Canada

Anthony Y. Stringer
Emory University School of Medicine
Atlanta, GA, USA

Anthanase Tzavaras
University of Athens, Greece

INTRODUCTION

1

Neuropsychology
A Twentieth-Century Science

Anthony Y. Stringer
Eileen L. Cooley

Definition and Introduction

Scholars disagree over when and how the term "neuropsychology" entered the clinical science vernacular. Bruce (1985) traced its origin to Sir William Osler's 1913 opening address for the Phipps Psychiatric Clinic of Johns Hopkins Hospital. In that address, Osler used the term to describe a new area of instruction that would encompass both the biological and psychological aspects of psychiatric disease. Karl Lashley also used the term, albeit in passing, in a 1936 presentation to the Boston Society of Psychiatry and Neurology (as cited in Bruce, 1985). Hebb (1949) had the distinction of being the first to use the term in a book title when he published *The Organization of Behavior: A Neuropsychological Theory*. "Neuropsychology" appeared again in the title of a 1960 collection of Karl Lashley's writings (Beach, Hebb, Morgan, & Nissen, 1960). The term, however, was neither used nor defined in the body of either of these books (Kolb & Wishaw, 1990).

The word began to acquire its modern meaning in a 1948 symposium at the American Psychological Association (APA) appropriately entitled "Neuropsychology." In this symposium, Hans-Lukas Teuber described procedures he and Morris Bender developed to study the behavioral effects of penetrating missile wounds to the brain (Benton, 1987). Teuber's seminal presentation not only brought the term into common use but may very well mark the beginning of neuropsychology's recognition as a distinct professional discipline.

Today, the field of neuropsychology centers on the study of the relationship between brain function and behavior. Its concern is the "role of individual brain systems in the organization of human psychological activity" (Luria & Haigh, 1992, p. 335), and in this regard it includes neuroscientific and cognitive research. The field also encompasses such clinical activities as the differential diagnosis of neurobehavioral disorders, detection of brain damage, lateralization and localization of brain lesions, establishment of functional baselines from which to measure deterioration or improvement, remediation of cognitive deficits, and competency determination (Parsons, 1991).

This chapter reviews the origins and development of neuropsychology as a science and profession. We briefly discuss the disagreement among scholars over whether new scientific disciplines represent evolutions or revolutions in thinking, and we contrast the ability of these two models to explain the emergence of neuropsychology. We trace the development of neuropsychology from its slow beginning to the dynamic profession of today. It will be evident that the success of the field directly results from the contributions of a remarkable generation of scholars and clinicians, many of whom share their stories in this book. We conclude with a preview of the chapters that follow.

The Origin of Neuropsychology: The Revolution that Wasn't

In seeking an origin for neuropsychology, one approach is to search for an event marking the historical transition from a pre-neuropsychological era to the current era of neuropsychology. This birth event may be akin to a revolution of the kind described by Kuhn (1970), in which a new paradigm for understanding data and conducting research emerges to supplant previous paradigms. This new paradigm will dominate a field (or in this instance, will create a new field) until it too encounters a crisis in which it must give way to another paradigm that provides a better explanation.

As no actual blood is spilled, scientific revolutions are in danger of going unnoticed by historians and the public. Consequently, Cohen (1985) and Porter (1986) suggested what may be considered "lines of evidence" to indicate when a revolution in science has occurred. These lines of evidence include

1. Presence of an entrenched orthodoxy within a field that garners intense resistance.
2. Documentation of a clear break with the entrenched orthodoxy. The break must be international in scope and be accompanied by a sense of urgency and an aura of grandeur.
3. Belief by contemporaneous scientists that a revolution occurred.
4. Treatment of the event as a revolution by later writers who discuss the period.
5. Judgment of later historians of science that a revolution took place.
6. Opinions from modern scientists supporting interpretation of the event as a revolution.

As these lines of evidence suggest, the consensus of contemporaries and historians provides the strongest justification for calling an event in the history of science "revolutionary."

The revolutionary model has been employed to construct a narrative of the history of general psychology. The birth event in this narrative is Wundt's founding, in 1879, of the first experimental psychology laboratory in Leipzig. Wundt established experimental introspective methods for studying mental events, a methodology that dominated the field until mentalism was overthrown by the behaviorists (circa 1913). The shift from introspection of covert mental events to observation of overt behavior lasted until the cognitive revolution of the mid-1950s. If Kuhn's model truly applies, we can expect that the Goliath of cognitive psychology will also eventually meet its David.

Leahey (1992) evaluated the "lines of evidence" supporting this narrative of psychology's history and concluded that with the *possible* exception of the founding of Wundt's laboratory, no true revolutions have occurred. Nonetheless, this narrative remains psychology's dominant "creation myth." If we follow Leahey's example and critically examine the events making up the history of neuropsychology, we will be hard-pressed to construct a creation myth paralleling that of experimental psychology.

Nonetheless, attempts have been made to identify a particular event or person that marks the transition from pre-neuropsychology to extant neuropsychology. Reitan (1989) cited the establishment of Halstead's laboratory for the psychological study of brain damaged patients in 1935. Hebb (1983) considered Karl Lashley to be "practically [the field's] founder" (p. 5) and also emphasized the "revolution" in neurology and neurosurgery stimulated by Wilder Penfield's exploration of the effects of frontal lobe ablation (circa 1936). Delis and Ober (1986) reached even further back to the late 1800s to find an origin in Broca's and Wernicke's descriptions of aphasic syndromes after focal lesions of the left hemisphere.

If indeed neuropsychology began in revolution, we should find at least a rudimentary consensus on when the first shot was fired. No such consensus is evident. Broca's description of the aphasic syndrome bearing his name appeared in 1861. Karl Lashley's seminal work was conducted from 1921 to 1930, and Halstead and Penfield began their separate contributions in the mid-1930s. Thus, we have events spanning a period of some 70 years vying for preeminence in the origin of neuropsychology. So great is the disagreement that the period during which Halstead founded his laboratory and conducted the bulk of his research is considered by others to be a time of "relative quiescence" (Delis & Ober, 1986, p. 244) when neuropsychology virtually disappeared (Hebb, 1983).

In contrast to the revolutionary model, Hartman (1991) argued persuasively that neuropsychology did not arise from one pivotal event. Instead, neuropsychology was the inevitable next step in the development of that portion of clinical science devoted to the study of the human brain. Hartman's view owes much to the evolutionary perspective of Boring (1963) and is similar to Leahey's (1992) evolutionary narrative of the history of psychology. This evolutionary model emphasizes continuity and the growing sophistication of enduring traditions within psychology and its subfields.

From the evolutionary perspective, historical context paved the way for neuropsychology's emergence. Instead of a single event marking the field's birth, we see many events conspiring to bring the new science into existence. Neuropsychology emerges neither at a precise time nor at a definite place. No individual can be singled out as the field's progenitor. Rather, neuropsychology has many pioneers, some working in isolation, others in varying degrees of collaboration, but all contributing something vital. In short, many pathways merged to create this new field.

The Evolutionary Pathways to Neuropsychology

When we try to date the emergence of neuropsychology, we are placed in a position not dissimilar from that of the paleontologist attempting to date the emergence of modern Homo sapiens. The best the paleontologist can say is that modern humans emerged somewhere on the plains of Africa some 200,000 years ago. Similarly, in determining the origin of neuropsychology, the highest precision we can achieve is to define a span of time during which the evolutionary pathways merged to create this new field.

While some (e.g., Delis & Ober, 1986) identify the medical studies conducted by the European neurologists Broca and Wernicke as a point of origin, it seems more accurate to conceptualize this pioneering work of the late 1800s within the context of the history of neurology. Their work represented a significant break from earlier pseudoscientific phrenological theories and techniques. Similarly, we place Korsakoff's work on amnesia, Dejerine's observations of alexia, and Leipman's description of apraxia—all cited by Delis and Ober as launching neuropsychology—within the history of neurology. As important as this work was in advancing the science of brain and behavior, it differs in methodology from the work that defines neuropsychology. While there is considerable continuity of theory and content between classical European neurology and the emergence of neuropsychology, we believe the following elements delineate neuropsychology as a distinct discipline:

1. The use of experimental psychology methods in both single case and group studies of brain-damaged patients.
2. The use of standardized, repeatable procedures and norm–referenced tests.
3. The quantification of behavior through the use of scores and summary indexes.
4. The use of various statistical methods, including factor analysis, in test development and in the analysis and reporting of data.

The issues investigated by Broca, Wernicke, Hughlings-Jackson, and other neurologists of the late 1800s are unquestionably significant in the history of both neurology and neuropsychology. The work of these neurologists laid the foundation for much of what was to come. But what distinguishes neuropsychology from the neurology of the late 1800s is the method by which these issues are investigated (Kolb, 1999). Neuropsychology is informed by the work of these pioneers in neurology, but their work is not truly neuropsychological in nature. Despite its scientific and historical importance, this work is best considered a forerunner—one of the many paths leading to later work that would be neuropsychological both in content and method.

Another pathway emerged in the 1880s when Galton opened a laboratory in London where individuals paid as little as a few pennies to take acuity, reaction time, and a variety of psychophysical tests. Out of this work grew the factor analytic method that has been so critical in the validation of mental ability tests. Galton's work saw its practical culmination in the testing program developed by Binet and Simon in early twentieth-century France to identify and place children in need of special education. A second practical offshoot of Galton's work emerged as World War I created the need to identify the strengths and weaknesses of large numbers of military recruits. It is estimated that as many as one million soldiers underwent mental ability testing during World War I (Franz, 1919, as cited in Hartman, 1991).

Clearly social and historical factors played a crucial role in the emergence of neuropsychology. Galton's work may have remained an esoteric curiosity had educational institutions not faced a crisis created by large numbers of children who were not benefiting from normal modes of instruction. Similarly, the mental ability testing movement was fostered by the need for increasingly large numbers of soldiers because of the new phenomenon of world war. The armament industry's production of increasingly sophisticated weapons technology, demanding greater skill from the soldier recruit, also contributed to the adoption of mental ability testing by the military.

Just after World War I, Shepherd Ivory Franz (1919) published a textbook detailing tests of tactile sensation, motor coordination, praxis, language, attention, memory, visuospatial perception, reasoning, and intelligence. By 1924, a dynamometer, a finger tapper, a motor steadiness test, a form board, and various tests of color vision, vibration sensitivity, attention, and memory were available (Hartman, 1991). Thus, by the time psychologists were ready to begin work that we would now call neuropsychological, many standardized and norm–referenced tests were ready for adoption.

Psychologists soon began putting such tests to use in the experimental study of clinical populations. Gatewood (1909) and Cotton (1912) contrasted patients diagnosed with dementia praecox with normal controls. Yerkes, Bridges, and Hardwick (1915) used standardized, norm–referenced tests to investigate a variety of patient populations including dementia praecox, chorea, epilepsy, syphilis, and hypopituitarism.

As psychologists were becoming increasingly aware of the relevance of their methods to the study of medical populations, they began to advocate for increased use of this scientific methodology. Franz did so in his series of lectures to the Government Hospital for the Insane starting in 1910 (Hartman, 1991). In a remarkably prescient 1917 address to the Toledo Academy of Medicine, Trettian advocated a role for psychology not only in the diagnosis of neural disorders but also in the reestablishment of function through retraining (Hartman, 1991).

While these psychologists were turning their attention to the study of clinical populations, Karl Lashley was conducting equally important animal investigations. It would be wrong to regard this work as unconnected to research with human subjects. Indeed, Franz was Lashley's teacher. Franz, in turn, was a student of Cattell. Lashley was undoubtedly aware of, and influenced by, the mental abilities testing movement and the new work being conducted with clinical populations.

Before Lashley, attempts to localize complex behaviors in discrete brain areas had been boosted by the clinical investigations of Broca, Wernicke, and others. From 1921 to 1930, however, Lashley's careful lesion studies dispelled any hope of finding a simple one-to-one correspondence between behavior and anatomy. Lashley systematically demonstrated the resistance of learned skills to brain ablation and began to reveal the true complexity of brain–behavior relationships.

From the foregoing, we can identify four pathways leading to the emergence of neuropsychology:

1. Investigations of aphasia, alexia, apraxia, amnesia, and other disorders by neurologists working in the tradition of the medical case study.
2. The mental ability testing movement beginning with the work of Galton and culminating in practical applications in educational and military institutions.
3. The early use of standardized, norm–referenced tests to study clinical populations and a growing recognition of the relevance of psychological methods to medical diagnosis, rehabilitation, and science.
4. Careful experimental studies with animals utilizing ablation techniques to delineate the complexity of brain–behavior relationships.

The 1930s: Quiescence or Beginning?

Hebb (1983) concluded that the investigation of brain–behavior relationships virtually disappeared after the 1920s as a direct result of Lashley's work. After Lashley's lesion studies, some thought that any further attempt to localize complex functions in discrete brain areas was a futile endeavor. Others, instead, cite the rise of behaviorism to explain this declining interest in brain–behavior relationships (Delis & Ober, 1986). Hebb even attempted to connect Lashley's work with the rise in behaviorism, but admitted that both Tolman and Skinner denied any such influence.

Contrastingly, we would argue that the period after the 1920s was far from quiescent. Rather, it might be conceived of as a beginning. By 1930, all that remained for the emergence of neuropsychology was one final and crucial step. Two laboratories were established in the 1930s for the study of neurological patients using psychological methods, but only one would point the way toward modern neuropsychology.

In 1930, Harriet Babcock began a longitudinal study of syphilitic patients. Babcock's work was strikingly modern not only in its subject matter—the cognitive effects of a neurologic disease—but also in its methodology. Babcock employed traditional psychological methods, incorporating normal controls in her research for comparison to her clinical sample. Babcock's methods were clearly defined and repeatable, and she tested her subjects with standardized psychological tests. Her approach included the quantification of deficits in discrete mental abilities as well as the use of an "efficiency index" to characterize the overall functioning of her patients. Virtually all the qualities of the modern neuropsychological study were present in Babcock's research. Nonetheless, Babcock's results were never consistently replicated, in part because of the imprecision with which patient groups were defined in psychiatric settings of the era (Hartman, 1991). In this respect, Babcock failed to transcend the limits of her time.

Five years later, in 1935, Ward Halstead opened a laboratory at the University of Chicago for the psychological study of neurology and neurosurgery patients. Halstead was an experimental psychologist trained in the use of ablation techniques. He brought the meticulous methodology of the animal laboratory to this new research endeavor and often returned to animal investigations for inspiration in designing procedures for testing humans. Indeed, the Category Test was inspired by Heinrick Klüver's work on stimulus generalization in monkeys following brain ablation (Reed, 1985). Since stimulus generalization decreased after brain ablation in monkeys, Halstead reasoned that a task that required generalization across stimulus sets might also be sensitive to brain damage in humans.

Halstead also found inspiration in his patients. He is reputed to have spent considerable time talking and socializing with patients and their families, and observing patients in such nontraditional settings as sports events (Reed, 1985). This undoubtedly gave him a unique perspective from which to design his test battery.

Like Babcock's approach before him, Halstead's approach was distinctly psychological, utilizing experimental design and control; standardized, repeatable, and objective examination methods; quantification of patient responses via test scores and summary indexes; and sophisticated statistical analysis of results. What may have allowed Halstead to succeed, in contrast to Babcock, was his close collaboration with neurologists and neurosurgeons, among them A. Earl Walker who was best man at Halstead's wedding (Reed, 1985).

Halstead undoubtedly benefited from the tradition of collaboration between psychology and psychiatry that had already been established (Hartman, 1991). Nonetheless, his laboratory was unique in creating an opportunity for psychologists to work with neurological patient populations that were more precisely defined than those available in psychiatric settings of the day. This may have made all the difference in establishing an enduring neuropsychological legacy.

In summary, nearly all the elements defining the field of neuropsychology had been established by 1920. In the 1930s, Halstead's laboratory, building upon what had gone before, added the final element—the study of carefully defined patient groups—allowing the emergence of the new field. While neuropsychology has no father (or mother), it has no shortage of pioneers—Franz, Lashley, and Halstead among them. Its origin is not to be found in some flash of revolutionary insight. Rather, neuropsychology evolved, under the influence of social and historical forces, from the neurological case study tradition, the mental testing movement, animal ablation studies, and the early collaborations between psychology and medicine. While we cannot identify a specific day and time when the field came into being, we can state with some confidence that between 1920 and 1940 the transition from pre- to extant neuropsychology quietly took place.

Scientific Neuropsychology in the United States: From Halstead to Geschwind

In founding his laboratory, Halstead's goal was to study the relationship between the brain and intelligence (Kane, 1991). As noted above, naturalistic observation, the already established tradition of psychological testing with medical patients, and brain ablation studies gave inspiration to the battery of tests Halstead developed in pursuit of this goal. Factor analysis of the test battery led to a four–factor theory of biological intelligence, which Halstead presented in his 1947 book *Brain and Intelligence.* Halstead's book was not well-received by his contemporaries (Wechsler, 1958), nor has posterity resurrected his theories (Hartman, 1991; Reed, 1985). Instead, Halstead's most enduring legacy remains the battery bearing his name—the Halstead–Reitan Battery.

Halstead's second legacy has been his students. Ralph Reitan, one of Halstead's most prolific students, established a laboratory at the University of Indiana Medical Center in 1950. Over the next 20 years, Reitan embarked upon perhaps the most thorough attempt to validate a test battery in the history of neuropsychology. To Halstead's original battery of tests, Reitan, his students, and colleagues added procedures for detecting aphasia and sensory perceptual impairment and for comparing the performance of the two sides of the body. Reitan's careful documentation of patient lesions; development of adult, adolescent, and child norms; use of discriminant function analysis; and investigation of the neuropsychological effects of a wide range of medical conditions set a standard of excellence for test development in neuropsychology.

The work of Reitan's students has been equally noteworthy (Reed, 1985). Hallgrim Kløve studied with Reitan in the 1950s and then established a laboratory at the University of Wisconsin. As of this writing, he is in the Department of Biological and Medical Psychology at the University of Bergen, Norway. Another student, Homer Reed, directed the Neuropsychology Laboratory at the New England Medical Center in Boston where he conducted extensive investigations into the use of the Halstead–Reitan Battery with pediatric patients. Phillip Rennick completed a fellowship with Reitan and then established a laboratory at Lafayette Clinic in Detroit. Rennick's Repeatable Cognitive Perceptual Motor Battery was designed for use in situations in which serial testing is needed (e.g., in the study of recovery of function). A wing in Lafayette Clinic was dedicated to Rennick after his untimely death from cancer.

Reitan's early work involved the examination of brain-injured World War II veterans. This population also provided the impetus for Hans-Lukas Teuber's work. Teuber immigrated from Germany and served as a noncommissioned naval officer before establishing the Psychophysiological Laboratory with the neurologist Morris Bender at New York University (Weinstein, 1985). After Bender left to chair Neurology at the Mount Sinai College of Medicine, Teuber assumed directorship of the lab. Like the laboratories established by Halstead and Reitan, Teuber's laboratory was home to many who went on to have prominent careers in their own right. Joseph Altman, Lila Ghent, Rita Rudel, Josephine Semmes, and Sidney Weinstein were all associated with Teuber's laboratory at various times. Teuber eventually left New York to continue his investigations at the Massachusetts Institute of Technology.

Teuber proposed the principle of double dissociation in 1955 (Delis & Ober, 1986). It was Teuber's contention that two conditions must be satisfied before a cognitive ability can be localized to a particular brain area: (a) the cognitive ability must be impaired after lesions to the brain area and (b) lesions outside the brain area must not impair the cognitive ability. This principle implies a different research methodology. In localizing functions, it is no longer enough to compare brain-damaged patients with normal controls. Comparisons also must be made between patient groups differing in the area and lateralization of their brain damage. Guided by this principle, Teuber and his colleagues set a new standard of rigor through their investigations of tactile pressure sensitivity; two-point discrimination; tactile point localization; size, pattern, form, and texture discrimination; body image; finger oscillation; grip strength; problem solving; and intelligence.

In 1948, the same year that Teuber's seminal presentation at APA put neuropsychology on the map, Arthur Benton began his tenure as professor of psychology at the University of Iowa. By 1950, Benton had established a small testing unit in the Department of Neurology of the University of Iowa Hospitals (Hamsher, 1985). Over the next several years, Benton and his students conducted basic normative studies and one of the first neuropsychological investigations of the effects of lateralized brain damage (Heilbrun, 1956). Then came a National Institute of Health Research Fellowship in 1957 that allowed Benton to expand his testing unit into a formal neuropsychological laboratory (Hamsher, 1985).

Over the next 20 years, Benton's laboratory became a pioneering center of neuropsychological research. The investigators who began their respective pathways to prominence in association with this laboratory included Max Fogel, Donald Shankweiler, Kerry deS. Hamsher, Nils Varney, Scott Lindgren, Otfried Spreen, and Harvey Levin (Hamsher, 1985). The work of Benton's laboratory epitomizes the early contribution neuropsychology made to medical science. Benton and his colleagues designed, standardized, and normed (taking into account the moderating effects of age, gender, and education) a variety of tests for use in studying what had previously been vaguely defined clinical disorders. One example, Benton's work on the Gerstmann Syndrome, will suffice to illustrate Benton's contributions.

The Gerstmann Syndrome has had a troubled history since it was first described (Gerstmann, 1940). Its cardinal features include a failure to recognize or localize stimuli to the fingers, a deficit in distinguishing right from left, a writing impairment, and a calculation disorder. The very existence of the syndrome has been questioned because of the low correlation observed among its cardinal features (Stringer, 1996) and the difficulty in localizing the syndrome to damage in a particular brain region (Benton & Sivan, 1993). Part of the problem in reliably characterizing the nature of the syndrome grew from the inconsistency in which its various components, finger agnosia in particular, were measured. Benton's application of neuropsychological methods advanced understanding of the Gerstmann Syndrome by standardizing assessment, systematically varying test parameters, and studying the normal development of the abilities that are impaired in the syndrome (Benton & Sivan, 1993).

Besides the work on the Gerstmann Syndrome, Benton and his colleagues developed and standardized tests of reaction time, double simultaneous stimulation perception, motor impersistence, aphasia, and so on (Hamsher, 1985). In addition, Benton's laboratory produced scores of papers on various aspects of cerebral dominance as it impacts face perception, judgment of line orientation, depth perception, constructional ability, auditory localization, and tactile perception (Hamsher, 1985).

In Benton's laboratory we also see the fields of aphasiology and neuropsychology coming together. The interest of neuropsychologists in aphasia grew after World War II, in part because of the increased number of soldiers whose brain injuries resulted in language impairment. The other stimulus that increased interest in aphasia was Kurt Goldstein's book *Language and Language Disorders*, published in 1948. Goldstein had already proposed that a loss of the ability to behave and think abstractly was the basis of most cortical syndromes (Goldstein, 1990; Goldstein & Scheerer, 1941). Goldstein's book combined his theories about abstracting ability with neurology's classic anatomico–clinical syndrome approach to aphasia. Both the numbers of aphasic patients available for study and Goldstein's approach attracted experimental neuropsychologists and psycholinguists to the study of language disorders (Goodglass, 1985). Aphasia research centers began to appear in the United States, Benton's laboratory being among them.

Besides Benton and his colleagues in Iowa City, Norman Geschwind, Davis Howes, and Harold Goodglass in Boston also were taking an experimental psycholinguistic approach to the study of the classic aphasia syndromes. Goodglass (1985) characterized the psycholinguistic approach by its use of experimental control group designs, psychological test construction methods, and statistical analyses in the study of aphasia. As such, the psycholinguistic approach to aphasia was consistent with the methods neuropsychology was introducing to the study of other brain syndromes.

Under Geschwind's influence, the Boston group also emphasized the functional anatomy of the brain as it pertains to the various aphasia syndromes (Goodglass, 1985). This emphasis helped repopularize the classical syndromes of aphasia: Broca's, Wernicke's, conduction, transcortical, and anomic. Later, a new technology—computerized axial tomography—confirmed the anatomico–clinical relationships intrinsic to this subtyping of aphasia (Hayward, Naeser, & Zatz, 1977).

Geschwind and his colleagues, however, extended their work beyond the study of aphasia. In 1965, Geschwind published "Disconnexion Syndromes in Animals and Man." This paper reintroduced the concept of the disconnection syndrome proposed more than half a century earlier by Dejerine and Leipmann. Geschwind contended that cortical syndromes result from disconnections of one hemisphere, or one brain region, from another. Alexia, for example, may result from disconnection of posterior language zones in the left hemisphere from left and right hemisphere visual association cortex. Conduction aphasia, as another example, may arise after disconnection of auditory cortex from speech centers in the left hemisphere. Similar disconnections presumably underlie subtypes of apraxia, agnosia, and the callosal transection syndrome.

Geschwind's paper powerfully impacted both neurology and neuropsychology. In ensuing years, Geschwind and his colleagues—Martin Albert, Harold Goodglass, and Edith Kaplan among them—would make Boston a premier center for research and clinical training in neuropsychology.

Scientific Neuropsychology in Canada

Though fewer in number, Canadian neuropsychological laboratories rivaled those in the United States in the vitality and significance of their work. Returning again to 1948, we find the opening of the animal laboratory in the Donner Building of McGill University (Hebb, 1983). In coming years, this facility would witness Peter Milner's development of techniques for electrode stimulation of subcortical brain regions, Olds and Milner's discovery of reward centers in the rat brain, work on the role of early stimulation in the development of later intelligence, and work on the effects of sensory deprivation on brain development and function (Hebb, 1983).

Neuropsychologists are focused largely on human brain–behavior relationships, and the role of animal brain research sometimes goes unappreciated. Such basic science research, however, often provides the theoretical base from which human neuropsychology develops and advances (Goldstein, 1985). The work conducted in the Canadian animal laboratories had such a significant impact that Hebb (1983), with some justification, can lay claim to Canada as the site for the revival of interest in brain–behavior relationships.

The animal laboratories of McGill University were only a short distance from the Montreal Neurological Institute where Brenda Milner conducted her investigations of human amnesia after temporal lobe resection (Milner, 1965, 1968, 1972; Milner, Corkin, & Teuber, 1968; Scoville & Milner, 1957). This surgery, performed to relieve intractable epilepsy, had the unanticipated consequence of producing a profound and unremitting amnesic syndrome. Milner's painstaking investigations not only correlated the severity of amnesia with the extent of hippocampal removal but also characterized the material–specific nature of the amnesia: left temporal resections produced amnesia for verbal information while right temporal resections affected memory for visuospatial material. Milner's work forms part of the foundation for neuropsychology's current understanding of human amnesic syndromes.

Scientific Neuropsychology in Western Europe

Neuropsychology did not plant its roots solely in North America in the 1950s; it found European soil just as fertile. Since space does not permit us to summarize all of the contributions made by European pioneers in the field, by way of illustration we will highlight briefly some of the work from England and France.

Beginning as early as the 1940s, the British neuropsychologist Oliver Zangwill began investigating the consequences of lesions in the so-called minor hemisphere. Benton (1994) described Zangwill as being sensitive and attentive to the needs of people around him. Perhaps it is these personal characteristics that drew him to study scientifically neglected patients with right hemisphere lesions. Prior to Zangwill, the prevailing viewpoint was that the left hemisphere was dominant for language and most other important functions, earning it the designation of "major" hemisphere. Zangwill's careful study of right hemisphere lesion cases began to democratize conceptions of hemispheric function (Benton, 1991). The hemispheres were not major and minor players in human cognition. They were instead specialized structures, each having a different distribution of functions that it performed. Such early work drew attention to the role of the right hemisphere in cognition and behavior, which in turn led to more sophisticated, dynamic models of hemispheric function that attempt to account for variance in cerebral dominance both within and between individuals.

A contemporary of Zangwill, Henry Hécaen, played a prominent role in establishing neuropsychology in France. The two men were apparently quite different in temperament (Benton, 1994). Where Zangwill was attentive, Hécaen was intense. While Zangwill possessed a keen sense of humor, Hécaen had a fierce, but unpretentious pride. After obtaining his medical degree from the University of Bordeaux in 1934, Hécaen studied psychiatry and neurology with Henri Ey and Jean Lhermitte (Boller, 1999). Hécaen studied with Wilder Penfield and Brenda Milner in Canada for only a few months in 1952, but the experience profoundly impacted his career. After returning to France, Hécaen began distinguishing himself through his prolific clinical investigations of aphasia, alexia, agraphia, agnosia, Balint's Syndrome, and the occurrence of hallucinations and illusions following focal brain damage. In 1962, he founded the Groupe de Neuropsychologie et de Neurolinguistique, a laboratory that attracted students from around the world. Hécaen was equally prolific as a teacher, and his students went on to impact the advance of neuropsychology throughout Europe and the United States.

At a dinner party hosted by Zangwill in 1949, Hécaen outlined an idea for an annual meeting in Europe focused on brain function and related issues (Zangwill, 1984). Beginning in 1951, a series of interdisciplinary conferences were held at a variety of European destinations including Mond Sec (Austria), Lake Constance

(Germany), Royaumont (France), Oxford (England), Amsterdam (The Netherlands), Fouesnant (Brittany), Hinterzarten (Black Forest Germany), and Steyning (England). These conferences brought together scholars and clinicians from diverse disciplines including neurology, psychology, electrophysiology, neuroanatomy, ophthalmology, and pediatrics. A commonality of interest in higher cortical functions united these scholars, along with a sense that this interest was outside the mainstream of their respective fields.

This interdisciplinary group met to discuss such topics as disorders of time sense, alexia, cerebral dominance, disorders of body schema, aphasia, constructional apraxia, and the effects of unilateral versus bilateral lesions. Besides Hécaen and Zangwill, the group included such well-known names as Denny Brown, Karl Pribram, and Teuber from the United States; Clemens Faust from Germany; Ennio DeRenzi and Luigi Vignolo from Italy; and many others from across the continent, truly reflecting the fecundity of European soil for neuropsychology. (For a more complete listing, see Boller, 1999.) By 1962 the group was formally calling itself the International Neuropsychological Symposium. At first, most papers were presented in German or French, the preferred languages for European scientific meetings. At the 1964 meeting, presentations made in English were translated into German by Teuber and Klaus Poeck (Boller, 1999). However, from 1976 forward, all papers were presented in English, and the practice of translation ended. English had replaced German and French as the language of choice for scientific discourse (Boller, 1999).

Scientific Neuropsychology in the Soviet Union

Once its march began in earnest, neuropsychology proved fairly unstoppable. The multiplicity of languages and national cultures in Europe was no deterrent. The field, however, faced a different kind of challenge in the Soviet Union. In communist Russia, politics could influence both the course of a scientist's career and the content of scientific research. Despite the challenges of being a scientist in the Soviet Union, it was in Russia that one of neuropsychology's earliest giants strode.

Aleksandr Romanovich Luria was chair of the Department of Neuropsychology at Moscow University, director of a laboratory at the Burdenko Neurosurgical Institute, and one of the most influential theorists in the field of neuropsychology. His accomplishments are all the more remarkable for the fact that shifting political tides compelled Luria to alter the focus of his research multiple times during his career (Cole, 1978; see also chapter 4). Thus, at various times, Luria studied the effect of emotion on motor behavior, the cultural and historical influences on the behavior of Central Asians, the developmental abnormalities seen in mental retardation, and the differences between identical and fraternal twins. When Luria's twin research encountered political opposition, he began to study Russian World War II veterans who had suffered penetrating missile wounds to the brain. In so doing, Luria founded Russian neuropsychology.

Luria's subsequent contributions to neuropsychology are numerous. Neuropsychologists throughout the world use his richly qualitative examination methods, compiled by Anne-Lise Christensen (1975). Luria was known for his willingness to work with students of varying nationalities. Though not as popular in the United States as the Halstead–Reitan Battery, Luria's investigational methods represent a viable alternative approach to neuropsychological examination and have received considerable attention outside of the United States. Luria also was an early exponent of neuropsychological approaches to rehabilitation and of the use of cholinergic drugs to enhance recovery of function (Gualtieri, 1988). His most influential contribution, however, was his reconceptualization of function and localization in neuropsychology.

If Lashley's work temporarily halted attempts to localize complex functions in the brain, Luria's work helped restart and reshape this endeavor. Luria defined functions as "complex adaptive activities aimed at the performance of some vitally important task" (Luria & Haigh, 1992, p. 340). The goal of a function is invariant, while the methods by which the goal is accomplished can vary widely. Drawing an analogy, Luria noted that respiration is normally accomplished through the action of the diaphragm; however, if diaphragm muscles are paralyzed, the action of the intercostal muscles can cause chest expansion and contraction. If these muscles too are paralyzed, air can be "swallowed" utilizing the pharynx and larynx; thus, respiration cannot be regarded as residing in any fixed set of tissue.

By analogy, brain functions represent the output of complex systems of interacting brain areas. Each area contributes something unique to the performance of the function, and the level of involvement may vary depending upon the integrity of other areas within the system. In this respect, complex brain functions do not reside in discrete brain areas. Rather, "all human behavioral acts take place with the participation of all parts and levels of the brain, each of which makes its own specific contribution to the work of the functional system as a whole" (Luria & Haigh, 1992, p. 346). In effect, each function is distributed throughout the brain. The neuropsychologist's task is not to localize functions to discrete brain areas but to describe how lesions in discrete brain areas characteristically impact functions.

Luria saw his redefinition of brain function as a revolution in neuropsychology that resolved the debate between localizationists and antilocalizationists (Luria & Haigh, 1992). Luria's redefinition led not only to his unique qualitative method of neuropsychological investigation but also provided the basis for understanding how brain lesions disrupt executive functioning, spatial orientation, phonemic perception, grammatical comprehension, visuospatial synthesis, and movement integration.

Luria's theories are consistent with late-nineteenth- and early-twentieth-century developments in the field of psychology. The trend was away from Faculty Psychology to Functionalist Psychology. Faculty Psychology described mental phenomena in terms of indivisible abilities, while Functionalist Psychology emphasized acts and goals over mental faculties. Luria gives credit to his mentor, the Russian psychologist Vygotsky, for contributing to this theoretical shift in psychology.

Here again, however, we see the difficulty of arriving at a historical consensus that a revolution in neuropsychology occurred. Wist's (1992) comprehensive review of the impact of Functionalism on neuropsychology mentions neither Luria nor Vygotsky. Regardless of whether we view Luria's contributions as revolutionary, his impact on modern neuropsychology has proven to be powerful and enduring.

Neuropsychology in Latin America

Neuropsychology spread across Europe largely undeterred by linguistic and cultural barriers but certainly challenged by the political climate in the Soviet Union. The challenges faced in Latin American were perhaps even greater.

In the early 1950s, two psychologists—C. Mendilaharsu and S. Acevedo de Mendilaharsu—traveled from Paraguay to study with Hécaen in France. Mendilaharsu and de Mendilaharsu subsequently established the first South American neuropsychological laboratory in 1958 at the Neurological Institute in Montevideo, Uruguay (Ardila, 1990). These South American pioneers went on to conduct investigations of constructional ability, dementia, and language. They additionally developed Spanish language versions of neuropsychological tests. Despite the initial connection with French neuropsychology, the early South American neuropsychologists worked mostly in isolation from their European and North American colleagues. The combination of language and geographic boundaries reinforced this isolation. Some South American pioneers also endured privation resulting from the economic challenges faced by their countries. Despite these less than optimal circumstances, neuropsychology expanded throughout Latin America, with neuropsychologists and neuropsychological societies springing up in Mexico, Peru, Columbia, Chile, Argentina, Brazil, Honduras, Nicaragua, and elsewhere.

Cognitive Neuropsychology: Modularity and Synthesis

By the early 1970s neuropsychology was forcing the adoption of a new, modular view of the brain. It became impossible to speak of the brain as if it were an undifferentiated whole. Instead, the brain seemed to be a system of independent, but interconnected, processing modules. Much of the work conducted in the United States, Canada, Western Europe, and Russia during the 1950s and 1960s pointed in this direction.

The classic disconnection syndromes revived and studied by Geschwind and his colleagues in Boston, Hécaen in France, and Ennio De Renzi in Italy assume a normal flow of information across otherwise independent brain regions. Disconnection of these regions does not so much impair information processing as prevent information from reaching or leaving an area of the brain critical for performing a task. A picture of more or less independent brain modules emerges from this approach.

Modularity is also implied in Luria's concept of brain organization. For Luria, the brain is an organ made up of functional systems. Functional systems, in turn, are composed of connected brain areas, each of which contributes something to the output of the system as a whole. Milner's studies of material–specific amnesia following left or right temporal lobectomy further contribute to this model of a brain capable of fractionation into specialized processing components.

Finally, modularity is starkly evident in Sperry (1964) and Gazzaniga's (1970) studies of commissurotomy patients. In these patients, each hemisphere seems to function with near total independence, even to the point of being unaware of information contained within, or actions initiated by, the contralateral hemisphere. Since this radical independence can be demonstrated simply by severing the commissural fibers that allow the hemispheres to communicate, it stands to reason that our subjective sense of wholeness, of being of one mind, may be an ephemeral illusion. Our brains are perhaps better understood as composed of dissociable modules, normally acting in concert but capable of autonomous functioning.

While neuropsychologists were discovering the modularity of the brain, cognitive psychologists were characterizing mental abilities in terms of processing steps or stages. In the mid-to-late-1960s, cognitive psychologists succeeded in expressing a wide range of mental tasks in terms of algorithms consisting of multiple serial operations or processing steps measurable by reaction time methods (Posner & DiGirolamo, 2000). The speed with which we accomplish even fairly complex tasks makes serial processing an unlikely model for all human cognitive functions. In the 1980s, alternative parallel distributed processing or neural network models began to appear. Using this approach, mental concepts could be represented by the parallel activation of a hierarchical set of nodes connected by various mathematical weights (Posner & DiGirolamo, 2000).

From the late 1960s through the 1980s, cognitive psychologists studied human information processing using these various heuristic models, none of which were directly tied to the human brain. Nonetheless, as cognitive psychologists parsed global mental abilities into component cognitive processes, the parallel with developments in neuropsychology could not escape notice. Cross-fertilization was inevitable, and soon cognitive psychologists began increasingly to consider the brain when formulating models of human cognition (e.g., Posner, Pea, & Volpe, 1982). Similarly, neuropsychologists began to incorporate cognitive models in their attempts to understand the effects of brain damage (e.g., Roeltgen, 1993; Shallice, 1981) and in their design of new and better test instruments (e.g., Delis, Kramer, Kaplan, & Ober, 1987).

The cognitive neuropsychological science that is under construction as we begin the twenty-first century is a far cry from the clinical science that began 50 years ago. It is a synthesis of clinical and experimental methods, anatomical and heuristic models, and neurological and cognitive perspectives. It is a science that is ever more interdisciplinary, possessing a perspective that grows ever broader. One way to gauge the impact of this new approach is to look at the shift in the topics that dominate the international meetings of neuropsychologists. The 1963 meeting of the International Neuropsychological Symposium in Austria focused on three topics: asymbolia, temporal lobe syndromes, and metamorphopsies (Boller, 1999). The 1998 meeting, held in Israel, was devoted to working memory, motor learning, and face and object perception. Clearly, a shift in the direction of cognitive science had occurred.

An interesting aspect of the shift forward in neuropsychology toward cognitive science is that it is partly associated with a shift back to the neurological case study, albeit in a different guise and format. Barry (1996) cited two published case studies as critical to the emergence of cognitive neuropsychology. First he cited the description of patient G.R., published in 1966. John Marshall and Freda Newcombe (1966) provided a detailed neuropsychological description of G.R.'s semantic and syntactic reading errors and interpreted those errors in terms of theories of normal information processing. Their study of G.R. went on to define the syndrome now known as "deep dyslexia." Irrespective of the clinical and theoretical status of this syndrome, the methods Marshall and Newcombe employed became a model for cognitive neuropsychology research—these methods being the detailed study of neurological patients with carefully constructed sets of experimental stimuli that focus on specific processing capabilities and the interpretation of intact and impaired performance in terms of models of normal information processing (Barry, 1996).

Elizabeth Warrington and Timothy Shallice published in 1969 the second case cited by Barry. Their patient, known as K.F., had a short-term–long-term memory dissociation. While having a short-term memory so limited that he could repeat only a single digit, K.F. still managed to learn and recall paired associates. The findings confounded the previously held notion that learning involved a transfer from short-term to long-term memory and pointed to the existence of a direct route to long-term storage. With regard to the development of cognitive neuropsychology, the significance of the case lies in the power of a single, well-studied case to challenge previous theories, even when those theories are based on control group investigations. Though this remains a controversial subject with contemporary scholars, some would argue that a well-designed case study can be as theoretically persuasive as a well-designed group study.

With regards to our earlier assertion that the classic neurological case study represents a forerunner of contemporary neuropsychology, we would argue that the "rediscovery" of the case study by cognitive neuropsychology supports our view. Although Broca's observations were a radical advance over other neurological theories of language of his day, the work of Broca and his contemporaries is qualitatively different from the case studies of contemporary cognitive neuropsychology. The distinction is in the methods of observation—clinical and naturalistic by Broca and his contemporaries a century ago; experimental, controlled, and theory-driven by Newcombe and her contemporaries today. The work of Broca and others allowed modern neurology to emerge. It may represent a revolution in neurology. Whether cognitive neuropsychology represents a contemporary revolution and how far it will take us in the new century remains to be seen. But without question, cognitive neuropsychology will play a prominent role in unraveling our mysteriously modular brain.

Technology in the Cognitive Revolution

Although we may need to wait for the final opinion of historians of science, some contemporary scholars not only view cognitive neuropsychology as a revolution but also point to technology as its stimulus. For example, Kolb (1999) wrote:

> It is clear that neuropsychological theory went through a revolution in the 1980s and 1990s and led to the development of a new way of thinking about the way cognitive functions are organized in the cerebrum. The changes in the last few years have been more methodological, with the advent especially of fMRI [functional Magnetic Resonance Imaging]. (p. 409)

Beginning again in the 1960s, new techniques became available for studying the mediation of cognition by the brain. The microelectrode, allowing the recording of the activity of single neurons or discrete neuronal populations was a significant advance, making possible the characterization of sensory and motor functions with unprecedented detail and precision (Hubel, 1987). Techniques also developed, such as the recording of event-related potentials (ERP), for studying brain electrical activity associated with cognition in humans.

In the 1970s, computerized tomography offered new confirmation of the localizationist ideas of the European neurologists of the 1800s (e.g., Hayward et al., 1977). During this same decade, Scandinavian investigators began using cerebral blood flow changes to identify areas of the brain that became active during reading (Lassen, Ingvar, & Skinhoj, 1978). From this early work, a variety of methods have evolved for associating brain modules with cognitive processing, including positron emission tomography, MRI and fMRI, and magnetoencephalography (MEG).

All of the above methods for studying the role of the brain in cognition have limitations (Posner & DiGirolamo, 2000). Some methods (e.g., ERP and MEG) have good temporal precision, being able to capture brain activities that occur in the millisecond range. These same methods, however, tend to lack spatial precision. Positron Emission Tomography (PET) and fMRI spatially localize areas of brain activation with good precision but depend on blood flow changes that take several seconds to occur. While each of the individual technologies will gain in precision, a promising future direction lies in the combination of imaging methods. Event-related fMRI for example improves on the time resolution of the standard fMRI by incorporating averaging techniques similar to those used in ERP

(Posner & DiGirolamo, 2000). Similarly, high temporal resolution data from techniques such as MEG can be co-registered with high spatial resolution data from MRI, combining the best of both technologies.

Future historians of the field may or may not agree that a cognitive revolution occurred in neuropsychology at the close of the twentieth century. But if such a revolution is judged to have occurred, it is doubtless that these technological advances fueled it.

Professional Neuropsychology Since 1950: Growth and Expansion

We have traced the history of scientific neuropsychology from its inception to the present period of growing synthesis with cognitive psychology. As scientific neuropsychology has grown, so too has the profession. The profession grew slowly at first, and indeed, it was not until 1963 that Hécaen established *Neuropsychologia*, the first journal devoted to the new field. One year later, De Renzi founded *Cortex*, and the stage was set for the explosion of scholarship that was to come.

At first Hécaen thought the field was too small for two journals, and he toyed with the idea of amalgamating them (Boller, 1999). From 1960 to 1974, an average of only 28 neuropsychology articles was published per year (Puente, 1992). From 1974 to 1985, the rate increased to 66 articles per year. Today, more than a dozen peer-reviewed journals are devoted exclusively to basic and applied papers in neuropsychology, including *Neuropsychology, Journal of Clinical and Experimental Neuropsychology, The Clinical Neuropsychologist, Journal of the International Neuropsychological Society, Archives of Clinical Neuropsychology, Cortex, Brain, Brain and Cognition*, and *Brain and Language*. These and other psychology, medical, and neuroscience journals annually publish over 4,000 scholarly papers related to the field. A similar pattern is evident in the growth of book publishing in neuropsychology. The field advanced from an average of one new title published a year in the 1960s to approximately ten per year in the 1980s (Puente, 1992). Currently, it is not uncommon for a single publishing house to have 50 or more titles in print related to the field. Neuropsychology is also well-entrenched in cyberspace, with upwards of 200 Internet websites devoted to news about brain research, brain disorders, and rehabilitation.

The field boasts many scientific and professional organizations. The International Neuropsychological Society (INS), the National Academy of Neuropsychology (NAN), and the American Psychological Association (APA) Division of Clinical Neuropsychology (Division 40) are the most well-known within the United States. Founded in 1967, INS reports a membership approaching 3,500, while NAN, formed in 1974, includes upwards of 3,000 members. Division 40 of the APA, incorporated in 1980, is the most recently formed of these organizations. Nonetheless, its membership exceeds 3,800, making it the fifth largest APA division. Besides the large organizations most familiar in North America, neuropsychologists have organized throughout Europe, Asia, South America, and Africa (see Jodzio, 1998; Nihashi, 1998; Preilowski, 1997).

In the early years, entry into neuropsychology was often on the basis of a self-declared area of research or clinical interest, with competence established through self-study and one-on-one mentoring. It was not until the mid-1960s that formal courses in neuropsychology began to appear, with one of the first offered in the Biological Psychology Doctoral Program at the University of Oklahoma Health Sciences Center (Parsons, 1991). Not surprisingly, the training and credentials of individuals calling themselves neuropsychologists varied widely even into the 1970s.

With the growth of professional organizations, entry into the field of neuropsychology became increasingly formalized. In 1979, Manfred Meier initiated the push to establish standards of training and competence for neuropsychologists in the United States. The work of Meier and many others eventually culminated in the founding, in 1981, of the American Board of Clinical Neuropsychology (ABCN), which affiliated with the American Board of Professional Psychology (ABPP) in 1984. Since 1984, ABCN/ABPP has been the principal organization responsible for peer review of the credentials, knowledge, and practice of clinical neuropsychologists in the United States.

Another important step toward setting professional standards in the United States was taken in 1987 when APA Division 40 published guidelines for doctoral, internship, and postdoctoral training in neuropsychology (APA Division 40, 1989). A year after training guidelines were published, this division formally adopted a definition of a clinical neuropsychologist. Most importantly, this definition made explicit the training, supervision, licensing, and peer review requirements that must be met by neuropsychologists. It also recognized attainment of the ABCN/ABPP diploma as "the clearest evidence of competence as a Clinical Neuropsychologist" (APA Division 40, 1989, p. 22). Interest in achieving this credential continues to grow, and currently over 250 practicing clinicians have attained diplomate status. One milestone likely to occur in the United States in the new century is the achievement of near universal ABCN/ABPP diplomacy among those identifying neuropsychology as their primary area of specialization.

By 1991, educational options in neuropsychology included 29 doctoral training programs, 40 internships, and 51 postdoctoral fellowships. These figures include only North American programs offering specialized training that adheres to Division 40 guidelines. The figures do not include the many other training institutions outside of the United States, the North American programs that offer limited experience and course work in neuropsychology, or the myriad opportunities for informal training and supervision negotiated among clinicians in private practice.

Overview of the Book

Although neuropsychology is little more than 50 years old, the field clearly has had a profound impact on our understanding of the brain and our assessment and treatment of brain disorders. At the start of the twenty-first century, we are witness to a passing of the torch from the generation of scholars who founded neuropsychology to the generation who are taking the field into the future. This book captures the stories behind the work and theories of many prominent, twentieth-century neuropsychologists. It attempts to go beyond a discussion of ideas and discoveries to explore the people and the paths they have chosen.

This book is divided into three major sections. Part I, "Pathways Unforgotten," highlights the contributions of Nelson Butters, Henry Hécaen, Aleksandr Luria, Roger Sperry, and Hans-Lukas Teuber, to contemporary neuropsychology. All but one of the chapters in this section were written by scholars, students, and colleagues with a close connection to the neuropsychologist they profile. The one exception is the chapter on Butters that includes a memoir he wrote shortly before his death in 1995 with an introduction and postscript written by Meryl Butters, his daughter and a neuropsychologist in her own right.

In Part II, "Pathways Remembered," ten pioneers of twentieth-century neuropsychology reflect upon the body of their work in the context of their personal development and professional pathway. The roles of social and cultural factors, scientific and technological advances, and serendipity become apparent in the pathways of many of these pioneering individuals. Contributors include Dirk Bakker, Anne-Lise Christensen, Kenneth Heilman, Edith Kaplan, Manfred Meier, Oscar Parsons, Karl Pribram, Ralph Reitan, Byron Rourke, and Otfried Spreen. Contributors come from the United States, Canada, and Europe and include individuals trained in the fields of psychology and medicine. Most have made contributions as both clinicians and scholars. Not only are these contributors pioneers in their own right, but they also reflect the influence of such luminaries as Arthur Benton, Ward Halstead, Norman Geschwind, Harold Goodglass, Karl Lashley, and others. Thus, these chapters indirectly cover and provide insight into the work of other prominent contributors to the field of neuropsychology who for various reasons could not have chapters devoted to them in the present volume.

Part III, "Pathways Imagined," assesses the current status of neuropsychology and envisions its future. Russell M. Bauer opens this section by pondering neuropsychology's present and future as a clinical profession. Laird Cermak, in a chapter completed just prior to his death, discusses the future of scientific neuropsychology. Finally, Anthony Y. Stringer concludes the book with a chapter on the role of the neurosciences, and neuropsychology in particular, in the alleviation of disability in the century ahead.

No single book can hope to achieve exhaustive representation of the twentieth-century pioneers in our field. Our intent is not to provide encyclopedic coverage of neuropsychology and its practitioners. If we had achieved such breadth of coverage, we would have necessarily sacrificed the contributors' depth of reflection. We have attempted, instead, to select a subset of the many prominent neuropsychologists—individuals who represent where the field has come and where it may be going. In some respects, our contributors are self-selected. Questions of time and health, as well as varying personal priorities, inevitably influenced the decision of some important figures in our field to not contribute a chapter. The omission of any individual, body of work, or nationality purely reflects these unavoidable practicalities and is not in any way a judgment on the relative importance of one individual, one theoretical perspective, or one country compared to another. We hope to provide a representative, if not exhaustive, sample of the many facets of contemporary neuropsychology. It is hoped that twenty-first century scholars and clinicians will find insight and inspiration in the reflections of this portion of the generation that preceded them.

REFERENCES

American Psychological Association Division 40. (1989). Definition of a clinical neuropsychologist. *The Clinical Neuropsychologist, 3,* 22.

Ardila, A. (1990). Neuropsychology in Latin America. *The Clinical Neuropsychologist, 4,* 121–132.

Babcock, H. (1930). An experiment in the measurement of mental deterioration. *Archives of Psychology, 117,* 1–61.

Barry, C. (1996). G.R., the prime "deep dyslexic": A commentary on Marshall and Newcombe (1966). In C. Code, C. W. Wallesch, Y. Joanette, & A. R. Lecours (Eds.), *Classic cases in neuropsychology* (pp. 189–202). East Sussex, United Kingdom: Psychology Press.

Beach, F. A., Hebb, D. O., Morgan, C. T., & Nissen, H. W. (1960). *The neuropsychology of Lashley.* New York: McGraw-Hill.

Benton, A. (1987). Evolution of a clinical specialty. In K. M. Adams & B. P. Rourke (Eds.), *The TCN guide to professional practice in clinical neuropsychology* (pp. 1–4). Amsterdam: Swets & Zeitlinger.

Benton, A. (1991). The Hécaen–Zangwill legacy: Hemispheric dominance examined. *Neuropsychology Review, 2,* 267–280.

Benton, A. (1994). Four neuropsychologists. *Neuropsychology Review, 4,* 31–44.

Benton, A., & Sivan, A. B. (1993). Disturbances of body schema. In K. M. Heilman & E. Valenstein (Eds.), *Clinical neuropsychology* (3rd ed.) (pp. 123–140). New York: Oxford University Press.

Boller, F. (1999). History of the International Neuropsychological Symposium: A reflection of the evolution of a discipline. *Neuropsychologia, 37,* 17–26.

Boring, E. G. (1963). *History, psychology, and science: Selected papers.* New York: Wiley.

Bruce, D. (1985). On the origin of the term "neuropsychology." *Neuropsychologia, 23,* 813–814.

Christensen, A.-L. (1975). *Luria's neuropsychological investigation.* New York: Spectrum Publications.

Cohen, I. B. (1985). *Revolution in science.* Cambridge, MA: Belknap Press.

Cole, M. (1978). Alexander Romanovich Luria: 1902–1977. *American Journal of Psychology, 2,* 349–352.

Cotton, H. A. (1912). Comparative psychological studies of the mental capacity in cases of dementia praecox and alcoholic insanity. *Nervous and Mental Disease Monographs, Series 9,* 123–154.

Delis, D. C., Kramer, J. H., Kaplan, E., & Ober, B. A. (1987). *California Verbal Learning Test Form II* (Research ed.). San Antonio, TX: The Psychological Corporation.

Delis, D. C., & Ober, B. A. (1986). Cognitive neuropsychology. In T. J. Knapp & L. C. Robertson (Eds.), *Approaches to cognition: Contrasts and controversies* (pp. 243–266). Hillsdale, NJ: Lawrence Erlbaum Associates.

Franz, S. I. (1919). *Handbook of mental examination methods* (2nd ed.). New York: Macmillan.

Gatewood, L. C. (1909). An experimental study of dementia praecox. *Psychological Monographs, 11*(45), pp. 1–71.

Gazzaniga, M. S. (1970). *The bisected brain.* New York: Appleton-Century-Crofts.

Gerstmann, J. (1940). Syndrome of finger

agnosia, disorientation for right and left, agraphia, and acalculia. *Archives of Neurology and Psychiatry, 44,* 398–408.

Geschwind, N. (1965). Disconnexion syndromes in animals and man. *Brain, 88,* 237–294; 585–644.

Goldstein, G. (1985). The history of clinical neuropsychology: The role of some American pioneers. *International Journal of Neuroscience, 25,* 273–275.

Goldstein, G. (1990). Contributions of Kurt Goldstein to neuropsychology. *The Clinical Neuropsychologist, 4,* 3–17.

Goldstein, K. (1948). *Language and language disorders.* Orlando, FL: Grune & Stratton.

Goldstein, K., & Scheerer, M. (1941). Abstract and concrete behavior: An experimental study with special tests. *Psychological Monographs, 53*(2) (whole no. 239).

Goodglass, H. (1985). Aphasiology in the United States. *International Journal of Neuroscience, 25,* 307–311.

Gualtieri, C. T. (1988). Pharmacotherapy and the neurobehavioural sequelae of traumatic brain injury. *Brain Injury, 2,* 101–129.

Hamsher, K. D. (1985). The Iowa group. *International Journal of Neuroscience, 25,* 295–305.

Hartman, D. E. (1991). Reply to Reitan: Unexamined premises and the evolution of clinical neuropsychology. *Archives of Clinical Neuropsychology, 6,* 147–165.

Hayward, R. W., Naeser, M. A., & Zatz, L. M. (1977). Cranial computed tomography in aphasia: Correlation of anatomical lesions with functional deficits. *Radiology, 123,* 653–660.

Hebb, D. O. (1949). *The organization of behavior: A neuropsychological theory.* New York: Wiley.

Hebb, D. O. (1983). Neuropsychology: Retrospect and prospect. *Canadian Journal of Psychology, 37,* 4–7.

Heilbrun, A. B., Jr. (1956). Psychological test performance as a function of lateral localization of cerebral lesion. *Journal of Comparative and Physiological Psychology, 49,* 10–14.

Hubel, D. H. (1987). *Eye, brain, and vision.*

Cambridge, MA: MIT Press.

Jodzio, K. (1998, Spring). Neuropsychology in Poland: Past and present. *International Neuropsychological Society Liaison Committee Newsletter, 5,* 1–3.

Kane, R. L. (1991). Standardized and flexible batteries in neuropsychology: An assessment update. *Neuropsychology Review, 2,* 281–339.

Kolb, B. (1999). The twentieth century belongs to neuropsychology. *Brain Research Bulletin, 50,* 409–410.

Kolb, B., & Wishaw, I. Q. (1990). *Fundamentals of human neuropsychology* (3rd ed.). New York: W.H. Freeman and Company.

Kuhn, T. S. (1970). *The structure of scientific revolutions* (Rev. ed.). Chicago: University of Chicago Press.

Lassen, N. A., Ingvar, D. H., & Skinhoj, J. (1978, October). Brain function and blood flow. *Scientific American, 239,* 62–71.

Leahey, T. H. (1992). The mythical revolutions of American psychology. *American Psychologist, 47,* 308–318.

Luria, A. R., & Haigh, B. (1992). Neuropsychology: Its sources, principles, and prospects. In F. G. Worden, J. P. Swazey, & G. Adelman (Eds.), *The neurosciences: Paths of discovery, 1* (pp. 335–361). Boston: Birkhauser.

Marshall, J. C., & Newcombe, F. (1966). Syntactic and semantic errors in paralexia. *Neuropsychologia, 4,* 169–176.

Milner, B. (1965). Visually-guided maze learning in man: Effects of bilateral hippocampal, bilateral frontal, and unilateral cerebral lesions. *Neuropsychologia, 3,* 317–338.

Milner, B. (1968). Visual recognition and recall after right temporal-lobe excision in man. *Neuropsychologia, 6,* 191–209.

Milner, B. (1972). Disorders of learning and memory after temporal lobe lesions in man. *Clinical Neurosurgery, 19,* 421–446.

Milner, B., Corkin, S., & Teuber, H.-L. (1968). Further analysis of the hippocampal amnesic syndrome: 14 year follow up study of H.M. *Neuropsychologia, 6,* 215–234.

Nihashi, N. (1998, Spring). Neuropsychology in Japan. *International Neuropsychological*

Society Liaison Committee Newsletter, 5, 1–3.

Parsons, O. A. (1991). Clinical neuropsychology 1970–1990: A personal view. *Archives of Clinical Neuropsychology*, 6, 105–111.

Porter, R. (1986). The scientific revolution, a spoke in the wheel? In R. Porter & M. Teich (Eds.), *Revolutions in history* (pp. 290–316). Cambridge, England: Cambridge University Press.

Posner, M. I., & DiGirolamo, G. J. (2000). Cognitive neuroscience: Origins and promise. *Psychological Bulletin*, *126*, 873–889.

Posner, M. I., Pea, R., & Volpe, B. (1982). Cognitive–neuroscience: Developments towards a science of synthesis. In J. Mehler, C. T. Walker, & M. Garrett (Eds.), *Perspectives on mental representation: Experimental and theoretical studies of cognitive processes and capacities* (pp. 251–276). Hillsdale, NJ: Lawrence Erlbaum Associates.

Preilowski, B. (1997). Establishing clinical neuropsychology in Germany: Scientific, professional, and legal issues. *Neuropsychology Review*, 7, 187–199.

Puente, A. E. (1992). The status of clinical neuropsychology. *Archives of Clinical Neuropsychology*, 7, 297–312.

Reed, J. (1985). The contributions of Ward Halstead, Ralph Reitan and their associates. *International Journal of Neuroscience*, 25, 289–291.

Reitan, R. M. (1989). A note regarding some aspects of the history of clinical neuropsychology. *Archives of Clinical Neuropsychology*, 4, 385–391.

Roeltgen, D. P. (1993). Agraphia. In K. M. Heilman & E. Valenstein (Eds.), *Clinical neuropsychology* (3rd ed.) (pp. 63–90). New York: Oxford University Press.

Scoville, W. B., & Milner, B. (1957). Loss of recent memory after bilateral hippocampal lesions. *Journal of Neurology, Neurosurgery and Psychiatry*, 20, 11–21.

Shallice, T. (1981). Neurological impairment of cognitive processes. *British Medical Bulletin*, 37, 187–192.

Sperry, R. W. (1964). The great cerebral commissure. *Scientific American, 210 (1)*, 42–52.

Stringer, A. Y. (1996). *A guide to adult neuropsychological diagnosis*. Philadelphia: F. A. Davis.

Warrington, E. K., & Shallice, T. (1969). The selective impairment of auditory verbal short-term memory. *Brain*, 92, 885–896.

Wechsler, D. A. (1958). *The measurement and appraisal of adult intelligence*. Baltimore: The Williams & Wilkins Company.

Weinstein, S. (1985). The influence of Hans-Lukas Teuber and the Psychophysiological Laboratory on the establishment and development of neuropsychology. *International Journal of Neuroscience*, 25, 277–288.

Wist, E. R. (1992). Functional influences on clinical neuropsychology. In D. A. Owens & M. Wagner (Eds.), *Progress in modern psychology: The legacy of American functionalism* (pp. 73–93). Westport, CT: Praeger.

Yerkes, R. M., Bridges, J. W., & Hardwick, R. S. (1915). *A point scale for measuring mental ability*. Baltimore: Warwick & York, Inc.

Zangwill, O. (1984). Henry Hécaen and the origins of the International Neuropsychological Symposium. *Neuropsychologia*, 22, 813–815.

PART I

PATHWAYS UNFORGOTTEN

2

Nelson Butters
One Step Ahead

Nelson Butters (1937–1995)

Introduction

*I*t has been a little more than four years since my father's death in November 1995, at age 58, from amyotrophic lateral sclerosis (ALS). He was at the peak of his career when he was diagnosed in March 1993 at the age of 55. His professional memoir, which follows, contains some facts about his education and career, but for the sake of completeness, I will outline it here. He attended high school at Worcester Academy, a private boarding school in Worcester, Massachusetts. There he became good friends with classmate and future radical Abby Hoffman, with whom he made frequent trips to Boston. He graduated first in his class and was class valedictorian. He went on to graduate summa cum laude with his B.A. in Psychology from Boston University and to earn his Ph.D. in Psychology from Clark University.

In his memoir, my father discussed many of the substantive scientific ideas that propelled his career in neuropsychology for almost 30 years. He authored or co-authored nearly 200 peer reviewed scientific articles, 60 invited monographs and book chapters, and reams of abstracts. He co-edited and co-authored six books and delivered a multitude of invited lectures and presentations. He was the subject of *Neuropsychological Explorations of Memory and Cognition: Essays in Honor of Nelson Butters*, edited by Laird Cermak. At the time he became ill, he was a tenured professor of psychiatry at the University of California School of Medicine at San Diego and Chief of the Psychology Service at the San Diego Veterans Affairs Medical Center. He was a Diplomate in Clinical Neuropsychology from the American Board of Clinical Neuropsychology/American Board of Professional Psychology. He was the first to obtain the "triple crown" in the field of neuropsychology, having been elected to the presidency of APA Division 40, the International Neuropsychological Society, and the National Academy of Neuropsychology. He was a member of the editorial boards of numerous scientific journals and was editor-in-chief of the APA journal *Neuropsychology*. He received many awards and honors, including the Distinguished Clinical Neuropsychologist Award from the National Academy of Neuropsychology (1991), the Meritorious Service Award from the Department of Veterans Affairs (1993), the Distinguished Service Award from the

Figure 2.1. Nelson Butters

American Board of Professional Psychology (1993), and the Distinguished Researcher Award from the Research Society on Alcoholism (1995).

Within weeks of receiving the diagnosis of ALS in March 1993, my father began to get his affairs in order. He had never learned to type, and his oral muscles were among the first to be affected. As a result, he had developed dysarthria and was worried that his spoken language soon would be incomprehensible. During May 1993 he spent several late evenings dictating into a small hand-held tape recorder. The resulting professional memoir, which was first published (due to the kindness of the then-editor, John DeLuca) in the APA Division 40 Newsletter (Vol.14, no. 3, 1996), appears below. It has undergone very minor editing, mostly in the form of putting common turns of phrase into proper grammar appropriate for publication. My father would have approved of the minor edits, and if he had the chance, as anyone who ever had a paper edited by him would attest, would likely have taken far more red ink to it. His words speak for themselves.

Meryl A. Butters, Ph.D.
University of Pittsburgh
School of Medicine
April 2000

A Memoir

I am going to begin tonight a series of recordings dealing with various aspects of my career.

On March 11 of this year, 1993, I received the diagnosis of ALS. Not only do I have ALS, but also I have the bulbar form, which is clearly affecting my ability to talk. I am making these recordings now while I still have some speech left and I can clearly express my thoughts on a number of issues. I am not going to make believe that this disease is pleasant or something that I would wish on anybody else, but it does have some secondary gains. One gain is that at least it allows me time to get my business affairs in order. I am lucky in that way, in that the clarity of my thinking has not been affected.

The disease, because of its chronic nature, also allows me to say good-bye to people. If I had died of a heart attack, as did Norman Geschwind, I would not have had the opportunity to say good-bye to my wife, my children, my students, my friends, and my colleagues and to say things that needed to be said. I think in everyone's life one enters into many relationships where things are not always talked through or said completely. This is certainly true in my relationship with my father. When he died on March 14 of this year, one of the things I mourned was my failure to resolve my relationship with him. My disease at least allows me the opportunity of not making the same mistake twice; it allows me to say those things that I need to say to some people, especially my children and my wife, that I would not or have not said over the years.

A third so-called secondary gain of this disease is that it gives me time to look back over my career and get a feeling of just how successful or unsuccessful I have been. Have I really achieved the goals I wanted, career-wise, in my life? Tonight I would like to reflect upon this issue.

I should point out as background that, when I went to college, I was really uncertain about what I wanted to pursue in life. My parents had pushed very hard for me to become a medical doctor or at the very least a lawyer. Neither of these professions appealed to me very greatly. I was very aware as a child, and as a teenager, of my awkwardness with my hands—that is, my difficulty of acquiring motor skills with my hands—and I really felt uneasy about being a medical doctor or trying to perform medical procedures for this reason. I did have confidence in my ability to talk and to speak publicly, but I found law, or the practice of law, to be rather boring and really not consistent with my desire to do something that would be of benefit to humankind. I had never really been able to convince myself that lawyers contributed much to society or did much other than satisfy their own needs. As an aside, I might note that at this date, that is many years later, I still have the same feeling about lawyers and am very glad I never entered that profession.

So, at the time I was in college, first at the University of Chicago and then at Boston University, I really was uncertain as to what I wanted to do. I would say that some time during the second or third year of college my focus on my career became much clearer, and I made a decision that I wanted to be a teacher of some sort. I didn't want to be a high school teacher, but I did like the idea of teaching in college. As I said, public speaking came rather easily to me, and the whole idea of being able to influence the lives of college students in a positive way was most appealing to me. So by my fourth year of college I had pretty much decided that I would go on into psychology with the goal of ultimately being a college teacher.

What happened in my career was a matter of serendipity. I entered the Ph.D. program at Clark University in the fall of 1960 with my intentions aimed at the idea of being a teacher. In fact, I had been awarded a Woodrow Wilson Fellowship for my first year of graduate school because of my commitment to college teaching. During my second or third year in graduate school, I happened to run across an article in the *Journal of Comparative and Physiological Psychology*, which was written, I guess in 1962 or 1963, by Mort Mishkin and H. Enger Rosvold. It was an article dealing with frontal lobe functions in monkeys and dealt with delayed alternation and reversal learning. At the time I had become very interested in Piaget's notions about cognition, and it seemed to me that there were some parallels between the work that Rosvold and Mishkin were doing with monkeys on the frontal lobe and the work Piaget was doing with children. More specifically, my feeling was that Rosvold and Mishkin were looking at the neurological structures, which were mediating the developmental changes that Piaget talked about in most of his writings. At that point I became fascinated with the idea of trying to actually explore, in a study with monkeys and humans, this possibility. I can concretize it a little bit better by saying I became interested in what went on in the brain or in what structures in the brain played a part in the development of concrete operations or formal operations in the thinking processes of children.

During those days at Clark, a program in physiological psychology was not available to me. So I decided that after I received my Ph.D. I would spend a couple of years trying to study physiological psychology and perhaps conduct a few studies on this issue of the neurological bases of cognition before I went on and pursued my teaching career.

At the end of my third year of graduate school, I wrote to Hal Rosvold at the National Institutes of Health (NIH) and asked if he would consider taking me as a postdoctoral fellow, 12 months from then. At the time I did not have much hope of getting such a fellowship because of my total lack of background in physiological psychology, so I was quite delighted when I received the invitation in July or August of 1963 from Rosvold to visit his labs at NIH, and I accepted.

I am sure I did not impress them with my knowledge of much of anything, but I was very much impressed with them and I very much wanted to pursue a postdoctoral fellowship. I was lucky enough in those days that fellowships were very easy to get, and despite my lack of background in physiological psychology, I did get the fellowship and worked with Rosvold and Mishkin from 1964 to 1966. My work at that time at the NIH dealt with the septal nuclei, the basal forebrain, and also with the caudate and their roles in reversal learning, delayed alternation performance, and so on.

After finishing my postdoc and spending one year at Wright State University, I returned to Boston in 1967 at the invitation of Harold Goodglass and Norman Geschwind to continue my work with monkeys at the Boston VA and to work with Dee Pak Pandya on the anatomy of the frontal lobes. While I went there initially to work mostly with animals, I realized, of course, that I would have an opportunity to also learn something about human neuropsychology. It was in this period of l967 to 1970 that I was conducting animal and human research simultaneously.

My 1970 paper with Mel Barton on the role of the frontal and parietal lobes in concrete operations (what Piaget called concrete operations or reversible operations in space) contained much of my philosophy about neuropsychology. That article is one I am particularly proud of because it was the first to really go into the issue of what brain structures are involved in visual imagery. A few years later, the whole topic about lateralization of visual imagery and the ability to do reversible operations with imagery became a major topic that people like Steve Kosslyn, Martha Farah, and Freda Newcombe all have investigated much more thoroughly than Barton and I did. However, I felt that my paper with Mel Barton really laid out for me the kind of research I wanted to do, namely, looking at the brain structures that were mediating abnormal cognition. I tried to show in that article that one could take the concepts that were popular in human cognition at that time and use them in a heuristic way to look at how different brain structures play a role in these cognitive processes. In many ways that first study with Mel Barton ultimately led to my studies on memory with Korsakoff patients.

What essentially happened is that I began to raise a basic question as to why patients with parietal lobe lesions could not do reversible operations. One could argue that the defect was related to an inability to reverse images; that is, one could not manipulate images very well if one had a parietal lobe lesion. On the other hand, it was possible that the deficit was not one of reversal but one of retention; that is, perhaps patients with right parietal lesions could not retain visual images. This led me to the studies I did with Ina Samuels in 1971, 1972, and 1973. Many of these studies were published in *Neuropsychologia*. Basically these were the first studies in which we used the Peterson technique with verbal and pictorial material in order to look at short-term memory or short-term retention. The initial studies were done with right and left hemisphere patients, and the Korsakoff patients were originally used as a control group—they were there so that we would have a group of brain-damaged controls that would be impaired on all the various tests that we used, both verbal and nonverbal.

While we were running those studies I met Laird Cermak and began to look systematically at Korsakoff's disease and to examine the role of interference and encoding in these patients' short-term memory defects. Again, this research reflected my basic belief that one could apply the concept of cognitive psychology to neurology; that is, one could combine the two and have a cognitive neuropsychology—a psychology in which one looked at the neurological basis of cognitive concepts, of cognitive processes.

My monkey work during those years, I think, was also of some importance. It was in the late 1960s and early 1970s that we did our research on localization of function within the sulcus principalis and actually demonstrated that the middle-third of the sulcus principalis was the critical region for delayed alternation and delayed response impairments. Along with Dee Pak Pandya, we were able to show that this particular region had a different pattern of efferent and afferent projections than did the anterior and posterior thirds.

It was during the early-1970s that I also worked with Don Stein and Jeff Rosen on recovery of function. These studies, I think, were among the very first to show that one could remove sections of the frontal lobes in monkeys in serial fashion, that is, over a series of operations, and basically have recovery of function. Serial lesions compared to one-stage lesions led to much milder and in many cases no impairments on delayed alternation and delayed response type tasks. Although I did not follow these studies up in great depth, I consider them to be important studies in my career. My reasons for not following them up are rather interesting in retrospect.

By 1973 monkeys had started to become somewhat expensive, and the animal laboratory conditions at the Boston VA were less than optimal. There were poor heating facilities and very poor ventilation, and Dee Pak Pandya and I lost numerous monkeys due to shigellae and other diseases that were directly traceable to the lack of an appropriate environment in which to house the monkeys. On top of that, my skill as a surgeon was very, very limited. As I noted before, one of the reasons I did not go into medicine was because of the great difficulty I had acquiring motor skills with my hands, and surgery, neurosurgery in particular, brought out all my deficiencies. I had a great deal of tremor and a great deal of instability with my hands, and I simply could not make the lesions I wanted to make in order to complete the studies that I wished to conduct. I also felt that it was inappropriate simply to delegate my lesion-making to other people and, although Jeff Rosen was a competent surgeon, I knew that Jeff would not be there forever. I eventually simply reconciled myself to the idea that I would cease to do animal research and concentrate on my human research.

By the mid-1970s my work with Laird Cermak had become well known and had already begun to have an impact on the field. More and more people were borrowing concepts, as we had from cognitive psychology, and testing them with various brain-damaged populations. At that time I also began to look at other patient populations. It was in the early- to mid-1970s that I became interested in Huntington's disease (HD) for the first time. In my initial studies on this disorder, the HD patients were used as a control group for the Korsakoff's patients. In my career it is rather interesting to note that many of my control groups in one study became a major focus of research in succeeding studies, and HD is a good example of that.

It was also in the mid-1970s that I became interested in looking at the issue of alcoholism in general, that is, cognitive deficits in long-term alcoholics who did not have Korsakoff's disease. Initially my interest in this was to simply see what the similarities between non-Korsakoff alcoholics and alcoholic Korsakoffs were. I am not going to review my findings on this, but I think it is fair to say that the papers that emanated from these studies, more specifically the papers with Chris Ryan and Jim Becker, Kathy Montgomery and Barbara Jones, all influenced the way that the neuropsychology of alcoholism is now viewed.

There was also another trend in my research during the mid- to late-1970s, which dealt with my desire to look at retrograde amnesia. I spent about 6–7 years looking at anterograde amnesia and was rather struck that no one had really studied retrograde amnesia in any systematic way. It was also obvious to me that the reason for this was the lack of suitable test instruments. At that time I was lucky to have Marilyn Albert join our laboratory, and she took on the task of developing the Boston Retrograde Amnesia Battery. She took this on with great enthusiasm, and ultimately our studies in 1979–1981 and our papers on patient PZ were a direct result of her great efforts in developing this battery.

Toward the end of the 1970s it became very clear to me that I could not stay in Boston for my entire career. There were a number of reasons why I came to this conclusion. I think ultimately I felt that I did not want to work in a hostile environment. I felt that the environment at the Boston VA, the environment that emanated from the administrators of the VA toward psychology research, was extremely hostile. I was also somewhat bothered that people in the medical school who should have defended us did not. In fact, I was very turned off by the lack of support that we received from the Dean and from the Chairman of Neurology.

I made up my mind toward the late-1970s that I would leave and build my own unit at some other medical school. I had many false starts at leaving. Moving to Pittsburgh, Houston, and Maryland were all possibilities at one time or another. In retrospect, I am very glad I did not go to any of these places because in 1983 I moved to University of California at San Diego (UCSD) at a most appropriate time for me and for UCSD. The UCSD Psychiatry Department offered me an opportunity that no other place did, namely, to take a clinical service and develop it with people who could do research as well as clinical work. In other words, I had a chance to prove that within a VA setting a clinical psychologist actually could do research and conduct major research programs at the same time that clinical services were provided to patients. As far as I knew, that was a rather rare occurrence in VA hospitals, which were generally quite hostile to research by clinical psychologists.

Another important consideration in my move to San Diego was the fact that clearly UCSD was going to be awarded a national Alzheimer's Disease Research Center. I also was aware that Boston University never had a chance of ever getting one of those centers, and I did want to continue my work that I began with Huntington's Disease and generalize it to cortical dementias such as dementia of Alzheimer's type (DAT). So, given the opportunities to develop my own psychology service and to be the Director of Neuropsychology at the Alzheimer's Center, in 1983, I moved to UCSD.

I think that my major accomplishments at UCSD involved both administration and research. I think on an administrative level I developed what I set out to develop, namely, a first-rate psychology service and, in particular, a superb neuropsychology group. I do not think that in terms of training, research, or clinical developments that another group in the country exists that is as good as the group I developed at UCSD.

I think my research accomplishments at UCSD fall into three distinct areas. One of my areas of research focused on the processes that underlie the memory disorders of cortical and subcortical dementias, and I think the work we have done comparing Alzheimer's and Huntington's patients in terms of the nature of their episodic and semantic memory defects has clearly demonstrated that all dementias are not alike. Different types of dementia manifest quite different types of memory impairments.

I think a second contribution has been in the early detection of dementia. Once we identified the neuropsychological characteristics that define a given type of dementia, they could be used for early detection of the disease. Work with the Consortium to Develop a Registry for Alzheimer's Disease (CERAD) Neuropsychological Battery, for instance, and with the Wechsler Memory Scale–Revised has shown that forgetting rates, or rapid forgetting, is a very good early indicator of DAT. In contrast, the rate of forgetting remains fairly normal in the case of patients with subcortical dementias like Huntington's Disease.

We made some significant contributions in a third area by showing the structures that underlie different types of implicit memory. By comparing patients with cortical and subcortical dementias, we have shown double dissociations between various implicit memory tasks and the two types of dementias. I think that our demonstration that patients with basal ganglia dementias are impaired specifically on implicit tasks that require the programming of motor movements is a very important demonstration, and I think that this will tend to hold up over time. I think, however, that our grasp of the nature of the implicit memory defect associated with Alzheimer's disease is still somewhat vague and I am not totally satisfied that we are on the right track with regard to this particular issue.

In terms of the research that I currently am involved in, I think there are two general projects that have great promise. I am extremely impressed with the work that has been done with Agnes Chan, using multi-dimensional scaling to develop two- and three-dimensional models of the semantic networks and semantic spaces of patients with Alzheimer's disease and subcortical dementias. I think that work is very creative and extremely unique, and I am hoping that Agnes will be able to continue that even when I am not here to help her.

The other area that I am very excited about at this time is the work that has recently begun with Mark Bondi looking at the pre-clinical signs of DAT; that is, can one, using neuropsychological tasks, pick out those healthy elderly individuals who will most likely develop DAT in the next three to four years? I think that Bondi's work with the California Verbal Learning Test, showing that particular indices such as intrusion errors and rapid forgetting are good early pre-clinical indicators of an upcoming DAT, is most promising and is an area that I believe will produce very important results in the long run.

I guess if I am going to be totally candid I should mention at least one area that I believe is going to go nowhere in the future. That is the area of so-called implicit memory. Over the last 10 years I have become more and more discouraged about the so-called separation of explicit and implicit memory, and although I have not said this publicly for political reasons, I think that this line of research is essentially going nowhere. I really do not think there are separate memory systems such as explicit and implicit; I think there is only one system. I believe what we are really seeing is that some patients can do some tasks but not others, that the reason they do some tasks and not others is because of the demands and the nature of the task and not because of two memory systems. Again, I think we only need posit one memory system. We need to look more clearly at the processes that the patients bring to bear on the demands of the task. I think that theorists who have proposed separate systems are going to find that their work is essentially going to hit a brick wall. I think conceptually it is weak, and I think it is nearing its end.

Now I would like to go back to a point I made about thirty minutes ago, namely, that when I went into this field my main objective was to be a teacher rather than a researcher. The outline I've provided here would lead one to believe that I have not met any of my objectives. In essence, I gave up being a teacher. Well, that is not quite correct. The thing I am most proud of in my professional life is the success of my former students, that is, my former postdocs and my former graduate students. The great delight that I always got out of doing research was seeing the great pleasure that my students found in this kind of scholarly endeavor. I always enjoyed, in a sense, teaching a student how to think and how to write. I would never have been much of a technician or methodologist. I think my strengths are that I could always write well and that I could think about a problem in a very logical manner. I think that one of the reasons I have always been seemingly one step ahead of the field is that I have always thought about problems in this very logical way. I have really delighted in training so many students to think the way I think. I am not sure where I acquired this skill, but it is something that I think I have successfully passed on to two or three generations of students. I am obviously extremely pleased to see people like Marilyn Albert, Jason Brandt, Jim Becker, Chris Ryan, David Salmon, and so on and so on, all do well in their professional careers. This is for me a great fulfillment of my desire to be a teacher. I think that for me the finest rewards I have received have been the thanks of students for the training I have given them, and I don't think they really have ever understood how much they also have given to me over the years, largely because I don't think many of them really understood that teaching was actually my initial career choice.

So, as I look back over my career I am obviously quite gratified and proud of the research that bears my name. But I am even prouder and happier about the students that I have trained. It is a wonderful feeling to know that you have had a positive effect on other people's lives. I think that knowing this makes my death much more acceptable and allows me to be at peace with myself, because I feel I have really made a difference in this world. The difference has been the way I have affected the lives of the students who have passed by me. I want to thank these students for allowing me to really have a wonderful and fulfilling life, at least professionally.

I know that some people think that it is quite tragic that I am facing death at a time when I've reached the pinnacle of my career, but I have a somewhat different philosophy about this whole situation. My view is that you can't judge a life or career by its length; rather you have to judge it by its quality. I feel I have accomplished a good deal on both the professional level and on a personal level during my life. You know, it's like a party; just because a party lasts a long time doesn't mean it's a good party. Some parties are much shorter but very sweet. And that's the way my life has been.

Nelson Butters, Ph.D.
May 16, 1993

Postscript

There are two remaining aspects of my father, one professional and one personal, that are important to highlight. On the professional level, my father spent much professional energy demonstrating the existence of distinct dissociations among cognitive functions within and between patients with various forms of cerebral dysfunction. He was unusually successful (perhaps uniquely so) at integrating neuroanatomy and cognitive theory with applied neuropsychology. As a result, one of the most distinguishing features of his career is that his work has been highly regarded by cognitive and clinical researchers as well as practicing clinicians. He was especially proud of his "cross–professional" appeal.

On the personal level, my father was a multi-faceted and complicated man who was many things to many people. Nevertheless, there are a number of consistent themes that run through the numerous tributes to him offered during his illness and following his death. Some come through clearly in this memoir, while others do not and therefore deserve mention here.

First, he was blunt, brash, and famously irreverent. While his lifestyle was decidedly mainstream, he was interested in those who chose to walk off the beaten path, and he liked to think of himself as something of a rebel. His role models included Marlon Brando, Lenny Bruce, and Woody Allen. He found humor in the darker side of life, though he never took himself too seriously. On more than one occasion he said, "If I wasn't a neuropsychologist, I would have been a comedian." But he was a neuropsychologist; he had a tremendous drive to perform well and held his students and colleagues to the same high standards he applied to himself. Every student he ever had has distinct memories of the red ink and blunt reviews accompanying their manuscript drafts. Having said that, while many perceived him as hard on his students, he was a very active and supportive mentor and colleague. He devoted much time and energy to providing a vast array of people with professional and personal advice and help. In his later years, he liked to think of himself as the "Godfather of Neuropsychology," often acting as a jobbroker for students and colleagues. When he became ill, he received hundreds of letters from concerned colleagues, staff, and friends. All conveyed concern and most also contained their favorite story or memory. Many contained anecdotes referring to ways he had helped someone.

Finally, it is important to mention my father's extreme devotion to our family. He and my mother were very young when they married, and she was always his sustaining light. Despite always having so much to do professionally, he always found time to nurture the individual in each of his three children, especially when we were young and needed it the most. He always recognized that his professional success was dependent upon the sustenance he received from his family.

M. A. B.

3

Henry Hécaen
Evolution of His Thought

Athanase Tzavaras
Martin L. Albert

To assert that Henry Hécaen was a powerful moving force in the creation of the contemporary field of neuropsychology during its fragile early years is merely to state the obvious. He was co-creator of the influential annual meeting of neuropsychologists, the International Neuropsychological Symposium (Zangwill, 1984), and was founding editor-in-chief of the journal *Neuropsychologia.* He published 346 scientific papers in the field and authored or edited 19 books or collections of essays. For years he was director of the world famous Research Laboratory for Neuropsychological Studies at Hôpital Sainte-Anne in Paris and the director of programs in human neuropsychology at the École Pratique des Hautes Études. His pioneering research discoveries are legendary. The purpose of this chapter, then, will not be merely to revisit his scientific corpus and comment on why this or that article was important (although we surely will do that), but rather to examine Hécaen's background, interests, and quirks with the goal of coming to understand the evolution of his thought. To this end we will explore Hécaen's passions as a seaman–mariner, an amateur Hellenist, a neuropsychiatrist, and above all a "Breton."

Perhaps we should begin with this last element, because it marks his sense of self-identification as a man *from* the outside and a man *of* the outside as opposed to a man from and of the mainstream. Hécaen was born in Brest, in Bretagne, in 1912, to a middle-class family and not in Paris to a wealthy or well-connected family. Throughout his life he persisted in declaring himself a Breton, not a Frenchman. To underscore this distinction he insisted on spelling his first name Henry in the Anglicized form and not Henri—a fact misunderstood by some journal editors who continue to "correct" the spelling to Henri, even to this day. This small but symbolic sign of self-identification is representative of Hécaen's independent-minded, provocative, and persistent (some might have said stubborn) willingness to stand out from the crowd and, indeed, even challenge the mainstream. That a man with such personal qualities might help create a distinctive new scientific domain and persevere in assuring its realization might not then be surprising.

Hécaen enrolled, while still relatively young, as a student in the Naval Medical

41

Figure 3.1. Henry Hécaen

School in Bordeaux. He graduated at the age of 22 with a thesis that was audacious for its time and place: "Artistic Inspiration and Its Relation to Madness." His dissertation, required for the medical degree in France, studied the case of the German composer Hugo Wolf and was inspired by sources that include ancient Greek literature, Freudian psychoanalysis, and phenomenology. His first teacher of neuropsychiatry was the senior neuropsychiatrist of the French navy, A. Hesnard, who was also his superior at the naval port in Toulon. Hesnard was famous at the time for helping introduce Freudian psychoanalysis to France.

For at least five years, Hécaen occupied various positions in the naval medical service and also served on warships at sea. Whenever possible, he would take the opportunity to attend teaching sessions by neurologists Jean Lhermitte and André Thomas in Parisian hospitals or spend time in cosmopolitan circles in Paris, including the surrealist set of Andre Breton. It is during this period that Hécaen consolidated his passion for art of the ancient world and improved his knowledge of ancient Greek. At the end of the 1930s, he married a talented violinist and daughter of an admiral. His naval career ended ingloriously (he used to call it a glorious end, with his characteristic self-directed irony). In the harbor of Dunkerque, when due to an error of a wireless operator, the navy oil tanker on which Hécaen served, instead of avoiding this channel harbor after the washout of the British landing, was trapped and seized, together with its crew, by German troops. During the skirmishes, a bullet accidentally hit Hécaen in the leg. A prisoner of war, injured, and on top of that suffering from malaria, Hécaen found himself in the privileged position of being released as a prisoner of the German army and discharged from the armed forces prestigiously due to this "luckily unlucky" conjuncture. Back in Paris, in collaboration with his close friend, the Basque political refugee de Ajuriaguerra, Hécaen began his true scientific career, mainly working with Jean Lhermitte but also with André Thomas.

At about this time Hécaen acquired the only official French hospital title he was to receive: Medecin des Hôpitaux Psychiatriques. A close look into Hécaen's scientific output published before the end of World War II reveals that his principal interests already lay at the borders of neurology and psychiatry. In an energetic dialogue with his friend, the French psychiatrist Henri Ey, Hécaen defended the doctrine of a *continuum* of the two disciplines or, better, the unity of neurologic and psychiatric concerns. Due to his areas of scientific interest that were only in later decades to capture the imagination of the world, but also due to the inability or unwillingness of the French hospital system to offer him an official, clinically responsible position, Hécaen for years remained professionally marginal.

Nervertheless, even in the clinical world of Paris after World War II Hécaen played a central role in the grand project of understanding the relation between brain and behavior, both by studying the psychiatric consequences of brain tumors or trauma and by studying the effectiveness of psychosurgery. By the end of the 1940s he had become the behavioral neurologist–neuropsychologist on the team of professor M. David, the well-known Parisian neurosurgeon, assigned to study the effectiveness and dangers of psychosurgery. The conclusions of this research, generally unknown to the international neuroscientific community, greatly influenced the practice of psychosurgery in France, resulting in its strict limitation well before limitations on psychosurgery were imposed in other countries.

Early in the 1950s Hécaen traveled to Montreal to work and study for a year at McGill University with the great neurosurgeon–neuroscientist Wilder Penfield. The year 1952 was to become a turning point in Hécaen's career. Working feverishly, he incorporated into his already rich clinical experience a strict experimental methodology. The scientific techniques of quantification in the study of brain–behavior relations and rigor of experimental design had not yet spread widely in France, and Hécaen was thirsty for them and passionate in his desire to introduce these new methods into his own work and the work of others.

Back in Paris after his year in Montreal, Hécaen continued in his role as Medecin des Hôpitaux Psychiatriques. It may be useful at this point to clarify the notion of "professionally marginal" for those readers who are not familiar with French academic medicine and clinical practice in the 1940s and 1950s. Hécaen never received an official major hospital appointment as a neurologist in charge of a neurological unit. The official hospital position offered Hécaen did not ensure his financial independence. Consequently, after his morning job at the hospital, he engaged in the private clinical practice of neuropsychiatry in the afternoons. After dinner, he would meet with his research collaborators, usually for a two-hour working session between 9:00 p.m. and 11:00 p.m. Into these sessions he introduced the ideas and research techniques he brought back with him from Montreal. Often, after the others had left, he would stay up into the early morning hours writing his professional papers and books.

Little by little, article by scientific article, he became recognized for his work in neuropsychiatry, especially in the world outside of France. Within France, recognition was slower in arriving; however, with research support of the Centre National de Recherches Scientifiques and the Institut National de la Santé et de la Recherche Medicale, he began to build a research team of scientists interested in the study of brain–behavior relations. Not until 1965, much later in his career, was he appointed Directeur d'Études of the École Pratique des Hautes Études. This was an academic appointment outside the hospital world but one with wide recognition, even within France, and one with a great potential for the development of interdisciplinary research programs. This appointment allowed him, finally, to close his private medical practice and engage undisturbed in his research and teaching activities. Nevertheless, it was only in 1970 that his research team was moved to autonomous and adequate research space. Hécaen remained director of this research center until 1982 when he retired. He continued to work actively and creatively, however, until his death in 1983.

This brief summary of Hécaen's career reveals two characteristics that persisted throughout his professional life and served as basic building blocks of his intellectual development. First, he combined a profound, almost encyclopedic, clinical knowledge with a detailed experimental study of clinical phenomena, using the most valid and reliable methods available at the time whether that meant applying few measurements to great numbers of subjects or great numbers of measurements to fewer numbers of subjects. Second, he brought to neuropsychiatry and neuropsychology information and techniques from other disciplines including neurobiology, linguistics, anthropology, philosophy, and statistics. Anyone who tried to classify the domains of research carried out by Hécaen and his research team during his lifetime would be astonished to discover that there were virtually no clinical neuropsychological phenomena that escaped study.

One of Hécaen's strategic techniques was to publish books periodically that gathered and summarized all existing, available research data in the field of neuropsychology, including, of course, his own. By reviewing these state-of-the-art publications, we can track not only the evolution of Hécaen's own work and thought but also that of the field itself. We also can see the steady growth of Hécaen's influence throughout the world. We might mention that Hécaen wrote most (85%) of his articles and books in French. His international influence and acclaim did not rest on the 15% of his publications in English, however, but on the many foreign accounts of his research, his numerous students (disciples might be a better word) from around the world, and his wide-ranging lecture tours.

Highlights of his state-of-the-art compendia include the 1944 to 1945 debate published in 1947 entitled "The Relation Between Neurology and Psychiatry," found in *The History of Psychiatry* (Alexander & Selesnick, 1966). Hécaen's ideas about the relation of neurology and psychiatry also are referred to in the complete list of Hécaen's publications prepared in 1984 by Galtier. Publications 124 and 129 are found in the special issue of *Neuropsychologia* compiled in memory of Hécaen (Jeannerod, 1984). In all of these works, Hécaen supported the position of continuity of the two fields.

In 1949 Ajuriaguerra and Hécaen produced an impressively dense and informed book considering the period immediately after the second World War, *Le cortex cérébral,* with the subtitle *Une étude neuro-psycho-pathologique.* This book presented in concentrated form almost all available data in neuropsychology. It was organized along two tracks—one in relation to the anatomic and functional specialization of cerebral hemispheres and/or lobes, the other in relation to major cerebral functions (i.e., speech, skilled movement, perception, etc.). This book constituted the major post-war point of departure for neuropsychology, served as the teaching manual for thousands of students and young neurologists and psychiatrists, and rendered Hécaen and Ajuriaguerra famous around the world. The first edition sold out, and a second revised edition appeared in 1960 and had similar publishing success. In the same spirit of comprehensiveness, Hécaen published his *Introduction á la neuropsychologie* in 1972 and, in 1978, in collaboration with Martin Albert, his text–reference entitled *Human Neuropsychology.* This book, translated into English and updated, systematized representation of Hécaen's line of thinking and research.

Hécaen's neuropsychological teachings were particularly well-expressed by the model concept of body schema. Although in the late-1940s and early-1950s the concept of body schema was considered by many to be a psychiatric or mentalist phenomenon belonging in the realm of philosophy, Hécaen provided one of the first views of this concept as the product of neurologic processing. Combining philosophy (with references to Merleau-Ponty and Thomas Aquinas), psychology (with reference to psychological aspects of conscious awareness), and neurology (with reference to selective losses of conscious awareness due to right hemisphere lesions which can cause anosognosia), Hécaen provided one of the earliest comprehensive neuropsychological formulations of conscious awareness of one's own body. This theorizing fit well within his general notion of the unity of neurology and psychiatry.

The successful collaboration of Hécaen and Ajuriaguerra produced the highly original monograph *Méconnaissances et hallucinations corporelles* in 1952, which reviewed all known apractoagnostic syndromes and all data related to agnosia for awareness of one's own body. Modern readers may find it useful to be reminded that in the journal *L'encephale* (1945 to 1946) Hécaen and Ajuriaguerra were the first to describe with nosographic clarity the syndrome of dressing apraxia, thus initiating, in coordination with other researchers around the world, the study of neuropsychological functions of the right hemisphere. This book, which had a frigid reception on the part of the scientific community at the time, can be usefully examined a posteriori, in parallel with its contemporary *Parietal Lobes* by Critchley (1953).

Together with his new collaborator, René Angelergues, Hécaen published a book that synthesized the problem of agnosias in 1963 and a book about aphasias in 1965 (Hécaen & Angelergues, 1963, 1965). These books, together with *Les troubles mentaux* in 1956 and *Les gauchers* in 1963, document the change in methodology used by Hécaen and his collaborators (Hécaen & Ajuriaguerra, 1956, 1963). After 1952, Hécaen's research began to be based on thorough and methodical examination of groups of brain-damaged patients, the results of which were quantified and subjected to statistical analysis. Hécaen's studies of brain-damaged subjects with carefully controlled experiments and statistical analyses led researchers around the world into the early modern phase of neuropsychological research. His insistence on the use of the scientific method in experimental neuropsychology in no way diminished Hécaen's passion for thorough study of unusual syndromes or clinical dissociations. Thus, Hécaen contributed not only detailed experimental analyses of classical neuropsychological syndromes but also new and rich clinical descriptions of rare syndromes such as visual agnosia, crossed aphasia, prosopagnosia, and Balint's syndrome.

In the 1960s, Hécaen again broke new ground in the study of brain–behavior relations by collaborating with linguists and creating an interdisciplinary research team that promoted, as few others have, neurolinguistics on the European continent. As is well known, the encounter between linguistics, speech pathology, and neurology has passed (not always comfortably) through various stages in its history, from a mere flirtation to frenetic mating. As Hécaen was studying neurolinguistics in the 1960s and 1970s, attempts were being made to illustrate Chomksy's theoretical constructs of "competence" and "performance" through analyses of aphasia. By the 1980s and even more so in the 1990s, the sophistication of neu-rolinguistic studies would have surprised even Hécaen.

As he moved into the 1970s, Hécaen began publishing in two domains—one looking backward, the other looking forward. Looking back, he produced with the historian Lanteri-Laura *Évolution des connaissances et des doctrines sur les localisa-tions cérébrales* (1977). Here he seized the opportunity of a historical review to adopt a final position on the issue of cerebral localization. He opted for a "yes, but" position. Although he was able, clearly and with abundant evidence, to support a firm belief in concepts of cerebral dominance of function and cerebral localization of function, he nevertheless was a sufficiently experienced clinician and a suffi-ciently objective scientist to recognize the merit of the arguments in favor of cere-bral plasticity. Looking forward, his second major work in this period, *Adaptation et restauration des fonctions nerveuses* (Jeannerod & Hécaen, 1979), was another state-of the-art document, opening the debate on cerebral plasticity that rages to this day.

Always provocative, always creative, always building new ideas on the solid foundations of the past, never afraid to explore new dimensions of brain–behavior relations, and never afraid to challenge existing dogmas and dogmatists, Hécaen managed to combine the proud regionalism of the Breton with the adventurous spirit of the navy seaman. As he lay dying from the consequences of a myocardial infarction, he summed up, telling one of us at his bedside: "I know I am dying. I want you to tell my friends I was proud of my career. I think I left a mark in the world of neurology and neuropsychology."

REFERENCES

Alexander, F. G. & Selesnick, S. J. (1966). *The history of psychiatry.* New York: Harper & Row.

Ajuriaguerra, J. de., & Hécaen, H. (1949). *Le cortex cérébral.* Paris: Masson.

Critchley, M. (1953). *The parietal lobes.* London: Hafher.

Galtier, A. (1984). Publications de Henry Hécaen. *Neuropsychologia, 22,* 647–59.

Hécaen, H. (1972). *Introduction et la neu-ropsychologie.* Paris: Larousse.

Hécaen, H., & Ajuriaguerra, J. de. (1952). *Méconnaissances et hallucinations cor-porelles.* Paris: Masson.

Hécaen, H., & Ajuriaguerra, J. de. (1956). *Les troubles mentaux au cours des tumeurs intracrâniennes.* Paris: Masson.

Hécaen, H., & Ajuriaguerra, J. de. (1963). *Les gauchers.* Paris: P.U.F.

Hécaen, H., & Albert, M. L. (1978). *Human neuropsychology.* New York: J Wiley.

Hécaen, H., & Angelergues, R. (1963). *La cécité psychique.* Paris: Masson.

Hécaen, H., & Angelergues, R. (1965). *Pathologie du language.* Paris: Larousse.

Hécaen H., & Lanteri-Laura, G. (1977). *Evolu-tion des connaissances et des doctrines sur les localisation cérébrales.* Paris: DDB.

Jeannerod, M. (Ed.). (1984). A special issue of *Neuropsychologia* dedicated to the memory of Henry Hécaen. *Neuropsychologia, 22,* 647–819.

Jeannerod, M., & Hécaen, H. (1979). *Adapta-tion et restauration des fonctions nerveuses.* Villeurbane, France: SIMEP.

Zangwill, O. L. (1984). Henry Hécaen and the origins of the International Neuropsycho-logical Symposium. *Neuropsychologia, 22,* 813–815.

4

A. R. Luria
Pursuing Neuropsychology
in a Swiftly Changing Society

Lena Moskovich
Dmitri Bougakov
Philip DeFina
Elkhonon Goldberg

A life, a human life, is not a life until it is examined; it is not a life until
it is truly remembered and appropriated; and such a remembrance is
not something passive, but active, the active and creative construction
of one's life, the finding and telling of the true story of one's life.
(Sacks, 1987, p. xvii)

I had very few opportunities to get normal systematic education.
Instead of that life offered me an incredibly stimulating atmosphere of
active and swiftly changing society. (Luria, 1982, p. 5)

*A*leksandr Romanovich Luria was born on July 16, 1902, in Kazan, Russia.
His father, Roman Albertovich Luria, was a famous gastroenterologist, and
his mother was a dentist. Possessing a strong, active, and dominant personality, Luria's father had a great authority over his children (which he continued
to have until the end of his life). Influenced by their father, both Luria and his sister ended up in a medical field. (Luria's sister, Lilly, became a psychiatrist.)

Both of Luria's parents were Jewish but, as in many Jewish families in Russia
and later in the Soviet Union, religion was never practiced in their house. Luria's
parents represented that group of professionals known as the "Russian Intelli-
gentsia" who were characterized by their appreciation of everything spiritual and
an ascetic attitude toward everyday living. There was no particular familial
warmth in the Luria household, but education was definitely a point of importance: Aleksandr and Lilly had a governess and were taught German, French, and
English from early childhood.

In 1918, Luria enrolled in the Law School of Kazan University (which shortly
after became the Public Science Department), from which he graduated in 1921.
There he discovered the world of psychology, and from that moment on, studied

Figure 4.1. Aleksandr Romanovich Luria

the field intensely. From the start, Luria was not satisfied with the psychology of his time. Thus, he began his search for a "scientific, real psychology" that would combine the investigation of individual human beings with the search for general principles of the human mind. As he expressed it, "I dreamt about [a] psychology that . . . studied simultaneously both concrete facts of life of [the] individual person and general laws that explained all of them" (Luria, 1982, p. 10).

Searching for "real life" psychology, Luria turned to the works of Freud. In 1922, he organized the (Russian) Psychoanalytic Association and wrote to Sigmund Freud. Surprisingly, Freud responded with a warm, supportive letter; however, after Luria reviewed the available literature, the young scientist quickly became critical of psychoanalysis. More specifically, he felt that psychoanalysis ignored the importance of social experience in cognition. Around this same time, Luria began to turn his attention toward experimental psychological methods, and he would go on to employ these methods to the study of psychoanalytic concepts.

One of his first investigations addressed the effects of toxic exposure on workers in a letter foundry. In addition to using reaction time as a main measure of fatigue, Luria introduced something "extravagant" to the experiment—the role of speech in reaction time regulation. Luria's involvement in this project had important consequences. He became fascinated with experimental psychology and started the journal *Problems of Psychophysiology, Reflexology and Hygiene of Labor*. Luria's work on the journal resulted in an offer of employment from the Moscow Institute of Psychology. Luria wrote, "All this period of my life was a period of naïve search of my own way in psychology. However, fifty years later, I feel that this period of my life was very important for my formation as a psychologist" (Luria, 1982, p. 14).

At this time Luria met his first wife—the actress V. Blagovidova. She inspired a poetic side of Luria not generally known to the scientific public. Much later, Luria's daughter Yelena (Lenochka) published a few of Luria's poems written for his first wife (Luria, 1994). The last line of one of the poems reads, "Life without tales is just a stupid joke" (p. 216).

Beginning in 1923, Luria lived in Moscow. He worked in the Institute of Psychology and lectured in the Academy of Communist Education. He wrote, "I was not older than my students and I did not know essentially more than they did, so I spent all the evenings preparing the next day lectures and hoping that I will [sic] be able to forestall them if only for a day" (Luria, 1982, p. 18). This period in his career also is significant because Luria met A. N. Leont'yev who became his friend and co-worker for the rest of his life.

Luria's interest in psychoanalysis resulted in the creation of a unique experimental design. He was interested in the objective measurement of responses during the process of free association, rather than just subjective interpretations. In his own words he explained, "I decided to start with my own 'experimental psychoanalysis,' using fluctuations of intensity of motor reactions as an objective measure of inner emotional conflicts" (Luria, 1982, p. 19). Luria came up with what he called the "conjugate motor method." In this method, participants were asked to free associate to both "neutral" and "critical" word stimuli while simultaneously giving a motor response. The motor response involved pressing a rubber bulb with their right hand while the left hand lay free on another bulb. Simultaneity of performance was a critical point because "the verbal response and the motor response should be combined into one functional system" (p. 19). Using this paradigm, Luria and Leont'yev investigated students just prior to their exams, as well as psychiatric patients and criminals. Analysis of reaction time data did not show significant differences in responses to the neutral and critical words; however, the supposedly "passive" left hand involuntarily reacted to the stimuli as well, particularly in response to the "critical" words.

In 1925, Luria began publishing the results of these investigations. In 1929 he presented some results at the International Psychological Congress at Yale, and in 1932 his book, *The Nature of Human Conflicts,* was published in the United States of America. Although this book gained Luria recognition in the outside world, it was never published in Russia. Luria's personal ambitions for this book were perhaps not realized:

> The theoretical basis of this work was naïve. . . . This work helped me to solve some of my early problems. . . . However its value was limited. Although the method synthesized . . . approaches that previously existed isolated from each other, it has not led to [a] fundamental reconstruction of psychology as a science. The fundamental reconstruction of psychology as a science . . . was a huge task that exceeded my limited abilities. I faced it unexpectedly in 1924 after I met Lev Semyonovich Vygotsky. . . . This event was a turning point of my life. (Luria, 1982, p. 23–24)

Luria met Vygotsky at a 1924 Neurology Congress in Leningrad. The 28-year-old teacher was giving a talk, "Consciousness as a Subject of Psychology," about the relationship between conditioned reflexes and human conscious behavior. Luria was inspired so much that he arranged a position for Vygotsky at the Moscow Institute of Psychology. Vygotsky joined Luria and Leont'yev, and subsequently became a guru for the other two. Together, they began to call themselves the "troika" or threesome.

The troika was interested in studying complex psychological phenomena in an experimental way, which was uncommon for the psychology of that time. They agreed that complex human psychological processes are qualitatively different from what is observed in animal behavior. They proposed that conditioned reflexes could not explain the complexity of human behavior and cognition and also noted that behaviors that appear to be similar in humans and other animals do not necessarily reflect the same psychological mechanisms.

Vygotsky referred to his theory as "instrumental," "cultural," or "historical" psychology. It was based on the premise that cognitive operations are to a large extent internalized cultural devices. As an extension of this idea, Vygotsky and Luria developed a theory that cognitive processes descend from the complex interaction of biological and cultural factors through the course of human history. These theoretical issues determined the main lines of Luria's subsequent research.

Luria, Leont'yev, and Vygotsky analyzed many important psychological issues (e.g., attention, memory, perception, etc.) and created new experiments to test the idea that the formation of higher forms of activity changes the structure of psychological processes. To that end, they embarked on experimental studies of child development. Their second line of research was a longitudinal study of identical and fraternal twins. A third line of investigation was a comparative study of normal and mentally retarded children. Finally, their fourth line of research focused on a cross-cultural investigation of specific forms of higher psychological processes in adults that grew up in a cultural environment different from European, industrialized Russia.

Results of their investigations supported their assumptions that human cognition can only be understood in the light of cultural anthropology and development. Human cognition is best viewed as the end product of the internalization of codes that pre-exist in the culture in an overt, external form. These codes, apart from their obvious function of communication, also provide cognitive strategies and representational systems, and thus are crucial for the development of self-regulation and volition. Children acquire cultural codes during the course of language acquisition. Likewise, children's capacity for self-regulating behavior develops from the internalization of what was initially a form of interpersonal verbal interaction. This conviction colored all of Luria's subsequent research into brain–behavior relations.

Luria and Vygotsky also embarked on the study of the disintegration of cognitive functions as a result of brain damage. In their work with aphasic patients, they sought to establish qualitative differences between normal and impaired verbal activity. They studied the regulatory influence of language on behavior as well as changes in other cognitive processes secondary to speech–language deficits.

Luria and Vygotsky also worked with patients diagnosed with Parkinson's disease. These patients had an impaired gait that resulted in frequent falls. To determine whether walking, an essentially automatized function in humans, could be improved in Parkinson's patients by bringing it under higher cortical control, Luria and Vygotsky ingeniously asked patients to step over pieces of paper scattered on the floor. By placing paper on the floor, Luria and Vygotsky hoped to recruit the participation of higher sensorimotor areas in the regulation of gait. As they expected, this manipulation improved the ability of Parkinson's patients to walk and therefore showed that transferring the neural regulation of a function to a different level in the brain could compensate for an impaired automatized process. This principle of reconstructing psychological processes by transferring them to another level of regulation was used later by Luria as well as by his followers in cognitive rehabilitation.

In another research project of that time, Luria and Vygotsky planned to investigate the intellectual activity of large groups of adults belonging to non-industrial, illiterate, "traditional" society. They chose remote parts of Central Asia to conduct their investigations where peasants were illiterate and isolated from western culture. They launched two expeditions to study the effect of literacy and social change on the forms of logical inference used by the indigenous inhabitants of these areas. To facilitate their work, Luria even learned the Uzbek language.

Luria was highly enthusiastic about the body of experimental data that was collected. The results confirmed both Luria's hypothesis and the value of the experimental design. Among the tests administered was an optical illusions task. After finding differences in the Asian participants' performance on this task compared to the typical performance of Westerners, Luria jokingly cabled to Vygotsky, "Uzbeks have no illusions!" (Homskaya, 1992, p. 32). Unfortunately, he underestimated the amount of censorship in the Soviet society. The innocent telegram was given an implicit ideological meaning, and it contributed to the government's crush of historico–cultural psychology.

The ideological watchdogs found the work of Vygotsky and Luria to be "reactionary and hostile to Marxism" (Luria, 1994, p. 67). Between 1932 and 1936, historico–cultural psychology was branded as "idealistic" (Luria, 1994, p. 68), not to distinguish it from "pragmatism" or "cynicism" but in contradistinction to "materialism." Such labelling misrepresented historico–cultural psychology as an extreme deviation from the dominant Marxist–Leninist ideology. Instead of interpreting the findings of Luria's expeditions as evidence that the social changes initiated by the Soviet regime facilitated the transition of logical structures used by rural non-westerners in the direction of cognitive maturity, Luria's report was misconstrued as implying that the tribespeople were uncivilized and cognitively unfit to join "the masses" in building "a better future" (Luria, 1994, p. 66). It was inconceivable, and ultimately anti–Soviet, that "the builders of communism" might think in a concrete and primitive manner. Ironically, Luria, who was Jewish, was branded as a "Great–Russian chauvinist" (Luria, 1994, p. 66). Logic is seldom important during a witch-hunt.

Thus the project in Central Asia was terminated and Luria never returned to hands-on cross-cultural studies. Luria's lab in the Moscow Institute of Psychology was shut down. He was forced to leave both the Institute and Moscow. Luria and his colleagues moved to the Ukranian city of Khar'kov where Luria organized the Psychological Department in the Psychoneurological Academy.

Luria's relocation resulted in changes in his personal life as well when he met the scientist, Lana Pimenovna Lipchina. They met by chance on the street, quickly fell in love, and soon were married. This tall, classically beautiful, aristocratic yet simple, quiet, and sincere woman was to become the pivot of the family and of all Luria's life. Luria's daughter Yelena (Lenochka) wrote:

> Their meeting was . . . rare luck. At that time, after his expeditions to Central Asia were denounced by authorities, he experienced a severe emotional crisis. He was compelled to stop . . . his investigations and spent the main part of his time working in Khar'kov. Mother helped him to hold out against these difficult years and survive in more hard times to come. (Luria, 1994, p. 78).

The hard times must have seemed unrelenting. In 1934, Vygotsky's life was cut short by tuberculosis. Although only six years younger than Vygotsky, Luria always considered him a mentor. Luria often emphasized Vygostky's influence on the development of his ideas and methodologies. After Vygotsky's death, Luria continued to be loyal to his mentor–friend. This was a difficult thing to do considering that Vygotsky's work was being denounced by the authorities. As soon as the political "thaw" of the late 1960s permitted, Luria organized publication of the collected writings of Vygotsky. Thus, it was not until 40 years later that the data acquired during Luria's expeditions to Central Asia reached a larger audience.

Luria came back to Moscow the same year Vygotsky died. He worked in the Moscow Institute of Genetics, conducting investigations of twins, and in the Institute of Experimental Medicine where he was in charge of the Department of Clinical Psychology. In 1936, however, medical–genetic investigations were prohibited, the director of the Institute of Genetics and some researchers were arrested, and Luria was forced to leave both his jobs. Luria's sister was also facing arrest for her work in psychiatry in these years.

Luria did the best he could in such a hostile environment. He returned to medical school to add a medical degree to his full professorship in psychology. In all likelihood, Luria's decision to pursue medicine was influenced by both intellectual and pragmatic considerations. In addition to being a natural stage in the unfolding of an internally consistent line of inquiry, it also might have been a move that was necessary to ensure his professional, and perhaps even his physical, survival. Regardless, it turned out to be the next logical step in pursuing his intellectual agenda. Luria graduated from medical school in 1937 and for two years worked as a neurology resident under Nikolai Nilovich Burdenko, the founder of the Institute of Neurosurgery in Moscow. Luria remembered the two years of residency as the most fruitful period in his life.

> I planned to be trained as a practicing neurologist and at the same time to develop psychological methods for focal brain damage diagnostics. I do not know whether professor Burdenko approved my plans, probably he decided that it would be amusing to have as a resident a full professor in psychology. (Luria, 1982, pp. 121–122)

It was not easy for Luria to pass from the logic of the experiment to the logic of clinical work. Instead of selecting a problem, creating a hypothesis, and then choosing a means for testing the hypothesis, he had to turn to another subject— the patient. In his autobiography, Luria described "the patient" as "an unknown complex of problems. The procedure and logic of clinical investigation seemed to be more like the work of a detective investigating a crime than the work of psychologist or physiologist" (Luria, 1982, p. 123). Stimulated by this challenge, Luria created and elaborated his own battery of tests targeting assessment of different cognitive processes.

From 1928 to 1934 and again in the end of the1940s I was focused on investigations of changes in cognitive processes which were associated with development. From 1936 till 1945 I concentrated my attention on the study of disturbances of cognitive processes and their improvement and on the brain mechanisms that managed them. (Luria, 1982, p. 45)

In establishing priorities of inquiry, Luria was guided by his belief in the preeminent role of language in the formation of representational and self-regulatory systems. He began with the study of different forms of speech–language deficits in patients with focal brain lesions. This led to the decision to write three volumes on three main forms of aphasia. He managed to write the first volume on sensory aphasia, for which he subsequently received his doctoral degree in medicine but found his work interrupted when World War II began.

People of the Soviet Union were called upon to contribute to the war effort, and the development of remedial programs to help head-injured soldiers was Luria's charge. He organized a hospital in the little town of Kissegatch (on the border of the European and Asian regions of Russia). A few thousand patients with brain wounds went through rehabilitation in this hospital through 1944. At the hospital, pharmacological, psychological, physiotherapeutic, educational, and vocational programs were combined with a large-scale research program.

Lev Zasetsky, the inspiration for Luria's (1972) book, *The Man with a Shattered World*, was one of the patients in this hospital. Zasetsky continued to correspond with Luria and the family for many years after his discharge. During Luria's years in Kissegatch, the main principles of rehabilitation were formulated: disinhibition of temporary inhibited functions, bringing into use functional abilities of preserved symmetrical areas of the other hemisphere, and utilization of preserved components of the impaired functional system.

In 1947, Luria published *Traumatic Aphasia* (Luria, 1968b). In this book, which was based on the examination of 800 patients with brain injuries that resulted in aphasias, Luria formulated his ideas on cerebral organization of verbal processes and the different forms of their impairment. Considering speech as a complex, functional, cognitive system, he showed its structure consisted of many components that are organized horizontally and vertically (i.e., hierarchically) and that are based on different structures of the brain. He also studied the relationship of this system with other cognitive systems and the dissolution of language in brain pathology.

Luria never considered his classification of aphasias to be complete and never stopped working on it. After World War II, Luria returned to his lab in the Burdenko Institute of Neurosurgery and resumed lecturing at Moscow State University. Both the hierarchic theme and the de-emphasis of the role of verbal mediation (thus setting the stage for considering other, nonverbal, representational systems) reflect another human interaction that left a powerful trace in Luria's work—interaction with Nicolas Bernshtein, a prominent Russian physiologist and mathematician who became a close friend of Luria's.

Several of Bernshtein's ideas powerfully affected Luria. Particularly influential were Bernshtein's pioneering work on the concept of internal representations and plans, the hierarchic nature of such representations and of self-regulating processes, as well as the concept of feedback and the idea that the "reflectory arc" should replace the "reflectory loop" as the building block of neural control. These ideas foreshadowed the pivotal concepts of cybernetics and cognitive psychology of later years. The idea of hierarchic cognitive controls guided by the images of the future and to-be-achieved products (*Solwehrt*, in Bernshtein's terminology) is central to the contemporary attempts to conceptualize the function of prefrontal systems and probably contributed significantly to Luria's own later interest in the frontal lobes.

Unfortunately, the third major intellectual influence in Luria's life shared the fate of the first two. Like Freud and Vygotsky (being branded "bourgeois pseudoscientists"), Bernshtein was ostracized in Russia for his incompatibility with Pavlovian doctrine, which by then had become the only sanctioned theoretical framework. For a number of years, Bernshtein could not pursue his research or publish his work, but did live to see the beginnings of his exoneration in the 1960s. A summary of Bernshtein's ideas was published only in 1966, more than three decades after these ideas had been formulated. As in the case of Vygotsky, Luria's loyalty to his friend at the time of adversity was exemplary.

The late-1940s and 1950s were the years that Soviet scientists would not forget. In 1948, genetics was labeled a "pseudo-science," putting an end to its existence in the Soviet Union. It is not easy for a western reader to conceive what this meant for the scientists who worked in this area: disgrace, defamation, loss of livelihood, loss of freedom, and sometimes even loss of life. Scientists were subjected to public pillory and shame.

Psychological science also fell under Soviet control. The "Pavlovian Session" in 1950 is well known, and its damage to biological, psychological, and medical sciences cannot be underestimated. For psychology it meant that human behavior and all psychological processes had to be reduced to conditioned reflexes. Besides the loss of one's job in times of general poverty, besides the confusion caused by being ostracized for one's lifelong work, the humiliating and cruel manner in which it was done left deep wounds in the researcher's soul. Luria, like many others, could not avoid censure. He was denounced as a representative of the anti–Pavlovian orientation in psychology. Like many others, he was forced to confess that his views had caused damage to the development of Soviet aphasiology.

Luria's laboratory at the Institute of Neurosurgery was closed. His painstaking work was demolished once again. At times, in the privacy of his own home, he was tearful. His wife, Lana Pimenovna, told him "Do not believe them, do not believe—they are wrong. This is a dark time" (Luria, 1994, p. 146). This remarkable woman's work in the biological sciences also was not spared: Tissue culture methodology was denounced as a pseudoscience, her lab was closed, and her future was thrown into uncertainty. Yet, she found enough inner strength to support her husband. Yelena Luria (1994) wrote, "I believe my mother was stronger than my father, and she always took his pain on her shoulders" (p. 134).

Luria found a refuge in the Institute of Defectology. Thus, once again he had to change the direction of his work. Then, in 1953, the process of "doctors-poisoners" began, resulting in Jewish physicians being charged with the intent to murder Stalin and other government members, and with the intent to harm all Soviet people. Many of the doctors were arrested and tortured, some of them died in prison, and some were rendered permanently disabled. Newspapers, radio broadcasts, and meetings were full of ranting denunciations of Jewish physicians.

This was the second time in Luria's life when arrest was an imminent threat. He knew that he was at the mercy of the prosecutors, and his friends followed him home after work to inform the family in case he was arrested in transit. A small suitcase containing underwear and dry bread was ready for the moment of arrest. Lana Pimenovna kept this suitcase for future students to see.

Remarkably, despite this severe political situation, Luria continued to work enthusiastically and productively. He created a new program of research and designed innovative methods of diagnosis for different forms of developmental abnormality. He worked on special educational programs for each form of developmental disability. This work helped him survive economically and spiritually.

Everything changed with Stalin's death in March of 1953. In April of the same year, all accusations were dismissed. At the end of the 1950s, Luria came back to the Burdenko Institute of Neurosurgery to continue the main line of his research—neuropsychology. The return could not have been easy; however, the Burdenko Institute of Neurosurgery played an important role in Luria's research, and Luria used every opportunity to come back to the Institute despite the adversities. It was a unique institution with a 300-bed hospital where a variety of neurosurgical conditions were treated and studied. Plenty of research facilities were available for the study of patients. Advanced surgical procedures made possible the study of cognition using multiple clinical models. It was a unique scientific environment for a researcher interested in the investigation of brain–behavior relationships. The director of the Institute today in 2000, Alexandr Nikolaevich Konovalov, considers himself Luria's student.

Patients with tumors and focal injuries became subjects for Luria's investigations. He was able to systematize investigation of the effects of damage to different brain areas on various cognitive processes. The results of his research culminated in *Higher Cortical Functions in Man* (1962), which provided the most complete account of Luria's work in neuropsychology. Luria dedicated this volume to the memory of Vygotsky. In this book, Luria presented a neuropsychological test battery and developed his strategy for uncovering the impaired cognitive factor that may underly a particular set of cognitive deficits (i.e., a syndrome) and for linking the syndrome to damage in a particular brain area.

In addition, and arguably of even more fundamental value, was the scientific theory advanced in this book. Luria's dual–competence—in dealing with cognition as a psychologist and with the brain as a neurologist—allowed him to go beyond the simplistic brain–behavior dilemma of the first half of the twentieth century, namely, narrow localizationism (phrenology style) versus equipotentialism. In his book, Luria formulated the concept of functional systems that were neither localized nor equipotential. He was probably the first to state that (a) behaviors, skills, and traits as they appear in the lay, real-life nomenclature are not the units appropriate for cerebral localization; (b) the identification of localizable elements of cognition is in itself a nontrivial task; and (c) the relationship between the "lay" and the "localizable" nomenclatures is not a simple one-to-one mapping. In Luria's terms, a behavior or trait is the product of interaction of many cognitive elements, each mediated by a different brain structure or region. Such a constellation of interacting brain structures, each mediating a particular cognitive dimension, constitutes a distinct functional system. Conversely, any given cognitive dimension enters a variety of behaviors and competencies as defined in terms of the lay nomenclature.

Luria's interest in executive functions led him to refine his understanding of the prefrontal cortex. His approach to the frontal lobe functions was reflected in the publication of *The Human Brain and Mental Processes* (1970). Later, discoveries in physiology turned Luria's attention from the cortex to the brainstem and limbic system. It led him to a somewhat simplistic, but didactically useful conceptualization. According to Luria, the brain consists of three processing blocks that control, respectively, perceptual integration, programming and executive functions, and arousal–activation and memory (Luria, 1973).

Luria also turned his attention to the right hemisphere and hemispheric interaction, medial and limbic cortices, and subcortical structures. Always ready to begin a new area of research, Luria supported his students in studies of neurotransmitter effects on cognition that were started in 1972 and led to a new approach to brain mapping based on neurochemistry. Other lines of investigation addressed ontogenesis and aging.

Luria subsequently studied neurolinguistics and in 1976 published *Basic Problems of Neurolinguistics* in which he added a new dimension to his approach to the aphasias. Some of his later books—*The Making of Mind* (Luria, 1979) (defined by Luria as a scientific autobiography) and *Language and Cognition* (Luria, 1981)— were published after his death. Two of Luria's "smaller books" were dedicated to the description of single cases. The first was *The Mind of a Mnemonist* (1968a) in which he described and followed longitudinally a man with a super-memory. (Sergey Eizenstein, the famous film director and Luria's friend, took part in this investigation.) The second book, *The Man with a Shattered World* (1972), described the longitudinal study of Lev Zasetsky, the patient with a parietal wound whom Luria knew from the hospital in Kissegatch. These books represented what Luria called "romantic science."

Beside his intensive research activity, Luria dedicated a great deal of time to education. Beginning in 1945, he was a professor of psychology at Moscow State University, where he later organized a Department of Neuropsychology and was its chair untill the end of his life. He also maintained two laboratories: the Neuropsychological Laboratory in Burdenko Institute of Neurosugery and the Aphasiological Laboratory in the first Moscow Medical Institute. Those who participated in daily laboratory meetings with Luria noted that he was always full of creativity and enthusiasm. "Luria as a teacher originated such a creative atmosphere that itself was an educational factor," recalled Evgenya Homskaya (1992, p. 161), Luria's student and colleague.

Luria's lab was full of activity, but the main focus was on testing patients. Without this, Luria felt that the day was empty. For Luria, an assessment was never routine. He was quick to generate new ideas and readily invented innovative tasks to test these ideas. The entire lab was a witness to this highly creative process. Luria was never as excited as during these sessions. The atmosphere was very democratic, and freewheeling discussions were common. Luria liked humor, and he could be both generous and charismatic. His labs were consistently crowded, and students and colleagues report scientifically and personally unforgettable experiences.

No account of Luria's career in neuropsychology can be complete without a word about his clinical contributions to neuropsychological diagnosis and remediation. Though this was clearly a subordinate, secondary facet of Luria's career, the fact remains that many neuropsychologists and behavioral neurologists know Luria mostly, or even solely, through his diagnostic techniques. His battery of tests allows one to obtain a substantial amount of information on cognitive processes by examining a patient for only 60 minutes. Luria's main contribution to applied neuropsychology is a matrix, rooted in a cohesive brain–behavior model, that offers an extremely systematic internal organization and dimensionalization of cognition. It also offers insights into how qualitative variants of a "failure" on a task can be utilized in a branching tree of hypotheses-testing. His clinical approach in many ways foreshadowed and served as the basis for the currently popular "process approach" to neuropsychological diagnosis.

In his later years, Luria lived in an old apartment on a quiet street close to the Kremlin. The three-room apartment was large by Soviet Union standards. When he lived in Moscow, Luria's regimen was simple: He woke up early and wrote until breakfast; from 10:00 a.m. to 2:00 p.m. he was in the lab. He came home for lunch, slept for 2 hours, and at 5:00 p.m. began working again. Usually after 7:00 p.m. he had guests, but these meetings were not just social occasions—it was difficult for Luria to focus on things not related to his work. Luria was far removed from the everyday necessities of life; his wife, Lana Pimenovna, took care of his diet, his regimen, and his health. She managed this despite having a career of her own as a full professor of biology. This allowed Luria to keep his focus on his work.

In 1977, Lana Pimenovna became severely ill and on June 2, 1977, she underwent surgery. An inoperable cancer was found. When Lana Pimenovna was discharged, she and Luria moved to a sanatorium. Luria tried his best to help relieve his wife's suffering. He died in the middle of a telephone conversation trying to obtain a new drug for her. Lana Pimenovna lived only five months more, suffering both emotionally and physically; however, she continued working on Luria's archive and helped organize Luria's memorial office at Moscow University, donating his entire library to the university.

Luria did not complete the task of designing a general theory of brain–behavior relations, yet he contributed mightily to the ongoing effort to develop one and to the emergence of neuropsychology as a mature science. Just like Luria, who himself divided his life into two parts—before he met Vygotsky and after that meeting—many of Luria's students consider meeting Luria a turning point in their own lives. The people who worked with Luria will never forget him.

REFERENCES

Bernshtein, N. A. (1966). *Outlines of the physiology of movements and the physiology of activity.* Moscow: Meditsina.

Homskaya, E. D. (1992). *Aleksandr Romanovich Luria. Scientific biography.* Moscow: Voyenizdat.

Luria, A. R. (1932). *The nature of human conflicts.* New York: Liveright.

Luria, A. R. (1962). *Higher cortical functions in man.* New York: Basic Books.

Luria, A. R. (1968a). *The mind of a mnemonist.* New York: Basic Books.

Luria, A. R. (1968b). *Traumatic aphasia.* The Hague: Mouton.

Luria, A. R. (1970). *Mozg cheloveka i psikhicheskie protsessy (The human brain and mental processes).* Moscow: Pedagogika.

Luria, A. R. (1972). *The man with a shattered world.* New York: Basic Books.

Luria, A. R. (1973). *The working brain.* New York: Basic Books.

Luria, A. R. (1976). *Basic problems of neurolinguistics.* The Hague: Mouton.

Luria, A. R. (1979). *The making of mind: A personal account of Soviet psychology.* Cambridge, MA: Harvard University Press.

Luria, A. R. (1981). *Language and cognition.* New York: John Wiley & Sons.

Luria, A. R. (1982). *Etapy proydennogo puti (The making of mind).* Moscow: Moscow University Press.

Luria, Y. (1994). *Moy otets A. R. Luria (My father A. R. Luria).* Moscow: Gnosis.

Sacks, O. W. (1987). Foreword. In A. R. Luria, *The man with a shattered world.* Cambridge, MA: Harvard University Press.

5

Roger W. Sperry

From Neuro–Science to Neuro–Philosophy

Antonio E. Puente

Introduction: The Uniqueness of Roger Sperry

A book on the history of neuropsychology should include biographies of luminaries. Deciding which ones to include can be difficult. Roger W. Sperry, however, is an obvious choice, as this chapter will amply illustrate. Sperry did groundbreaking work in the areas of both neuroscience and neurophilosophy and is the only person with a graduate degree in psychology to have received a Nobel Prize. Even the lay public knows about his discovery of left and right brain differences in split–brain patients. He published over 300 articles in the most rigorous scientific journals, often as the sole author. He provided training to nearly 100 visiting scientists, graduate students, and postdoctoral fellows from 12 different countries and several different disciplines, ranging from medicine to philosophy. Finally, historians of psychology consider Sperry one of the major figures in the discipline's century-old pursuit of the scientific understanding of the mind and behavior. His scientific methodology was highly rigorous, on par with the best contemporary research. Yet the questions he asked were the same ones that were asked by William James at the start of the twentieth century: what is consciousness and what is the origin of behavior?

This chapter is divided into three sections. The first section presents an overview of Sperry's personal and professional development, including his relationships with his mentors, students, and collaborators. As will be shown, Sperry's commitment to neuropsychology began as early as his adolescence and spanned 65 years. The second section of the chapter discusses "the four turnarounds," as Sperry called them, of his scientific career. Although the focus of his research shifted during each of the turnarounds, Sperry was unwavering and relentless in his focus on simplicity and elegance in research methodology. Sperry also had a uniquely far-sighted understanding of historical questions in psychology. The final section of the chapter centers on Sperry's concern about society and the

Figure 5.1. Roger W. Sperry

implications of his research and ideas for the solution of societal problems. Sperry was always uncomfortable with the limited role of psychology in solving societal predicaments. Without question, Sperry embodied both a unique personality and a remarkable life.

Personal and Professional Development

As a teenager, Sperry was exposed to the ideas of William James when his father brought home James's (1890) *Principles of Psychology* from the public library. Reading and scholarly achievement clearly were valued in the Sperry home. Roger was one of two boys, both competitive and good students. Sperry was to come in contact again with James's ideas in his "Introduction to Psychology" course taught by William Stetson at Oberlin College. These proved to be two defining events: Sperry's entire career was subsequently devoted to answering the questions posed by James and presented by Stetson. Neuropsychology provided Sperry with the methodology to answer these questions.

While he was a student, it would have been almost impossible to predict that Sperry would choose a research career. His interests appeared to be in sports, and he was captain of some of his high school teams. He was a fashionable dresser and apparently quite popular with his peers. His early experiences revolved around the typical things a boy might do in the rural areas of Hartford, Connecticut; however, a sign of his early scientific curiosity can be found in his habit of searching for dead animals to dissect.

The untimely death of his father had an adverse effect on the family's income, resulting in their move to East Hartford, Connecticut, where Sperry continued his interest in sports. So strong was this interest that Sperry listed athletic coaching as his primary goal in his college applications. As a second choice, he indicated medical research. Sperry and his brother were admitted to Oberlin College in Ohio, a rigorous liberal arts college with a strong tradition in athletics. Again, he continued with his pursuit of sports, lettering in baseball, basketball, and track. While his brother pursued chemistry, Sperry drifted toward English. Although he went on to receive his undergraduate degree in English, near the end of his undergraduate career, his interests began to shift to psychology.

Sperry was particularly impressed with Raymond Stetson and his research. Stetson had gone to Harvard to obtain his Ph.D. with William James. Unfortunately, by the time of Stetson's arrival, James had changed his focus to religion, so Stetson studied with others, including Hugo Münsterberg. Nevertheless, the indirect impact of James's ideas prevailed at Harvard, probably because of the use of James' publications for teaching purposes. After Harvard, Stetson secured a position at Oberlin College, remaining there for the rest of his career.

Stetson was not a particularly prolific researcher, although he was well liked as a professor. Stetson's field of expertise was speech therapy and his papers, for the most part, were published in European journals. Oberlin College in general, and

Stetson in particular, had a great impact on Sperry during his training. This is evidenced by two facts: (1) Sperry's notes on the first day of Stetson's "Introduction to Psychology" class served as the foundation for Sperry's entire future research program, and (2) Sperry left his papers to Oberlin College upon his death. The admiration appears to have been mutual, as the neuroscience building on campus is named after Sperry, and he received an honorary doctorate degree from Oberlin.

After completing his master's degree with Stetson, Sperry wanted additional training. He decided to study at the University of Chicago under the tutelage of Paul Weiss, a prominent scientist working in the Department of Zoology. Weiss's research was prolific, continuing well into the 1960s. Weiss' basic premise was that the nervous system is plastic. This idea became the focus of Sperry's first research turnaround. Using nerve regeneration techniques, Sperry set out to prove that his advisor's idea was incorrect, a pattern that would repeat throughout his entire career. That is, Sperry seemed to enjoy challenging the intellectual status quo, whether it was his own graduate advisor or the intellectual zeitgeist of the day.

After Sperry's academically prosperous time in Chicago, Weiss suggested that Sperry apply for a postdoctoral fellowship at Harvard with Karl Lashley, another prominent scientist of the middle-1900s. Lashley, like Sperry, originally was trained as a zoologist but had migrated over time to study the brain and its relation to behavior. Lashley was the director of the Yerkes Primate Research Center in 1941. Robert Yerkes had originally established the Center at Harvard but, due to the inclement weather in Boston, it eventually was moved to Orange Park, Florida. There Lashley worked with other prominent (e.g., Donald Hebb, Henry Nissen) as well as promising (e.g., Karl Pribram) scientists of the time. The focus was on behavior, but the conduit to understanding behavior was the nervous system. Again, Sperry went on to challenge his advisor, resulting in his second research turnaround. Both at Yerkes and later back at Chicago, Sperry developed simple experiments that were to challenge Lashley's equipotentiality theory that proposed that brain lesions have nonspecific effects such that the exact placement of a lesion may be unrelated to the degree and type of resulting behavioral deficit.

After completing his postdoctoral training at Yerkes, Sperry secured a tenure-track position in the Department of Anatomy at the University of Chicago. It was during this time that Sperry became involved with a wide variety of young scientists. Some of them became lifelong colleagues. Robert Doty, now at the University of Rochester, included Sperry as part of his doctoral thesis committee in 1950. Sperry also worked with several other researchers, including Nancy Miner and Ronald Myers. Despite Sperry's productivity, and for reasons not clearly understood, the University of Chicago decided not to grant him tenure.

Subsequently, Sperry obtained an appointment as section chief in the Division of Neurological Diseases and the Blindness Laboratory, under Seymour Kety, at the then recently formed National Institutes of Health. Sperry, however, never resided in Bethesda, Maryland, the eventual home of this agency. Tuberculosis, probably contracted while working with monkeys at Yerkes, forced him to leave his position. He spent six months in Saranac, New York, recovering his health. Sperry used this time to contemplate more seriously the role of consciousness in brain function. Indeed, the last section of the article "Neurology and the Mind–Brain Problem" (1952) provides a glimpse of his research focus for the next 40 years. This signaled the beginning of the third turnaround in his thinking.

Sperry continued forging ahead with his theories and writing. After a particularly successful symposium talk, Sperry was invited to the California Institute of Technology (Caltech) by Norman Horowitz to present a lecture. That lecture so impressed the faculty that Sperry was offered a tenured position, and Caltech's Hixson Fund was converted into the Hixson Chair of Psychobiology, a position Sperry held until his retirement in 1984. Sperry and Horowitz developed a lifelong friendship, and Horowitz supported Sperry's behavioral research at Caltech's molecular-based Division of Biology.

Caltech was an odd place for Sperry. There was no question that he felt right at home with the likes of other world-class scientists and students. The Division of Biology not only was extremely well funded and productive, it also was on the cutting edge of a then emerging field—microbiology. Sperry, however, was the only behavioral scientist on the staff. This isolation continued until his death. Thus, he was surrounded by some of the best and brightest scientists of his time but worked in geographical isolation from the colleagues he most wished to impact—psychologists and neuropsychologists. Sperry often shared that he felt that neither Caltech nor the field of psychology truly appreciated his work.

Nonetheless, while at Caltech, Sperry became as productive as at any time in his fifty-year research career. By the peak of his productivity during the 1960s, Sperry was occupying large areas of laboratory space—eventually occupying an entire wing. He had up to 10 different scientists and/or graduate students working on a variety of projects. During this time, he kept a relatively low profile, opting to stay in his office, often with his feet on the desk and "thinking."

Sperry could be a daunting supervisor. Meetings often were prefaced with questions such as, "Is this important? Will your ideas make a difference?" Unprepared contacts with Sperry were highly inadvisable. To some, Sperry came across as cold, distant, and aloof. In reality, however, Sperry simply was quite shy and preferred to avoid public contact. Simultaneously, Sperry was driven. He challenged his students and colleagues, but never more than he challenged himself. For example, his writings were reviewed a number of times, not only by himself but also by colleagues as well as his spouse. He rewrote and edited manuscripts numerous times. Manuscripts with theoretical or philosophical ideas were sent to colleagues outside the laboratory to see whether there were any flaws in his thinking. Sperry often read drafts of his papers at laboratory seminars for criticism. This rigorous approach resulted in extremely high quality manuscripts from Sperry's laboratory and brought constant funding from a variety of sources for the entire length of his career.

As at the University of Chicago, the focus of Sperry's work at Caltech initially was nerve regeneration with students such as Nancy Miner. By the late 1950s, however, he had shifted focus to examining the split–brain phenomena, initially in cats

(1956), later in monkeys (1958), and finally in humans (1962). The research with cats was done in collaboration with Harbans Arora, Nancy Miner, John Stamm, Ronald Myers, A. M. Schier, and Theodore Voneida. Sperry also did work with chicks in conjunction with Larry Benowitz. Sperry's work with monkeys involved Mitchell Glickstein, A. M. Schier, Colwyn Trevarthen, Richard Mark, Evelyn Lee-Teng, and Charles Hamilton. When his corpus callosum work shifted to humans, another set of young scientists collaborated including Joseph Bogen, Michael Gazzaniga, Jerre Levy, Harold Gordon, Robert Nebes, Eran Zaidel, Leah Ellenberg, G. Plourde, and R. Saul. It is important to note that there was extensive collaboration in the laboratory and investigators shared subjects for experiments.

At his peak, Sperry's lab at Caltech resembled more of a highly organized research factory than a standard research laboratory. For example, in 1976 Sperry's intellectual assembly line included his research associate Charles R. Hamilton; his visiting associates Evelyn Lee-Teng and Colwyn B. Trevarthen; his research fellows Laura Franco-Testa, Ronald L. Meyer, and Eran Zaidel; and his graduate students Sheila Gillard Crewther, Karen E. Gaston, Karen F. Greif, David S. Isenberg, Larry E. Johnson, Margaret Y. Scott, and Betty A. Vermeire. In addition to these colleagues, there were one student assistant and ten research staff members including Lois E. MacBird, Sperry's long-time secretary, and Dahlia Zaidel, a long-standing collaborator, technician, and assistant.

Other individuals played a role in Sperry's professional development. These include Brenda Milner, Professor of Neurology at McGill University; Robert Galambos, Emeritus Professor of Neuroscience at the University of California School of Medicine; William Burbanck, Emeritus Professor of Biology at Emory University; Jerry Kollros, Emeritus Professor of Zoology at the University of Iowa; and Kao Liang Chow, Emeritus Professor of Neurology at the Stanford University School of Medicine. There is little question that Sperry interacted both with his students and with colleagues around the country, relying on them for feedback on the development of his concepts.

Sperry's articles have been published and/or translated into several languages including Russian, Chinese, Japanese, and Spanish. A large percentage of his articles are single-authored although I believe he was generous in many instances by placing himself as second or even last author despite the fact that he generated the research designs. Several of his articles, especially those involving the human split–brain work, have been reprinted in numerous journals and books; however, it is interesting to note that subsequent researchers and reviewers have at times failed to cite Sperry's original split–brain research.

Toward the 1990s, Sperry stopped collecting data, and almost all his students and collaborators secured positions in other academic and research settings. Sperry contracted a neurological motor disease late in life, and as it increasingly affected him, he began to focus primarily on the fourth turnaround of his career—Sperry's writings became almost exclusively philosophical in nature. Sperry's colleagues and students delivered his presentations, as he opted to stay out of the public eye. He ceased giving almost all lectures by 1980 because of slowed and slurred speech. He chose instead to split his time between his office at Caltech and his home where he furthered his ideas by publishing in a variety of journals both in the United States and abroad.

In contrast to his earlier work, Sperry's work on consciousness and neurophilosophy was undertaken almost exclusively alone. While he collaborated and sought the advice of fellow colleagues and past-students, including Colwyn Trevarthen, Theodore Voneida, and Joseph Bogen, almost all of his publications in this area are single-authored. In fact, at the time of his death, Sperry was still working on the revision of at least one manuscript.

The Four Turnarounds

As already noted, Sperry's first psychology class, taught by Raymond Stetson, profoundly affected him. Sperry wrote two questions on the first page of his class notes:

1. Where does behavior come from?
2. What is consciousness?

These two questions, which arose from William James's view of psychology, provided the foundation for Sperry's half-century of research. Sperry often shared with me that Stetson had the greatest impact on his intellectual development. It should not be surprising to note, then, that Sperry's research program followed a systematic road of attempting to answer these two provocative and central questions in the history of psychology. While Sperry divided his research program into four phases, or "turnarounds," he attempted to address the above two questions in each phase. The four turnarounds were as follows:

1. Nerve regeneration research
2. Studies involving equipotentiality
3. Split–brain studies
4. Consciousness research

Sperry's research program was systematic, despite the shifts in direction, and each phase evolved into the next one. There are several pieces of evidence supporting this contention. Sperry repeatedly indicated this to me as well as to others. He kept a scientific diary for a number of years that attested to the flow of his research. Finally, Sperry's most recent writings, especially during the 1990s, allude to this fact although not often in straightforward terms.

There are specific overlapping periods of time for each of the four major phases (see Table 5.1). The first phase began in 1937 and ended in 1975. The second phase was rather short—1952–1955. The third phase began in 1950 and lasted until 1985. The fourth and final phase probably began with a lecture at Caltech in the spring of 1962 and continued until his death in 1994. What is curious is that each time a particular line of research evolved, its focus would fade only slowly. For example, Sperry published his first article on nerve regeneration in 1939 and his last one in 1975, although his major focus in this area lasted just 20 years.

Table 5.1 also lists the number of publications resulting from each phase of Sperry's career according to the years in which that particular research was carried out and the number of articles produced that focused on that particular area. It is almost impossible to be specific about these estimates because in some review articles, Sperry addressed research that involved more than one of the turnarounds and in some rare instances, the empirical research involved two areas simultaneously. The estimates provided, however, are good approximations.

Several issues need clarification. First, Sperry always kept a small portion of his research allocated to areas that were no longer central to his interests. Hence, even though the peak of his nerve regeneration research occurred during the 1940s and early-1950s, he and a small number of his students continued doing research in this area for another 10 to15 years. Second, it appears that he devoted equal time, in terms of publications, to the three areas that were most important to him. I believe he felt that Lashley's theory of equipotentiality was well answered by the five or so studies devoted to this topic. Indeed, I questioned him on the validity of including this as a turnaround in his research program. Sperry considered this phase of his research quite important. It disproved Lashley's electrical field theory and confirmed principles of vertical organization within the cerebral cortex.

Third, the consciousness research spans the longest time—almost half a century. The first article, published in the *American Scientist* (Sperry, 1952), contains in the summary section a blueprint of what was to come from his research program for the next 30 to 40 years—an unbelievably clear and well-laid-out plan for attacking the second question from his "Introduction to Psychology" course. There was little doubt that Sperry was interested in using science to answer age-old philosophical questions. In fact, I believe that he considered this last phase of his research to be potentially the most important.

In reviewing his publication record, we observe that Sperry clearly preferred to publish empirical articles in rigorous scientific journals. In fact, his first review article was published only after 37 empirical articles had been published. And, it was not until his 45th article that psychological issues crept into his discussions. By the 1960s, Sperry's ideas were starting to have an international impact as his

TABLE 5.1: SPERRY'S FOUR TURNAROUNDS

Phase	Years	Articles Published
Nerve Regeneration and Chemoaffinity	1937–75	75
Equipotentiality	1952–55	5
Split–brain	1950–85	80
Consciousness and Values	1962–94	70

research began to be translated and published in other languages. It is worth noting that it was not until 1946 that Sperry published his first article in a psychological journal, the *Journal of Comparative Psychology*. Another article that qualifies as a psychology article was "On the Neural Basis of the Conditioned Response" which appeared in the *British Journal of Animal Behaviour* (1955). This is interesting in light of the fact that, historically and vocationally, Sperry considered himself much more of a psychologist than a zoologist or even a biologist.

Each of Sperry's turnarounds was well funded, mostly by governmental agencies. He received his first research grant in 1940 and his last one in 1980—though he was funded until his death. Further, his research was funded continuously for nearly 50 years. Funding came from federal agencies ranging from the National Institutes of Health to the Public Health Service. In addition, he received support from various other sources including the Penrose Fund (American Philosophical Society), Eli Lilly and Company, and the Caltech Hixson Fund. Further details are presented in Table 5.2.

I will characterize briefly the research done during each of the four turnarounds. In the first turnaround, nerve regeneration, Sperry was interested in addressing the nature versus nurture question. He saw a challenge and an opportunity in the work of his new doctoral supervisor, Paul Weiss, who provided both techniques and a theoretical framework from which to attempt to answer this question. Weiss had postulated that the nervous system was plastic and, indirectly, had provided support to the then emerging theory of behaviorism (i.e., nurture).

TABLE 5.2. SAMPLING OF FUNDING ACTIVITY BY SOURCE OF FUNDING, DATE, AND TYPE OF RESEARCH

Source	Date	Type of Research
Penrose Fund	1940	Muscle Transposition
National Institutes of Health	1955	Visual Pattern Perception
Public Health Service	1955	Visual Pattern Perception
Southern California Society for Mental Hygiene	1955	Visual Pattern Perception
National Science Foundation	1956	Perceptual Integration
Mental Health Foundation	1956	Perceptual Integration
Eli Lilly & Company	1957	Myotypic Respecification
National Science Foundation	1960	Split–brain Rhesus Monkeys
Commonwealth Fund	1961	Central Nervous Pathways
Hixson Fund	1968	Hemispheric Disconnection
Public Health Service	1970	Absence of Neocortical Stimulation
Institutes of Health	1971	Developing Brain
Public Health Service	1973	Interhemispheric Interaction
Public Health Service	1977	Hemispheric Lateralization
Public Health Service	1980	Lateralized Functions

Thus, Sperry's overall goal was to determine whether this theory was correct. In other words, is the peripheral nervous system sufficiently malleable that nerves can be interchanged while functioning remains intact?

In order to answer this question, Sperry began a series of studies involving muscle transplantation in rats. He then added nerve crossing. After coming to the conclusion that little plasticity was evident with these nerves and muscles, Sperry proceeded to work on sensory functions, including vision and olfaction. He also expanded the research from rats to other species including amphibians, monkeys, and fish. By the early-1950s, Sperry was fairly convinced that plasticity in motor and sensory activities in a wide variety of animals was limited in scope. After conducting a research program lasting two decades, Sperry had successfully challenged the ideas of Weiss, thus supporting the role of nature over nurture.

Sperry's second turnaround occurred during his postdoctoral years with his next supervisor, Karl Lashley. Sperry developed relatively simple experiments to test and challenge Lashley's theory of equipotentiality. To briefly restate, equipotentiality theory proposed that brain lesions have nonspecific effects. Lesion location, consequently, is unrelated to the nature of the resulting behavioral deficit. The mechanism by which these nonspecific effects arise is a hypothetical spread of electrical impulses. To test Lashley's theory, Sperry used dielectric plates initially, and later used subpial slicing and tantalum wire and mica plate implants in the visual cortex. The spread of electrical impulses that Lashley hypothesized did not occur. The experiments were simple, elegant, and methodologically robust. Sperry had been able to express Lashley's concepts in simple behavioral terms that, in turn, were translated into experimental paradigms. Sperry concluded after three to four years of work in this area that it was probably time to move on to more complex issues.

The work in Lashley's laboratory left Sperry wanting for more of a challenge. There was little question that he had become very interested in the brain, in contrast to his earlier work that had focused almost exclusively on the peripheral nervous system. Further, I believe he wanted to challenge his own ideas by focusing on both the brain and higher-order mammals. Sperry's return to the University of Chicago during the mid-1940s signaled the beginning of a shift in his focus toward the brain in monkeys and eventually in humans. This led to the third phase in Sperry's career—split–brain research.

Sperry is most known for his split–brain research and, unfortunately, this is the area in which his ideas are the most misunderstood. He began by focusing on the transfer of sensory information across the corpus callosum in cats and monkeys, presenting his findings for the first time to a group of psychologists at the 1960 convention of the American Psychological Association. In 1961, Sperry published "Cerebral Organization and Behavior" in *Science*, noting how the separated hemispheres in many respects behaved like individual brains. For example, Sperry showed that after severing the fibers connecting the cerebral hemispheres (i.e., the massive corpus callosum, the smaller anterior commissure, and the optic chiasm), visual discriminations could be taught to a single hemisphere by closing one of the animal's eyes. The opposite hemisphere would have no knowledge of these discriminations when it, in turn, was tested.

A surgical procedure for the treatment of epilepsy made it possible to study the split–brain effect in humans. In the 1940s, William Van Wagenen had cut the connections between the cerebral hemispheres in 26 epileptic patients, reasoning that this would prevent the spread of seizure activity from one hemisphere to the other (Gazzaniga, 1985). In direct contradiction to Sperry's animal research, the initial studies of these patients suggested that the surgery left them behaviorally unchanged and with negligible improvement in their seizure control. Michael Gazzaniga, who was beginning his work in Sperry's laboratory, attempted unsuccessfully to gain access to and test Van Wagenen's original cases.

Fortunately, Joseph Bogen, a neurosurgical resident at White Memorial Hospital, and his neurosurgery professor Peter Vogel, were interested in giving the procedure another try for the treatment of intractable epilepsy. Bogen had done a postdoctoral fellowship at Caltech with Anthony Van Harreveld. Harreveld's office was next to Sperry's, a fortuitous configuration as it allowed Bogen to learn of Sperry's split–brain effect (Gazzaniga, 1985). Bogen's review of reports on the original split–brain cases suggested that at least some showed improvement in their seizure control. This motivated him to perform his first commissurotomy on a war veteran with intractable epilepsy. Bogen made the patient available for study, and this patient began Sperry's extension of the split–brain effect to humans.

The original study in humans by Gazzaniga, Bogen, and Sperry (1962) laid out the foundation for the research that was to continue for another 25 years. Starting with the war veteran case, Sperry slowly expanded the program to include a dozen research volunteers with similar conditions. Based on studies of these patients, Sperry and his colleagues eventually concluded that each cerebral hemisphere had quite a different functional specialization. The left hemisphere readily names stimuli presented to it alone, while the right hemisphere struggles and typically cannot do so. When allowed to use the left hand, which the right hemisphere controls, the right hemisphere can point, find, or otherwise indicate stimuli about which it is verbally silent. Further, and possibly more importantly, when the two hemispheres are disconnected, the person functions with an apparently divided consciousness (Sperry, 1966). Each hemisphere seems to possess an independent capacity to perceive, process, react to, and store information (Gazzaniga, 1985).

The notion of right– and left–brain differences has become widespread in western popular culture. Sperry did not believe, however, that the left–brain was dominant, nor did he believe that people could be classified as left– or right–brained. Such ideas have little empirical foundation. What Sperry did believe is borne out by the close to 100 studies that he and his students and colleagues at Caltech performed in cats, monkeys, and eventually humans.

What emerges from these meticulous studies is that the left hemisphere is more analytical than the right and, in contrast, the right is more appreciative of gestalt and emotional behavior. An elegant and simple approach to understanding hemispheric functioning and the function of the corpus callosum across three species was Sperry's singular most important scientific accomplishment, resulting in his receipt of the Nobel Prize in 1981 (Sperry, 1981).

The fourth and final turnaround of Sperry's research centered on the concept of consciousness. This phase could probably be further subdivided into two parts. The first part involves the idea that consciousness arises from the unified interaction of both hemispheres in the intact normal individual. Each hemisphere produces a type of consciousness in its own right; however, behavior is not as purposeful and goal-directed as when both hemispheres work in unison. Consciousness emerges from brain activity and, in turn, consciousness has a unique downward causation effect, controlling and directing the brain's activity.

The second part of this phase of research involves the consideration of value systems. Sperry asked two obviously value-laden questions: what thoughts ought to arise in consciousness, and which values can be deemed the most useful? Thinking about what ought to arise in consciousness automatically invokes a value system that permits such thoughts to emerge in the first place. Sperry proposed that a system of thinking in which scientific methodology is applied to values might enhance the development of consciousness. He also thought that nature and time would ultimately determine the values that are most useful to the human species.

Future Directions: Neuropsychology and Society

There is little question in my mind that Sperry believed that his work was misunderstood. For example, historically he believed that Caltech focused too much on molecular biology and that his work, at the level of behavior and mind, was considered too "soft," especially for the "hard" science focus of Caltech. He believed that the split–brain work was over-interpreted, especially by non-scientists. In addition, he thought that his work on nerve regeneration was best appreciated by neuroscientists but largely ignored by psychologists, the group with whom he most strongly identified. Sperry's ideas on consciousness were considered by some to be misguided efforts at philosophy. Finally, I believe Sperry felt very strongly that a consciousness revolution began in the 1960s—a revolution he thought could be as significant as the Copernican revolution. Sperry believed that psychology could contribute to this revolution. Again, these ideas have yet to be fully appreciated by the scientific community.

Sperry's work nonetheless has had a significant impact on both psychology and society. Continuing surveys about major historical figures in psychology typically include Sperry. Sperry's work has produced ripple effects such as the development of the *Declaration of Human Responsibilities* by a group of distinguished scientists from around the world. The document is being considered by the United Nations as the next step to follow the 50th anniversary of the *Declaration of Human Rights*.

Sperry was interested in the brain from the very beginning but needed to know how it functioned before he could draw any conclusions about higher-order activities. Behavior is dependent to a large degree on the structure and the physiology of the nervous system. Sperry believed that a more accurate understanding of this brain–behavior relationship was seminal to the development of a consciousness revolution. Such an understanding could serve as the foundation for the solution of modern-day problems. The integration of science and mind, combined with a focus on consciousness and brain function, will serve as the legacy of Roger W. Sperry.

REFERENCES

Gazzaniga, M. S. (1985). *The social brain.* New York: Basic Books.

Gazzaniga, M. S., Bogen, J. E., & Sperry, R. W. (1962). Some functional effects of sectioning the cerebral commissures in man. *Proceedings of the National Academy of Sciences U.S.A., 48,* 1765–1769.

James, W. (1890). *Principles of psychology.* New York: Holt.

Sperry, R. W. (1946). Ontogenetic development and maintenance of compensatory eye movements in complete absence of the optic nerve. *Journal of Comparative Psychology, 39,* 321–330.

Sperry, R. W. (1952). Neurology and the mind–brain problem. *American Scientist, 40,* 291–312.

Sperry, R. W. (1955). On the neural basis of the conditioned response. *British Journal of Animal Behaviour, 3,* 41–44.

Sperry, R. W. (1961). Cerebral organization and behavior. *Science, 133,* 1749–1757.

Sperry, R. W. (1966). Brain bisection and mechanisms of consciousness. In J. C. Eccles (Ed.), *Brain and consciousness experience* (pp. 298–313). Heidleberg: Springer-Verlag.

Sperry, R. W. (1981). Some effects of disconnecting the cerebral hemispheres: Nobel lecture. *Les Prix Nobel.* Stockholm: Almqvist & Wikesell.

6
Hans-Lukas Teuber
Envisioning Neuropsychology

Mary Brown Parlee[1]

*H*ans-Lukas Teuber (1916–1977) posed a question, laid out a research program and, according to one historian (Benton, 1994), gave an emerging field its name in a paper he gave at the 1948 American Psychological Association (APA) meeting in Boston (Teuber, 1948). He asked, "What is the psychologist's role in the neurological laboratory?" The vision he articulated was of "the coalescence of experimental psychology and experimental neurology." Contributions would come from clinicians and experimenters, "the most advantageous constitution being that of the centaur, who combines the human head of the clinician with the horse trunk of the brass instrument psychologist. The brass instrument portion is required because of the need for specialized tests and procedures in the border region of psychology and neurology" (Teuber, 1948, pp. 1–2).

In Teuber's (1948) vision of neuropsychology, the specialized tests would be used not simply to identify "the" brain injured patient as such, but also would be used by the psychologist "with the eyes of a theorist" who asks "the fundamental question: how does living structure, especially neural structure, 'mediate' psychological functions?" (p. 1). Using detailed experimental results from his World War II research with Morris Bender on brain-injured soldiers, and under the guise of a "methodological" critique that in fact advanced important theoretical points, Teuber concluded that an answer could not be found until some difficulties of testing and of interpreting test results were resolved. "The coalescence of psychology and neurology is not an achievement, but a goal," he concluded (p. 13).

It was a goal Teuber would pursue all his life, and in retrospect it is surprising to realize how early in his scientific life he committed himself to it. He was 31 years

1. I was a graduate student in the Massachusetts Institute of Technology Psychology Department from 1965 to 1969, although I did not do my dissertation research with Teuber. Like other students, I took courses with him, went to the weekly colloquia followed by dinner at the Teubers's home in Arlington, and during one summer was a part-time research assistant to Teuber and Suzanne Corkin. As I have become immersed in archival material that provokes memories of the department Teuber created, I realize that his interest in the history of science influenced me and perhaps other students from that period (e.g., Squire, 1996).

I want to thank Stephen Chorover, Suzanne Corkin, Charles Gross, and Richard Held for their thoughtful and informative comments on an earlier draft of this chapter. Responsibility for the final version is my own.

Figure 6.1. Hans-Lukas Teuber

old when he gave the APA paper in Boston. He had a newly awarded Ph.D., was newly discharged from the U.S. Navy, had a job in a new city, and had a new (his second) son. His U.S. citizenship and his third language (English) were of only slightly less recent vintage.

After Hans-Lukas Teuber's untimely death on January 4, 1977, memorials of his life and career appeared in scientific journals and in the National Academy of Science's *Biographical Memoirs* (Benton, 1994; Gross, 1994, 1999; Hécaen, 1979; Held, 1979; Hurvich, Jameson, & Rosenblith, 1987; Pribram, 1977; Richards, 1978; Weinstein, 1985; Weiskrantz, 1977).[2] He is described as "one of the most influential neuropsychologists of his generation" (Gross, 1994, p. 451), someone who made "an enormously significant contribution to the form and content of the field of neuropsychology as we know it today" (Benton, 1994, p. 31). He was the founder of the influential Psychophysiological Laboratory at New York University (NYU)–Bellevue Medical Center and later of the Massachusetts Institute of Technology (MIT) Psychology Department, which at the time of his death "had grown into a center of psychology and the brain sciences that came to be known and admired the world over" (Hurvich et al., 1987, p. 461).

These obituaries and memorial tributes outline, with more or less detail depending on the forum, Teuber's family and educational background in Germany and Switzerland in the 1920s and 1930s, his graduate work in psychology at Harvard in the 1940s, and his research on effects of brain injuries, first while serving in the U.S. Navy and then in his Psychophysiological Laboratory at NYU in the 1950s. They recount his 1960 move to MIT, where he founded a highly unorthodox psychology department, and his teaching and scientific work in the 1970s as he became even more active nationally and internationally as "a consummate organizer, synthesizer, and sponsor of research on the brain, as well as the mentor of many of today's leading brain researchers" (Gross, 1994, p. 451). The tributes refer to and in some cases list Teuber's many publications, memberships in professional associations, awards, and honors. And they try to convey—each from the perspective of an author who knew Teuber in different settings and roles—the enthusiasm, intellectual style and vigor, and personal qualities of the man.

The personal reminiscences and anecdotes in the memorial essays are varied and often vividly detailed, and the authors highlight different aspects of Teuber's

2. A short biography of Teuber also will appear (Parlee, in press) in the American Psychological Association's forthcoming *Encyclopedia of Psychology*.

The most detailed published account of Teuber's family background and early education is the essay by Leo Hurvich, Dorothea Jameson (both colleagues of Teuber at NYU), and Walter Rosenblith (a colleague and then provost at MIT when Teuber headed the Psychology Department), prepared with assistance from Marianne Teuber (Hurvich et al., 1987). This essay seems to follow the general outlines of a narrative *vita* Teuber wrote in the late-1950s that is now in the MIT Archives.

I too follow this outline, drawing as well on other material in the MIT Archives, from Teuber (1994), and from other details provided by Marianne Teuber. I want to express my deep appreciation to Marianne Teuber for her generosity, kindness, and valuable insights; the photograph included in this chapter also is courtesy of Marianne Teuber.

scientific contributions to neuropsychology, psychology, and neuroscience. But there is, inevitably, a certain sameness about these brief appreciations. The general outlines of Teuber's education, scientific life, and career do not vary much from account to account—both for the obvious reason that the basic biographical facts do not change with the teller and probably also because the genre (obituaries written by colleagues and published in scientific journals) is limited in length and viewpoint and, by convention, does not explicitly discuss historical context. At the suggestion of the editors of this volume, and with the luxury of greater length, this essay will try to fill in the general outline by considering some of the people, institutions, ideas, and scientific developments that shaped and were influenced by Teuber's scientific life and work.

Background and Education

Hans-Lukas Teuber was born in Berlin on August 7, 1916, oldest son of Eugen Teuber and Rose (Knopf) Teuber. A second son, Ulrich, was born in 1920. Both parents were musical (they both played the piano well and enjoyed dancing); Ulrich went on to become an organist and historian of music. Early years were spent in Doberan, west of Rostock near the Baltic Sea.

Teuber was educated first at a private preparatory school in Berlin and then at the Collège Français, a Huguenot school founded in 1689, where he studied Latin, Greek, Ancient History, and the Natural Sciences—all taught in French. He received the baccalaureate degree in 1934. When he was in his 40s Teuber wrote that the greatest single influence during his childhood and early years had been his father, who had shared with young Hans-Lukas his seemingly disparate interests in literature, animal behavior, and mathematics, and stimulated in the son a search for integrative principles that continued throughout his student and later years.[3]

3. Eugen Teuber (1889–1958), also educated at the Collège Français, had been a young student of philosophy and psychology at the University of Berlin when he was sent by the Prussian Academy of Sciences in 1913 to Tenerife (in the Spanish Canary Islands) to install a Primate Station for behavioral observations of chimpanzees. As its first director he secured a suitable site and buildings for research, hired staff, and with Rose Teuber began systematic observations of chimp social behavior and physical development.

When Wolfgang Kohler (1887–1967) came to Tenerife to direct the Primate Station in late-1914, Eugen and Rose Teuber participated as observers in the fruit basket experiments, the first of Kohler's famous experiments on intelligence in anthropoid apes. Some of the Tenerife chimpanzees were housed in the Berlin Zoo after Kohler returned to Berlin in 1920. When Eugen Teuber took young Hans-Lukas to visit the animals, Marianne Teuber (1994) later recounted, they still evidently remembered their scientist–friend from Tenerife: as father and son approached, "the animals would come to the fence, grab it and shake it vigorously, uttering the staccato 'o, o, o' of joy and greeting on spotting Teuber in the crowd" (Teuber, 1994, p. 574).

After leaving Tenerife, Eugen Teuber served in the German army as a communications officer on the Eastern front during World War I and then returned to doctoral studies at the University of Rostock, where he earned a Ph.D. degree in 1921 (with a dissertation on the philosophy of art

Another important influence was the neurologist Kurt Goldstein, a family friend whom Teuber first met in Berlin in the early 1930s. Goldstein was at that time well known for his extensive investigations of brain injured World War I soldiers whose altered perceptual and intellectual functions he interpreted holistically in his "organismic theory" (Teuber, 1966).

After traveling in Italy, France, and Switzerland, Teuber enrolled in 1935 at the University of Basle in Switzerland. There he concentrated in philosophy with an emphasis on philosophy of science and took courses and laboratory training in biology, comparative anatomy, and embryology. Teuber (1959a) dated the beginnings of his interest in the physiology of the nervous system to these university days, being particularly influenced by the work of embryologist Hans Spemann, which suggested that "problems and methods of study of CNS [Central Nervous System] functions might be similar to those found in experimental embryology (equipotentiality, vicarious functioning, organizers)" (Teuber, p. 2). Teuber also in later years mentioned the importance—in this case personal as well as intellectual—of his participation in "a small interdisciplinary group in Basle, composed of young instructors and students, who explored the methodology of various sciences and attempted to bridge the gap between biological and social science"[4] (p. 2).

One of the fellow students in this interdisciplinary group was Marianne Liepe, who was studying art history at Basle—and who was strikingly beautiful and intelligent, widely read, and from an academic family.[5] Liepe left for the United States in 1939 to continue her study of art history at Vassar College, and in that year Teu-

of Jean-Baptiste Dubos). Financial pressures resulting from post-war inflation, combined with a strong pragmatic bent, led Eugen Teuber to turn away from the prospect of an academic life. He joined ADREMA, a German business machine company (similar to IBM), first as director of research, then also as director of exports. He became interested in what would now be called information processing machines and had several patents on a system for a simple addressing and sorting machine. (This account of E. Teuber's life and work is drawn from an article by M. Teuber, 1994; some of the same information also appears in Hurvich et al., 1987.)

In an interview given in the 1960s, Hans-Lukas Teuber said that his father's example was perhaps partly responsible for what he described as his own "tendency not to identify with any one field entirely" (Teuber, October 30, 1968, interview with Steve J. Heims). Like his father, Hans-Lukas Teuber was remarkably adept at both the practical (e.g., securing research sites, hiring staff, improvising equipment) and intellectual sides of scientific research.

4. The lure of excitement and the challenges of interdisciplinary groups like the one in Basle were probably strengthened for Teuber not only by his later research with neurologist Morris Bender but also by his participation in some of the interdisciplinary Macy Foundation conferences on cybernetics in the early-1950s (Heims, 1991). Between 1958 and 1960, Teuber also participated in the Macy Foundation conferences on the central nervous system and behavior organized by Horace Magoun (Brazier, 1959).

5. Marianne Liepe's father, Dr. Wolfgang Liepe, chaired the Department of German Literature at the University of Keil before leaving Germany for the United States, where he was a professor of German literature at the University of Chicago.

ber was awarded the Holtzer Fellowship at Harvard and planned to leave for the United States as well.[6]

With the outbreak of World War II, Teuber's entry to the United States was delayed until 1941. Immediately upon his arrival, Liepe and Teuber were married, and he enrolled as a graduate student in Harvard University's Psychology Department. Teuber was a student at Harvard from 1941 to 1944 and from 1946 to 1947. From 1944 (when he and Marianne Teuber became naturalized American citizens) through 1946, he served in the U.S. Naval Reserve, stationed, after basic training in Geneva, New York, at the U.S. Navy Hospital in San Diego.

While at Harvard, Teuber supported himself and his growing family (Andreas Wolfgang was born in 1942, Christopher Lawrence in 1946) by working as a research assistant on the staff of the Ella Lyman Cabot Foundation. The Foundation was then engaged in a ten-year experiment to see whether (in the language of the time) delinquency could be prevented among underprivileged boys by interventions consisting of guidance, counseling, and psychotherapy. Teuber—learning English at breakneck speed through total immersion[7]—conducted interviews, trained interviewers, constructed questionnaires, and evaluated interactions between counselors and boys.

This work, he later said, "impressed me with the need for quantitative indices in the evaluation of behavior, and with the necessity of obtaining adequate control groups in assessing behavior change" (Teuber, 1959a, p. 3). His doctoral dissertation, "Dyadic Groups: A Study in Counseling Relationships," grew out of this work. Gordon Allport was his supervisor; Jerome S. Bruner and Robert F. Bales completed his committee.[8] It is possible to see some influences of this "excursion into social field work" (as he later described it) in Teuber's later research and writing, but by far the more decisive influences on his developing commitment to understanding brain structure and function came from other sources. Fortunately, these are described in Teuber's own words (Teuber 1959a; also quoted by Hurvich et al., 1987, pp. 466–467):

> My original biological interests had been fostered at Harvard through contacts with Lashley, through avid reading of the work of J. W. Gibbs, L. J. Henderson, and W. B. Cannon. The possibility that the logic of Gibbsian systems

6. In 1929, Charles W. Holtzer established the Holtzer Fellowship in Harvard's Graduate School of Arts and Sciences "for students of German birth who have received their preliminary education in German institutions of learning. Open to students in any department of the University."

7. Teuber failed the required German language examination at Harvard the first time he took it because he did not know enough English to translate the German texts.

8. In the preface to his dissertation (already showing indications of the vigorous English prose style he would develop later), Teuber said: "Our indebtedness is greatest to our teacher, Professor Gordon W. Allport, of Harvard University, who has always wanted a monograph to be written on the dyadic group, and for some reason felt that the author should make this first attempt. From the very conception of the problem down to the cleansing of the writer's English, he has helped to see this thorny matter through."

(set up for physical chemistry) might be equally applicable to biological and social systems was considered more and more seriously.

A more direct influence was that of Kurt Goldstein's, who at that time (1941) was Visiting Professor and William James Lecturer at Harvard. Frequent personal contacts made me aware of the strategic role of experimental neurology within the framework of general biological science, and suggested a reconsideration of the earlier German work (Bethe, Uexkull, Weiss) in comparative physiology of nervous systems and problems of sensorimotor integration.

The final and decisive "push" in the direction of my chosen field was provided almost fortuitously by a two-year period in the U.S. Navy. In 1944, I arrived at the San Diego Naval Hospital where Dr. M. B. Bender was in charge of the neurology wards. He was interested in studying peripheral nerve injuries, causalgia, and sensory disturbances after cerebral injury. Hearing of my acquaintance with Goldstein's work, he suggested that I stay with him at the Naval Hospital. An improvised laboratory was set up early in 1945, and men with acute battle injuries [from the Southwest Pacific] of the nervous system were studied by us for nearly two years. The unique opportunity of observing effects of acute brain injuries resulted in a number of joint papers. . . . In these papers, we tried to continue the tradition of Goldstein and Gelb, of Poppelreuter, of Head and Holmes, considering the injuries as experiments of nature and studying the disturbances of brain function as a clue to normal modes of central nervous system functioning.

Following discharge from the Navy, and after completing my work at Harvard, I came to New York University College of Medicine to build up there, under the original sponsorship of M. B. Bender and S. B. Wortis, a small laboratory for the study of effects of brain injuries. (pp. 4–5)

Morris Bender gave a more vivid, backstage view of their joint research in San Diego and relocation to New York University[9]:

When I first met Luke . . . it was in the Personnel Office at the San Diego Naval Hospital during World War II . . . Luke was well versed in experimental psychology, even though he did his work in social psychology, and [was] especially knowledgeable of the German literature on battle injuries of the brain sustained by victims of World War I.

Once connected, we studied our patients with great enthusiasm, often

9. Bender was speaking at the January 19, 1977, gathering to remember Hans-Lukas Teuber held at MIT after his sudden death on January 4. On January 19, Teuber was to have delivered his James R. Killian Faculty Award Lecture—"Mood, Motives, Memory, and Values"—in the same auditorium.

working long hours and well into the night. I particularly enjoyed his imaginative and insightful interpretations of our data and the lively discussions we had in writing our papers. Since no equipment was made available to us, Luke would improvise by using discarded motors and whatever else he could liberate from the Navy junk pile. We continued in this manner until the end of the war.

In April 1949, when we were separated from the Service, we took along one of these motors and drove, still in our uniforms, across the United States. It was less of a drive and more of a harrowing flight, because during the trip Luke has the constant feeling that we might be stopped by the Military Police, who would catch us red-handed with the Navy goods. We finally reached New York, and Luke immediately set up the motor for experiments on flicker fusion in a small office of the Bellevue Psychiatric Hospital. Shortly afterwards, he was appointed to the Department of Psychology at New York University ... [where] he became an extremely popular and influential teacher, attracting many gifted students into psychology and medicine.

Psychophysiological Laboratory, New York University

As Bender's remarks suggest, the research with brain-injured World War II veterans begun in San Diego was continued and expanded in the Psychophysiological Laboratory at NYU, directed first by Bender, until he left to head the Neurology Department at Mount Sinai College of Medicine, and then by Teuber. In 1948 Teuber became area consultant (for the greater New York area) to the U.S. Veterans Administration, and the laboratory received support from the Committee on Veterans Medical Affairs of the National Research Council (NRC) to recruit and test men with battle injuries of the brain due to penetrating missiles. Although the NRC would not fund research on a control group of veterans, Teuber and Bender recruited a control group (veterans who had sustained peripheral nerve injuries from penetrating missiles, with no signs of CNS involvement) through collaboration with Harry Grundfest at the Neurological Institute in New York.[10]

With the patient recruitment procedures in place (186 active cases and 101 control subjects were being tested by the summer of 1953), the Psychophysiological Laboratory was up and running, and Teuber embarked on a productive decade of research, teaching, lecturing, and writing. His first doctoral student was Stan Battersby, his second Sidney Weinstein, and he soon attracted the nucleus of a

10. From an unpublished transcript of a lecture by Teuber, "Experimental Psychology (Neuropsychology)," presented in January, 1952, in the Basic Sciences Course, Army Medical Service Graduate School, Walter Reed Army Medical Center (MC417, MIT/IASC).

research group—augmented by visiting students and researchers—that included Lila Braine (then Lila Ghent) and Josephine Semmes as well as Sidney Weinstein.[11] During the 1950s, the laboratory produced a steady stream of papers and two classic monographs: *Somatosensory Changes after Penetrating Brain Wounds in Man* (Semmes, Weinstein, Ghent, & Teuber, 1960) and *Visual Defects after Penetrating Missile Wounds of the Brain* (Teuber, Battersby, & Bender, 1960).

Both the biographical essay by Hurvich et al. (1987) and Weinstein's reminiscences (Weinstein, 1985) highlight some of the methodological innovations developed by Teuber and his group at NYU: rigorous experimental testing of the performance of large groups of patients; use of control groups; and development of specific tests for assessing performance in somatosensory, visual, and auditory domains. During this period, Teuber also developed more general methodological and theoretical principles for testing strategies and interpreting performance deficits: double dissociation of symptoms, cerebral differences and hemisphere interactions, and corollary discharge (Teuber, 1959b, 1960). He also wrote two major papers, which proved influential, both of them theoretically rich and comprehensive in their coverage. One was on physiological psychology, in the *Annual Review of Psychology* (Teuber, 1955) and one on perception, in the *Handbook of Physiology* (Teuber, 1960).[12]

The influence of these and other contributions to neuropsychology is discussed in the memorial tributes to Teuber by colleagues cited at the beginning of this essay and may be well known to some readers of this volume. A few examples will be briefly described, however, to give a flavor of the work for those who may be less familiar with it.

11. The core people in the small laboratory at NYU represented a remarkable convergence of significant trends—personal influences, ideas, and techniques—in neuropsychological research at that time. Lila Ghent was newly arrived in New York City from Montreal, where Donald Hebb was a major figure in physiological psychology. Josephine Semmes had been a student of Lashley, had worked with him at the Yerkes Laboratory of Primate Biology in Orange Park, Florida, and had earlier worked in the research group of Warren McCollough and Walter Pitts in Chicago.

12. According to Charles Gross, neuroscientist, member of the National Academy of Sciences, and historian of neuroscience, the *Annual Review of Psychology* paper on physiological psychology "set the program for the field for the next decade" (Gross, 1994, p. 452). Teuber was active in the APA throughout the late 1940s, 1950s, and 1960s, and was much involved (and Sidney Weinstein played a key role) in the reestablishment of APA's Division of Comparative and Physiological Psychology in 1962 (Dewsbury, 1996). Teuber served as president of the division from 1965 to 1966.

Teuber's much cited "Perception" chapter in the authoritative *Handbook of Physiology* was written in part while Teuber was in hospital, recovering from injuries suffered in an automobile accident caused when the driver of an oncoming truck lost control and veered into Teuber's lane. Though badly injured in the accident, Teuber remained conscious at the scene and insisted that no one move him until trained medical help arrived, thereby sparing himself possible damage to the nervous system. Hospital visitors recall Teuber, bandaged and in traction, with books and papers piled high on the bed, and a drawing of a skeleton mounted inside the closet door of his room marked with 15 or so red lines showing where his bones had been broken.

Arthur Benton, a leading neuropsychologist and contemporary of Teuber, has provided a concise description and evaluation of the research on somatosensory function reported in the 1960 monograph by Semmes et al.

> This study showed that bilateral and ipsilateral sensory defects were a fairly frequent consequence of unilateral brain disease; that these defects occurred more frequently after left hemisphere injury; that the cerebral representation of somatosensory function was more diffuse in the right hemisphere than in the left; and finally, that the patterns or combinations of sensory defect were different in the two hands. Thus the study modified traditional concepts of contralateral innervation, and at the same time, demonstrated hemispheric asymmetry in the mediation of somatosensory performance. These findings, which were in the main confirmed by later investigators, had a profound impact on thinking in this field. (Benton, 1994, p. 38)

Other work from the Teuber group bore on the question of recovery of function following brain injuries and led to modification of the widely-held belief (the "Kennard" principle) that brain injuries incurred early in life nearly always cause less impairment than similar lesions incurred at maturity (Teuber, 1975). When the researchers compared performance on visual, motor, and somatosensory tests, administered to soldiers 10 or more years after they had sustained their injuries, with records of initial examinations conducted immediately following their wounding, Teuber and his colleagues found support for the Kennard principle (despite the restricted age range of the men at the time of injury and the greater sensitivity of the laboratory assessments). The picture grew more complex, however, when children with brain injuries early in life were also tested on a wider variety of tasks:

> By following cohorts of 25 children with right and 25 children with left hemiplegias of early onset, we observed . . . that language does indeed tend to be "spared" after sufficiently early lesions of the left cerebral hemisphere; but this escape is not complete—there are subtle changes on tests of syntactic competence—and the escape is not without its price. The child often develops speech under these conditions by sacrificing some of those complex nonverbal capacities that would normally depend on the right hemisphere. . . . It is as if language development had precedence and as if reliance on the atypical (right) side for linguistic tasks exerted a crowding effect on that side, compromising its normal function. (Teuber, 1975, p. 475)

Teuber's methodological principle of "double dissociation of symptoms" (a strategy for inferring an underlying neural mechanism from behavioral symptoms) is described in his own words in the context of the group's research using a visuo–spatial task:

In cases of double dissociation, one symptom is found with one particular lesion but not with a contrasting lesion, and conversely, thereby suggesting separable mechanisms . . . [For example,] "double dissociation" can be seen in the test of setting a luminous line to the visual vertical, where it turned out that lesions of the anterior brain regions produced difficulties in setting the line when the patient's head and body were tilted; those with parietooccipital lesions had much less difficulty in this respect. Conversely, patients with such parietooccipital penetrations performed much more poorly than those with frontal ones on a somewhat different task: that of setting a line to the vertical while their own body was upright, but the line had to be adjusted against an interfering (obliquely striped) background. By searching for such patterns of symptoms and by systematically varying the tasks employed we can hope to get at root changes in perception or in other aspects of behavior. (Milner & Teuber, 1968, p. 274)

Finally, Teuber's empirical efforts over many years to solve the "riddle of frontal lobe function" (e.g., Teuber, 1964; Teuber, Battersby, & Bender, 1952) and his wide-ranging knowledge of the scientific literature led him to formulate the concept of "corollary discharge" (Teuber, 1960), which he incorporated into his thinking for the rest of his life (e.g., Teuber, 1964, 1975, 1978). "Corollary discharge" is part of a system in which

. . . self-induced motion of the eye (efferent pattern) causes peripheral motor effects and, concurrently, a central discharge back into the appropriate sensory system (corollary discharge) which normally matches (i.e., cancels) the sensations produced by the active movement (re-afferent pattern). Under normal conditions, corollary discharges and re-afferent patterns balance, so that signals from the environment are perceived (e.g., motion of external objects) and distinguished from relative motions due to the perceiver's own movements. . . . Although entirely conjectural at this point the hypothesis [a corollary discharge from motor to sensory structures which prepares the latter for anticipated change] is attractive, since it can subsume normal and abnormal phenomena, and can perhaps be elaborated into a more general theory of constancies and illusions, and of perceptual identification. (Teuber, 1960, p. 1648)

Teuber goes on to say, "We have come to the conclusion that disturbances . . . on the level of the corollary or anticipatory discharge, represent an important common denominator in many forms of frontal lobe pathology in man" (Teuber, 1964, p. 419).

In summarizing the impact of these and other contributions, Henri Hécaen described Teuber as "la fondateur et l'animateur de Neuropsychologie contemporaine" [the founder and guiding spirit of contemporary neuropsychology] (Hécaen, 1979, p. 122). The overall scientific significance of the work is signaled by awards and honors Teuber received during his lifetime, including the Karl Spencer Lashley Award for Research in Neurobiology from the American Philosophical Society (1966), election to the American Academy of Arts and Sciences (1962), election to the National Academy of Sciences (1972), the Eastman Professorship at Oxford (1971–1972), and honorary degrees from the Universite Claude Bernard, Lyons, France (1975) and the Universite de Geneve, Switzerland (1975).

Lest we lose sight of the concrete realities behind Teuber's influential contributions during the NYU years, however, glimpses of his work "backstage" remind us that neuropsychology depends not only on the scientist and his or her ideas, but also on instruments and research sites, the human participants called patients or subjects, and networks of professional colleagues extending beyond the laboratory. Sidney Weinstein's reminiscences of the early days of the Psychophysiological Laboratory provide engaging detail about some of these components:

[W]e started our lab on a virtual shoestring. Using penknives and cardboard we created testing boxes. From scraps of material we created tests of texture discrimination. Cardboard and children's construction paper and library paste provided the ingredients for many of our tests of problem solving and I still recall that the first Semmes–Weinstein Pressure Aesthesiometer was housed in a small cigar box labeled "El Paso Cigars, The Cowboy's Payday Smoke." (Weinstein, 1985, p. 282)

Richard Held's reminiscences tell how Teuber transmuted these seemingly unpromising materials into scientific substance:

I first met Lukas Teuber in the late 1940s on a visit to his Psychophysiological Laboratory at Bellevue Hospital in New York City. The quarters were old and dingy. Debilitated neurological patients and harried physicians filled the halls. During my visit, however, this initial unsettling impression quickly gave way to the sense of excitement generated by the activity going on in the laboratory. Lukas characteristically imbued his surroundings with a particular tension. His presence made a great difference, not only in the general ambiance, but also in the style and substance of what was communicated in the informal discussions that were an inevitable part of a visit to his quarters. By his very manner of raising questions and pointing at the crucial issues, he breathed life into what might have been simply recitation. (Held, 1979, p. 117)

Weinstein (1985) described how this intellectual atmosphere was translated into networks of people and ideas:

[A]t the Psychophysiological Lab, with Luke, Joji [Josephine Semmes], and Lila [Braine nee Ghent] we . . . [had] informal luncheon meetings every Thursday. These weekly talks by many eminent, visiting scientists were conducted while we sat around a rather decrepit table and munched on rather large hero sandwiches. It was these Thursday lunches that provided much of the interaction between the NYU group and the outside world of neuropsychology. (p. 280)

Recalling some of these visitors, Weinstein provided a long list of names that would figure prominently in any history of the field.[13] Teuber's location in New York City, his broad range of knowledge, and his connections with European scientists (he read their publications in German and French and undertook an extensive trip to visit laboratories in England, France,and Germany in the summer of 1957)—all contributed to the networks of professional–cum–personal friendships Teuber formed during the NYU years. One gathers from the correspondence and reminiscences, furthermore, that these ties were strengthened through hospitality he and Marianne Teuber offered visiting scientists and their families in their home.[14]

A further revealing glimpse into another side of Teuber's work during the 1950s

13. Weinstein's list includes "in no particular order of chronology, subject matter or eminence . . . Harry Harlow, Donald Hebb, Ed Evarts, Joe Zubin, David Wechsler, Karl Pribram, Oliver Zangwill, Kurt Goldstein, Art Benton, Heinrich Kluver, Roger Sperry, Otto Lowew, George Ettlinger, Harold Goodglass, Ennio de Renzi, Henry[sic] Hécaen, Klaus Poeck, Wolfgang Kohler, Saul Korey, Karl Lashley, Brenda and Peter Milner, Mortimer Mishkin, Joseph Altman, George Krauthamer, Norman Geschwind, Donald Meyer, Lou Gerstman, Eckhard Hess, Murray Jarvick, Alvin Liberman, Don Lindsley, Joseph Gerstmann, Robert Cohen, Frank Beach, Jerry Lettvin, Walter Pitts, Pedro and Tauba Pasick, Walter[sic] McCulloch, Carl Pfaffman, David Raab, Austin Riesen, Jay Rosenblatt, James Olds, Hal Rosvold, Mark Rosenzweig, Eberhard Bay, Jerome Bruner, Albert Ax, Larry Weiskrantz, Jerzy Rose, Konarsky, Sy Wapner, Robert Galambos, Hans Wallach, Luigi Vignolo, Alexander Luria, Danny Lehrman, and many, many, many others" (Weinstein, 1985, pp. 279–280).

Some of the names Weinstein mentioned also figure prominently in Teuber's correspondence from the NYU years (including especially Karl Pribram), as do others not on the list. These include (in no particular order) Herschel Leibowitz, Donald M. MacKay, Walter Rosenblith, Richard Solomon, Richard Held, George Miller, Thorne Shipley, Alberta Gilinsky, Ulrich Neisser (then a Harvard undergraduate), Margaret Mead, Edwin Newman, Martin Scheerer, Paul Schiller, Walle Nauta, Joseph Brady, and many others.

14. When networks like these condense at a particular time and place—say at the 1948 APA symposium, or the 1950 Pennsylvania State University meeting of APA (which Pribram [1977] named as the beginning of an era in physiological psychology), or the 1955 Eastern Psychological Association meeting (where George Miller gave the influential "Magic Number Seven" invited address and Karl Pribram, with Teuber as Chair, gave a talk on "Neocortical Functions in Behavior")—then, sometimes, scientific fields are changed or new ones formed. It may be a decade or more before most researchers feel the effects. Teuber did not attend the now famous "Moscow Colloquium" of 1958, which one historian suggests marked a turning point in the emergence of the neurosciences as a new field (Marshall, Rosenblith, Gloor, Krauthamer, Blakemore, & Cozzens, 1996), but he was a participant, and usually an active one, at a surprising number of events of this kind. An attempt to document this persuasively would require more space than is available here.

(but one completely intertwined with the activities described above) comes from Daniel Robins, in words read at a gathering to remember Hans-Lukas Teuber held at MIT after his death in January 1977 (Pfeiffer, 1977):

> I shall remember Dr. Teuber—remember him from a different perspective perhaps than most of you gathered here today. I was one of the first of the group of World War II veterans who volunteered for Dr. Teuber's investigations into head injuries almost 25 years ago. My remembrances of him are from glimpses, glimpses from time to time over the years. He was always "Dr. Teuber." I was always "Mr. Robins." But that doesn't express our relationship. It does not express his warmth at every meeting we had, his concern for my well-being, his interest in what I was doing as a person. I think back to those early days at Bellevue Hospital, the battery of tests—"Don't let us tire you, Mr. Robins. We can go on next week. Call me whenever you feel the need to." And last year, when on a business trip to Boston, I stopped by at MIT. Dr. Teuber was never too busy to see me. We talked and the years rolled back: the same warmth, the same personal interest and concern were there in that quiet voice. I remember him as a modest man, a concerned man, an interesting man, a gentle man, a gentleman. (Daniel Robins, quoted by Stephen Chorover, pp. 15–16 of Pfeiffer, 1977)

Remarks by Rita Rudel on the same occasion provide a view of Teuber's work from yet another perspective:

> I was riding home on the bus one day from Columbia Presbyterian [Hospital] where I work now and idly looking through a paper by someone in Montreal on the subject of "effects of brain damage." And a man sitting on the bus next to me peered over my shoulder and said to me, "Do you know something about this field?" And I said, "Yes, a little." [Rudel was a researcher in the NYU Psychophysiology Laboratory during the 1950s.] And he said, "You know, I went to City College, the city university. And one time they had an invited lecture by someone named Hans-Lukas Teuber. It had to be the greatest lecture I ever heard. I can't remember what he said, but this had to be the most exciting thing I ever heard. If I'd had my life to live over again, I would have tried to get into that field." I never found out what his name was, but I knew exactly what he meant. (Unknown man, quoted by Rita G. Rudel, p. 17 of Pfeiffer, 1977)

As these glimpses behind the stage of public honors and published papers suggest, Teuber's appointment diaries from the NYU years show a dense intermingling of activities involving different people, knowledge, skills, and goals. They included testing patients; teaching; traveling to local, national, and international meetings; participating in APA organizational affairs; hosting visiting scientists from the United States, Europe, and the Soviet Union; attending operas and plays.[15] The "Teuber group" at NYU was becoming increasingly prominent nationally and internationally, and Hans-Lukas and Marianne Teuber enjoyed living in their house in Dobbs Ferry, which was both lovely and within commuting distance of the art, music, and plays of Manhattan. Then in early-1960, newly in receipt of a seven-year National Institutes of Health program grant for research and graduate training in neuropsychology at NYU, Teuber received a call from MIT asking if he would consider moving his laboratory to Cambridge and heading the institute's psychology section.

Psychology Department, Massachusetts Institute of Technology

More than ten years of in-house discussion and dissention over "the problem of psychology" at MIT lay behind the call to Teuber.[16] The problem from the

15. In reading appointment books and correspondence from the 1950s, I was struck by how active Teuber was as a speaker/presenter of papers and by the very wide range of groups and organizations he addressed (neurologists, psychologists of every stripe, psychiatrists, undergraduates; to university-wide, regional, state, and national organizations) and by the interest and warm responses he evoked, well beyond the conventional level of thanks and commendation. I also was struck by the extremely detailed discussions of methods and data in his correspondence with Karl Pribram, Heinrich Kluver, and other scientists in the late 1940s and early 1950s. Teuber maintained an active schedule as lecturer and conference participant after his 1960 move to MIT; as his department-building administrative activities increased, his engagement with day-to-day work in the laboratory decreased.

16. Given his background and experiences, Teuber certainly knew that the interdisciplinary, scientific–clinical nature of neuropsychology (a "border region" field) meant that it did not have a natural home in academic institutions organized, as most are, along disciplinary and departmental lines. MIT, on the other hand, had (and has) a well-deserved reputation as a place where problem-oriented rather than discipline-oriented research is the norm. Even in such an environment, however, psychology and psychologists at MIT posed an administrative challenge during the 1950s that seems to have had little to do with the particular personalities involved.

Unlike most major research universities in the United States, MIT did not have a psychology department until the 1960s. MIT was predominantly an engineering school until the 1930s when, under Karl Compton's presidency, faculty research strength and course offerings in the sciences were substantially expanded. In 1949 a post-World-War-II survey led a faculty committee to recommend that MIT strengthen its curriculum in the humanities and social sciences, and in 1950 a School of Humanities and Social Studies was added to the existing schools of Engineering, Science, and Architecture and Planning.

Psychology does not seem to have been an issue for MIT administrators until 1947, when Kurt Lewin died. Lewin, a distinguished German-born psychologist, had built the MIT Research Center for Group Dynamics into a thriving, nationally visible center for "action research" and had developed a graduate program leading to a Ph.D. in Group Dynamics. But the Center was only loosely affiliated with the Department of Economics and Social Science, and MIT made little effort to keep the Center or its students from moving to the University of Michigan after Lewin's death. Subsequently, references to the "problem of psychology" began to creep into MIT administrators' correspondence.

administration's point of view was that, in the absence of a separate psychology department, psychologists had been added to the MIT faculty and staff during the 1940s and 1950s by departments and interdepartmental laboratories of the Institute because psychological expertise was needed in support of ongoing, externally funded research projects. By 1959 there were four main groups of psychologists at MIT, with little in common except the name "psychology" on their degrees and no coordination or consultation among the groups regarding new appointments.[17]

Undergraduate students continued to ask for courses in psychology and alumni testified to its potential importance in their jobs as engineers and businessmen. And MIT was committed—in principle at least—to providing its undergraduates with a coherent curriculum in the humanities and social sciences, including psychology. What administrative mechanism could be used to develop a psychology curriculum taught by psychologists who were outstanding researchers?

Repeated attempts were made to resolve the problem throughout the 1950s (external and internal committees formed, reports written, meetings with administrators, followed by more of the same) until finally MIT president Julius Stratton decided that enough was enough. There was a psychology section within the Department of Economics and Social Science, which was in the School of Humanities and Social Science. The hope was that, with a clear commitment of support for psychology from the president, this section could provide an administrative umbrella under which all of the psychologists at the institute would gather (regardless of the school or department or laboratory of their research group and/or appointment) to plan a Ph.D. program in psychology and coordinate the undergraduate psychology curriculum. An outside advisory committee was formed to advise the MIT administration in selecting the right man (in the language of the time) to head the section. Hans-Lukas Teuber's name came up almost immediately, and negotiations proceeded swiftly.

Teuber's letter of appointment from MIT's President Stratton (May 4, 1960) indicated that he was to head the psychology section in the Economics Department, but the understanding was that he would work with the other psychologists to propose the formation of a Ph.D.–granting Department of Psychology. It did not work out quite that way.

Teuber had a clear vision of the kind of psychology department he wanted to build at MIT. He was a skilled grant-writer, in the early 1960s federal funding for research (including support for faculty, student, and administrative staff; equipment; and building renovations) was flowing more freely than ever before or since, and procedures for recruiting and hiring faculty were much less formal than they are today. Within three years, most of the psychologists who had been affiliated

---

17. The two main groupings included psychologists interested in organizational behavior, associated with the School of Industrial Relations, and a larger group interested in communications sciences, associated with the Research Laboratory of Electronics and the Lincoln Laboratories (where they worked mostly on the "human factor" in "man–machine" systems).

with the psychology section when Teuber arrived had left MIT or withdrawn from activities of the section. New psychology faculty had been hired, Teuber's proposal that an independent Psychology Department be established had been approved, and the first graduate students had been admitted.

As Teuber himself said three years later, in a letter to John Burchard, Dean of the School of Humanities and Social Science, "These were rough years, from 1961 on, when I came onto the campus. . . . You called me to the Institute at a time when you had every right to distrust psychology and psychologists. There had been more than a decade of bickering and in-fighting, of half-hearted starts and sudden defections. I came and started out by letting practically everybody go."[18]

To build the kind of psychology department he envisioned, Teuber raised the outside money necessary to hire new faculty and staff, to support visiting scientists and graduate students, and to move the new department into its own, newly renovated building. This was a remarkable achievement, made possible both by Teuber's hard work and acumen and by MIT administrators' willingness to allow him, if he could (with their help) attract the necessary funding from external sources, to implement his vision of what a psychology department at MIT should look like. Equally remarkable was the vision itself.

In the early 1960s, the central core of most psychology departments was learning, and faculty and curriculum reflected (with different emphases) the scientific sub-fields of the discipline (experimental, physiological, comparative, social, personality, developmental, abnormal). Teuber created a very different kind of psychology department, one that neuroscientist and historian Charles Gross said "helped change the concept of a psychology department and led to the founding of neuroscience departments across the country (Gross, 1994, p. 453). By the mid-1960s, the MIT Psychology Department faculty consisted at the senior level of a world–famous neuroanatomist (Walle Nauta), an experimental psychologist (Richard Held), and Teuber; and at the junior level a philosopher (Jerry Fodor) and a psycholinguist (Merril Garret), as well as physiological, comparative, and experimental psychologists (including Stephen Chorover, Peter Schiller, Alan Hein, Joseph Altman, Charles Gross, Wayne Wickelgren, and Herbert Saltzstein).[19]

18. The quotation is from a letter from Teuber to Burchard, June 8, 1964 (MC417, MIT/IASC). Teuber also moved quickly on another front shortly after arriving at MIT. He discovered that MIT undergraduates were being used without their knowledge as subjects in an experiment on posthypnotic suggestion (by a part-time, visiting faculty member). He put a stop to this practice and helped MIT form a Review Committee on Human Subjects to safeguard human participants in research projects in the future—several years before such review committees were required by NIH.

19. Chorover and Altman had come with Teuber from NYU, as did Louise Pfeiffer who was secretary and then administrative assistant to Teuber from 1953 to 1965. After Pfeiffer retired and until Teuber's death, his secretary/administrative assistant was Eva Ritter (later Ritter-Walker). Like Teuber, Ritter-Walker was fluent in German and French as well as English; before working in the Psychology Department she had been secretary to Norbert Weiner and to Noam Chomsky.

Many of the faculty had undergraduate degrees in the biological or natural sciences or in engineering, as did most of the graduate students admitted into the program in its early years.

Research groups and teaching in the department were organized into three "prongs," an image derived from the Greek letter psi, the symbol of psychology: physiological psychology (later called brain and behavior), general experimental psychology, and social and developmental psychology.[20] The social-developmental prong was relatively downplayed, however, as it was never possible to find the "right person" for a senior appointment in social psychology.

Within a few years and at the urging of his faculty, Teuber petitioned the MIT administration (unsuccessfully) to change the department's name to "Psychology and Brain Sciences" and move it into the School of Science.[21] In 1970 the Alfred P. Sloan Foundation designated the MIT Psychology Department a "center of excellence" in the emerging new field of "the neurosciences" (or of "behavior in relation to the neural sciences"), and for the next five years Sloan provided general support to the department's activities. The Sloan grant, together with National Institute of Mental Health training grants and large research grants from other sources to Teuber and other faculty, constituted the majority of the department's funding under Teuber's chairmanship during the 1970s. MIT administrators helped smooth the way for Teuber at some foundations when he sought outside funding, but MIT itself provided a relatively small proportion of the Psychology Department's total budget.[22]

20. Teuber inherited the elements of this tripartite structure, a legacy from earlier efforts by psychologists at MIT (including, at various times, Donald Marquis, George Miller, J. C. R. Licklider, Roger Brown, Ronald Melzack, and Michael Wallach) to develop a coherent undergraduate psychology curriculum. He stamped it with his own vision, however, selectively limiting the range of existing courses to be included, adding other disciplines, and presenting the whole as an integrated approach to a set of fundamental, clearly-delimited scientific questions about the relation between behavior and brain function.

21. Teuber renewed this request for change of departmental name and school affiliation many times, but it was never granted. The School of Humanities and Social Sciences would agree to the name change, but—even without a change of school—was increasingly uneasy about allowing natural-science-oriented psychology courses to count as part of the undergraduate humanities and social sciences requirement. The School of Science would agree to the name change if the department were moved under its aegis (where Biology Department faculty could scrutinize its appointments more closely). After Teuber's death in 1977, Richard Held succeeded him as head of the Psychology Department. The department's name was subsequently changed to Department of Brain and Cognitive Sciences, and it is now located in the School of Science. An undergraduate, interdepartmental "Concentration in Psychology" has evolved in the School of Humanities and Social Sciences to meet the needs of undergraduates interested in a broader and more traditional range of psychology courses than was offered by the Department of Brain and Cognitive Sciences. In many ways it seems that the "problem of psychology" at MIT remains unresolved.

22. In the late-1960s, less than 20% of the Psychology Department's total budget came from MIT. MIT is an institution where faculty research and graduate education have high priority, but it seems likely that the institutional strength of the Psychology Department Teuber created rested in part on the popularity of its undergraduate classes. Enrollment in these classes climbed

While at MIT, Teuber continued to be active in international, interdisciplinary groups of scientists and clinicians interested in behavior and brain function, including the International Neuropsychological Symposium, the International Brain Research Organization, the European Brain and Behavior Society, and the French Psychological Society. His preface to the English translation of Aleksandr R. Luria's *Higher Cortical Functions* shows his considerable interest in differences among national traditions in neuropsychological research (Teuber 1966/1980).[23] And even though the American Psychological Association was increasingly being abandoned by physiological psychologists during the late 1960s and 1970s (Davis, Rosenzweig, Becker, & Sather, 1988), Teuber continued to participate in North American psychological organizations, including not only APA and the more experimentally oriented Eastern Psychological Association, but also the Psychonomic Society and the elite Society of Experimental Psychologists. He was also a member of the Society for Neuroscience, whose president, when the "younger generation" of neuroscientists began to assume leadership, was Larry Squire, an early graduate of the MIT Psychology Department (Squire, 1998).[24]

Teuber's many connections with European and North American brain scientists enabled him to mount a colloquium series every year that showcased his vision of psychology as he thought it should be—multidisciplinary in method, focusing on the behavior of organisms.[25] He was famous for his elegantly witty, scholarly—

steadily from 1962 on, the most popular class being Teuber's famous "Introduction to Psychology," which was so large that for a few years he had to give each lecture two times in the same day. (Telling students they could attend either lecture, he used to say, teasingly, "The facts may change, but not the jokes.")

23. On one of his European trips, he and Marianne Teuber visited Aleksandr Luria's country retreat, where Teuber jokingly teased Luria about their meal being served to them at table—in a supposedly egalitarian country.

24. Squire, now Professor of Psychiatry, Neurosciences, and Psychology at the University of California, San Diego, is a member of the National Academy of Sciences, as is another early graduate of the MIT Psychology Department, neuroanatomist Ann Graybiel. In the early-1970s, when the Psychology Department was still relatively small, Teuber used to be modestly proud of the fact that three of its senior faculty (Nauta, Held, and Teuber) were members of the National Academy of Sciences and of the American Academy of Arts and Sciences.

25. Teuber used many different terms to refer to the "border region" field he envisioned, including "neuropsychology," "physiological psychology," "biological psychology," "brain and behavior," and "behavioral biology." The latter was the term he urged the Sloan Foundation to adopt in 1969 when the Foundation was planning its new interdisciplinary program focusing on behavior in relation to the neural sciences, but "neuroscience," already beginning to gain currency by the late-1960s, was chosen instead.

Correspondence with MIT administrators about changing the name of the department suggests something of the way he viewed the term "neuropsychology" in 1972. According to Teuber, "'Psychology and Neuropsychology' was considered [by the faculty as a new name for the department] and rejected because it seemed redundant to some people, and because the word 'neuropsychology' has acquired an unfortunate meaning of a limited clinical specialty involving the psychometric testing of patients with neurologic illness" (Teuber, 1972, p. 1).

and lengthy—introductions of the speakers, and the colloquia were attended by scientists from throughout the Boston–Cambridge scientific community (including, on occasion, Warren McCullough, Jerome Lettvin, Marvin Minsky, Seymour Papert, Patrick Wall from MIT, David Hubel, Torsten Wiesel, and Norman Geshwind from Harvard). As had been the case when he was in New York, Teuber made his department a stopping-off place for national and international visitors, and the hospitality offered by the Teubers in their Arlington home further strengthened scientific networks and friendships.

In addition, Teuber worked tirelessly to promote research done by faculty and students in the new and unorthodox department he created, guiding visitors through the laboratories (preceded by "Hurricane alert!" memos from his office if they were site visitors from a funding agency) and sending copies of his elegantly written and eye-catchingly illustrated annual report to hundreds of psychologists, brain scientists, and psychology departments. Gerald Schneider, one of the first students to graduate from the MIT Psychology Department (and later to join its faculty), spoke of this side of Teuber's work at the January 19, 1977, gathering held at MIT after Teuber's death:

> He so much loved to talk about the research in the Department. . . . Thinking about that quality reminded me of when I was a graduate student at MIT, sitting around with a bunch of students talking about a new finding in the Department, you know, where should this be published. "Of course, you should send it to *Nature.*" Another one said, "No, we should send this to *Science*, of course." Then someone said, "Why not just tell it to Lukas?" You see, he was one of our means of publication. And I found out later as I went to give talks at many places that many people I met had heard of my work first, or the work of other people in the Department first, by listening to Lukas Teuber. (p. 12 of Pfeiffer, 1977)

Although Teuber worked tirelessly and with infectious enthusiasm to promote his vision of psychology and research in the department he created, so much activity must have been tiring. He spent a year at Oxford University in 1971 to 1972 as the Eastman Professor—a period characteristically filled with several return trips to the MIT department, grant proposals, and manuscripts, as well as his duties in the Eastman professorship—and returned looking thinner than before. He was taking a well-deserved vacation with Marianne in the British Virgin Islands when he died while swimming, possibly from a heart attack, on January 4, 1977; his body was lost at sea.

One of the speakers at the January 19, 1977, gathering to remember Hans-Lukas Teuber was Jerome Wiesner, who had been, among many other distinguished positions and accomplishments, provost and then president of MIT during part of the time Teuber was there. He reflected the following:

[T]he MIT Psychology Department, with all its diversity and quality and rigor, is indeed Luke's creation. . . . In the 15 years that Luke was at MIT, he created a great Department and hundreds of friends—a department poised, as he believed the entire field to be, on the edge of deep understandings of the human mind, how it functions and how it learns. His influence will remain here forever, but we, his close friends, will miss him deeply. (p. 3 of Pfeiffer, 1977)

The "entire field" to which Wiesner referred was the emerging new field Teuber had spoken of 30 years earlier at APA as "the coalescence of experimental psychology and experimental neurology" and had called "neuropsychology" (Teuber, 1948, p. 2). He envisioned the field then as a goal, not an achievement. That goal is closer three decades later thanks to Hans-Lukas Teuber and his work—work that his zest, wit, and enthusiasm always made seem like fun to those whose lives and minds he touched.

REFERENCES

Benton, A. (1994). Four neuropsychologists. *Neuropsychology Review, 4,* 31–44.

Brazier, M. A. B. (Ed.). (1959). *The central nervous system and behavior: Transactions of the second conference, February 22, 23, 24, and 25, 1959, Princeton, NJ.* New York: Josiah Macy, Jr. Foundation.

Davis, H. P., Rosenzweig, M. R., Becker, L. A., & Sather, K. J. (1988). Biological psychology's relationships to psychology and neuroscience. *American Psychologist, 43,* 359–371.

Dewsbury, D. A. (1996). A history of Division 6 (Behavioral neuroscience and comparative psychology): Now you see it, now you don't, now you see it. In D. A. Dewsbury (Ed.), *Unification through division: Histories of the divisions of the American Psychological Association* (Vol. 1, pp. 41–66). Washington, DC: American Psychological Association.

Gross, C. G. (1994). Hans-Lukas Teuber: A tribute. *Cerebral Cortex, 4,* 451–454.

Gross, C. G. (1999) Hans-Lukas Teuber. In R. A. Wilson & R. Kiel (Eds.), *Encyclopedia of cognitive science* (pp. 832–833). Cambridge, MA: MIT Press.

Hécaen, H. (1979). H. L. Teuber et la fondation de la neuropsychologie experimentale. *Neuropsychologia, 17,* 119–124.

Heims, S. J. (1991). *The cybernetics group.* Cambridge, MA: MIT Press.

Held, R. (1979). Hans-Lukas Teuber. *Neuropsychologia, 17,* 117–118.

Hurvich, L. M., Jameson, D., & Rosenblith, W. A. (1987). Hans-Lukas Teuber, 1916–1977. In National Academy of Sciences (Ed.), *Biographical memoirs* (Vol. 57, pp. 461–490). Washington, DC: The National Academy Press.

Marshall, L. H., Rosenblith, W. A., Gloor, P., Krauthamer, G. K., Blakemore, C., & Cozzens, S. (1996). Early history of IBRO: The birth of organized neuroscience. *Neuroscience, 72,* 283–306.

Milner, B., & Teuber, H.-L. (1968). Alteration of perception and memory in man: Reflections on methods. In L. Weiskrantz (Ed.), *Analysis of behavioral change* (pp. 268–375). New York: Harper & Row.

Parlee, M. B. (in press). Hans-Lukas Teuber (1916–1977). In A. E. Kazdin (Ed.), *Encyclopedia of psychology.* Washington, DC: American Psychological Association.

Pfeiffer, L. (1977). Transcript of a gathering to remember Hans-Lukas Teuber, Kresge Auditorium, Massachusetts Institute of Technology.

Pribram, K. H. (1977). Hans-Lukas Teuber: 1916–1977. *American Journal of Psychology, 90,* 705–707.

Richards, W. (1978). Obituary: H.-L. Teuber, 1916–1977. *Vision Research, 18,* 357–359.

Semmes, J., Weinstein, S., Ghent, L., & Teuber, H.-L. (1960). *Somatosensory changes after penetrating brain wounds in man.* Cambridge, MA: Harvard University Press.

Squire, L. (1996). Preface. In L. R. Squire (Ed.), *The history of neuroscience in autobiography* (Vol. 1, p. 607). Washington, DC: Society for Neuroscience.

Squire, L. (1998). Interview with Larry Squire. *Journal of Cognitive Neuroscience, 10*, 778–782.

Teuber, H.-L. (1948). *Recent advances in diagnostic psychological testing: Clinical neurology.* Paper presented at the 56th Annual Meeting of the American Psychological Association, Boston. (Included in the Teuber Collection, MIT Archives and Special Collections, MC417, Box 21).

Teuber, H.-L. (1955). Physiological psychology. *Annual Review of Psychology, 6,* 267–296.

Teuber, H.-L. (1959a). Narrative vita, circa 1959. Teuber Collection, MIT Archives and Special Collections, MC417, Box 17.

Teuber, H.-L. (1959b). Some alterations in behavior after cerebral lesions in man. In A. D. Bass (Ed.), Evolution of nervous control from primitive organisms to man (pp. 157–194). Washington, DC: American Association for the Advancement of Science.

Teuber, H.-L. (1960). Perception. In J. Field, H. W. Magain, & V. E. Hall (Eds.), *Handook of physiology, neurophysiology* (Vol. 3, pp. 1595–1688). Washington, DC: American Physiological Society.

Teuber, H.-L. (1964). The riddle of frontal lobe function in man. In J. M. Warren & K. Akert (Eds.), *The frontal granular cortex and behavior* (pp. 410–444). New York: McGraw-Hill.

Teuber, H.-L. (1966). Kurt Goldstein's role in the development of neuropsychology. *Neuropsychologia, 4,* 299–310.

Teuber, H.-L. (1966/1980). Preface. In A. R. Luria (Ed.), *Higher cortical functions in man* (2nd ed.) (pp. xi–xiv). New York: Basic Books.

Teuber, H.-L. (1972). Letter to Walter A. Rosenblith. Teuber Collection, MIT Archives and Special Collections, MC417, Box 40.

Teuber, H.-L. (1975). Effects of focal brain injury on human behavior. In D. B. Tower (Ed.), *The nervous system, Vol. 2: The clinical neurosciences* (pp. 457–480). New York: Raven Press.

Teuber, H.-L. (1978). The brain and human behavior. *Proceedings of the Twenty-First International Congress on Psychology,* Paris, 119–163.

Teuber, H.-L., Battersby, W. S., & Bender, M. B. (1952). Effects of cerebral lesions on intellectual functioning in man. *Federation Proceedings, 11,* 1.

Teuber, H.-L., Battersby, W. S., & Bender, M. B. (1960). *Visual field defects after penetrating missile wounds of the brain.* Cambridge, MA: Harvard University Press.

Teuber, M. L. (1994). The founding of the Primate Station, Tenerife, Canary Islands. *American Journal of Psychology, 107,* 551–581.

Weinstein, S. (1985). The influence of Hans-Lukas Teuber and the Psychophysiological Laboratory on the establishment and development of neuropsychology. *International Journal of Neuroscience, 25,* 277–288.

Weiskrantz, L. (1977). Hans-Lukas Teuber. *Nature, 2,* 485–486.

PART II

PATHWAYS REMEMBERED

7

TEACHING THE BRAIN

Dirk J. Bakker

As Things Were

Holland is a small country, largely forged from polders. A polder is land claimed from the sea; it is low, flat land, extending to the far horizons. At the end of World War II, the land seemed flatter than usual as buildings were destroyed, and many polders were covered by water again. As a child during the war, I saw Rotterdam being burned down. Some years later, I received my secondary education in this same town. The noise of the drop hammers, as the town was being rebuilt, still echoes in my ears.

After finishing secondary school, I decided to study psychology. I had to tell my father how to say the word "psychology": "say the 'ps' like in the word 'psalm.'" Indeed, psychology was not a very popular choice for college students in the 1950s, although many European universities offered a major in the field. German authors wrote most of the available literature at that time. Osgood's *Method and Theory in Experimental Psychology* (1953), was one of the few exceptions. At the Free University of Amsterdam, psychology was taught jointly by faculty from philosophy and medicine. Consequently, students faced piles of philosophy books—over five hundred pages on the history of philosophy before Plato and Aristotle alone. But the bookshelf changed dramatically within a period of ten years. By the end of the 1960s, most psychology texts came from North America and Britain. At the same time, less and less philosophy was being offered in the psychology curriculum—unfortunately so.

As a student of developmental psychology, I chose "The Development of Bilateral Transfer" as the topic of my master's degree thesis. In essence, I asked, "does one hand profit from exercising the other one?" Analyzing the data was laborious, as computers were not available. A simple analysis of variance took a full day using paper and a pencil. My thesis topic was clearly neuropsychological in nature, causing the supervising professor a problem, since at that time, this branch of psychology did not exist in the academy. A number of psychologists, however, had learned to appreciate brain–behavior relationships while working in neurological clinics. These clinicians, being thus trained on-the-job, were practicing in a manner that could be described as neuropsychological. There even was a "Netherlands Society for Neuropsychology" founded in 1963.

Birth of an Interest

Investigating the development of bilateral transfer is, in fact, dealing with the inter-hemispheric transfer of information and thus touches upon the concept of laterality. Was it in view of these connections that the prospect of filling a vacancy in the Paedological Institute of Amsterdam was so tempting to me? The vacant position was that of a researcher in the field of reading disabilities. My knowledge of this subject matter was very limited, but I knew that handedness had something to do with it and that an American investigator was claiming that handedness reflected something called "hemispheric dominance." Later I learned that the investigator was Samuel Orton.

It is amazing to reflect on the "silent" influence Orton had in this part of the world—silent because only a few knew the name behind these concepts, although many primary school teachers could tell you that the "wrong" hand preference could lead to reading difficulty and school failure. Thus, the initial focus in this field was on reading difficulty or dyslexia, as related to handedness and hemispheric dominance. Professional books and journals of the time did discuss these ideas, but Herbert Birch's concept of inter-sensory integration was in the limelight instead. Consequently, inter-sensory integration, operationally defined as cross-modal transfer, became the starting point of my research.

Holland is a small country, about the size of Massachusetts. It only can survive by forging connections with other countries; as a result, the country has a strong international focus. The same holds true in my country's approach to science; thus, international publishing was fashionable, and scholars came to the Netherlands to visit us. Renowned neuropsychologists and dyslexia specialists including Arthur Benton, Margaret Rawson, Paul Satz, and many others landed in Amsterdam to see how and what we did in the Birch tradition. These consultations were of great importance to me. For instance, I first learned to write scientific articles as a result of these professional interactions. I occasionally find myself wondering if these visiting scholars learned anything from us; I do hope so.

Ten years passed before I went to North America. Arthur Benton arranged for me to present at the Academy of Aphasia meeting in Rochester, New York in 1972. Emotionally, I would describe it as a bipolar event: I experienced both a high degree of nervousness and the satisfaction of being taken seriously. In the same year, Margaret Rawson took me to the annual conference of the Orton Dyslexia Society in Seattle, while Paul Satz came to Amsterdam to present in a meeting I had organized. A book resulted from that latter meeting entitled *Specific Reading Disability* (Bakker & Satz, 1970), with chapters by Satz and Sparrow, Annett, Kinsbourne, Spreen, and others. These events were highly stimulating and of great value in the development of child neuropsychology in Holland and probably elsewhere in Europe.

I continued my research on dyslexia, in line with Herbert Birch's ideas, with even more enthusiasm. I published a number of papers on this topic and finally my dissertation entitled "Temporal Order Perception in Disturbed Reading" (Bakker, 1972). Arthur Benton came to The Netherlands and asked me some tough questions during my dissertation defense (but he had given me the answers the night before!).

Temporal Order in Disturbed Reading

Why was I focusing on temporal order perception when Birch and many others had published on "inter-modal matching"? Several investigations had shown that disturbed readers have difficulty matching visually and aurally presented information. In this line of research, subjects matched patterns of short and long taps with patterns of dots and dashes, a task that appeared demanding for children with dyslexia.

This being the case, I asked what causes the problem in performing such a task. In trying to get an answer, I considered that the subject had to match temporally ordered information presented in the auditory modality with spatially ordered information presented in the visual modality (or the other way around). It seemed possible that reading-disabled subjects experienced difficulty, either with the act of matching visual–auditory information or the matching of spatial–temporal information. I went a step further and queried whether these subjects could even accurately perform a basic temporal and/or spatial task when matching was not required.

I chose to investigate temporal order processing in normal and disturbed readers. Such an investigation is not easy for at least two reasons. First, talking about temporal order is talking about time. Though very basic, the concept of time is also very complex. When we speak about time, we are addressing duration or succession. In the case of succession, we may be asking the subject whether one or two tones were presented (succession versus simultaneity) or, perhaps, which of the tones was presented first and which one last (temporal order). In the latter case, the tones have to be different in order to make an answer possible. But different in what respect(s)?

At this point we face a second problem in dealing with temporal order perception, as it is always something that is temporally ordered. We must realize a priori that a finding from a study on the perception of temporal order may be related to that something, rather than to the ordering process itself. We can circumvent the problem to some extent by randomly displaying the items (the somethings) during the response phase. If these items are visual, the subject can point to or name the items that came first or last. But interpretation is confounded further by the fact that pointing and naming are quite different ways of responding, possibly resulting in different outcomes.

The complexity of doing this research should now be apparent, but I persevered nonetheless. What my colleagues and I found in several large samples of normal and dyslexic readers is that these two groups differed in the perception of temporally ordered verbal (or verbally codifiable) items but were not so different when items were nonverbal in content. This conclusion is more limited than the global claim that reading or language-impaired subjects have a problem with the perception of temporal order as such. If that were the case, such a person would also find it difficult to do such nonverbal tasks as pointing to the leg that moved first or second when walking.

Similarly, Luria (1968) described a number of brain-damaged cases who were not able to beat out a temporal pattern (such as —...—...) but who were quite able to reproduce the same pattern with words. More recently, Studdert-Kennedy and Mody (1995), in explaining that "rate of perception" is something different from the "perception of rate" and "temporal processing," highlighted how careful we should be in dealing with time concepts. This article and related studies (Reitsma, 1998) indeed do reflect the renewed interest in the relationship between the processing of temporal order and developmental language disorder.

I found that reading-disabled children did not have difficulty in naming single letters (given that they have sufficient time to do so) but that they do show problems when they have to reproduce the order of presentation of these letters. Thus, I concluded that these children do not have a verbal labeling problem nor—as argued above—any temporal ordering problem. Instead, difficulties occur when verbal items are presented in a time scheme. In other words, "the interaction between time and verbal code is disturbed and not so much the main factors" (Bakker, 1972, p. 67).

Frank Vellutino (1978) disagreed with my hypothesis and, in an extended discussion, he claimed that the basic problem in dyslexia is the processing of verbal information, irrespective of whether this information is or is not ordered. Vellutino's publication represents the beginning of a continuing line of investigators who stress the crucial importance of linguistic competence, especially phonological analysis capacity, in learning to read.

One of the last chapters of my dissertation is on hemispheric specialization in temporal order perception. The answer to the question of which cerebral hemisphere predominates in the mediation of temporally ordered information appeared to depend on the verbal or nonverbal nature of that information. The chapter testifies to my growing interest in reading and dyslexia as related to hemispheric asymmetry of function. There were three sources of this interest:

1. The long and steady scientific interest in this relationship, initiated by Samuel Orton.
2. The development of new techniques to trace hemispheric asymmetry of function including dichotic (and monaural) listening, bilateral (and unilateral) viewing, dichaptic (and unilateral) touching, and various electrophysiological techniques (EEG/ERP).
3. An undisguised personal curiosity.

Reading, Dyslexia, and the Cerebral Hemispheres

Which neuropsychologists were not dealing with hemispheric asymmetry of function in the 1970s and 1980s? The journals bulged with articles on this subject. Take reading and dyslexia—here is the reasoning that prevailed (and still prevails): language is predominantly mediated by the left hemisphere in most individuals; text is printed language, thus the reading of text should be mediated predominantly by the left hemisphere. When we administer a verbal listening, viewing, or haptic test, we expect to find that proficient reading goes with firm right ear, right visual field, and right hand preference. What did investigators actually find? The predictions were confirmed, but not always. It was sometimes found that dyslexics showed weaker right lateral plane preferences, no preferences, or left plane preferences— findings that were explained as indicating atypical hemispheric asymmetries in the processing of verbal inputs. But what about the majority of dyslexic subjects who, like their counterparts without a reading problem, show the typical right plane advantage?

Intriguingly enough, some studies reported that the hemisphere–reading relationship depends on the reading age of the child. Reading in the higher grades of primary school was associated with a right plane advantage, but this did not hold up for reading in the lower grades. Could this mean that initial and advanced reading are subserved predominantly by different hemispheres—initial reading by the right and advanced reading by the left hemisphere? But that would imply that initial and advanced reading are qualitatively different processes.

What do primary school teachers see when observing their pupils while reading? They find that early reading is, above all, slow and fragmented. That is fine with the teacher since accuracy is the desired goal at this stage of learning. Slow reading is not only acceptable, it is a necessity since the very novice reader is faced with a problem: letters do not meet the law of shape constancy. Turn a cup upside down and it still is a cup. Do the same with the letter "p" and one gets something different—a "b." Moreover, whereas a cup and a saucer, while having different forms also have different names, a "d" and a "D" have the same name in spite of their different forms. Thus, the novice reader has to master text as a perceptual complexity. Over the course of development, reading should become increasingly fluent. Fluency is incompatible with laboriously analyzing every letter and word. In advanced reading, perceptual analyses have sunk below the level of consciousness (Fries, 1963); it rather requires the application of learned syntactical rules and the use of an acquired, rich lexicon (Goldberg & Costa, 1981). The sentences of Figure 7.1 demonstrate the idea I am describing: being a fluent reader one probably grasps the essence, but reading again, word by word this time, draws the secret out of these sentences (Hagen, 1984).

Early reading entails processing of perceptually demanding text, with slow, fragmented, but accurate processing as a result. Could this type of reading be the province of the right hemisphere rather than the left? Advanced reading, with perceptual demands no longer in the forefront, clears the way for fluency. Could the

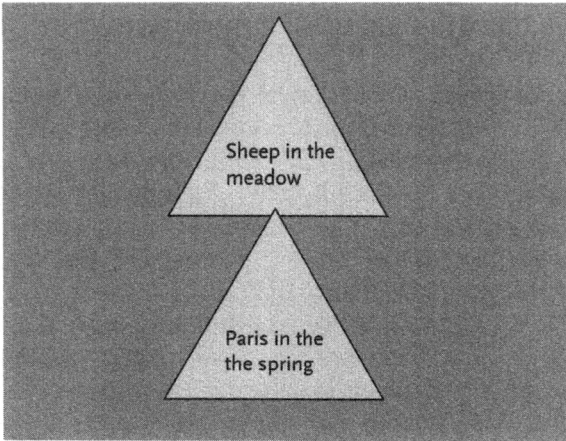

Figure 7.1. Two sentences with the same, well-known syntactic structure.

left hemisphere, rather than the right, mediate this type of reading? Diller and associates (Diller, Ben-Yishay, Gerstman, Goodkin, Gordon, & Weinberg, 1974) reported on a large sample of brain-damaged children who had to cross out a particular letter in rows of different letters; those with left hemispheric lesions were relatively slow but accurate, whereas those with right hemispheric lesions were relatively fast but sloppy. Several investigators (e.g., Bakker, Hoefkens, & Van der Vlugt, 1979; Bjørgen, 1998; Carmon, Nachshon & Starinsky, 1976) also found a right field advantage for verbal inputs in older, but certainly not in younger, primary school children.

The so-called Balance Model (Bakker, 1979, 1983, 1990; Rourke, Bakker, Fisk, & Strang, 1983) of learning to read thus was born: early reading is predominantly mediated by the right, advanced reading by the left cerebral hemisphere. This right-to-left shift occurs at some point during the learning-to-read process—a risky idea in the scientific community of those days (perhaps these days as well).

So, how do we gather evidence to support these ideas? Behavioral techniques such as dichoptic viewing were valuable, but in terms of validity they are two or three steps away from the hemispheric activity we wanted to tap. Fortunately, electrophysiological expertise and EEG/ERP equipment were available, enabling us to get close to (evoked) cerebral activity. A four-year longitudinal study was designed consisting of normal children from kindergarten through primary school grade 3. Words were flashed in the central visual field, ERPs were registered at parietal and temporal locations, and reading tests were administered. Principal components of the ERPs were established, reading scores were factor-analyzed, and correlations between ERP–parameters and separate factor scores were calculated for each hemisphere (Bakker, 1990; Licht, 1988; Licht, Bakker, Kok, & Bouma, 1988). The results are summarized in Figure 7.2.

In support of the hypothesis, reading performance is more strongly associated with right than with left hemisphere activity in kindergarten and the first grade of the

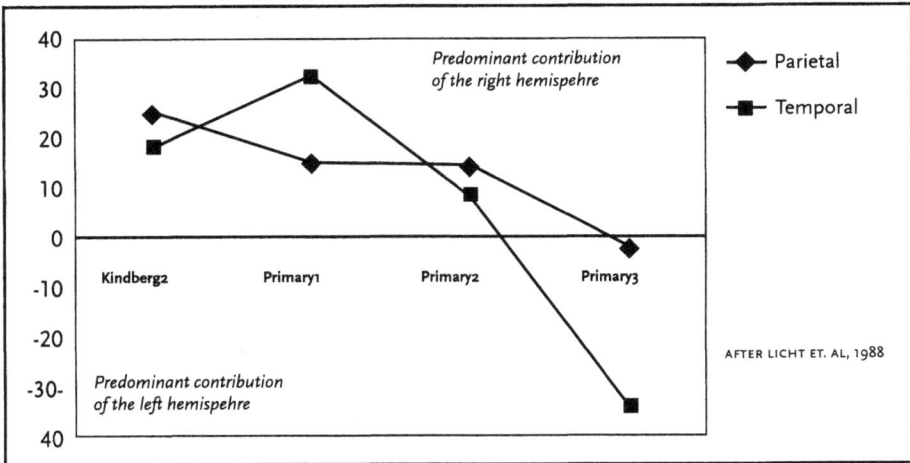

Figure 7.2. Relative contribution of the right and left cerebral hemisphere to the processing of text (Licht et al., 1988).

primary school (early reading), but more strongly with left than with right hemisphere activity in the third grade of the primary school (more advanced reading).

Now, more than ten years later, I have not seen much evidence contradicting the claimed role of the right and left hemisphere in early and advanced reading, respectively. The prominence of the right hemisphere in early reading has been underscored by the results of recent research (De Graaff, 1995; De Graaff & Licht, in press).

In the years before ready access to computer technology, researchers had ample time to think. Deductive thinking prevailed. My problem was how to move from normal to disturbed reading. Considering the upper part of Figure 7.2, I reasoned that some children may not be able to make the hemispheric shift in the mediation of reading. If so, we could predict that those children, while getting stuck in the predominant generation of right hemispheric strategies would continue to show a fragmented style of reading (i.e., no fluency). Since these children, presumably, remain focused on the perceptual features of text, I classified the problem as "P-type dyslexia."

At the same time, one could imagine other children whose reading is mediated by the left hemisphere from the very onset of their learning-to-read process. While trying to generate left hemisphere, linguistic strategies, they would overlook the perceptual text features, resulting in both fast and inaccurate reading. I classified this hypothetical reading disorder as "L-type dyslexia." Do "P" and "L" exist in reality? Teachers have indeed observed these styles of reading in the classroom; however, more was needed to ascertain the validity of this classification.

Subsequent studies provided evidence for the validity of the P/L–classification. P– and L–dyslexic children appeared to differ on quite a few parameters: the amplitudes of some word-elicited peaks in the right versus the left hemisphere; the pattern of eye movements; the reaction times to graphemic, lexical, and semantic task demands; the decay of words stored in memory; and so on (Aro,

Licht, & Lyytinen, 1994; Bakker, Licht, & Van Strien, 1991; Donders & Van der Vlugt, 1984; Jonkman, Licht, Bakker, & Van den Broek-Sandmann, 1992; Masutto, Bravar, & Fabbro, 1994; Morton, 1994; Van der Vlugt, 1991; Van Strien, in press). In view of these findings, there seems to be a clear basis for this classification. How far the P/ L–classification parallels other classification systems remains an unanswered question.

From Etiology to Treatment

One day the director of the Paedological Institute, where I had a part-time job, came to see me. Obviously he had something important to say. The message came down to the following: I appreciate your work, but remember that you are employed by an institute that provides clinical services. He continued by suggesting that I develop a method to effectively treat dyslexic children. This chat was the beginning of one of the most challenging and exciting phases in my scientific career. Of course, the issue of treatment had been present in the back of my mind for quite some time. Why was I hesitating to explore treatment issues? Perhaps I was avoiding the logical pitfalls of a treatment based on my own model of dyslexia.

For instance, take an "L"-type dyslexic child. According to the model, such a child had "skipped" the early phase in the learning-to-read process that requires predominant control by the right hemisphere. Logically one then would have to stimulate the right hemisphere in an effort to get it to take the lion's share in reading. One might say, "okay, just try." But what should we expect as a result of right hemisphere stimulation? We expected to find long-lasting change in the hemisphere, but can brain parameters be changed by psychological interventions?

Please do not laugh in hearing that; as a result of a sort of silliness, I once believed that the brain was an autonomous organ with its primary task being to carry out a genetic blueprint of behavior. I believed that psychological interventions would fail to bring about any lasting change in the brain. Thus, I was, at first, skeptical about the idea of stimulating a cerebral hemisphere. Forget it. But when I thought about it further, I noted that psychotherapy brings about behavioral changes that supposedly are accompanied by changes in the brain itself. In the process of carrying out behavior, the brain itself is altered. What an exciting idea!

The excitement caused by a discovery may be hard for other people to understand. I remember like it was yesterday the day I came across an article by Rosenzweig and his group (Rosenzweig, Bennett, & Diamond, 1972) on the impact of the environment on brain development in rats. In their study, rats were raised either in isolation without stimulating toys (the impoverished environment group) or were raised socially in a cage with play toys (the enriched environment group). The basic maintenance of the two groups (i.e., food and water administration) was the same. Brain differences were found, with the enriched animals showing a heavier and thicker occipital cortex, larger amounts of neurotransmitter, an increase in glial cells, larger neuronal cell bodies, greater RNA–DNA ratios, and more—wow!

Let us contrast impoverished versus enriched learning environments by comparing two rats—one who finds food right under its nose versus a second who, upon awakening, must master a maze in order to obtain food. The brain of the latter animal is better off. In a similar vein, I used to tell my students, "After the lecture you can bike home, put some coins in the slot of a food machine and eat, or, alternatively, you can bike home, select a recipe, prepare a meal, and then eat. Think about the differences in these two experiences for the brain."

Inspired by these ideas, I searched for more research on the impact of enriched environments on brain development. Greenough and his group (Greenough & Juraska, 1979) found that enriched environments were associated with more dendrite bifurcations and spines. Davenport's work (Davenport, 1976) on impoverishment versus enrichment during the early development of animals, with or without brain damage, showed that the enriched animals with brain damage appeared almost as smart in mastering a maze as the non-damaged impoverished subjects. Thus, evidence was accumulating that demonstrated the effects of educational and learning environments on the brain.

Some twenty-five years after Rosenzweig's et al. publication (1972) I came across "The Social Construction of the Human Brain" by Eisenberg (1995); the title alone caught my interest. It seemed that this line of investigation was finally being extended to human brain development. Thus, I finally had scientific justification for stimulating the left hemisphere of P–type dyslexic children and the right hemisphere of L–types, with the goal of inducing changes in the stimulated hemisphere and hopefully, as a result of these changes, improving aspects of reading. Stimulation of the left hemisphere should particularly improve fluency, and stimulation of the right hemisphere should particularly improve accuracy.

Wonderful plan—but I was concerned that the idea of stimulating the right hemisphere in order to improve reading would not be readily accepted by the scientific community, to say the least. That is why we decided to begin modestly and to include as many control conditions as we could. One of the things we wanted to do, from the very onset, was a series of treatment studies to trace the proposed treatment-induced cortical changes. In contrast to animal studies, we could not "look into" the brain of treated dyslexic subjects; in those days, technologies such as functional MRI were not available. The only thing we could do was record ERPs to flashed words, before and after treatment.

The first, small-scale study (Bakker, Moerland, & Goekoop-Hoefkens, 1981) was intended to provide initial support for the continuation of this line of research. The results were encouraging. We found treatment-induced changes in the hemispheric distribution of electrophysiological activity, improvement of reading and, most importantly, significant correlations between changes in hemispheric activity and improvement in reading. All of this resulted from sixteen, 45-minute sessions. The treatment during these sessions aimed at stimulating the left hemisphere of P–dyslexics and the right hemisphere of L–dyslexics. Stimulation was accomplished through one of the visual half-fields and the fingers of the right or left hand, both providing for hemisphere-specific stimulation (HSS).

Soon a computer program, HEMSTIM, became commercially available for fixation-controlled stimulation through the visual half-fields; however, computers were not very common in the 1970s. The headmaster of one of the schools where we wanted to recruit subjects commented, "Imagine you are successful with your HSS–treatment. What would be the benefit for our school as we have no computer?" He continued by suggesting that we develop a non-computerized method that would be as effective as HEMSTIM and would be transferable to the classroom setting.

As a result of this discussion, the HAS–procedure was designed, providing for "hemisphere-alluding stimulation." With HAS, P–dyslexic children read phonetically and semantically enriched texts, presumably encouraging predominant processing by the left hemisphere, and L–dyslexic children read perceptually demanding text, presumably encouraging predominant processing by the right hemisphere.

A second, extended investigation followed (Bakker & Vinke, 1985). There were two experimental groups—HSS and HAS—and three control groups, with a sample of P– and L–dyslexic children in each group. ERPs were recorded and scholastic achievement tests administered, prior to and after 22 treatment sessions. In general, the results paralleled the findings of the pilot study. When we submitted the manuscript for publication we received a favorable response, but one nagging question remained: Where is your crossed–control condition (i.e., P–types receiving right hemisphere stimulation and L–types receiving left hemisphere stimulation)? Good question, but in order to get parental permission we had promised parents that we would give their children the experimental, rather than the crossed–control, condition. The reviewers of our submission kindly accepted that argument.

At the same time, another challenge presented itself. Robin Morris (Morris, 1989) inquired about the possible mechanism underlying the treatment effects, and he suggested that "narrowing of attention" could be the crucial factor. In flashing words to one visual field, one narrows attention to one hemisphere (Marcel Kinsbourne would agree). If Morris were correct, we would expect the results of stimulation to be independent of the visual field used for presentation.

After this discussion, we decided to design a challenge study (Bakker, 1995): L–type dyslexic children received either stimulation of the left hemisphere or the right hemisphere. Subsequently, children who had received stimulation of the left hemisphere showed increased fluency and decreased accuracy in reading; children who had received stimulation of the right hemisphere showed the reverse pattern of outcomes. Thus, it seems that stimulation of the right or left hemisphere makes a difference.

Treatment as a Construct

At the beginning of my career I had a mentor whose task was to initiate me into the secrets of research methodology. Once he told me that he had received an invitation to investigate the effect of milk consumption on the intelligence of school children. A union of milk dealers had heard of a foreign study suggesting that milk, consumed daily by children, could raise level of intelligence. The mentor asked me how I would design such an investigation. I proposed a group of children receiving milk on a daily basis, a group not receiving milk, and another control group receiving lemonade on a daily basis. The mentor agreed. We never heard from the union again.

Lemonade is almost entirely water and, as milk also is largely water, we wanted to check out whether this component of milk could be the major factor causing a possible increase of intelligence. But the union probably was not interested in that possibility. We could have planned other control conditions, as milk has many components—water, proteins, vitamins, calcium, and other minerals. It certainly could be the case that any one of these, a particular combination of these, or even an interaction of components would cause an effect. Milk can be conceptualized as a construct of many (possibly interacting) components.

What about the same reasoning applied to hemisphere-specific and hemisphere-alluding stimulation (HSS and HAS) in the treatment of dyslexia? Since both are constructs of various components, we can ask which components are critical in producing the effects on reading. In HSS, stimuli are flashed in the right or left visual half-fields. We need to know which stimuli are effective and how long they should be administered. What would happen when just plain light was flashed? What about factors of stimulus brightness and color? Such issues may seem trivial, but they are not.

Consider the issue of stimulus presentation time. Usually words or letters are flashed for less than 300 milliseconds. With practice, flashing times are reduced across treatment sessions; lowering occurs every time a subject makes less than two mistakes in a series of twenty words. Thus a child may start with 300 milliseconds in the first session and finish with 30 milliseconds. Thus, information processing speed increases across treatment sessions. Tallal and associates (Merzenich, Jenkins, Johnston, Schreiner, Miller, & Tallal, 1996) recently claimed positive effects of what they call temporal processing enhancement on language and reading in dysphasic (and dyslexic?) children. Because a similar factor is part of the HSS procedure, it is important to consider temporal factors in the reading performance of our HSS-treated dyslexics.

We recently confronted this issue as some puzzling results emerged from treatment studies (Dryer, Beale, & Lambert, 1999; Glaudé, 1994) here and abroad. Bilateral stimulation—that is to say, stimulation through the central visual field or stimulation of either visual field—may produce results that match those produced by single hemisphere stimulation. A common factor of these various treatment designs is the lowering of flashing times across sessions, which comes down to enhancing speed of processing.

In reflecting on these results, one thing immediately becomes apparent: increasing processing speed, if found to be effective at all, cannot be the only factor affecting the outcomes of our treatment procedures. First, not all studies using HSS produce similar effects of right versus left hemisphere stimulation (Bakker et al. 1981; Bakker & Vinke, 1985; Grace & Spreen, 1994). Second, in some treatment studies,

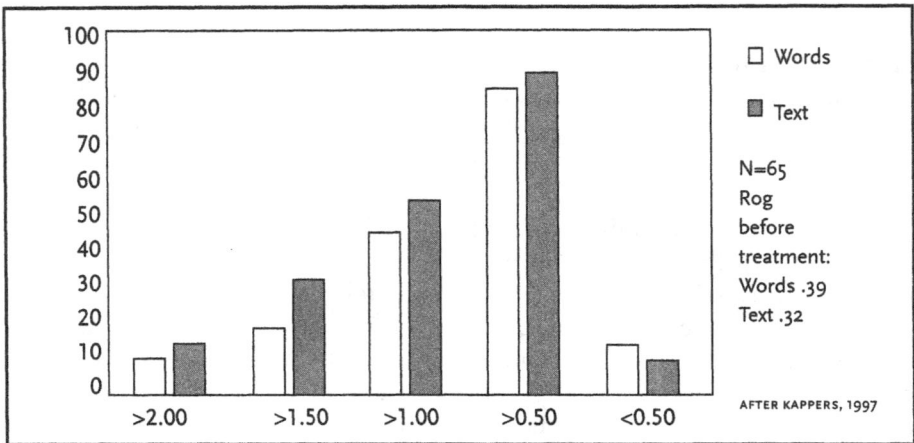

Figure 7.3. Percent of children by rate of gain (ROG) after treatment for severe dyslexia (Kappers, 1997).

processing speed does not play a role (i.e., when flashing times are kept constant across treatment sessions, when HSS is administered through the fingers, or when HAS is the treatment). Yet the results still show the predicted right versus left hemisphere effects (Bakker, Bouma, & Gardien, 1990; Goldstein & Obrzut, 2001; Robertson, in press). Thus, enhancement of processing speed can be only one of the factors responsible for treatment effects.

Another important factor may be the nature of the words that are presented in the left or right lateral plane of dyslexic children. Van Strien, Stolk, and Zuiker (1995) flashed emotionally threatening versus emotionally neutral words in the visual half-fields of P– and L–type dyslexic children. The authors predicted that flashing threatening words to the right hemisphere would have a greater positive impact on reading accuracy than the flashing of neutral words. Their hypothesis was supported.

The treatment of dyslexia through hemisphere stimulation is now practiced on a daily basis in the outpatient clinic of the Paedological Institute, as it is in a number of institutes elsewhere in the country and abroad. Kappers (1997), the former director of the outpatient clinic previously mentioned, recently published the results of this clinical treatment program. Figure 7.3 presents an overview of the results.

The dyslexic children treated by Kappers and colleagues were very poor in reading at intake: while a "rate of gain" (ROG) of 1.00 reflects a normal reading level, these children, on average, showed ROGs lower than .40. After treatment 40–50% of these children demonstrated normal reading or better (ROGs > 1.00).

Between Sleeping and Waking

It is sometimes said that the richest ideas arise in the twilight of the day. The idea that the brain is willing to respond, in a lasting fashion, to stimulation from an educational environment, often tumbles through my mind during those early morning hours. "The Brain as a Dependent Variable" was the title of my presidential address to the International Neuropsychological Society (INS) (Bakker, 1984). The brain as a dependent variable means no less than that we are in the position to teach the brain.

As neuropsychologists, we are well prepared to assume the challenge of teaching the brain. As good psychologists, we know what stimulus patterns are all about. As neurobehavioral scientists, we are informed about the brain mechanisms that parallel various behavioral functions. As clinicians, we know appropriate techniques for therapeutic stimulation of the brain.

Despite our strengths in this domain, present-day neuropsychologists are mainly involved in assessment and diagnosis. They seem to feel less comfortable with neuropsychological approaches to treatment. In addition, most of us, including our students, are only vaguely aware that the brain can be influenced psychologically. Based on traditional conceptualizations of the brain and the current emphasis on genetics, most of us take it for granted that the brain is an independent, rather than a dependent, variable. This, in spite of the emergence of a new branch on the scientific tree called psycho–neuro–endocrinology. (Note the sequence of suggested causation: it begins psycho, comes to neuro, and ends with endo. Neuropsychologists, mind your business!)

The brain is shaped by both genetic and environmental conditions. Environments not only impact on an existing brain, environmental conditions possibly played a role during its evolution. It seems no longer heretical to consider this possibility, as ". . . genomes are showing that they can help themselves cope with a changing environment" (Arber, as cited in Pennisi, 1998, p. 1134). These changes are brought about by physical and chemical parameters. Nevertheless, some evolutionists talk of "adaptive or directed evolution." This is a far cry from claiming that mutations occur only randomly during evolution. Thus, environments not only directly impact the brain but possibly also impact brain evolution.

Why emphasize so strongly the importance of environmental influences on the brain? Such an emphasis legitimizes our therapeutic activities. In addition, humans shape environments for other living creatures. Consequently, humankind needs to realize that there always are two environments—one out there and a copy inside the head; the latter may remain for generations to come. We must consider the environments we create for the current generation and for those to come.

Neuropsychology in the Polder: Then and Now

During my early years in university, fewer than 20 new students entered psychology each year. Oral exams were given at the professor's private home. We arrived wearing a blue suit, black shoes, and a necktie. The professor offered a cigar or cigarette, his wife coffee or tea. Then the questions, tough questions usually, were presented. If you passed, the professor signed your examination card. When you had enough signatures on your card, you completed the overall exam for your master's degree a few years later. University life was simple indeed. These exams covered everything within psychology, but not so neuropsychology, as this branch of the field did not exist.

Over the years, the picture has changed dramatically. Now over 150 new psychology students enroll in my university every year. Written exams are administered to massive numbers of students who also fill out multiple-choice forms on the quality of the teacher and his or her teaching. I was the first (part-time) professor of neuropsychology in The Netherlands. At that time I was under the division of developmental psychology. Now neuropsychology is a division in itself, with some 40 new students each year. Over the years, professors of neuropsychology have been appointed at other universities in the country.

Two political and societal developments have had a dramatic impact on life in general and on the university in particular. First, Holland embraced the idea of a European Union from the very outset. My country is internationally oriented by tradition, and being part of the European Union is an economic necessity for us. One of the related questions was what language should be used in the university—Dutch? But our native language is not very appropriate for attracting students from abroad. Thus, English is now used in postdoctoral courses. The European Union encourages collaboration among European scientists. This is not to say that North America is out, not at all; it just says that something brand new has been added here in Europe.

The second event, having a world-wide impact, was the oil crisis and its numerous consequences. This country developed the so-called polder model for its economic future. One salient element of this model is the agreement between employers and employees that employment has priority over better earnings; another element addresses cuts in public spending. The model appears to work well in Holland. In North America, something similar is called "the third way." So far so good, but the model has its price. It requires cutting expenses, increasing collaboration, enhancing quality, and encouraging private enterprise—in other words, a no-nonsense approach.

The universities in Holland changed radically as a consequence of this model. Universities are required to establish so-called inter-academic "research schools" (read: less expenses for the government). These schools are open to "scientifically qualified" researchers from different universities working in similar fields. Scientifically qualified means that a person produces a sufficient number of publications. This translates into taking a given publication, counting the number of pages, and giving one point for every five pages. This number is then multiplied by four if the publication is in an international, refereed journal; by two if it is a chapter in an international book; and so on. The goal is to have 72 points in a period of four or five years. Even if one achieves the status of being scientifically qualified one time, one must qualify again after five years.

Take this chapter as an example. It will have some fifteen pages equalling three points and, as it is international, it totals to two times three for six points. Not bad for a "qualified" person over 60 years old—lucky me!

I recall going to North America several times in the 1970s. My wife often found me enthusiastic and motivated after my return. I would talk of the good science there, conducted by nice people. I was hesitant to stay there and begin a career, however, because I perceived keen competition in North America. Ironically, now I would love to know how a North American colleague would feel after experiencing our system of evaluation in Holland.

Private enterprise is another element of the polder model. Some ten years ago I could not sleep one night because of an exciting business idea: since we are entering the European Union, why not develop a European school devoted to child neuropsychology? In the cold light of day, I thought it better to forget the whole idea. When I told my colleagues about the idea with which I was then struggling nightly, they surprised me by enthusiastically encouraging me to go on. I did persevere, and with my long time associate, Robert Licht, I founded and continue to co-direct the European Graduate School of Child Neuropsychology. Ten to fifteen students come, stay for a year, take their exams, and then go back to their home countries holding valuable certificates. To date, we have trained students from 25 countries and 6 continents. Though the numbers of our graduates are small, we have trained enough students for the school to survive. It is wonderful to enjoy the company of these young, highly motivated people.

Just like in Holland, neuropsychology is becoming a visible science and profession in many places around the globe. It is the science that deals with the reciprocal relationship between the brain and behavior. Our model is not Brain → Behavior, but rather Brain ↔ Behavior. I am confident that future generations of neuropsychologists will find this reciprocal relationship to be as fascinating as I do.

REFERENCES

Aro, M., Licht, R., & Lyytinen, H. (1994). Do probe evoked potentials reveal differences between subtypes of dyslexia? In R. Licht & G. Spyer (Eds.), *The balance model of dyslexia* (pp. 57–70). Assen, The Netherlands: Van Gorcum.

Bakker, D. J. (1972). *Temporal order perception in disturbed reading.* Rotterdam, The Netherlands: Rotterdam University Press.

Bakker, D. J. (1979). Hemispheric differences and reading strategies: Two dyslexias? *Bulletin of the Orton Society, 29,* 84–100.

Bakker, D. J. (1983). Hemispheric specialization and specific reading retardation. In M. Rutter (Ed.), *Developmental neuropsychiatry* (pp. 498–506). New York: Guilford Press.

Bakker, D. J. (1984). The brain as a dependent variable. *Journal of Clinical Neuropsychology, 6,* 1–16.

Bakker, D. J. (1990). *Neuropsychological treatment of dyslexia.* New York: Oxford University Press.

Bakker, D. J. (1995). The willing brain of dyslexic children. In R. M.Yoshi & C. K. Leong (Eds.), *Developmental and acquired dyslexia* (pp. 33–39). Dordrecht, The Netherlands: Kluwer.

Bakker, D. J., Bouma, A., & Gardien, C. J. (1990). Hemisphere-specific treatment of dyslexia subtypes: A field experiment. *Journal of Learning Disabilities, 23,* 433–438.

Bakker, D. J., Hoefkens, M., & Van der Vlugt, H. (1979). Hemispheric specialization in children as reflected in the longitudinal development of ear asymmetry. *Cortex, 15,* 619–625.

Bakker, D. J., Licht, R., & Van Strien, J. W. (1991). Biopsychological validation of Land P-type dyslexia. In B. P. Rourke (Ed.), *Neuropsychological validation of learning disability subtypes* (pp. 124–139). New York: Guilford Press.

Bakker, D. J., Moerland, R., & Goekoop-Hoefkens, M. (1981). Effects of hemisphere-specific stimulation on the reading performance of dyslexic boys: A pilot study. *Journal of Clinical Neuropsychology, 3,* 155–159.

Bakker, D. J., & Satz, P. (1970). *Specific reading disability: Advances in theory and method.* Rotterdam: Rotterdam University Press.

Bakker, D. J., & Vinke, J. (1985). Effects of hemisphere-specific stimulation on brain activity and reading in dyslexics. *Journal of Clinical and Experimental Neuropsychology, 7,* 505–525.

Bjørgen, G. (1998). *Hemisfaerespesifikt engasjement i startfasen av normal leseinnlaering* [Hemisphere-specific engagement in early phases of learning to read]. Master's thesis, University of Trondheim, Norway.

Carmon, A., Nachshon, I., & Starinsky, R. (1976). Developmental aspects of visual hemifield differences in perception of verbal material. *Brain and Language, 3,* 463–469.

Davenport, J. W. (1976). Environmental therapy in hypothyroid and other disadvantaged animal populations. In R. N. Walsh & W. T. Greenough (Eds.), *Environments as therapy for brain dysfunction* (pp. 71–114). New York: Plenum.

De Graaff, M. B. (1995). *Hemispheric engagement during letter and word identification in beginning readers: An event-related potential study.* Doctoral dissertation, Free University, Amsterdam.

De Graaff, M. B., & Licht, R. (in press). Event-related potentials in letter identification tasks: Developmental changes during the first year of reading instruction. *Developmental Neuropsychology.*

Diller, L., Ben-Yishay, Y., Gerstman, L. J., Goodkin, R., Gordon, W., & Weinberg, J. (1974). *Studies in cognition and rehabilitation in hemiplegia.* New York: New York University Medical Center.

Donders, J., & Van der Vlugt, H. (1984). Eye-movement patterns in disabled readers at two age levels: A test of Bakker's balance model. *Journal of Clinical Neuropsychology, 6,* 241–256.

Dryer, R., Beale, I. L., & Lambert, A. J. (1999). The balance model of dyslexia and remedial training: An evaluative study. *Journal of Learning Disabilities, 32,* 174–186.

Eisenberg, L. (1995). The social construction of the human brain. *American Journal of Psychiatry, 152,* 563–575.

Fries, C. C. (1963). *Linguistics and reading.* New York: Holt, Rinehart & Winston.

Glaudé, S. W. D. (1994). Prevention of dyslexia in latent P- and L-type kindergarten children: A three year follow-up. In R. Licht & G. Spyer (Eds.), *The balance model of dyslexia* (pp. 71–99). Assen, The Netherlands: Van Gorcum.

Goldberg, E., & Costa, L.D. (1981). Hemisphere differences in the acquisition and use of descriptive systems. *Brain and Language, 14,* 144–173.

Goldstein, B. H. & Obrzut, E. J. (2001). Neuropsychological treatment of dyslexia in the classroom setting. *Journal of Learning Disabilities, 34,* 276–285.

Grace, G. M., & Spreen, O. (1994). Hemisphere-specific stimulation of L– and P–types: A replication and a critical appraisal. In R. Licht & G. Spyer (Eds.), *The balance model of dyslexia* (pp. 133–181). Assen, The Netherlands: Van Gorcum.

Greenough, W. T., & Juraska, J. M. (1979). Experience-induced changes in brain fine structure: Their behavioral implications. In M. E. Hahn, C. Jensen & B. C. Dudek (Eds.), *Development and evolution of brain size* (pp. 295–320). New York: Academic Press.

Hagen, P. (1984). *Hoe wij leren lezen* [How we learn to read]. Tilburg, The Netherlands: Zwijsen.

Jonkman, I., Licht, R., Bakker, D. J., & Van den Broek-Sandmann, T. M. (1992). Shifting of attention in subtyped dyslexic children: An event-related potential study. *Developmental Neuropsychology, 8,* 261–278.

Kappers, E. J. (1997). Outpatient treatment of

dyslexia through stimulation of the cerebral hemispheres. *Journal of Learning Disabilities, 30,* 100–125.

Licht, R. (1988). *Event-related potential asymmetries and word reading in children.* Doctoral dissertation, Free University, Amsterdam.

Licht, R., Bakker, D. J., Kok, A., & Bouma, A. (1988). The development of lateral event-related potentials (ERPs) related to word naming: A four year longitudinal study. *Neuropsychologia, 26,* 327–340.

Luria, A. R. (1968). The directive function of speech in development and dissolution, part II. In R. C. Oldfield & J. C. Marshall (Eds.), *Language* (pp. 353–365). Harmondsworth, England: Penguin.

Masutto, C., Bravar, L., & Fabbro, F. (1994). Neurolinguistic differentiation of children with subtypes of dyslexia. *Journal of Learning Disabilities, 27,* 520–526.

Merzenich, M. M., Jenkins, W. M., Johnston, P., Schreiner, C., Miller, S. L., & Tallal, P. (1996). Temporal processing deficits of language-learning impaired children ameliorated by training. *Science, 271,* 77–81.

Morris, R. (1989). Treatment of learning disabilities from a neuropsychological framework. In D. J. Bakker & H. Van der Vlugt (Eds.), *Learning disabilities: Neuropsychological correlates and treatment, Vol. I* (pp. 183–190). Lisse, The Netherlands: Swets & Zeitlinger.

Morton, L. L. (1994). Interhemispheric balance patterns detected by selective phonemic dichotic laterality measures in four clinical subtypes of reading-disabled children. *Journal of Clinical and Experimental Neuropsychology, 16,* 556–567.

Osgood, C. E. (1953). *Method and theory in experimental psychology.* New York: Oxford University Press.

Pennisi, E. (1998). How the genome readies itself for evolution. *Science, 281,* 1131–1134.

Reitsma, P. (1998). Time, order, and reading disorder. In R. Licht, A. Bouma, W. Slot, & W. Koops (Eds.), *Child neuropsychology: Reading disability and more* (pp. 67–83). Delft, The Netherlands: Eburon.

Robertson, J. (in press). Neuropsychological intervention in dyslexia: Two studies on British pupils. *Journal of Learning Disabilities.*

Rosenzweig, M. R., Bennett, E. L., & Diamond, M. C. (1972). Brain changes in response to experience. *Scientific American, 266,* 22–29.

Rourke, B. P., Bakker, D. J., Fisk, J. L., & Strang, J. D. (1983). *Child neuropsychology.* New York: Guilford Press.

Studdert-Kennedy, M., & Mody, M. (1995). Auditory temporal perception deficits in the reading-impaired: A critical review of the evidence. *Psychonomic Bulletin and Review, 2,* 508–514.

Van der Vlugt, H. (1991). Neuropsychological validation studies of learning disability subtypes: Verbal, visual–spatial, and psychomotor abilities. In B. P. Rourke (Ed.), *Neuropsychological validation of learning disability subtypes* (pp. 140–159). New York: Guilford Press.

Van Strien, J. W. (in press). Verbal learning in boys with P–type dyslexia, L–type dyslexia, and boys without learning disabilities: Differences in learning curves and in serial position curves. *Child Neuropsychology.*

Van Strien, J. W., Stolk, B. D., & Zuiker, S. (1995). Hemisphere-specific treatment of dyslexia subtypes: Better reading with anxiety-laden words? *Journal of Learning Disabilities, 28,* 30–34.

Vellutino, F. R. (1978). Toward an understanding of dyslexia: Psychological factors in specific reading disability. In A. L. Benton & D. Pearl (Eds.), *Dyslexia: An appraisal of current knowledge* (pp. 61–111). New York: Oxford University Press.

8

Lifelines

Anne-Lise Christensen

Aleksandr Romanovich Luria's approach to neuropsychology has had a profound influence on my life's work. In an unpublished draft of a manuscript that became the introduction to his final book, *The Making of Mind,* Luria (1979) wrote

> People come and go. Their ideas and actions remain. Nevertheless, a retrospect of one's life in science can be of certain value. . . . It can reflect the atmosphere in which the scholar worked, the factors that influenced his work, the basic ideas that dominated during the period of his activity, and the influences of outstanding men he met.[1] (A.R. Luria, personal communication, April 11, 1976)

In keeping with this sentiment, I shall try to illustrate "the atmosphere" of my life.

The Beginning: Education in Denmark and the United States

In this chapter I shall describe fragments of the development of neuropsychology in Denmark, where I have lived my life and worked in the field since the late-1950s. Luria praised the "ascending to concreteness." In contrast, my own life began concrete and later became more abstract.

The last part of my school years was marked by the German occupation of Denmark. German soldiers were marching and singing through the streets; our school was overtaken. Resistance was on our minds and took place in the dark. Graduation to the University of Copenhagen was a happy event coinciding with liberation on May 5, 1945. The overwhelming experience of freedom and peace continued during that summer. The borders were opened, and we were full of hope and expectations for the future.

At the time, the first year in University consisted of obligatory courses called *Filosofikum* (an introduction to philosophy and sciences). I enrolled. I also married a fellow student, Niels Egmont Christensen, who had been my classmate for

---

1. The original, non-gender-inclusive language has been preserved in my direct quotes of Luria's texts and letters.

five years. This was much to our parents' concern; we were both 19. I embraced marriage and motherhood (our son, Mads Egmont, was born in 1947) with more enthusiasm than I did my studies, although we nevertheless each completed *Filosofikum*. My husband continued in philosophy and logic. I would feel his strong influence on my way of thinking when, after devoting myself exclusively to the role of mother and housewife for six years, I reinitiated my studies.

I was divided between studying literature and studying psychology. It was the summer of 1952, and an institution called Nordic Summer University had its first meeting in Denmark. Eminent scientists such as Niels Bohr and Mogens Fog participated—making the experience very special. The events that took place at this summer university influenced my choice to study psychology.

The Gestalt psychologist Edgar Rubin, known for his work in figure–ground perception, was the senior professor in the Psychology Department at the University of Copenhagen, which was founded in 1872 by Alfred Lehman and boasted of being the second experimental laboratory in Europe. Traditional psychophysiology was the main discipline; however, a strong phenomenological ideology also prevailed and was expressed by the younger professors, among them Franz From who wrote a book in 1953 called *Om oplevelsen af andres adfærd (Concerning the Experiencing of Other Persons' Behavior)*.

By 1954, my husband Niels had completed his degree. He received two grants, which enabled our small family to go to the United States and to, of all places, Harvard and Radcliffe Universities. The world truly opened up to us. Mads attended an advanced, private school—Brown & Nichols—which influenced his later wish to attend the University of Southern California (USC) and study film. I had the good luck of being accepted at Radcliffe, even if my qualifications were sparse; this may have been due to the fact that it was shortly after the war. Courses with Talcott Parsons, Gordon Allport, Gardner Lindzey, and George Mandler (Henry Murray was on sabbatical leave at the time) in the Department of Social Relations provided me with new food for thought.

My greatest influence in Cambridge, however, was Jerome S. Bruner. His and Jacqueline Goodnow's course about "thinking" took place in Memorial Hall. I had read Wertheimer and Duncker, but attending the Bruner lectures fascinated me to an extent that I had never experienced before. Was it possible that a professor could stimulate my interest to such a degree? The early Bruner and Goodman paper, "Value and Need as Organizing Factors in Perception" had been on the curriculum in Copenhagen. This was the paper that started the New Look movement in psychology. In Jerome Bruner's (1983) autobiographical book, *In Search of Mind*, there is a quotation from Matthew Erdelyi's 1974 paper, "A New Look at the New Look" that reads as follows:

> The proceedings, at least formally, started some quarter century ago with a series of publications . . . which suggested that the perception of external stimuli is not free of the shackles of internal events: attitudes, values, expectancies, and psychodynamic defenses all impinge upon perception. This view became loosely known as the New Look. (p. 68)

Bruner added the following:

It was psychophysics all right, but psychophysics in the market place rather than in the shielded laboratory where such matters were ordinarily conducted. Instead of having our "subjects" judge the magnitude of controlled, neutral "stimuli," we set them the task of estimating the sizes of coins, ordinary U.S. mintage right out of my pocket. And in place of "trained observers" as subjects, we used ten-year-old school children. Their job was to adjust a patch of light to match the size of a nickel, a dime, a quarter, and a half-dollar. That was all. Half of the kids were from schools in affluent parts of Boston; the others from the city's slums.

The findings had an almost Dickensian quality. The more valuable the coin, the greater the over-estimation of its size. And the poorer children over-estimated more than the affluent ones. (p. 70)

There was more to it: New Look psychology did not consist of dry, experimental studies but of experiences from the ordinary day-to-day. Bruner gave his lectures in a language that expressed the meaningfulness of concrete, everyday life and with an unexpected, creative use of words and associations that was very much in tune with my thinking and expectancies of psychology. I had never experienced science in this way before, and thus I listened with overwhelming joy.

The second semester, I was invited to participate in a small, advanced seminar about "transfer of training" at Bruner's home. I had been asked to present my readings in German and forgot all of my materials on the bus. Being more familiar with Freud than I, everyone laughed sweetly at what I had done, and I did not understand why. After that experience, I realized the need to become acquainted with psychoanalysis (which had not been taught at the Psychology Department in Copenhagen). I took a course taught by Edwin Semrad about analytic group procedures at Boston Psychopathic Hospital, where six to eight post-graduate students kindly welcomed me. I later learned that Semrad has been inspirational to several well-known group psychoanalysts.

The year at Harvard had changed my outlook on psychology. My horizons were broadened: I had made new friends and had become inspired to widen the scope of the work that lay ahead of me.

When I returned to Denmark in 1955, I continued my studies and finished my degree in 1957. My need for further knowledge, however, was acute. I enrolled in a course given by Lise Oestergaard, who would become the first professor of clinical psychology at the University of Copenhagen. She became a giving but also a demanding friend. Years later, her support for the establishment of the Center for Rehabilitation of Brain Injury (CRBI) at the University of Copenhagen would be essential. At that time, Lise was head of psychology at the University Hospital's Psychiatry Department and encouraged me to do clinical work there while I took the course. This is the road I took into clinical psychology and psychiatry.

Continued Education in the Psychiatric, Neurological, and Neurosurgical Clinics

My husband had accepted a position at the University of Aarhus (Jutland) in 1959, where he became Chair of the Philosophy Department in 1968. The University was about 25 years old and embodied a pioneering spirit. We went, and I secured a position as clinical psychologist at the University's Psychiatric Hospital. The professor was Erik Strömgren, one of the most influential European psychiatrists of his time. Through the years, until his death in 1993, he was a strong supporter of neuropsychology, and he would later play an active role as CRBI's first Chairman of the Board.

After having worked in psychiatry for one year, however, I felt that I knew too little about the diagnostic symptoms of the patients I examined. I realized that intensive studies on the central nervous system, as manifested in neurology and neurosurgery, were a necessity. I succeeded in obtaining a medical position at the University's Neurological and Neurosurgical Departments, although there had never been a psychologist working there before. A year later, I became the neuropsychologist on the neurosurgical staff, a position that I kept for nine years. The head of the department was Richard Malmros, a professor and neurosurgeon of the "old tradition" in which physicians took pains to care for their patients' needs. He obviously cared deeply for his patients, often visiting them in the middle of the night to check on their status. He investigated his patients' lives and looked after their personal needs, helping them whenever possible. For example, he made sure that wigs were immediately made available and left by the nightstand of the female patients who had undergone surgery. Malmros was also profoundly interested in neuropsychological findings and wanted me to accompany him on his rounds. He was research-oriented and innovative in his methods. I gained experience in various brain diseases, and a close follow-up of patients with acute conditions of brain injury led to my interest in outcome research.

Once during these nine years, an Armenian professor from the Bourdenko Neurosurgical Institute in Moscow visited the Department. While he was giving a presentation, someone asked him about the influence of neuropsychology on neurosurgery. He answered in his special brand of Russian humor by telling a story: "Imagine a water mill, where the flow of water has decreased. Then happily, a little mouse passes by the river and pees into the water. Suddenly the water flows again, resulting in new prosperity. The little mouse is neuropsychology; neurosurgery is the water mill." Without neuropsychology, neurosurgery would not have flourished.

Initially, in these nine years, I participated in clinical work with patients, mainly in the area of assessment. I used traditional clinical psychological tests, but it soon became clear to me that these were not fit for examining patients in the acute stage of their illness or recovery. Then in 1966 I was asked to review the newly published English translation of A. R. Luria's *Higher Cortical Functions in Man*. The meaningfulness of his method was clear to me, and I realized that here was what I needed. In this book, Luria presented a theory of brain function that ingeniously combined the divergent ideas of narrow localization with Lashley's suggestions of mass activity and equipotentiality. Luria provided a thorough evaluation procedure of higher cortical functioning that could be used at the patient's bedside. The benefit of the approach was that the tasks were developed from a comprehensive theory of brain functioning. Thus, each task examined different aspects of brain functioning in a manner meaningful to the patient, while also providing a diagnostic summary consistent with the neurosurgeons' way of thinking. The method also made it possible to determine changes in functioning by delineating new areas of damage affecting the overall patterns of function, therefore allowing for evaluation of progression or healing. The method was difficult to perform as intended, however, without direct instruction. I therefore began to translate the theory and practical procedures into Danish for my own purposes in order to get further insight into the mechanisms of its application.

In the daily work at the Department, attempts to apply the method gave rise to a common understanding among staff members. Everyone was involved in the treatment and care of the patients. Test results from the neuropsychological evaluation facilitated the understanding of the patients' reactions; therefore, the patients' behavior could be understood. Feedback in relation to the patients' disturbances improved their insight at the same time that it increased the possibilities for a better treatment. The importance of neuropsychological assistance became clear.

One area of research in the Department was Parkinsonism. In a study about the sequelae of stereotaxic surgery, the psychological findings suggested no decline in intellectual functioning after surgery. In the publication, the Luria approach was combined with traditional testing (Christensen, Juul-Jensen, Malmros, & Harmsen, 1970).

A controlled study of a group of amateur boxers using the method also was conducted. The results indicated that the method identified a pathology where the neurological examination did not (Thomassen, Juul-Jensen, de Fine Olivarius, Bræmer, & Christensen, 1979). This study was conducted in collaboration with the staff neurologist, Palle Juul-Jensen, who would become an important friend.

Visits to the Bourdenko Neurosurgical University Institute

In 1969, Luria attended the General Psychology Conference in London. Jerome Bruner also was present. Bruner had told me some years before that the right place to study higher cortical functions was in Luria's laboratory in Moscow. During the opening reception of the conference, Bruner insisted that I introduce myself to Luria. I did so and told him about my early attempts at using his method. Luria asked, "Why don't you come to Moscow?" After that reception, Luria suffered a heart attack and could not deliver his lecture. Instead, Hans-Lukas Teuber read Luria's paper, which was entitled, "The Origin and Cerebral Organization of Man's Conscious Action." I did not see Luria again during the conference but soon after

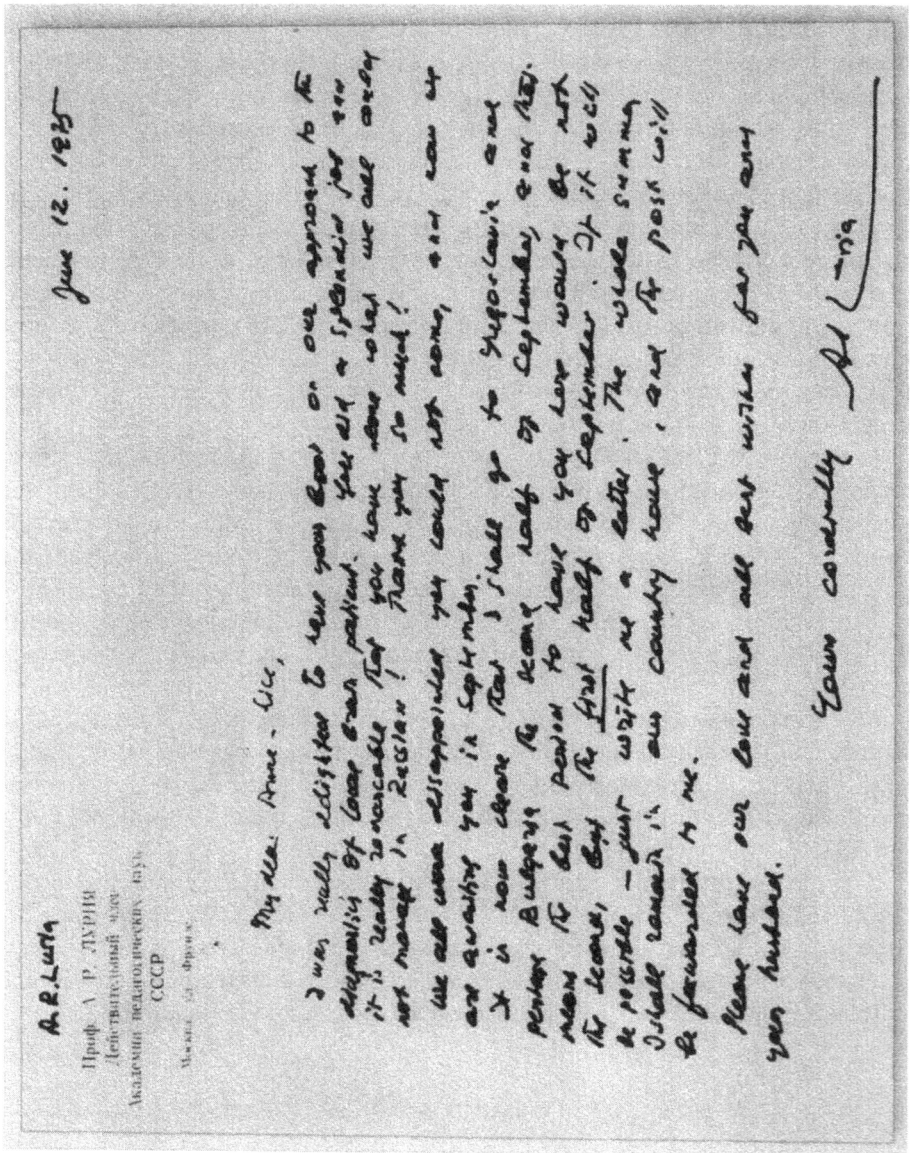

Figure 8.1. Letter of June 12, 1975, after Luria received the book, *Luria's Neuropsychological Investigation*, in Moscow.

received an official invitation to visit him in Moscow. I went in September of 1970. While there, I participated in his examination of patients at the Bourdenko Neurosurgical University Institute and was presented with reprint after reprint to read during the evenings.

The neuropsychologist who was chosen to assist me in all possible ways—I did not speak any Russian—was Elkhonon ("Nick") Goldberg. He has been a very special friend and collaborator since that time. Nick went to the United States under difficult circumstances. (For a more detailed account of his exodus from the Soviet Union see Goldberg, in press.) Over the years he has proven himself to be an eminent neuropsychologist through his work and publications. Presently, he is director of the Institute of Neuropsychology and Cognitive Performance in New York, as well as Clinical Professor of Neurology at the New York University School of Medicine.

On that visit, I had brought along a copy of my Danish version of Luria's examination method. Professor Luria, as I addressed him (to all others he was Aleksandr Romanovich), exclaimed, "Of course it is a vulgarization. But I have always wanted someone to do what you have done." Professor Luria told me to return after I had completed an English translation of the manuscript, saying that "the world needs it."

Thus I paid him a second visit three years later, together with a group of 20 Danish neurosurgeons, neurologists, and psychologists with whom I had a shared interest in Luria's work. Luria read the manuscript and suggested the title, *The Luria Neuropsychological Investigation* (LNI). He corrected and added to the manuscript, gave me a paper to translate as the first chapter, and also wrote the foreword.

When the LNI book was published (Christensen, 1975), Luria was given a copy and wrote me a letter shortly thereafter saying, "I was really delighted to have your book; you did a splendid job and it is really remarkable that you had done what we all could not manage in Russia!" (See Figure 8.1.)

When the textbook, manual, and cards were being published in 1975, a third visit to Moscow followed. Two Scandinavian neurophysiologists, pioneers in regional Cerebral Blood Flow Imaging (rCBF), David Ingvar from Lund and Niels Lassen from Copenhagen, had visited Luria in Moscow two months earlier. When I arrived in September, Luria's laboratory was plastered with pictures of imaging studies. The method provided a direct and clear verification of the concept of functional systems and was the first in the series of functional imaging methods that are available in brain–behavior research today. When I landed, Luria was waiting for me at the stairs to the plane and immediately told me that my book was being translated into Russian.

Reactions to Luria's Neuropsychological Investigation

The first presentation of the practical application of the Luria methodology was given at the International Neuropsychological Society (INS) conference in Noordwÿkerhout, Holland, in June of 1979. Kenneth Walsh, from Australia, invited me to take part in a symposium called "Single Case Methodology." The symposium abstract stated

> Luria's (1966) theory about the working brain offers an approach that has proven effective in both diagnostic neuropsychological work and rehabilitation. According to the theory, the significance of symptoms and signs can be understood only in the context of the notion of a functional system. A functional system in the brain consists of a number of parts. Each is very specific, particularly but not exclusively cortical, since fibral connections are included. The system operates in a concerted manner to form a substratum of psychological functions. The more complex the symptom, the more complicated the psychological function.
>
> The main task of the neuropsychologist is to find ways to learn what each part of the brain contributes to the organization of a functional system. The way in which this can be done is through a thorough and careful analysis, that is, a qualification of the symptoms. A main assumption is that these functional systems are dynamic and individual since they are developing in accordance with the brain's experience and its integrative processes.
>
> The case report concerns a patient from the neurosurgical department operated on for a parietal tumor, localized in the secondary and tertiary areas of the right hemisphere. The common factor in this case was found to be disturbed projection of elements in space due to lack of predominance of the usual visual gestalts.

There seemed to be a general acceptance of the concrete illustration. A number of the well-known neuropsychologists who were present at the meeting later became close collaborators and friends, among them Edith Kaplan and Muriel Lezak, as well as Leonard Diller, whose support has been of extreme importance.

The LNI became known in the United States and elsewhere, and was translated into several languages. Two of the most extraordinary publications were in Zulu, by S. Tolman and N. B. Msengana, and Japanese, by Tsuyoshi Nishimura. Invitations to give presentations and lectures followed. Among them was an invitation to Ward 7D of the Veterans Administration (VA) Hospital in Boston. The Chief of Neurology was Norman Geschwind. Edith Kaplan was his neuropsychology collaborator. My first visit was the beginning of a close relationship with her. We would engage in stimulating discussions about similarities and differences between the process-oriented examination method and the LNI; her influence on my clinical work was significant. Participation in the supervision of her post-graduate students was a rewarding experience, often taking place around midnight.

My trips to Boston occurred at least once a year between 1981 and 1985, and I was often given the opportunity to teach Edith's class at Boston University. She repaid my visits by coming to Denmark or other places in Scandinavia to give lectures. Her visits were always extremely intense; they generated new knowledge and unexpected happenings.

One time while I was in Boston, we visited Clark University. I was introduced to Professor Donald Stein who, together with Stanley Finger, had just published *Brain Damage and Recovery: Research and Clinical Perspectives* (Finger & Stein, 1982), which he gave me after an almost day-long discussion about Luria's theory of brain function and developments in neurosciences. Don has become a very important contributor to the CRBI rehabilitation programs, participating in the Center's international conferences, to which I shall return later. His personal friendship has been extremely valuable, both in support and critique.

Luria sent me a letter some time later that said, "By the way, have you seen Reitan's review...?" Ralph Reitan (1976) had published a review in *Contemporary Psychology* called "Neuropsychology: The Vulgarization That Luria Always Wanted," a title that had been taken from my foreword. Reitan wrote: "Luria's procedures for neuropsychological evaluation seemed to come closer to the conventional neurological evaluation than to psychological assessment as it is customarily performed in the United States" (pp. 737–738). For Reitan, as he went on to quote in the same review, Luria's neuropsychology opened up "new paths to answer the question of the inner structure of psychological processes." All the same, he continued, "Luria's approach is one in which he attempts to analyze the nature and interrelationship of deficits rather than measured abilities." In this way, Reitan failed to recognize the need for a qualitative analysis of the deficits in order to understand their impact on the patient's intact functions—the mental abilities.

In contrast, Kolb and Wishaw (1990) stressed positive aspects of the LNI:

(a) it is based on the theoretical principles of neuropsychological functioning, making the interpretation a logical conclusion of the theory; (b) it is thorough, inexpensive, easy to administer, flexible, and brief, taking only about 1 hour to administer; and (c) measures the actual behavior of the subject rather than inferred cognitive processes, thus making interpretation more straightforward. The disadvantages are: (a) the scoring is subjective and based on clinical experience. It is unlikely that a novice to neuropsychology or neurology could easily master the interpretation without extensive training. On the other hand, experienced neuropsychologists or neurologists ought to find the battery easy to learn; (b) because the manual that accompanies the battery offers no validation studies, it must be taken on faith that the tests really do measure what Luria claims they do. This criticism is the most serious, because most Western neuropsychologists are likely to continue to use psychometric assessment tools reporting validation studies. (pp. 737–738)

Muriel Lezak (1983) commented on the LNI, stating that her concerns were (a) it is not comprehensive enough; (b) the lack of normative data creates difficulties in evaluating, especially subtle learning and memory deficits; and (c) certain tasks are not useful in detecting mild or diffuse impairments.

Much of the criticism regarding the LNI is related to the qualitative approach that it represents. This critique would apply to any approach that is primarily qualitative in orientation. The LNI method leads to a qualitative analysis of the patient's level of functioning. The examiner has the task of identifying the disturbed functions. In addition, the examiner is responsible for clarifying how a patient is trying to cope with the difficulties with which he or she is presented. Proper use of this method further allows for the formulation of very specific hypotheses about the fundamental defect through the selection of different tasks in which the defect is an essential component.

The task analysis performed during the investigation can teach the neuropsychologist how to structure a task in order to make the patient use intact functions in the service of reorganization—in other words, how to compensate in the most effective way. A close therapeutic relationship between the patient and neuropsychologist in this process strengthens the effectiveness of cognitive training and provides emotional and social improvement. Since it is my conviction that neuropsychology needs to change its methods of assessment for rehabilitation to have future recognition and growth, I shall return to these matters at the end of the chapter.

Soon after these varied reviews appeared in the United States, Charles Golden and his group showed an interest in the LNI and even suggested a collaboration. Golden and his colleagues wanted to develop a quantitative approach based on Luria's theory. They wanted to standardize administration, set time limits, and create functional profiles. I firmly rejected their offer of collaboration because their proposition was in total contrast to Luria's method. Nevertheless, their Luria–Nebraska Neuropsychological Battery was published (Golden, Purisch, & Hammeke, 1979), using the material developed in Denmark. My view of the publication, however, was supported in articles written by a number of distinguished neuropsychologists, among them Edith Kaplan and several of her former students.

The Golden approach, all the same, overshadowed the LNI in these years. It met the American need for numbers and, as such, was in correspondence with the quantitative approach.

Teaching Neuropsychology

In 1969, I was offered a teaching position with the medical faculty of the University of Aarhus where, as assistant professor, I taught psychology to medical students for ten years. My courses were a new addition to the medical curriculum; they were a success and have gradually expanded since then. Teaching appealed very much to me and led to the publication in 1979 of a textbook: *Neuropsykologi: Klinisk praksis*. The book also became part of the curriculum at the Psychology Department at the University in Copenhagen.

The professorship meant that I had to change departments and return to psychiatry. I proposed the establishment of a clinical psychological department. My proposal was accepted. In the following years, this department grew to include all branches of adult clinical psychology and neuropsychology, each reciprocally influencing and enriching each other. Close and stimulating collaboration with staff from the diverse psychiatric areas generated research and publications (Christensen & Nielsen, 1981; Fromholt, Christensen, & Strömgren, 1973; Nielsen & Christensen, 1974).

Life had been full of inspiration and development throughout the 21 years that we spent in Aarhus. My son Mads had completed degrees in Copenhagen and at USC and was working as a TV and film producer. That period ended abruptly with my husband's suicide in May of 1980. Niels had, in the beginning of the 1970s, suffered bipolar psychiatric episodes. He had come to feel cured, so that when his depression returned, the experience was unbearable for him.

The Return to Copenhagen

I returned to Copenhagen, where my first appointment was a research position in the department where I had started my clinical work 25 years earlier. The chief of the Clinical Psychological Department was Professor Alice Theilgaard; during my work in Aarhus, we had been in close contact and our collaboration now continued. I spent the years traveling and participating in the Department's clinical work, primarily engaged in the neuropsychological issues in psychiatry.

I was asked to present the LNI mainly in Europe and the United States, and was invited to Bergen, Norway, where Halgrim Klöve, was professor of neuropsychology. We had met earlier and had become good friends. I returned to Bergen in 1982 for the INS meeting and met Lance Trexler, who was the initiator of the first rehabilitation conferences that took place in Indianapolis, Indiana. He invited me to participate in the second conference. These meetings were of great importance for the development of the field. Lance worked at the Community Hospital in Indianapolis at that time; he later started his own Center for Neuropsychological Rehabilitation (CNR). In the following years, we visited each other and exchanged ideas and methods. In 1983 he stayed at the CRBI for three months as a visiting professor and to this day participates in the Center's research. I also met George Prigatano, in Indianapolis and visited him in Oklahoma City and later in Phoenix. His influence and his friendship have been valuable as well.

The work I was doing generated interest in my own country and resulted in a grant from the Danish Egmont Foundation for the purpose of establishing a neuropsychological assessment and rehabilitation center. Yehuda Ben-Yishay and Leonard Diller offered their support during this period. The chairman of the Egmont Foundation, Esben Dragsted, was also in New York while I was there. He was invited to the New York University Rehabilitation Center in order to get acquainted with the Institute and became so interested that he took part in the day's full program. In the evening, Leonard Diller had tickets for a Mozart opera at the Metropolitan—Esben Dragsted's favorite entertainment. His interest in our work continued, and he provided strong support in many ways throughout all the years that he served as the Foundation's chairman.

The grant became, in the beginning, however, a little of a nightmare. The professors from the involved departments—psychiatry, neurology, and neurosurgery—at the University Hospital opposed the plan, stating that they did not believe in brain injury rehabilitation. The situation was solved ingeniously by asking the psychology faculty at the University of Copenhagen to accept the Center, which they did, although hesitantly at first.

The new institute was named the Center for Hjerneskade (or as noted above, the Center for Rehabilitation of Brain Injury—CRBI). The name was chosen after much consideration; we wanted to communicate precisely the Center's concern: brain injury. Initially, some of the brain injured patients and their families objected to the name, but it gradually came to be accepted because of the positive reputation that it achieved. The fact that the Center was at the University brought with it an unexpected advantage: The patients could say that they were "taking courses" at the University, which strengthened the self-image of the brain-injured patients.

The grant was for 3.2 million Danish Kr., money that was allotted for the first three years. During this time, the Center was expected to prove effective enough to obtain funding for rehabilitation from the counties and municipalities, thereby becoming a publicly funded, privately run institution. We succeeded. A three-year follow-up study, using improved social functioning as an outcome variable, demonstrated the effectiveness of our training. The areas evaluated were living conditions, leisure activities, and return to work. Improvement was shown in the statistical results one year after completing the rehabilitation program. The 3-year follow-up showed that these gains were maintained, as there was no statistically significant decline. At the same time, an evaluation conducted by a county research group showed economic gains for all involved parties—state, county, and municipalities.

The Center had a Board of Governors established by the Egmont Foundation. Originally, the goal of the CRBI was described in the founding papers as follows: "The purpose of the institution is to undertake neuropsychological investigations in the service of rehabilitating brain-injured persons and at the same time perform research and teaching within the area." Through experiences and research in the years that followed, gradual changes occurred. Research and teaching were still main tasks, but the rehabilitative goal broadened; some aspects were emphasized and additions were made. The main issue was to support brain-injured individuals in regaining the ability to live their lives to the fullest and the ability to master the constant changes that are a part of human life: physically, socially, and cognitively.

My Thirteen Years at the CRBI

During my thirteen years as director of the CRBI, 937 patients were examined and/or treated—320 in the Center's comprehensive day program. The treatment was most often provided for one semester; there was group as well as individual training. All patients referred were initially neuropsychologically assessed using the LNI and other neuropsychological tests and thereafter either took part in the Center's day program, received individual treatment, or were sent for treatment elsewhere. All patients were followed to the extent needed. The staff consisted of neuropsychologists, clinical psychologists, speech therapists, and special education teachers. The addition of physiotherapists further advanced the effectiveness of the program. Consults from neurology, neurosurgery, physiatry, and psychiatry were available, and one member from each group participated in the referral team. The collaboration was interdisciplinary, and the administrative staff was closely involved.

The daily schedule was always full of activity, open to creative ideas and at the same time strictly structured. Events such as lectures, musical performances, and sports provided additional stimulation and kept up motivation. Advancement in the field owes much to patients' need to overcome their difficulties and engage in life; as the patients learned, we all learned.

Members of the staff taught at the University and elsewhere. In 1992, I was appointed Professor of Neuropsychological Rehabilitation. The Center served as a clinic where neuropsychology students could do their clinical practice. International collaboration provided the opportunity to also receive students from countries of the European Union. Guests from Denmark and abroad, from all disciplines in rehabilitation, came and stayed for either short or long periods of time. This diversity further enhanced the atmosphere of activity and optimism.

David Ellis, who had worked in rehabilitation for several years in Philadelphia, participated in the work the first four months. We had met at a conference, and David was interested in the planning of the new Center and in gaining new experiences. We later co-edited a book called *Neuropsychological Treatment after Brain Injury* (Ellis & Christensen, 1989).

Research was essential and a main part of the Center's image. Thomas Teasdale, was made head of our research in 1990. He fulfilled this task successfully: members of the staff published a significant number of papers and book chapters. Among the latest were two publications regarding the European Brain Injury Questionnaire (EBIQ) that were a result of the European collaboration; one was published by Teasdale (Teasdale et al., 1997) and the other by Gerárd Deloche (Delouche et al., 1996). This contributed to the growth of knowledge and to the benefit of the patients. In 1995, Carla Caetano, from the United States, joined our staff and research group, co-authoring several papers and book chapters with me (Christensen & Caetano, 1996, 1999a, 1999b).

Collaboration in Denmark has, through the years, taken place with the establishment of eight new centers for post-acute treatment of brain injury and two new centers for acute treatment located throughout the country. Vejlefjord, Jutland, established in 1985, was the first, and its director at the time, Joergen Braemer had been one of my close collaborators from Aarhus. Unfortunately, he died a few years later at the age of 41. Interaction with that center suffered for some years, however, due to political interference regarding the geographical position of a reference center.

A successful collaboration took place with the Danish Brain Injury Association, started in 1985 by Aase Engberg. Her husband had suffered a severe head injury in 1973. Her experiences during his treatment made her leave a career as a clinical engineer to study medicine. She is now a neurologist with a doctorate in epidemiology. In collaboration with George Zitnay from the International Brain Injury Association (IBIA), "The First International Brain Injury Conference" was held in Copenhagen in 1994. Collaboration with George continues to this day.

The 1985 European INS conference was the first of several international conferences that took place at the Center's initiative over the years. Two Finnish neuropsychologists, Anna Ritta Putkonen and Ritva Laksoonen, began Nordic meetings in partnership with Halgrim Klöve, Jarl Risberg, and myself. These meetings continued, with varying intervals, until 1995, when the fifth meeting was taken over by the neuropsychological societies that had been established in each respective country.

Collaboration with Sweden was strong throughout all of this time. Professor Jarl Risberg was a member of the Center's Board of Governors, and patients from the CBRI were examined at his rCBF laboratory in Lund. In addition, I began to lecture on neuropsychological assessment and rehabilitation at Lund and Gothenberg Universities and continued to do so for many years.

In 1990, in collaboration with the Psychology Laboratory at the University of Copenhagen, several Russian neuroscientists were invited to give a series of lectures, which were published in a book called *Luria Lectures* (Forchhammer, 1991). One of the Russian guests was Elena, Luria's daughter, who was a doctor of medicine. Elena wrote the first chapter of this book in which she described her father. She had earlier suffered depressive periods and, at Luria's request, we had sent her medicine that was unobtainable in Moscow. During the lecture series, she stayed in my home, enjoying the atmosphere of what she called "our fairy tale country."

Collaboration with Russia has continued. I am a member of the European Multiprofessional Neurotraumatologica (EMN), whose initiator and president is Klaus von Wild of Münster University in Germany. In 1997, I participated in a neurosurgical meeting at the Volga River in Russia that was arranged by Professor Alexander Potapov of the Bourdenko Neurosurgical University Institute. I spent three days after the congress at the Institute working with the neuropsychologist Nathalia Gogitidze, who later visited the CRBI.

In 2001 a second congress took place in Moscow, this time in the buildings of the new Bourdenko Institute. A few of the neuropsychologists I knew from my first visit in the seventies came to meet me. The work at EMN, of whose presidium I recently became a member, is emphasizing the interdependence between neurosurgery and neuropsychology, and the need for mutual recognition of their complementary knowledge and skills in the service of the brain damaged patient. Klause von Wild champions early rehabilitation because of his deep interest in his patients. He has established a rehabilitation unit in his neurosurgical department, where neuropsychology plays an important role, a fact that for me has meant a renewal of the very fruitful collaboration I had with neurosurgeons in my early years.

Most important, however, were three invited meetings, all resulting in international publications and all edited in collaboration with Barbara Uzzell (Christensen & Uzzell, 1988, 1994, 2000). Nathan Cope (2000) wrote in his foreword to the latest:

> This handbook is the result of the most recent of a series of conferences held in Copenhagen, Denmark, at five year intervals over the past 15 years under the guidance and leadership of Dr. Anne-Lise Christensen and under the sponsorship of the Egmont Foundation, which must be acknowledged as well for its constant support of this international effort.
>
> The participants in these conferences are all internationally renowned clinicians and scientists. These experts represent not only the area of neuropsychology, but disciplines ranging from fundamental neurophysiology and neuroanatomy, to medical and financial perspectives on neurological injury and recovery. The participants have, to a significant extent, remained remarkably constant over this period and this has allowed increasing intimacy among them, both professionally and personally. One felicitous result of this camaraderie has been that the conferences have evolved with an increased focus on topics of the broadest interest across disciplines. One aspect of such a continuing dialogue across disciplines is that specific areas of mutual interest are explored in depth, allowing cross-fertilization of ideas to occur. (p. ix)

I turned seventy years old during the Third International Conference. Jan Frøshaug, the Chairman of the Board, hosted a dinner. The dinner took place in a small, beautiful castle overlooking the sound between Denmark and Sweden. It was a happy and joyful event; the Board of Governors, the staff from the CRBI, and the invited guests participated, as well as my family. In accordance with Danish habit, some speeches were given. The trio of Yehuda Ben-Yishay, Don Stein, and George Prigatano performed elegantly. Yehuda's part was an analysis of the chemical compounds of my personality. This birthday, however, meant retirement. My successor was not easily found; there were fourteen applicants—Danish, Swedish, German, and American. It would be the Chairman of the Board's decision. One member of the Board disagreed about how the process was carried out and withdrew from the Board. In the end, Mugge Pinner was appointed in May of 1998. She had been a supporter of the establishment of the CRBI during its early periods.

The years at the Center gave me much personal gratification. In 1989, I became a *Ridder af Dannebrog*, an honor bestowed on me by the Queen of Denmark, and in 1994 received the *Doctor Honoris Causa* title in Lund. I was made honorary member of many international, neuropsychological societies and became the Neuropsychologist of the Year in 1998 in Sweden.

Retirement and Future Goals

Retiring from CRBI has not stopped my work and my interest in the field. I continue to take on new endeavors. For example, I have been appointed senior consultant at the Institute of Neuropsychology and Cognitive Performance in New York.

New horizons also have opened up for me. Shortly after retiring, I was invited to visit Brasilia, Brazil, and the SARAH Network of Hospitals for the Locomotor System. I was invited by the Network's executive director, Lucia Willadino Braga, who is also a neuropsychologist, and by Aloysio Campos da Paz Jr., the Network's president and surgeon-in-chief. I have been made an honorary member of the Board of Consultants. I encountered at SARAH an atmosphere of scientific knowledge and overall superior technical expertise, incorporated within a true humanistic approach. The Network is also characterized by an architecture that elevates mind and soul, and that facilitates visualization of the ideal rehabilitation institution. (See Figure 8.2.)

The SARAH Network began as a single hospital complex. Over time, it developed and consolidated principles, concepts, and methods that eventually led to the Center's edification as a national and international point of reference for quality care. The system blends the aesthetic with the functional and reflects our dynamic, ever-expanding knowledge of spatial, architectural, and function-specificity concepts. What takes place at SARAH is in accordance with the winds that, at present, seem to be blowing in medicine, psychology, and rehabilitation toward a merger of humanistic and empirical scientific viewpoints. A. R. Luria expressed this same idea in a different way. He believed that one of the most important and challenging tasks to solve was the old problem of the nomothetic versus the ideographic scientific approach. Luria formulated the dilemma as the crisis between (1) explanatory, physiological psychology and (2) a descriptive, phenomenological psychology of the higher psychological functions. The problem is still with us. SARAH may be a concrete example of how the goal of bridging the chasm between humanistic and empirical scientific approaches can be achieved.

The Stork

Danish author Karen Blixen (1937) has a story called "The Roads of Life" from her book *My African Farm*, about a little man who lives in a little round house with a round window and a little triangular garden. It is a tale from Blixen's childhood, and as the story is told to her she is shown a drawing that the storyteller creates right before her eyes. Each of the man's experiences results in a line being added to the drawing. As he moves through the experiences of his life, he reacts with unceasing effort to the tasks that are demanded of him, the obstacles he encounters, the hard work he must perform. He never gives up. In the end, when he looks at the whole picture crafted from the lines of his experience, what does he see? He beholds a picture of a stork emerging from these lifelines.

Figure 8.2. The SARAH—North Lake, inaugurated in 2000 (Architect: João Filgneiras Lima—Lélé).

If in your life there comes a moment when all the roads you have taken converge and allow you to see your own "stork," what experience could possibly surpass this? An expanded theory of brain function that is applicable to daily life and that may ultimately have the power to reinstate function—this is what could make my lifelines converge and a stork appear.

REFERENCES

Blixen, K. (1937). *My African farm.* New York: Random House.

Bruner, J. (1983). *In search of mind: Essays in autobiography.* New York: Harper & Row.

Christensen, A. L. (1975). *Luria's neuropsychological investigation. Manual and test materials.* New York: Spectrum Publications.

Christensen, A. L. (1979). *Neuropsykologi: Klinisk praksis.* Kobenhavn: Munksgaard.

Christensen, A. L., & Caetano, C. (1996). Alexandr Romanovich Luria (1902–1977): Contributions to neuropsychological rehabilitation. *Neuropsychological Rehabilitation, 6,* 279–303.

Christensen, A. L., & Caetano, C. (1999a). Luria's neuropsychological evaluation in the Nordic countries. *Neuropsychological Review, 9,* 71–78.

Christensen, A. L., & Caetano, C. (1999b). Neuropsychological rehabilitation in the interdisciplinary team: The postacute stage. In D. T. Stuss, G. Winocur, & I. H. Robertson (Eds.), *Cognitive neurorehabilitation* (pp. 188–199). Cambridge, UK: Cambridge University Press.

Christensen, A. L., Juul-Jensen, P., Malmros, R., & Harmsen, A. (1970). Psychological evaluation of intelligence and personality in parkinsonism before and after stereotaxic surgery. *Acta Neurologica Scandinavica, 46,* 527–537.

Christensen, A. L., & Nielsen, J. (1981). A neuropsychological investigation of 17 women with Turner's syndrome: Luria's theory applied to Turner's syndrome. In W. Schmid & J. Nielsen (Eds.), *Human behaviour and genetics: Proceedings of the Symposium of the European Society of Human Genetics* (pp. 151–166). Amsterdam: Elsevier.

Christensen, A. L., & Uzzell, B. P. (Eds.). (1988). *Neuropsychological rehabilitation.* Boston: Kluwer Academic Publishers.

Christensen, A. L., & Uzzell, B. P. (Eds.). (1994). *Brain injury and neuropsychological rehabilitation: International perspectives.* Hillsdale, NJ: Lawrence Erlbaum.

Christensen, A. L., & Uzzell, B. P. (Eds.). (2000). *International handbook of neuropsychological rehabilitation.* New York: Kluwer Academic/Plenum Publishers.

Cope, N. (2000). Foreword. In A. L. Christensen & B. P. Uzzell (Eds.), *International handbook of neuropsychological rehabilitation* (pp. ix-x). New York: Kluwer Academic.

Deloche, G., North, P., Dellatolas, G., Christensen, A. L., Cremel, N., Passadori, A., Dordain, M., & Hannequin, D. (1996). Le handicap des adultes cérébolésés: Le point de vue des patients et de leur entourage. *Annales de Réadaptation et de Médecine Physique, 39,* 1–9.

Ellis, D. W., & Christensen, A. L. (Eds.). (1989). *Neuropsychological treatment after brain injury.* Boston: Kluwer Academic.

Finger, S., & Stein, D. G. (1982). *Brain damage and recovery: Research and clinical perspectives.* New York: Academic Press.

Forchhammer, H. (Ed.). (1991). *Luria lectures.* Copenhagen: Luria Lectures.

From, F. (1953). *Concerning the experiencing of other persons' behavior: A contribution to the phenomenology of human behavior.* Copenhagen: Nyt Nordisk Forlag.

Fromholt, P., Christensen, A. L., & Strömgren, L. S. (1973). The effects of unilateral and bilateral electroconvulsive therapy on memory. *Acta Psychiatrica Scandinavica, 49,* 466–478.

Goldberg, E. (in press). *The executive brain: Frontal lobes and the civilized mind.* New York: Oxford University Press.

Golden, C. J., Purisch, A. D., & Hammeke, T.

A. (1979). *The Luria–Nebraska neuropsychological battery.* Lincoln: University of Nebraska Press.

Kolb, B., & Wishaw, I. Q. (1990). *Fundamentals of human neuropsychology* (3rd ed.). New York: Freeman.

Lezak, M. (1983). *Neuropsychological assessment.* New York: Oxford University Press.

Luria, A. R. (1966). *Higher cortical functions in man.* New York: Basic Books.

Luria, A. R. (1979). *The making of mind: A personal account of Soviet psychology.* Cambridge, MA: Harvard University Press.

Nielsen, J., & Christensen, A. L. (1974). Thirty-five males with double Y chromosome. *Psychological Medicine, 4,* 28–37.

Reitan, R. (1976). Neuropsychology: The vulgarization that Luria always wanted. *Contemporary Psychology, 21,* 737–738.

Teasdale, T. W., Christensen, A. L., Willmes, K., Deloche, G., Braga, L., Stachowiak, F., Vendrell, J. M., Castro-Caldas, A., Laaksonen, R., & Leclercq, M. (1997). Subjective experience in brain-injured patients and their close relatives: A European Brain Injury Questionnaire study. *Brain Injury, 11,* 543–563.

Thomassen, A., Juul-Jensen, P., de Fine Olivarius, B., Bræmer, J., & Christensen, A. L. (1979). Neurological, electroencephalographic and neuropsychological examination of 53 former amateur boxers. *Acta Neurologica Scandinavica, 60,* 352–362.

9

The Making of a Behavioral Neurologist–Neuropsychologist

Kenneth M. Heilman

From Brooklyn "Burro" to Medical Student

*I*was born in Brooklyn, New York, on June 2, 1938. My mother was a homemaker and an insurance broker. My father was a sports fan and an accountant. To my knowledge no one in my family was a scientist. I do not know what makes someone a scientist. I have trouble writing the word "scientist" because many scholars do not believe that the research that my colleagues and I do is really science. I do know, however, that I have always been one of those people who wanted to know how things work. Since no one in my family had this same "disability," I guess this phenotypic trait is not entirely inherited.

My mother told me that when I was a young boy and something in our home broke, I would not let her throw it out. I wanted to take it apart to find out how it worked. To her surprise, once in a while, I actually would fix something—like her old kitchen clock. My mother must have thought that this activity was important, because, in spite of being a compulsive housecleaner, she allowed me to spread the inner workings of that old clock across the floor—at least for a few hours.

When I went to P.S. 103, an elementary school in Brooklyn, I learned that people who want to know how things work are called scientists. Although I told my teachers that I wanted to be a scientist, they were not impressed. I almost flunked out of elementary school because the teachers did not like the way I spelled or read aloud. Because I was still too young to work, they just held me back in the third grade instead of asking me to leave school. I do not think repeating the third grade helped my spelling, which remains so bad that the computer spell-check does not even give me choices. I did manage to graduate from elementary school and went on to P.S. 227, Shallow Junior High School. The only way a student could fail to graduate this junior high was to be sent to prison or be killed. I was in some fights that, at the time, I thought might lead to one of these outcomes. But I survived, with a crooked nose.

When my friends were taking placement tests for college preparatory high schools in New York such as Brooklyn Tech or Peter Styvesant, I was not allowed to even attempt the tests. I had scored too low on standardized tests back in the third grade, and I was steered toward trade school. I knew, however, that if I went to trade school I could not be a scientist. With my mother's help, I was admitted to New Utrecht, the local high school, where I could take college preparatory courses.

I did not do well in my academic courses. For example, my Spanish teacher, Mrs. Lena Grossman, had the class stand up and read in Spanish. After I read, she would call me a "pinhead" and a "burro." She also failed to understand why I could not spell in Spanish, since Spanish has complete sound–letter correspondence. Mrs. Grossman told me that I was not "college material" and repeatedly failed me, I suspect, to prevent me from getting my college preparatory degree. Fortunately, there were other Spanish teachers who did not share her teaching methods or her low opinion of me. In contrast to Spanish, I found science and math courses easier and more interesting. I especially enjoyed chemistry. My high school yearbook says, "Ken wants to perform medical research." My peers clearly knew me better than Mrs. Grossman did.

In spite of Mrs. Grossman's efforts, I was admitted to the University of Virginia. I majored in chemistry because I wanted to perform medical biochemical research. At the same time, I was curious about how the brain works and controls behavior. My wrestling coach, Dr. Frank Finger, taught an Introduction to Psychology course. Because he was an excellent coach and a nice person, I thought I would take his class. It was an excellent course, but behaviorism dominated psychology at the University of Virginia in the 1950s. We read books such as Skinner's *Of Science and Human Behavior* and *Walden II*. To the behaviorist, the brain was irrelevant, and nothing in this course addressed how the brain worked. I, therefore, continued my study of chemistry.

In my third year, I enrolled in a graduate level course in organic chemistry. I already had taken the prerequisites. Professor Lutz, an outstanding chemist and teacher, lectured about atoms, molecules, and quantum mechanics using topological explanations. I did not understand his lectures and often had no idea what he was talking about. One day I leaned over to a friend and asked, "Do you understand what Professor Lutz is speaking about?"

He said, "Sure. Don't you?"

I said, "No!"

He said, "But you are the one who always gets A's."

"That is a different story," I said. I was disappointed with myself for reaching an intellectual ceiling. Maybe my junior high school advisors were correct when they directed me to trade school.

One day as I walked by the medical school, I thought, "Medicine may not be a bad trade. You could find out how things work and even fix some things." I went to the admissions office and completed an application. Several weeks later, although I was still in my third year of college and never had taken a biology course, I was admitted to medical school for the following year. I never did graduate from college, but fortunately, it was not because I could not spell, read aloud, or learn Spanish.

A Case of Neglect

In medical school, I took my first neuroscience course. This course covered human neuroanatomy, brain embryology, and neuronal cellular physiology—but again, nothing about how the brain works. Consequently, I hoped the clinical courses and rotations would teach me about how the brain mediates behavior. In psychiatry, I learned about the different forms of mental illness and their treatments, including the use of drugs and psychoanalysis. I again learned about operant techniques and behaviorism. In the neurology lectures, I learned about motor units, diseases of the peripheral nerves and the myoneural junction (e.g., myasthenia gravis), and diseases of the muscle (e.g., dystrophy). Lectures on the central nervous system focused on stroke and epilepsy, with almost no mention of the behavioral problems associated with these diseases. My last hope, therefore, was the clinical neurology rotation.

I finally began the clinical neurology rotation during my third year of medical school. While on my way to see a patient diagnosed with myasthenia gravis, I passed a middle-aged man who was sitting on the edge of his bed eating his lunch. He said, "Doc, can you come over here?"

I walked over to this man's bed and said, "I am not a doctor yet, but I would be happy to try to help you."

He said, "Being a medical student is good enough for me to call you 'Doc.'"

"Thank you," I replied. "How can I help?"

"What kind of weird place is this? They only serve me vegetables. I am not on a special diet. How do I get some meat?" he asked.

I looked down at his tray. He had one of those plates they used in hospitals that had a raised divider down the middle of the plate to stop the meat from oozing into the vegetables. The vegetables were on the right side of the plate and the meat, which didn't look quite edible, was on the left. On rounds, I had heard that this man was admitted for a stroke. I thought that perhaps the stroke had injured his right occipital lobe, preventing him from seeing to the left side. I turned the dish around 180 degrees so that now his meat was on the right. He saw the meat and said, "Thank you, doctor."

After the patient finished eating, I returned to examine his vision. I expected him to be unable to see my right hand move in his left visual field and was surprised when he, in fact, did see my hand move on his left side. I did not understand, then, why he had been unable to see the left side of his plate.

The attending physician that month was Dr. Fritz Dreyfus. In addition to being a superb neurologist and teacher, Dreyfus also was very approachable. The next day, I asked him to explain this patient's neurological slips. Dreyfus said the patient, a 67-year-old, retired civil engineer, had a condition called unilateral or hemispatial neglect. Although Dreyfus' major interest was in epilepsy, he was strongly interested in the mechanisms underlying this behavioral disorder. Thus, he directed me to the articles of his colleague from New Zealand, Dr. Derek Denny-Brown.

After we finished rounds, I went to the library and began reading everything I could about neglect and learned about several tests for this disorder. When patients with unilateral neglect try to draw or copy a figure, they often will leave out the side of the picture contralesional to, or opposite, their brain injury. When shown a horizontal line, patients with neglect will displace the center of the line toward the side of their lesion. Dr. Martin ("Marty") Albert described a test used by Dr. Horenstein that also was a sensitive measure of neglect. In this test, you draw many little lines, about an inch or two long, randomly distributed over a page. You then ask the patient to cross out or cancel all of the lines. They will, again, neglect the contralesional lines.

After my research, I went back to the wards to see the man with unilateral neglect. I spoke with him for several minutes and was surprised that he appeared so calm and indifferent when he was so weak on his left side. I asked if I could perform some tests on him, and he again was agreeable. "You are the doctor," he said. So with the approval of the patient's medical team, I began my examination.

The first test I gave him was line bisection. I drew a 10-inch line on a blank piece of paper, put the line directly in front of him, gave him a pencil, and asked him to mark the middle of the line.

He said, "Doc, you mean bisect the line?"

I nodded.

"Doc, you probably remember from geometry that the way you bisect a line is to draw either an equilateral or isosceles triangle and then drop a meridian."

The patient proceeded to draw an isosceles triangle. The two sides of the triangle were equal, as they should be. The right side of the triangle did come down to the right end of the horizontal line; however, the left side terminated at the middle rather than the left end of the line. The patient then attempted to bisect the line by dropping a meridian. Not surprisingly, his meridian intersected the horizontal line several inches to the right of center, because the base of the triangle was only the right half of my original line. He darkened this intersection, pointed with his right index finger, and concluded, "There. The line has been bisected."

I next drew a simple picture of a daisy that I asked him to copy. His drawing also showed neglect. He failed to draw petals on the left side of the daisy, and he placed the entire drawing on the right side of the page.

Although I would have enjoyed spending more time with this patient, I had many chores to do as a medical student. Medical students are given the jobs that no one else wants. As I was performing some of these chores, the patient called me again.

"Hey, Doc. Over here."

When I came over to his bed, the patient lifted his weak left arm with his right one. As he showed me his left arm he asked, "Could you get this guy out of my bed?"

I was surprised by his request. I thought that I might not have heard him correctly. "Could you repeat that?" I asked.

"Yes! I want this person out of my bed."

I told him that the arm he had lifted was his own arm.

"You know," he said. "It looks like my arm , but it does not belong to me."

I showed him that the hand he was lifting was connected to a wrist, the wrist was connected to a forearm, the forearm was connect to an arm, the arm was connected to the shoulder, and the shoulder was attached to his chest. Unfortunately, I was not able to convince him that it was his own arm. Subsequently, the patient lifted his left hand with his right arm and attempted to throw it out of his bed; however, because of his stroke, his left arm was spastic. The increased tone was like a spring. When he attempted to throw his arm out of the bed, it sprang back and hit him in his chest. After repeating this several times, the patient announced, "You see, this guy will not get out of my bed." When I explained to the patient that his left arm may feel dead because it is weak and numb, he replied, "There is nothing wrong with my left arm."

I was concerned that this patient would get frustrated attempting to get his left arm out of bed. Therefore, during rounds the next day, I told Dreyfus about the man's behavior and asked how we could help.

"Lightly restrain his left arm to the left side of the bed," Dreyfus instructed.

"Will restraining his left arm be uncomfortable for him?" I asked.

"No it will not," Dreyfus explained. "As far as he is concerned, it is not his left arm. Remember that he also has a spatial neglect. Therefore, once you get the arm into his left space he will be unaware that it is even restrained."

Later that morning, I went to see the patient and asked him if he still wanted me to get his arm out of bed.

"Yes," he said. "I do not want this person in my bed."

I gently picked his arm up and loosely restrained it so that it was on the left side of his body. As soon as I did this, he said, "Thanks, Doc; I do not know what that guy was doing in my bed."

Later that morning, the patient called me over to his bed again and said, "Doc, I think this guy you took out of bed this morning may be holding me down." I asked him if he would rather have that arm in bed with him or be held down.

"Neither," he replied.

I told him that I would release his left arm so that he could roll over. I shared with him my hope that as he got better he would realize that the arm he thought belonged to someone else actually belonged to him.

This patient's inability to recognize a part of his body is called asomatognosia (a = without, soma = body, gnosia = knowledge) or personal neglect. Personal neglect is often, but not always, associated with unilateral neglect. The inability to recognize that an arm is paralyzed is called anosognosia (a = without, noso = disease, and gnosis = knowledge). These were the most striking disabilities I had ever seen. Although I have seen hundreds of other patients who have these disorders, I still am awed whenever I see one of these unfortunate individuals.

A Powerful Means

Although I did not understand why this man was unaware of the left half of space and the left side of his body, I learned that studying patients with brain damage may be a powerful means of learning how the brain works. Since the time of Paul Broca's description of his aphasic patient, "Tan," some of the greatest advances in understanding the brain have come from studies of individual patients. Study of individual subjects with brain damage remains an important and productive research method. Although the standard for quality research is the population-based experimental paradigm used to study new drugs and therapies, some questions are best tested by well-designed case studies. We can learn a great deal about brain–behavior relationships from carefully designed and methodologically rigorous case studies of rare neuropsychological syndromes. Unfortunately, many scientists who perform population studies have not learned the difference between case studies and anecdotal reports.

If I Had Only Had Velcro

Shortly after examining the patient with unilateral neglect, my neurology rotation was completed and I moved on to general surgery. On this rotation we performed surgery on dogs. The surgeons thought that I was pretty deft. In addition, my beagle was one of the few to survive. While the fact that surgeons fix things appealed to me, I was not sure that they were in a position to learn how the brain works. As when I was a child taking apart my mother's clock, in surgery, I again found pleasure in working with my hands. While I enjoyed taking the body apart and putting it back together, I found that a lot of stitching and knotting was very tedious. If surgeons only had Velcro rather than sutures, I may have ended up a surgeon! Besides the lack of Velcro, I resented not being allowed to adopt my beagle, and I resented the sacrifice of so many of those cute dogs. Fortunately, medical students today do not perform dog surgery as a regular part of their curriculum.

I was thinking seriously about becoming a neurologist; however, people kept telling me that while neurology was interesting, neurologists could do little to help patients. I therefore decided to take a medical internship and residency at Cornell University. At that time, New York Hospital did not have an ambulance service, so I decided to train primarily at the Cornell Division of Bellevue Hospital. During the years I spent at Bellevue, I had many opportunities to try to fix sick people. Although I worked terribly hard, these two years were extremely happy ones for me.

After two years of general training, residents were expected to pick a sub-specialty of internal medicine. I was still unsure about what I wanted to do. The Vietnam War was intensifying, and the military had a shortage of physicians. Although I was in the reserves and had a deferment until I completed my medical training, I decided to sign up for active duty. After basic training, I was sent to a small hospital in the beautiful city of Izmir, Turkey. As Chief of Medicine in this hospital, I had the opportunity to treat patients for strep throat, ear and urinary tract infections, dermatitis, and gonorrhea. I found that treating (or fixing) patients with these diseases, while rewarding, was boring. When I received a letter from the

Chief of Medicine at Cornell, inviting me to return to complete my training, I decided instead to apply for a neurology residency.

A Case of Pure Word Deafness

At that time, Derek Denny-Brown was the only neurologist in America who I knew was interested in the relationship between the brain and behavior. I applied for a position at his Harvard Neurological Unit at Boston City Hospital. Denny-Brown accepted me. When I was discharged from the service, I moved to Boston. Prior to my beginning this residency, Denny-Brown had a heart attack, stepped down as Chair, and began to spend most of his time at the regional primate center in Framingham. Because he had accepted neurology residents, however, Denny-Brown periodically came to make rounds with us.

During the first year of my neurology residency, I was called by Psychiatry to examine a 58-year-old engineer named Tommy, whom they wanted to admit. Although they thought Tommy had a psychiatric disorder, they were concerned that he might also have a neurological condition. Tommy's wife brought him to the hospital because he was acting strangely. While shopping at Filene's, a Boston department store famous for their basement sales, she called Tommy at home to let him know she would be late. He must have heard the phone ring because he picked it up, yet after his wife spoke a few words Tommy said, "Doreen, stop mumbling!"

Doreen said, "Tommy, I am not mumbling."

"I cannot understand a word you are saying. Maybe it is the connection. Call me back." Tommy hung up the phone and waited for Doreen to call back. When the phone rang, he again answered, recognized Doreen's voice, but still accused her of mumbling. Tommy eventually became angry because he could not understand a word she said, so he hung up again. Doreen realized that something might be wrong and immediately took a taxi home.

When Doreen arrived home, Tommy looked perfectly fine. Every time she spoke, however, Tommy did not understand her and said, "Stop it—it's no longer funny."

Because Tommy was getting progressively agitated, Doreen called three of their children to come home. When the children tried to talk with him he said, "Are you in this with your mother?" The family realized that something terrible was happening, and they brought him to the emergency room.

Except for rheumatic heart disease that required a prosthetic stainless steel valve, Tommy was healthy and not taking any medicine. He had no history of any psychiatric problems. On general examination, I could hear his prosthetic valve, but otherwise everything was normal. When I examined Tommy's speech, I found he could speak normally and name objects that I held in front of him. He could not, however, understand anything I said. He also could not repeat or imitate what I said. The remainder of his neurological examination was normal. Out of frustration I wrote down, "I would like to admit you to the hospital. " He replied, "Why?" His family and I were delighted that we had found a means of communicating with him. I then wrote, "I think you had a stroke."

The next morning during our rounds, I presented Tommy to our attending neurologist. After the attending heard my presentation and examined the patient, he asked me what I thought was wrong with this man. I told him I thought he had a stroke. We moved away from the patient's bed and the attending asked me, "How can he hear the phone ring and recognize his wife's voice, but not understand words? If he were deaf he would not hear anything, and if he were aphasic he should not be able to read and speak normally. You admitted a hysteric! Call psychiatry and get this faker off our service."

Since I was worried about Tommy, I told the attending that the type of artificial valve that Tommy had was famous for sending emboli (blood clots) to the brain. I had begun to anticoagulate him and wanted Tommy well-regulated with oral medicine before we transferred him to Psychiatry. Fortunately, the attending agreed to let me keep him on our neurology service.

After rounds, the chief resident told me that Norman Geschwind, the Chief of Neurology at Boston University, had a strong interest in language disorders. Perhaps I could invite him to Boston City Hospital to see this patient. Traditionally, on Saturday mornings we had grand rounds in which we presented one or two cases to Denny-Brown. Since Denny-Brown would be out of town during the next grand rounds, I had a perfect opportunity to invite Dr. Geschwind. When I called, Geschwind was extremely warm and friendly. I invited him to do grand rounds, and he said he would be there.

On Saturday morning we all met in our conference room. The room usually held about twenty to thirty people. On that day it was packed. I thought about whether or not Geschwind would think that this patient was a faker and how embarrassed I would be in front of everyone on our service. After I introduced Geschwind, I presented Tommy. Geschwind examined the patient and found exactly what I had described: this patient spoke and named objects normally. Although Tommy could not understand or repeat speech, he was able to understand written commands. After Geschwind completed his examination and the patient returned to his room Geschwind said, "Terrific case!"

Geschwind went on to explain that this man had a disorder that was first described at the turn-of-the-century and was called "pure word deafness." Geschwind reviewed the contributions of Broca and Wernicke to our understanding of how specific aspects of language are mediated by discreet brain areas. Geschwind then described what happens when the left primary auditory cortex is injured.

A lesion in the left primary auditory cortex can interrupt auditory information coming to the left hemisphere from the thalamus, as well as prevent auditory information crossing over from the right hemisphere. As a result, auditory information is not able to access Wernicke's area, the part of the brain that contains memories of how words sound. Consequently, the patient cannot understand spoken words. Repetition of speech may be impaired, again because auditory signals cannot get to language cortex. In contrast, patients such as Tommy can read and write words since written words enter the brain via the visual system, and can therefore access the language cortex. Similarly, an intact visual system–language cortex pathway allows the patient to name viewed objects. In addition, the selective sparing of more anterior brain areas allows for the preservation of spontaneous speech.

Geschwind thought the patient had an embolus from his heart that destroyed the primary auditory cortex, just anterior to Wernicke's area. I was relieved to learn that Geschwind also thought that this person had a stroke, and I was amazed at how clearly he explained the patient's signs and symptoms. Then I saw my attending's hand being raised. Geschwind recognized him. "Norman, how come he was able to recognize the telephone was ringing and that his wife was the one who had called him?"

Geschwind explained that sound and voice recognition are not verbal processes and therefore probably can be mediated by the nondominant right hemisphere. In patients with pure word deafness, the primary auditory cortex in the right hemisphere is intact and connected to the auditory association and other ipsilateral cortical areas.

In 1967, Computerized Tomography (CT) or Magnetic Resonance Imaging (MRI) scans did not exist; however, a new technique for scanning the brain with radioisotopes injected into the bloodstream was available. More isotope would leak from the blood to parts of the brain that were injured by the stroke, allowing these parts to be distinguished from brain areas that were normal. Tommy's brain scan showed that he had a stroke exactly where Geschwind said it would be.

A Curious Finding

In the second year of my neurology residency, I saw a patient on Peabody Ward of the Harvard Medical Service. The patient had the sudden onset of left-sided weakness. I examined the patient, who did indeed have a left hemiplegia. In addition, I tested this patient with some of the measures used to assess unilateral neglect. On the line bisection task, this patient thought that the midline was two inches to the right of the actual midline. In addition, on the line cancellation test, he cancelled only the lines that were on the right half of the page. Like my first neglect case, this patient was unaware that anything was wrong with him, including his left-sided weakness. When I asked why he came to the hospital he replied, "Because my family brought me." I diagnosed this patient as having a stroke of his right parietal lobe. When we obtained a radioisotope scan, however, we learned that rather than having an abnormality in the parietal lobe as I had suspected, the patient had a lesion in his frontal lobe. Before this case, I never knew that patients could get neglect from frontal lobe damage.

After Denny-Brown retired, Norman Geschwind took over as Chief of the Neurological Unit at Boston City Hospital. This was especially nice for me, because I had planned to take a fellowship with him since hearing him explain pure word deafness in grand rounds—that is, if he would have me. Now that Geschwind was coming to City Hospital, he was stuck with me.

Geschwind had his morning coffee in a small meeting room that had several chairs around a table. Residents or faculty could sit down and have their morning coffee with Geschwind and chat about anything that was on their mind. During morning coffee, I showed Geschwind the brain scan from the patient with neglect from a frontal lobe lesion. He said, "Interesting. In almost all the reports of experimental neglect in monkeys, the neglect was induced by making frontal lobe lesions." He told me that the most recent report was written by Welch and Stuteville and was published in the journal *Brain*.

Two things struck me about this article. Although investigators going all the way back to the late-nineteenth-century had reported neglect-like behavior in animals with frontal lesions, there was no mention of humans suffering neglect from similar lesions. At the same time, it was not entirely clear that neglect could be induced from parietal lesions in monkeys.

A Test of a Hypothesis

After Geschwind came to the Neurological Unit at Boston City Hospital, he recruited Deepak Pandya, a neuroanatomist who was interested in the connections of different parts of the cortex. Studying the monkey brain, Pandya and Kuypers found that each of the primary sensory areas connects only with its own association area. In other words, the primary visual area connects to visual association areas, the primary auditory area projects to the auditory association area, and the primary somatosensory area (e.g., touch) projects to its association area. Each of these sensory or modality-specific association areas projects to multimodal or polymodal sensory areas. These polymodal sensory areas are in the inferior portion of the parietal lobe and in both banks of the superior temporal sulcus (Pandya & Kuypers, 1969).

Reading Pandya and Kuyper's paper reminded me of the paper on neglect written by Denny-Brown and Banker (1954) who suggested that all the sensory modalities come together in the parietal lobes of humans and this synthesis allows us to be aware of stimuli in the opposite half of space. Pandya and Kuypers (1969) demonstrated in monkeys that the polymodal areas where all the senses came together are in the monkey's parietal lobe and in both banks of the superior temporal sulci. Since all the senses came together, according to Denny-Brown and Banker's hypothesis, destruction of these areas in one hemisphere should induce neglect of stimuli presented in contralateral space. To test this hypothesis, I asked Pandya if we could ablate this area in a few rhesus monkeys and see if this lesion would induce neglect. In other (control) monkeys, we would make an equal-sized lesion in a different part of the brain that is not a synthetic or polymodal area. The monkeys that had the temporal–parietal lesions demonstrated unilateral neglect and the control monkeys did not (Heilman, Pandya, & Geschwind, 1970). These observations appeared to support Denny-Brown and Banker's hypothesis.

Something troubled me, however, when I examined these monkeys. If a stimulus was presented to the side opposite their temporal–parietal lesion, the monkeys were aware of the stimulus. When both the right and the left sides were stimulated at the same time, however, the animals only appeared to be aware of the stimulus on the same side of the body as their cerebral lesion (ipsilesional side). If, according to Denny-Brown, these temporal–parietal lesions destroyed the representation of contralateral space, why could these monkeys at times detect single stimuli applied to the contralesional side but fail to detect these same stimuli under conditions of bilateral simultaneous stimulation? This phenomenon of failing to feel a stimulus on one side when stimulated on both sides had been reported in humans by Dr. Morris Bender (1952). Bender called this phenomenon "extinction to simultaneous stimulation." Bender described this phenomenon but did not speculate about the underlying attentional mechanisms.

Attention as Mental Triage

Attention is difficult to define, but everybody knows what it is, observed William James, one of the founders of American psychology. Attention may be difficult to define because it is a process rather than an entity. Our brain receives more information than it can simultaneously process. If you find this book interesting, you pay attention to the words on the page and are unaware of how your left foot feels—until I mention your left foot and cause your attention to shift to it.

An analogy from my days in the Air Force may clarify how attention operates. I entered the Air Force in the mid-1960s and went to Alabama for basic training. One part of my military training involved how to deal with a disaster when medical personnel cannot, simultaneously, care for all injured people. In such a disaster, one doctor must serve as the triage officer. This officer categorizes the injured based on the urgency with which they must be treated and then labels them accordingly.

Attention can be conceptualized as a mental triage process. We attend to those stimuli that are most important to us. The significance of a stimulus is determined by several factors. We attend to novel stimuli because we have not yet determined their meaning. We also attend to stimuli that are important to us as determined by our immediate needs (drives) and future goals (conations).

When reading this chapter, attending to your left foot is not important to you because it is not a novel stimulus, and paying attention to it satisfies no immediate needs and helps you realize no future goals. Therefore, you probably stopped attending to your foot until I brought it up again. However, if a bug crawled on your foot while you were reading this chapter, you would immediately detect the novel sensation and shift attention to your foot. If you had pain in this foot, you would attend to it because pain induces immediate needs or drives. If you were Cinderella waiting for your glass slipper, you also would attend to your foot because of its role in achieving your future goals.

Pandya, along with Kuypers, made another important anatomic discovery. They found that the monkey dorsolateral frontal lobe, on each side of the brain, projects to the temporal–parietal areas on the same side. The temporal–parietal area of each side of the brain also projects back to the frontal lobes. Along with other investigators, Luria (1966), a Russian neurologist, demonstrated that patients with frontal lobe injuries often lose their ability to engage in goal-oriented behavior. Therefore, when the dorsolateral frontal lobe is injured, it can not supply information about future goals and motives to the temporal–parietal regions. In the absence of this information, people cannot correctly triage stimuli and therefore may not attend to the important things. Important stimuli to which they should pay attention become insignificant, not unlike how your left foot becomes insignificant when no novel stimuli, no pain, and no glass slippers draw your attention to it.

While sensory areas in the temporal, parietal, and occipital lobes monitor the external world, other parts of the brain monitor the body. These portions of the brain are widely distributed and form a complex network called the limbic system. In order to influence behavior, the limbic system has to communicate with other brain systems involved in behavior. This communication function falls to the cingulate gyrus, a portion of the limbic system that has strong connections with both the frontal lobes and the temporal–parietal regions.

Understanding the Neglect Syndrome

Since the 1970s, I have conducted my research in the Department of Neurology at the University of Florida. There, my colleague Ed Valenstein and I were searching for patients who had neglect from frontal lobe lesions. We found several people who had neglect from lesions of the cingulate gyrus (Heilman & Valenstein, 1972); however, naturally occurring lesions often involve more than one brain structure. To learn if a cingulate gyrus lesion was the area critical for inducing neglect, we surgically removed the cingulate gyrus from one side of the brain in monkeys and demonstrated that these animals indeed developed neglect for contralesional stimuli (Watson, Heilman, Cauthen, & King, 1973).

Barbara Haws, our chief technician at the time, made an interesting and serendipitous observation. Our monkeys had large homes, part of which were enclosed (for when it rained or was cold) and part of which were open. Rural North Florida has many snakes, some poisonous but most harmless. Our monkeys were protected so that snakes could not enter their homes, and we never had a monkey who received a snake bite. Nonetheless, Barbara noticed that when these monkeys were outside and saw a snake, they would panic. After removing one cingulate gyrus from a monkey, Bob Watson brought a plastic snake to our laboratory. When he showed the monkey the wiggling snake on the same side as the injured hemisphere, the monkey became panicked. When he showed the monkey the snake on the side of the body opposite the injured hemisphere, however, the monkey showed no evidence of panic.

In summary, directed attention depends on goals and drives. Consequently, the frontal lobe and the cingulate gyrus are important in the triage of stimuli. The output of the frontal lobe and cingulate gyrus is passed to the parietal lobes, but what then is the function of the parietal lobes? The parietal lobes may make attentional computations and therefore act as the triage officer. As we discussed, the triage officer categorizes and labels injured victims and, based on these labels, physicians and surgeons decide which patients to attend to immediately.

Besides its attentional computations that are important to the triage process, the parietal lobe has other functions it must perform. Studies of patients with injuries to the superior portion of their parietal lobes have revealed that they are impaired at making spatial computations. Spatial coding is one of the most efficient means our brain has of labeling stimuli as relevant or irrelevant. We attend to the portion of space that has the important stimuli and do not attend to the portion of space that has irrelevant stimuli.

When patients have bilateral lesions of the ventral or inferior portion of their occipital and temporal lobes, they develop visual object agnosia. These individuals may have normal vision such that they may be able to draw the objects they see; however, they cannot name these objects or describe the use or actions associated with these objects. They also may have problems recognizing faces of people they know (which is termed prosopagnosia). Ungerleider and Mishkin (1982) studied the visual system in monkeys and observed that after visual stimuli enter the primary visual cortex these stimuli subsequently are analyzed and processed by two visual streams. The ventral stream goes to the inferior portions of the temporal lobe, and the dorsal stream travels to the parietal lobes. The ventral stream appears to be important in recognizing objects or people and has been called the "WHAT" system. The dorsal stream is important for spatial location and has been called the "WHERE" system.

As we discussed earlier, we could induce neglect in monkeys by making lesions in the monkey's inferior parietal lobe and superior temporal sulcus. Monkeys do not have the same inferior parietal lobe as humans. Many scientists believe that the monkey superior temporal sulcus corresponds to the human inferior parietal lobe, and the monkey inferior parietal lobe corresponds to the human superior parietal lobe. Others have thought the monkey inferior parietal lobe is actually homologous with the human inferior parietal lobe. We wanted to learn whether injury to the monkey superior temporal sulcus or inferior parietal lobe would cause the type of hemispatial neglect that was associated with injuries to the human inferior parietal lobe.

When we lesioned monkeys, we found that injury to the posterior superior temporal lobe induced spatial neglect (Watson, Valenstein, Day, & Heilman, 1994). The monkey's "WHAT" and "WHERE" systems converge in this area. This same area (the region of the superior temporal sulcus in monkeys and the inferior parietal lobe of humans) also receives input from the frontal lobes. The frontal lobes input important information about drives.

Bob Watson and I (Watson & Heilman, 1979) saw a patient who had severe hemispatial neglect. A CT scan of his brain revealed that he did not have an injury to his parietal lobe. He did not even have an injury to his cerebral cortex. Instead, he had a hemorrhage deep in the brain that injured his reticular activating system. This called to mind research Moruzzi and Magoun (1949) conducted 50 years ago. Moruzzi and Magoun anesthetized cats and inserted electrodes in the cats' reticular activating system. With electrical stimulation to the reticular activating system, the cats became aroused and alert. Based on these and subsequent studies, neuroscientists believe that the reticular system is important in arousing or alerting the brain.

Moruzzi and Magoun also performed electroencephalographic (EEG) recordings when they stimulated the reticular system and found that the cats not only became aroused but their EEG waves also increased in frequency. We reviewed Moruzzi and Magoun's classic paper and noted that they found laterality effect when they stimulated the cat's reticular system. The EEG recorded on the stimulated side of the brain showed a greater arousal response than did the EEG recorded from the opposite side. Although these authors did not comment on this observation, these recordings suggest that if one side of the reticular system is injured, that same side of the brain may become "comatose." If one side of the brain is comatose, it may not process stimuli in the opposite side of space.

To test this hypothesis, we made small lesions on one side of monkeys' mesencephalic reticular system to see if this caused neglect of contralateral space. After receiving these lesions, the animals demonstrated the most severe neglect we had ever seen. We recorded EEGs from the monkeys and found, as we had hypothesized, that the hemisphere ipsilateral to the reticular lesion was, in fact, very slowed.

Normally we become aroused because there is an important stimulus in a particular part of space. Stimulus relevance is, in part, determined by the frontal–cingulate–parietal system we discussed above. When investigators stimulated different parts of the cerebral cortex, they found the dorsolateral frontal lobes, the cingulate gyrus, and the parietal lobes induced the greatest arousal. These are the same areas that we thought were critical in making attentional computations. Based on these findings, we proposed that a cortical-(frontal-parietal)-limbic (cingulate)-reticular network was important in mediating attention to stimuli in the opposite side of space (Heilman, 1979; Watson, Valenstein, & Heilman, 1981).

A New Hypothesis

After we demonstrated in both humans and monkeys that neglect could be induced by both frontal and parietal lesions, we wanted to learn if lesions in these two different areas produced different forms of neglect. In order to perform tasks such as cancellation and line bisection, a patient has to be aware of stimuli in all parts of space and must be able to act in all parts of space. In the clinic we see patients, such as those with Parkinson's disease, who are not weak but fail to act (i.e., akinesia). Because the monkeys with frontal lesions did not appear to be weak and did not respond to contralesional sensory stimuli, we thought that their failure to respond was induced by sensory neglect or unawareness. An alternative explanation, however, is that their neglect was related not to sensory neglect but rather to a failure to respond (i.e., limb, hemispatial, or directional akinesia).

To test this hypothesis, we trained monkeys on a crossed response task. They were taught to respond in left space with the left arm to right-sided stimuli and to respond in right space with the right arm to left-sided stimuli. After the monkeys were trained in this task, we ablated their right frontal lobe. We found that the monkeys could respond normally to contralesional (e.g., left-sided) stimuli by reacting with the ipsilesional (e.g., right) arm. When we stimulated the ipsilesional (e.g., right) side, however, the animal failed to correctly respond with the left arm. The results of this study suggested that frontal lesions induce neglect because there is a premotor or intentional defect (Watson, Miller, & Heilman, 1978). Subsequently, we performed a similar experiment on humans with either frontal or parietal lesions and found that while parietal lesions induce sensory neglect, frontal lesions are associated with intentional or action neglect (Coslett, Bowers, Fitzpatrick, Haws, & Heilman, 1990).

Asymmetrical Attention

Neurologists have long noticed that the lesion in patients with neglect is much more likely to be in the right than left hemisphere. In order to account for this asymmetry, we suggested that the left hemisphere attends to stimuli primarily on the right side of the body, but in contrast, the right hemisphere can attend to stimuli on both the left and right sides of space. Therefore, if the left hemisphere is injured, the resulting neglect is not severe because the right hemisphere can attend to both contralateral and ipsilateral hemispace. In contrast, when the right hemisphere is injured, the left hemisphere can attend only to the right side of space, and therefore the patient is inattentive or unaware of stimuli in left hemispace.

To test this hypothesis, we attached EEG electrodes over the area of the scalp over the right and left pareital lobes of normal college students (Heilman & Van Den Abell, 1980). The subjects sat in front of an apparatus that had three lights— one in the middle, one on the left side, and the third on the right side. Directly in front of each subject's chest we placed a telegraph key. Subjects were instructed to press the telegraph key as soon as they saw the middle light come on. The lights on the right or left side came on shortly before the middle light to act as a warning stimulus.

One of the reasons warning stimuli may reduce reaction times is because they instruct the subject to attend to the start stimulus. As predicted, reaction times were faster when the onset of the middle light was preceded by a warning stimulus. When we analyzed the EEG recording, we found that the right hemisphere became activated when the warning stimulus was delivered on the left side. When the warning stimulus was delivered on the right side, both hemispheres showed activation. These results support the hypothesis that the left hemisphere attends primarily to stimuli on the right side of space while the right hemisphere attends to stimuli on both sides. Subsequently, functional imaging studies provided further support for this asymmetrical hemispheric attentional hypothesis.

Mrs. Grossman Would Be Surprised

Although I have focused in this chapter on my work in attention and awareness, my colleagues and I have performed similar studies to explore many other brain–behavior relationships. Our goal has been to learn the architecture of the modular systems that mediate complex behaviors. I have been a behavioral neurologist now for nearly 30 years. Today we can "fix" many more patients with brain diseases than we could in the 1960s when I began my career. We also have learned much about how the brain works; however, we still have a long way to go.

I am proud that, along with my friends, colleagues, and students, I have helped to contribute to this body of knowledge. I think that my third-grade teacher, my junior high advisors, and Mrs. Lena Grossman would be surprised that I graduated high school, got into college, attended medical school, and contributed to the growth of scientific knowledge. When they predicted failure for me, they could not have known that I would be fortunate to have wonderful mentors, friends, and colleagues. It is the support, guidance, and knowledge of these people that allowed me to make contributions to our understanding of the brain. We have, however, just begun, and we still need to learn how to fix it!

REFERENCES

Bender, M. B. (1952). *Disorders of perception.* Springfield, IL: C. C. Thomas.

Coslett, H. B., Bowers, D., Fitzpatrick, E., Haws, S. B., & Heilman, K. M. (1990). Directional hypokinesia and hemispatial inattention in neglect. *Brain, 113,* 475–486.

Denny-Brown, D., & Banker, B. Q. (1954). Amorphosynthesis from left parietal lesions. *Archives of Neurology and Psychiatry, 71,* 302–313.

Heilman, K. M., Pandya, D. N., & Geschwind, N. (1970). Trimodal inattention following parietal lobe ablations. *Transactions of the American Neurological Association, 95,* 259–261.

Heilman, K. M. (1979). Neglect and related

disorders. In K. M. Heilman & E. Valenstein (Eds.), *Clinical neuropsychology* (pp. 268–307). New York: Oxford University Press.

Heilman, K. M., & Valenstein, E. (1972). Frontal lobe neglect in man. *Neurology, 22,* 660–664.

Heilman, K. M., & Van Den Abell, T. (1980). Right hemisphere dominance for attention: The mechanisms underlying hemispheric asymmetries of inattention (neglect). *Neurology, 30,* 327–330.

Luria, A. R. (1966). *Higher cortical functions in man.* New York: Basic Books.

Moruzzi, G., & Magoun, H. W. (1949). Brainstem reticular formation and activation of the EEG. *Electroencephalography and Clinical Neurophysiology, 1*, 455–473.

Pandya, D. N. & Kuypers, H. G. J. M. (1969). Cortico-cortical connections in the rhesus monkey. *Brain Research, 13*, 13–36.

Ungerleider, L. G. & Mishkin, M. (1982). Two cortical visual systems. In D. J. Ingle, M. A. Goodale, & R. J. W. Mansfield (Eds.), *The analysis of visual behavior* (pp. 549–586). Cambridge, MA: MIT Press.

Watson, R. T., & Heilman, K. M. (1979). Thalamic neglect. *Neurology, 29*, 690–694.

Watson, R. T., Heilman, K. M., Cauthen J. C., & King, F. A. (1973). Neglect after cingulectomy. *Neurology, 23*, 1003–1007.

Watson, R. T., Miller, B. D., & Heilman, K. M. (1978). Nonsensory neglect. *Annals of Neurology, 3*, 505–508.

Watson, R. T., Valenstein, E., & Heilman, K. M. (1981). Thalamic neglect: The possible role of the medial thalamus and nucleus reticularis thalami in behavior. *Archives of Neurology, 38*, 501–507.

Watson, R. T., Valenstein, E., Day, A., & Heilman, K. M. (1994). Posterior neocortical systems subserving awareness and neglect. Neglect associated with superior temporal sulcus but not area 7 lesions. *Archives of Neurology, 51*, 1014–1021.

10

Serendipity in Science
A Personal Account*

Edith Kaplan

*I*was born on February 16, 1924, in New York City, of immigrant parents. I was raised as an only child, though I had had a brother who died of diphtheria in Europe prior to World War I at the age of four. I spoke only German until I entered kindergarten. My father was a baker and bought and sold bakeries as one would invest in the stock market, so we moved about quite a bit. At one point, my father owned a bakery in Boro Park on Thirteenth Avenue, right across from the Yeshiva. I have since learned that both Norman Geschwind and Ken Heilman once lived in that neighborhood (though none of us knew each other at the time).

Those early years were rather lonely and uneventful. The only books at our home were Hebrew prayer books, and the only newspapers were in Yiddish. So prior to going to school, my time was spent with my mother learning crafts. I was quite a skilled knitter before I was five years old and still enjoy knitting. In kindergarten I learned the English alphabet and thought that reading consisted only of naming the letters. During elementary school, however, I became an avid reader and developed an idiosyncratic pronunciation. For example, I read the word "misled" as "myzeld." To this day, the two pronunciations have different affective significance for me. For example, "misled" represents a benign process, whereas "myzeld" suggests premeditated malice.

I attended elementary and secondary public schools in Brooklyn, New York. By the time I entered middle school, I had become interested in medicine and organized a medical club of which I was the self-appointed president. I arranged for visits to local psychiatric institutions. For example, the chairman of the Department of Psychiatry at The King's County Psychiatric Hospital agreed to interview psychiatric patients demonstrating a variety of disorders (e.g., schizophrenia, para-

*I want to thank Dr. Carmen Armengol for her critical reading and thoughtful editing of this chapter. Carmen, when the heart is truly touched, not many words are needed. Thank you!

To Patti Miliotis, many thanks for the countless ways you have been helpful during the writing of this chapter. I should also like to express my gratitude to Noreen Donovan of Suffolk University for her able assistance in the preparation of this manuscript. Finally, I wish to acknowledge Dr. Aurelio Prifitera for his encouragement and years of unwavering support throughout the various stages of test development with The Psychological Corporation.

noid psychosis, obsessive compulsive disorder, as well as dementia) and to provide a question-and-answer period for us.

I also was interested in creative writing and journalism. I joined the school newspaper and wrote a weekly column (with a byline). My creative writing instructor at that time, Mr. Waiser (could this have presaged my later interest in the WAIS–R?), on one occasion demonstrated what he considered to be the best example of a dangling participle by quoting the following from my column: ". . . and the boys come to school with their shirttails, among other things, hanging out."

In elementary school I developed a close relationship with a girl whose mother was a schoolteacher. When my friend told me about her intentions to go to college, I decided this was something I should do too. So I later enrolled at Brooklyn College, and this is where my story truly begins.

At Brooklyn College I met Heinz Werner who introduced me to developmental psychology. He presented developmental psychology as a means of conceptualizing psychological phenomena. Werner sought to apply developmental analysis to all aspects of mental behavior. It was probably his seminal paper, entitled "Process and Achievement: A Basic Problem of Education and Developmental Psychology" (published in the *Harvard Educational Review* in 1937), that had the most profound effect on me. In this paper, published over 60 years ago, Werner expressed great concern about the growing use of standardized tests to assess cognitive functioning—tests that are predicated on the idea that the final solution to a problem is an objective measure of an underlying *unitary* mechanism. Werner believed that psychologists and educators had failed to appreciate the multifactorial nature of these instruments.

Even today, test items are, for the most part, scored in a binary fashion (i.e., right or wrong) and then summed to yield an overall global score. In fact, final solutions may be arrived at via diverse processes that reflect the activity of distinctly different structures in the central nervous system. Werner, in his paper, presented a convincing argument that close observation and careful monitoring of behavior en route to a solution (process) is likely to provide more useful information than can be obtained from right or wrong scoring of final products (achievement). The focus on process, a process-oriented approach to assessment (sometimes referred to as the Boston Process Approach), has directed and dominated my professional life (Kaplan, 1988).

During my junior year at Brooklyn College I became interested in studying with Werner the development of word meanings. Convinced that meaning is largely inferred from the cues of the contexts in which words appear, Werner and I endeavored to investigate experimentally the processes underlying the acquisition of word meaning through verbal contexts. To this end, we designed the Word–Context Test. Briefly, the test is composed of 12 artificial words, signifying either an object or an action and varying in degree of concreteness. Each word is embedded in six sentences ordered in such a way that as a child moves from one sentence to the next, the clues increase in specificity. The children are told that they will see 12 unfamiliar words and that their task is to figure out what each word means.

For example, the first of the 12 series contains the word CORPLUM (a piece of wood). The sentences, presented sequentially, read as follows:

1. A CORPLUM MAY BE USED FOR SUPPORT.
2. CORPLUMS MAY BE USED TO CLOSE OFF AN OPEN PLACE.
3. A CORPLUM MAY BE LONG OR SHORT, THICK OR THIN, STRONG OR WEAK.
4. A WET CORPLUM DOES NOT BURN.
5. YOU CAN MAKE A CORPLUM SMOOTH WITH SANDPAPER.
6. THE PAINTER USED A CORPLUM TO MIX HIS PAINTS.

Each sentence was printed on a card. After each sentence was presented, the child had to try to figure out what the artificial word might mean and explain how that meaning fit into each sentence.

One hundred and twenty-five school children between the ages of 8.5 and 13.5 years were tested individually. Based on the verbatim responses, our analyses focused on correctness of final solutions (although this was not the primary focus of the study) and, more importantly, on such processes of signification as word–sentence fusion; aggregation of individual solutions; pluralization; transposition; and the grammatical, linguistic, and semantic characteristics of responses. Criteria were derived and subjected to both qualitative and quantitative analyses. In general we found that, as expected, correctness increased with age and that the younger children lacked differentiation between the meaning of the word and the given verbal context. Developmentally, there was a growing comprehension of the test sentence as a stable grammatical structure (Werner & Kaplan, 1952).

It is of interest that in 1957, Ralph Reitan developed a Word Finding Test. Though the procedures he used were very similar to ours, he indicated that his test was developed without prior knowledge of our test. In 1972, Reitan reported that the problem-solving aspect of his Word Finding Test was sensitive to cerebral lesions in a heterogeneous brain-damaged population. On this verbal problem-solving task, his patients performed significantly worse than matched controls without brain damage.

In 1976, Byron Rourke and his colleagues (Pajurkova, Orr, Rourke, & Finlayson, 1976) generated a children's version of Reitan's Word Finding Test (the Children's Word-Finding Test). They reported that 40 normal control children (grades 3, 4, and 5) performed significantly better than 20 children with diagnosed learning disabilities. These authors also reported some indications that the learning disabled children differed *qualitatively* in their approach to the test and suggested that this qualitative difference be investigated further.

In 1949, I received my Bachelor of Arts degree from Brooklyn College and immediately followed Heinz Werner, who had moved on to Clark University in Worcester, Massachusetts, the year before. In 1952, our monograph on the development of word meanings was published, I received my Master of Arts degree, and I gave birth to my son, Michael. That was certainly a banner year!

As a predoctoral student at Clark from 1949 to 1952, I was influenced by Piaget's (1951) *Play, Dreams and Imitation* and by Vygotsky's (1934) *Thought and Speech* (revised and edited by Alex Korzulin in 1986). I began to pilot some studies on the development of gestural representation and finally settled on the study of speech-for-the-self (inner speech) and speech-for-others (external speech) for my master's thesis (Kaplan, 1952). What prompted this research was the controversy between Piaget and Vygotsky. Piaget maintained that for young children speech for the self is not differentiated from speech for others (i.e., it is "egocentric"). As the child matures, egocentrism declines and finally disappears. For Vygotsky, however, egocentric speech does not disappear but rather goes underground to become inner speech differentiated from external speech.

To test these competing perspectives, 20 college students served as subjects. Each subject was required to write a sentence describing each of six stimuli: two visually articulated line drawings, two visually diffuse configurations (water colors), and two relatively unfamiliar synthesized odors. The sentences were intended for two different audiences: (1) the self—to serve as an aide for the subject to identify the stimulus at some later date; and (2) an unknown other—another person relying on the written sentence to identify the stimulus. These different audiences permitted a comparison between self-directed and other-directed communication (i.e., inner- and external-speech).

The analysis of the written sentences primarily focused on explicitness of expression, communicability of the expression, and idiomatic referents (e.g., assimilation to personal experience). Briefly, analyses revealed that changes in the linguistic description of the stimuli were a function of the variation in addressee (self/other) and in stimuli (visual/olfactory). For a more detailed description, see chapter 17 in Werner and Kaplan (1967).

It was after I had fulfilled all the requirements for the Ph.D., except for the qualifying examinations and the German exam, that I separated from my husband, Bernard Kaplan, and left Worcester in 1956 to seek my fortune in Boston. I had heard Harold Goodglass lecture on the examination of cognitive deficits in patients with brain injury (Goodglass & Kaplan, 1979). I had been so impressed with Harold's clinical approach, testing of clinical limits, and his emphasis on the importance of identifying the strategies a patient utilizes to solve a problem that I turned to him to ask whether he knew of any possible positions in the Boston area.

Serendipitously, he had just received money for six months' worth of salary left over from the Social Science Research Council Study Group that had ended just the month before. Most importantly, the money had been earmarked for the study of gesture in aphasia. Though it would only last for six months, I thought it would be a wonderful opportunity, and I could look for another job afterward. Given my early interest in gestural and language development in normal children, the study of impaired gesture and language functions in the adult was certainly an exciting prospect. So when Harold offered me the job, I enthusiastically accepted. Harold often says that it was one of the best investments that he ever made, because the six months that had been supported by the grant parlayed into my 29 years at the Boston Veterans Administration Hospital!

In the beginning, Harold and I set to work on the development of a gesture and pantomime test to study patients with left and right hemisphere lesions. The question we addressed, which dictated the structure of the test, was the extent to which the impaired gestural behavior of aphasics was secondary to a central communication disorder or to a disorder of praxis (apraxia). We formulated several hypotheses. If impaired gestural behavior was a communication disorder, then there should be a significant correlation between the severity of the aphasia and the gestural score. Further, there would be a hierarchy of difficulty as a function of the level of abstraction of the test items. If, however, the deficit was attributable to an apraxia, the symbolic level of the item would not have an impact on performance but, more importantly, the opportunity to imitate the examiner should not improve performance. The findings were thought to support apraxia as the explanation for the gestural impairment seen in aphasia (Goodglass & Kaplan, 1963).

Many of the qualitative characteristics of the impaired performance of the aphasics were childlike. For example, when the patient was asked to show how he or she would pretend to brush his or her teeth, the patient would rub the teeth with the forefinger as if it were the toothbrush. This behavior, which we termed "body-part-as-object," raised questions in my mind about the normal development of praxis. This led me to undertake the study of the development of gestural representation for my doctoral dissertation (Kaplan, 1968).

Children between the ages of 4 and 12 were required to demonstrate how they would use highly familiar implements with which they were likely to have had daily transactions (e.g., a toothbrush, comb, etc.). In contrast, they also were required to show how they would use implements that they had experienced only vicariously when an adult had used the object (e.g., a razor, an iron, etc.). Both the action and its spatial orientation had to be appropriate. The results demonstrated a clear developmental progression: (a) diffuse movements (unrelated to any part of the command); (b) manipulation of the object of the action (e.g., rubbing hair with a few fingers for *comb*); (c) deictic or indexical behavior, (i.e., pointing to where the action should take place—pointing to head for comb, mouth for toothbrush); (d) body-part-as-object (e.g., index finger as a toothbrush, or fingertips as the teeth of a comb); (e) holding without extent (i.e., the hand is positioned to hold the implement but empty space is not used to represent the extent of the implement, e.g., the fist holding the toothbrush is too close to the mouth, so that if the subject were actually holding a brush it would be too far to the side of the mouth); and finally (e) holding with the extent of the implement represented.

Another serendipitous event took place in the early days at the Boston Veterans Administration Hospital. Dr. Fred Quadfasel, Chair of the Neurology Service, organized a weekly seminar to study pure neurological disorders. He assigned the disorder of pure motor agraphia to me because the only papers on that topic were in German; because at that time I was still studying for my German qualifying exam at Clark University, I was the most likely candidate to fully benefit from this assignment. The first German paper I read was by Bouman and Grunbaum (1930). These authors argued that what appeared to be a motor agraphia was really secondary to a grasp reflex. If one carefully observed the patient while writing, one would note that all the letters were present but that the illegibility was due to the overwriting secondary to the grasp reflex.

Walking down the corridor of 7D, a neurology ward that for years primarily housed the Aphasia Unit, I noticed a patient, PJK, grabbing door knobs and having great difficulty letting go. Serendipitously here was a patient who appeared to have a grasp reflex, thus providing an opportunity to check out Bouman and Grunbaum's thesis. I immediately brought PJK into my office. PJK had suffered the surgical removal of a large glioblastoma multiforme lateralized to the left frontal lobe. (During the surgery the neurosurgeon had tied off the anterior cerebral artery to control for bleeding. This procedure not infrequently results in infarcts, which is what had occurred in this case.) On examination, he did have a grasp reflex in his right hand and not in his left. From observing the patient's writing with his right hand, it was clear that he had formed each letter correctly but because of his grasp reflex there was marked overwriting which rendered the product illegible. Bouman and Grunbaum were correct.

Unexpectedly, however, I noted that PJK's writing with his left hand, unencumbered by a grasp reflex, also was strikingly impaired. He was unable to write the alphabet, words, and sentences to dictation, nor could he name objects held in his left hand or follow commands to perform movements with this hand. He appeared to be both aphasic and apractic but only with his left hand. Outside of the motor problems secondary to his right grasp reflex, his performance with his right hand was *not* aphasic. This was puzzling since PJK had a unilateral left frontal lobe lesion, which would naturally lead one to expect him to have aphasic problems with the contralateral (and not just the ipsilateral) hand.

Many Wednesday seminar meetings were devoted to trying to understand PJK's problem. Suggestions for studies and novel tests would be discussed. I would take these ideas back to the laboratory and then report my findings the following Wednesday. On one occasion, the Chair of Psychiatry facetiously said, "His left hand doesn't know what his right hand is doing," and left the room.

It was finally Norman Geschwind, my behavioral neurology colleague at the VA, who correctly concluded that the most likely explanation was a deconnection syndrome. He had been reading the early German and French cases reported in the literature that shared features with our patient, PJK. It was the behavior of Roger Sperry's surgically callosotomized cats, however, that provided the information that allowed us to really understand PJK. Sperry's animals showed many interesting anomalies in the performance of the two sides of their bodies as a result of the callosotomy—a surgery that deconnected their two cerebral hemispheres. In a similar manner, the results of our special studies of PJK clearly indicated that he could perform most tasks if the stimulus and response were confined to one hemisphere. If, however, the stimulus was presented to one hemisphere and the response was to be mediated by the other hemisphere, the task could not be completed correctly.

Geschwind and I submitted this case study to *Neurology* (Geschwind & Kaplan, 1962). While the paper was being reviewed, PJK died. Jose Segarra, the VA neuropathologist, performed the post-mortum and verified the presence of a left anterior cerebral artery infarct as well as the thinning of the anterior two thirds of the corpus callosum. When we received the galley proofs, we were able to include the pathology report as a footnote. In 1998, this article was chosen as a landmark paper and republished in the May issue of *Neurology* (Geschwind & Kaplan, 1998).

In 1972, Harold Goodglass and I published the first edition of the *Assessment of Aphasia and Related Disorders* and the *Boston Diagnostic Aphasia Examination* (BDAE). In 1983, we published the second edition of the *Assessment of Aphasia and Related Disorders*, the *BDAE*, and the *Boston Naming Test* (Kaplan, Goodglass, & Weintraub, 1983) for the evaluation of word finding problems. Since all patients who have lesions in the language zone of the left hemisphere have some form of word finding difficulty, an analysis of the kinds of errors (phonemic paraphasias, verbal paraphasias, circumlocutions) has diagnostic significance. An achievement score (i.e., the total number of correct responses) would not be diagnostically helpful. As a matter of fact, a relatively poor score might not even differentiate between the cerebral hemispheres. A patient with a right hemisphere lesion may show nonaphasic misnaming, which is perceptually based.

For example, in the sample of errors made for the line drawing of a harmonica (a stimulus included in the Boston Naming Test), a patient with a right frontal lesion may be pulled to the reeds, and based on an incomplete perceptual analysis, respond "a double decker bus," "a garage," or "a factory." Such patients do not have a naming problem. Based on their faulty percepts they access their lexicon correctly. In contrast, characteristic aphasic errors in response to a harmonica might include, "a musical thing you blow," "a marhonika," "mon-ka," "a frelisha," "an accordion," and "I know it; I can't say it."

Not only has the BDAE been widely used in the United States and other English-speaking countries, it has been translated into many languages (e.g., Spanish, French, German, Italian, Dutch, Finnish, Japanese, and Chinese). The third edition (Goodglass, Kaplan, & Barresi, 2000) of these publications consists of a major revision. We felt the pressure to introduce a short form of the BDAE to meet the needs of examiners who are pressed for time but want a reliable instrument for the diagnostic classification of the aphasias.

The BDAE standard form and the added extended testing form are based on recent research in neurolinguistics, allowing the clinician to probe into syntax comprehension, category-specific difficulties in word comprehension and word production, as well as grapho–phonemic processing. The Boston Naming Test now contains a 15-word short form, as well as the original 60 line-drawn items. To help sort out word finding problems from word knowledge issues (especially in children), a recognition (multiple choice) format also has been introduced. This addition is particularly important in assessing children as well as adults with depression or semantic dementia.

In 1976 I took over the VA pre- and postdoctoral clinical neuropsychological training program, which rapidly expanded both because it was nested in the neurology service and because it was one of the rare centers to have such a distinguished interdisciplinary faculty (e.g., Norman Geschwind, Nelson Butters, Laird Cermak, Marlene Oscar Berman, Margaret Naeser, Frank Benson, Michael Alexander, Nancy Helm-Estabrooks, and, of course, Harold Goodglass). This rich environment provided an exciting opportunity to learn about aphasia and cognitive neuroscience and offered opportunities for collaborative research. Our program received international recognition and attracted scholars who came on sabbaticals or shorter visits (e.g., Luigi Vignolo, Malcolm Piercy, Felicia Huppert, Franco Dennis, Carlo Semenza, Teddi Landis, and Theodor von Stockert). Some came from abroad to study with us having obtained Fulbright or Guggenheim awards (e.g., Jane Holmes Bernstein from Scotland, Gilbert Desmarais from Montreal, Lieve Vercryuse from Belgium, Evelyn Hornung from Lausanne, Matti Lane from Finland, and Donald Stuss and Connie Delamalva from Ottowa). In addition, many graduate students in the greater Boston area elected to do their dissertations with us as members of their committees.

In June of 1978, I was invited to Oxford, England to present a paper on a lifespan overview of symbolic, motor, and spatial components of praxis at the International Neuropsychology Symposium (Kaplan, 1978). My presentation was well received, and I had an opportunity to discuss apraxia with neurologists and psychologists such as Luigi Vignolo, Ennio De Renzi, Oliver Zangwill, and Claus Poeck, whose work on apraxia I had been reading. It was too good to be true! Subsequently, I was elected to membership in the International Neuropsychology Symposium, a society that, at that time, had a limited membership of 100 (33 from North America). Annual, week-long meetings in European settings offered an opportunity to engage with such distinguished leaders in the field as Norman Geschwind, Henry Hécaen, Hans-Lukas Teuber, and Oliver Zangwill (all of whom are now deceased). The more contemporary active members included Sue Corkin, Guido Gainotti, Doreen Kimura, Brenda Milner, Mortimer Mishkin, and Eran Zaidel, to name a few who are at the cutting edge of neuroscientific research. I felt very privileged indeed to have been invited to be a member of such an illustrious group.

The 1970s and 1980s were the golden years. In addition to the above-cited visiting scholars, we were fortunate to have annual visits from Anne-Lise Christensen who has been a clinical role model for me as well as for my interns. Each year, we all looked forward to her visit. She would lecture in my neuropsychological assessment course, demonstrate the administration of her Luria Neuropsychological Investigation for our staff, and work with some of the patients. We all felt so privileged to have the opportunity to witness her skilled "testing of clinical limits," her sensitivity, perceptiveness, gentleness, and empathic responsiveness to each patient with whom she worked. I have learned much from Anne-Lise and continue to hold her in very high esteem and to treasure our friendship as it has grown over the years.

Kevin Walsh, whose clinical approach to assessment I also hold in high regard, is another kindred soul. His remarkable ability to do a detailed analysis of test behavior, which he shared with us during his visits and in his lectures and writings, has left an indelible mark on all of us. His zest for life, good humor, and gentle teasing make him very special.

In 1980, the American Psychological Association (APA) declared the beginning of the "Decade of the Brain." As then president of the International Neuropsychological Society, I was asked to recommend speakers for the APA Master Lecture series. The five Master Lectures were published as a monograph entitled *Clinical Neuropsychology and Brain Function: Research, Measurement, and Practice* (Boll & Bryant, 1988). The contributors were Don Stein, who addressed recovery of function; Richard Thompson, who covered brain substrates of learning and memory; Maureen Dennis, who presented language and the young damaged brain; Michael Posner, who covered structures and functions of selective attention; and myself, presenting on a process approach to neuropsychological assessment (Kaplan, 1983, 1988).

As director of clinical neuropsychological services and clinical internship training, conducting and supervising neuropsychological evaluations of patients with known or suspected central nervous system dysfunction, it again became obvious that "neuropsychology by the numbers" (a phrase borrowed from Muriel Lezak) was not very helpful. Final global scores are not nearly as informing (and in some instances may be misleading) as observing, noting, identifying, and quantifying the behaviors of patients while they are working *toward* a solution. An analysis of the strategies an individual may employ en route to either a correct or incorrect solution may speak to the role of the non-compromised hemisphere and may suggest prescriptive interventions. In 1976, Hans-Lukas Teuber invited me to discuss the role of the non-compromised hemisphere in a symposium he had organized on the topic of hemispheric specialization at the New York meeting of the American Psychological Association (Kaplan, 1976).

Analyses of the processes by which adult patients passed or failed various subtests of the Wechsler Adult Intelligence Scale–Revised (WAIS–R) led to modifications in administration and scoring procedures which ultimately resulted in the development of the WAIS–R as a Neuropsychological Instrument (WAIS–R NI) (Kaplan, Fein, Morris, Kramer, & Delis, 1991) published by The Psychological Corporation. Careful documentation and quantification based on finer analyses of performance, together with the modality of input and output and the nature of the task and stimulus parameters, can provide new insights into brain–behavior relationships. The process-oriented approach also yields expanded scores that are more useful in monitoring a recovery course over time as well as the efficacy of an intervention, be it surgical, pharmacological, or behavioral. The WAIS–R NI served as a model for the Wechsler Intelligence Scale for Children–Third Edition (WISC–III) as a Process Instrument (WISC–III PI) (Kaplan, Fein, Morris, Kramer, & Delis, 1999).

The WISC–III PI provides an approach to the assessment of cognition that permits the identification of profiles of spared and impaired functions. The emphasis on finer analyses of problem-solving behavior and the parsing of component factors contributing to performance provide an understanding of the level of information processing of the child and generate prescriptive individualized interventions.

Because the WISC–III surveys a broad range of cognitive functions, it is widely used in the early stages of an evaluation to help identify specific areas that may be problematic for a child. The process-oriented approach to the WISC–III also identifies the strategies that are employed to solve a task and examines the nature of the errors that are made, the particular context in which they occur, and the nature of the stimulus parameters. For example, the information subtest has at least five different content areas: number facts, directions, geography, science, and names. A child may demonstrate selective difficulty with one or more of these areas. Since a number of verbal subtests require the articulation and elaboration of a verbal response, multiple-choice versions were created to permit a distinction between lack of knowledge and difficulty expressing that knowledge. Furthermore since the multiple-choice foils were selected from the WISC–III original standardization sample (non-clinical and clinical populations), the error choices of the child may have particular diagnostic relevance.

Wherever possible, following the directive of Hans-Lukas Teuber to investigate the issue of double dissociation, a given function is tested in another modality (e.g., the visual analog for orally presented Digit Span is Spatial Span; for Picture Arrangement we created a Sentence Arrangement subtest). In a different vein, the necessity to distinguish between word knowledge and the ability to express it led to the development of various ways to assess Vocabulary (e.g., the verbal and pictorial multiple-choice subtests). Similarly, analysis of performance subtests is facilitated by the separation of perception from motor or constructional aspects. For example, a motor-free (multiple-choice) version of the Block Design subtest was created to evaluate the perceptual component of this task without the contamination of motor dysfunction. The introduction of the adaptation of the Elithorn Mazes (Elithorn, Kerr, & Mott, 1960) provides an opportunity to analyze aspects of executive function such as planning ability, working memory, and impulse control.

I have been actively involved in developing other clinical instruments that focus on parsing the multifactorial aspects of the functions under investigation and developing finer analyses of processes, strategies, and errors. Dissatisfied with such existing instruments as the Rey Auditory Verbal Learning Test (RAVLT), my interns and I, especially Dean Delis during his postdoctoral year with us, began to expand the analyses and bit-by-bit modify the RAVLT. We continued this work after Dean left for California. After a long distance ongoing collaboration with Dean at the helm and Joel Kramer joining us, the adult and children's versions of the California Verbal Learning Test (CVLT) came into being (Delis, Kramer, Kaplan, & Ober, 1987, 1994).

By design, the CVLT lends itself to a finer analysis of the processes involved in learning a categorized word list over five trials, followed by a distractor list, recall of the first list, cued recall, short delay and long delay recall, and a recognition trial. The recall after each of the five learning trials yields information on the patient's learning curve, consistency of learning, and use of active versus passive learning strategies (semantic clustering versus serial order learning, and primacy versus recency). Provision of the distractor list to be learned followed by recall of the first list permits the evaluation of proactive and retroactive interference. Error analyses such as perseveration, quality of intrusions, and so on, all have been found to have diagnostic value. And now the second edition of the CVLT (Delis, Kramer, Kaplan, & Ober, 2000), to which we have added a 9-word Mental Status Version, has further refinements of diagnostic relevance. David Libon (another former VA intern) found an error analysis that he generated on his 9-word version of the CVLT to be very useful for the differentiation of cortical from vascular dementia (Libon, Mattson, Glosser, et al., 1996).

Over the years, Dean and I have enjoyed developing tests, conducting workshops, and participating in symposia together. We founded the Boston Neuropsychological Foundation as a non-profit organization to fund internships for deserving and promising students. And now, last but not least, the long awaited Delis–Kaplan Executive Function System (D-KEFS) has been completed (Delis, Kaplan, & Kramer, 2001). This last test pulls together under one umbrella distinctive, executive functions and serves as an excellent example of the importance of parsing the traditional multifactorial tests used by neuropsychologists (e.g., the Trail Making Test, the Stroop Test, and Word List Generation) to better identify the underlying component(s) contributing to the difficulties a child or adult is experiencing. In addition, the D-KEFS includes a number of subtests addressing a variety of verbal and nonverbal problem-solving tasks, most notably the California Card Sorting Test. It was Dean's idea to include an adaptation of the Word–Context Test that Werner and I first published in 1952. Yes, what goes around comes around!

Worth mentioning here are a few other tests that I have had a hand in developing such as (1) MicroCog: A Computerized Assessment of Cognitive Functioning (Powell, Kaplan, Whitla, Weintraub, Catlin, & Funkerstein, 1993); (2) the Kaplan–Baycrest Neurocognitive Assessment (Leach, Kaplan, Rewilak, Richards, & Proulx, 2000); (3) Clock Drawing: A Neuropsychological Analysis (Freedman, Leach, Kaplan, Winocur, Shulman, & Delis, 1994); and (4) The Boston Qualitative Scoring System (BQSS) for the Rey–Osterrieth Complex Figure (Stern, Javorsky, & Singer et al., 1999).

Currently, I am a Professor of Psychology at Suffolk University in Boston. I continue my long-standing affiliation with Boston University School of Medicine as Adjunct Professor in the Departments of Neurology and Psychiatry and as a member of the core faculty of the Behavioral Neuroscience doctoral program. I am also an Affiliate Professor of Psychology at Clark University.

I have been president of the International Neuropsychological Society and the Clinical Neuropsychology Division of the American Psychological Association (Division 40). I have been on the board of the Academy of Aphasia. Currently I am

still the president of the Boston Neuropsychological Foundation that Dean Delis
and I founded in 1983.

My work has been recognized in many ways. In 1977, I received the Distinguished Service Award from the Massachusetts Speech and Hearing Association.
In 1982, the National Head Injury Foundation recognized me for my services. In
1984, the Massachusetts Psychological Association presented me with the Ezra
Saul Psychological Service Award. In 1993, I was the recipient of the Distinguished
Clinical Neuropsychologist Award from the National Academy of Neuropsychology. In 1994, the Edith Kaplan Neuroscience Scholarship Fund was established by
the MeritCare Medical Center in Fargo, North Dakota. In 1996, I received the Distinguished Contributions Award from the New England Psychological Association, and in 1997 I received the Distinguished Career Contributions award from
the Massachusetts Psychological Association. Also in 1997, I was inducted into the
Psi Chi Honor Society at St. Anselm College in Manchester, New Hampshire.

In 1999, the Edith Kaplan Award was established and announced at the formal
celebration of my seventy-fifth birthday. What an event that was! Carmen Armengol, Elisabeth Moes, Deborah Fein, and Clare O'Callahan (all former pre- and postdoctoral interns, now colleagues and dear friends) orchestrated the occasion. During the day there was a scientific conference celebrating my life and work,
cosponsored by the Edith Kaplan Award Committee and the Massachusetts Neuropsychological Society. Marlene Oscar-Berman, my colleague and close friend,
chaired the day's program and introduced each of the following speakers and topics:

1. Anne-Lise Christensen—"Edith Kaplan: Neuropsychologist, Source of Inspiration, Friend"
2. Kenneth Heilman—"Apraxia"
3. Nancy Helm-Estabrooks—"The Influence of Edith Kaplan's Teachings on
   Methods for Treating Aphasia"
4. Jane Holmes Bernstein—"The Rey–Osterrieth Complex Figure: The View
   from Visuospace"
5. Ursula Kirk—"The Process Is the Message: The How and What of Copying
   the Rey–Osterrieth Complex Figure, Clock Drawing, and Assessing Neuropsychological Development with the NEPSY"
6. Deborah Fein—"Neuropsychology of Communication in Autism"
7. William Milberg—"Meeting Edith Kaplan in Cold Minnesota"
8. William Barr—"Historical Reflections on Edith"
9. Penny Prather—"Developing the IDEA"
10. Paul Spiers—"Listening to Dr. Kaplan Listening to Patients"
11. Gail Hochanadel—"The Edith Kaplan Approach to Aging"
12. Sandra Weintraub—"Behavioral Classification of Dementia Syndromes"
13. Morris Freedman—"Clock Drawing in Aging and Dementia"
14. Dean Delis—"New Process-oriented Tests of Executive Function"
15. Aurelio Prifitera—"The Impact of Dr. Kaplan's Work on Test Development
    and Assessment"

It was a glorious day—approximately 250 people attended. There was a wonderful mix of science and humor. That evening there was a formal banquet, dancing, roasting, a slide show of memorable moments in my life (presented by Carmen Armengol), and a skit written and directed by Clare O'Callahan with Sandra Weintraub acting incredibly like me. It was like the formal wedding I never had. My biological family—son Michael and granddaughter Rachel—along with my academic family—former students, interns, and colleagues, were all there. All in the family.

Though I have many credits to my name, my greatest sense of achievement comes from the accomplishments of the people I have trained (both formally and informally). Many of them have distinguished themselves in research and test development. Many also direct highly regarded programs that are training the third and fourth generations of prominent neuropsychologists.

(Editors' Note: Thus, what began as serendipity has become a legacy.)

REFERENCES

Boll, T., & Bryant, B. K. (Eds). (1988). *Clinical neuropsychology and brain function: Research, measurement, and practice.* Washington, DC: American Psychological Association.

Bouman, L., & Grunbaum, A. (1930). Uber motorische momente der agraphie. *Monatsschrift Fuer Psychiatrie undd Neurology, 7,* 223.

Delis, D. C., Kaplan, E., & Kramer, J. H. (2001). *Delis–Kaplan Executive Function System.* San Antonio, TX: The Psychological Corporation.

Delis, D. C., Kramer, J. H., Kaplan, E., & Ober, B. A. (1987). *The California Verbal Learning Test.* San Antonio, TX: The Psychological Corporation.

Delis, D. C., Kramer, J. H., Kaplan, E., & Ober, B. A. (1994). *The California Verbal Learning Test–Children's Version.* San Antonio, TX: The Psychological Corporation.

Delis, D. C., Kramer, J. H., Kaplan, E., & Ober, B. A. (2000). *The California Verbal Learning Test* (2nd ed.). San Antonio, TX: The Psychological Corporation.

Elithorn, A., Kerr, M., & Mott, J. (1960). A group version of a perceptual maze test. *British Journal of Psychology, 51,* 19–26.

Freedman, M., Leach, L., Kaplan, E., Winocur, G., Shulman, K., & Delis, D. C. (1994). *Clock drawing: A neuropsychological analysis.* New York: Oxford University Press.

Geschwind, N., & Kaplan, E. (1962). A human cerebral deconnection syndrome: A preliminary report. *Neurology, 12,* 675–693.

Geschwind, N., & Kaplan, E. (1998). A human cerebral deconnection syndrome: A preliminary report. 1962 [Classical article]. *Neurology, 50,* 1201–1212.

Goodglass, H., & Kaplan, E. (1963). Disturbance of gesture and pantomime in aphasia. *Brain, 86,* 708–720.

Goodglass, H., & Kaplan, E. (1979). Assessment of cognitive deficit in the brain-injured patient. In M. Gazzaniga (Ed.), *Handbook of behavioral neurobiology, vol. 2* (pp. 3–24). New York: Plenum Publishing Corporation.

Goodglass, H., & Kaplan, E. (1972, 1983). *The Assessment of Aphasia and Related Disorders.* Philadelphia: Lea & Febiger.

Goodglass, H., Kaplan, E., & Barresi, B. (2000). *Boston Diagnostic Aphasia Examination* (3rd ed.). Baltimore, MD: Lippencott, Williams and Wilkens.

Kaplan, E. (1952). *An experimental study on inner speech as contrasted with external speech.* Unpublished master's thesis, Clark University, Worcester, MA.

Kaplan, E. (1968). *Gestural representation of implement usage: An organismic–developmental study.* Unpublished doctoral dissertation, Clark University, Worcester, MA.

Kaplan, E. (1976, August). *The role of the non-compromised hemisphere in patients with focal lesions.* Invited paper presented at the American Psychological Association Meeting, New York, NY.

Kaplan, E. (1978, June). *Symbolic, motor, and spatial components of praxis: Lifespan overview.* Invited paper presented at the International Neuropsychology Symposium, Oxford, England.

Kaplan, E. (1983). Process and achievement revisited. In S. Wapner & B. Kaplan (Eds.), *Toward a holistic developmental psychology.* Hillside, NJ: Lawrence Erlbaum Associates.

Kaplan, E. (1988). A process approach to neuropsychological assessment. In T. Boll & B. K. Bryant (Eds.), *Clinical neuropsychology and brain function: Research, measurement, and practice* (pp. 125–167). Washington, DC: American Psychological Association.

Kaplan, E., Fein, D., Morris, R., Kramer, J. H., & Delis, D. C. (1991). *The WAIS–R NI.* San Antonio, TX: The Psychological Corporation.

Kaplan, E., Fein, D., Morris, R., Kramer, J. H., & Delis, D. C. (1999). *The WISC–III as a process instrument.* San Antonio, TX: The Psychological Corporation.

Kaplan, E., Goodglass, H., & Weintraub, S. (1983). *The Boston Naming Test.* Philadelphia: Lea & Febiger.

Leach, L., Kaplan, E., Rewilak, D., Richards, B., & Proulx, G. B. (2000). *Kaplan Baycrest Neurocognitive Assessment.* San Antonio, TX: The Psychological Corporation.

Libon, D. D., Mattson, R. E., Glosser, G., Sands, L. P., Kaplan, E., Malamut, B. L., Swenson, R., & Cloud, B. S. (1996). A nine-word dementia version of the California Verbal Learning Test. *The Clinical Neuropsychologist, 10,* 237–244.

Pajurkova, E. M., Orr, R. R., Rourke, B. P., & Finlayson, M. A. J. (1976). Children's Word-Finding Test: A verbal problem-solving task. *Perceptual and Motor Skills, 42, 851–858.*

Piaget, J. (1951). *Play, dreams and imitation.* New York: Norton.

Powell, D., Kaplan, E., Whitla, D., Weintraub, S., Catlin, R., & Funkenstein, H. (1993). *MicroCog: Assessment of Cognitive Functioning.* San Antonio, TX: The Psychological Corporation.

Reitan, R. (1972). Verbal problem solving as related to cerebral damage. *Perceptual and Motor Skills, 34,* 515–524.

Stern, R. A., Javorsky, D. J., Singer, E. A., Singer Harris, N. G., Sommerville, J. A., Duke, L. M., Thompson, J. A., & Kaplan, E. (1999). *The Boston qualitative scoring system (BQSS) for the Rey–Osterrieth Complex Figure.* Odessa, FL: Psychological Assessment Resources.

Vygotsky, L. (1934). *Myshlenie I rech' [Thought and speech].* Moscow: Sotsekriz. [Revised and edited by Korzulin, A. (1986). *Thought and language.* Cambridge, MA: The MIT Press.]

Werner, H. (1937). Process and achievement: A basic problem of education and developmental psychology. *Harvard Educational Review, 7,* 353–368.

Werner, H., & Kaplan, E. (1952). The acquisition of word meanings: A developmental study. *Monographs of the Society for Research in Child Development, 15,* 3–120.

Werner, H., & Kaplan, B. (1967). *Symbol formation.* New York: John Wiley & Sons.

11

In Search of Knowledge and Competence

Manfred J. Meier

A Milwaukee Childhood

*I*t seems both daunting and daring to embark on a reflection upon one's work in the context of personal and professional history. Such an effort seems to require both a lifespan developmental perspective and a degree of self-criticality that may have waned with the well-known central nervous system changes that occur with age. However, the task offers an opportunity to reconstruct some of the salient experiences and developmental transitions in my personal and professional life. In retrospect, the events in my career that seem worthy of discussion also seem both era-bound and the result of fortuitous circumstances rather than forethought and planning.

I grew up in the 1930s as a first generation kid in a Milwaukee working-class neighborhood. The bullying I received from some of my physically and emotionally abused peers and the apparent wide range of individual differences in the people I knew contributed to a later interest in human behavior. The multiplicity of languages spoken in the area also contributed to a sense of wonder at the diversity of human beings. These early stirrings of interest in human behavior were perhaps out of place in my childhood environment that encouraged interest in fields like engineering. Similarly, I felt the impact of my father's skills and work ethic acquired during an extensive German railroad apprenticeship. Through incredible persistence (32 years without a day off), he developed a successful American career that allowed the family to survive the Great Depression.

My high school experiences also favored such practical pursuits over more esoteric interests in behavior. The advent of World War II and the substantial industrial expansion during those years provided a further impetus toward an engineering or technical career. Indeed, psychology courses had not yet appeared in the high school curriculum of most American schools. Fortunately, my good academic record and pursuit of science and mathematics courses prepared me for potential achievement in many fields. What was most impressive about my high school experience was that it gave me the opportunity to meet classmates from higher socioeconomic levels who had parents, and sometimes even older siblings, who had attended college. Although my specific educational and vocational goals had not emerged, by my sophomore or junior year I had at least resolved to pursue a post-secondary education.

Fashioning A Career

After a stint in the U.S. Army, fortunately following the cessation of conflict, the logical choice for me was to continue my education with the help of the GI Bill. I enrolled at the University of Wisconsin in Madison and began to consider a career in medicine. Psychology was not taught until the beginning of the sophomore year, but I decided that psychology would provide an optimal undergraduate major whether or not I went to medical school. To conclude that this was a mature interest at that time would not be justified. For that matter, I did not find the early psychology courses particularly gratifying, but I hoped that they would improve by the time I reached the more advanced courses.

The introductory psychology classes were quite large at the University of Wisconsin. It was the custom that the department head would teach one of the introductory sections. The already-famous Harry F. Harlow was at the University and was known as a superb lecturer. Unfortunately, his classes filled so rapidly that it was almost impossible to access them. This left my introduction to psychology to less exciting lecturers. Nevertheless, the subject matter was of sufficient merit to adequately engage my attention, and I continued on to graduate school at Wisconsin. There I had the good fortune of finally taking a course with Harlow—a graduate proseminar offered the very first semester.

This exposure to Harlow in the winter of 1952 constituted my first encounter with what later became known as neuropsychology. I had been admitted to the clinical psychology graduate program, which had the same first-year requirements as other more established branches of the field of psychology. I frequently have asked myself why I didn't enter medical school instead and am compelled to conclude that I lacked the kind of daily discipline that medical school required. I enjoyed the flexibility and lower time requirements of a graduate curriculum in psychology. This orientation derived not so much from laziness as from social needs, the gratification of which required more time than a medical school curriculum would permit. Such socializing did sharpen my bridge playing skills and provided an opportunity to enjoy one of the most beautiful campuses in the United States, including the student pub—one of the few such establishments for college students anywhere in the country during the 1950s.

The graduate curriculum in psychology also provided an opportunity for a "minor." I elected to minor in the philosophy of science—an interest driven partly by the writings of Paul E. Meehl, already a distinguished professor at the University of Minnesota where the Minnesota Multiphasic Personality Inventory (MMPI) had just been constructed. I had the good fortune of corresponding with Meehl about research I was conducting in a Veterans Administration (VA) hospital. The base rate for predicting a clinical outcome was favorable in a population of VA patients with active tuberculosis who were not required to remain in the hospital by law and who frequently left against medical advice. Profile analysis of their MMPIs led to a series of sorting rules that effectively predicted, with very low false negative and false positive rates, who would leave the hospital against medical advice. In any case, the more distant influence of Meehl and the contiguous influence of Harlow began to sharpen and level my career focus.

Harlow's proseminar was devoted largely to the research he and his graduate students were conducting on the effects of localized cortical ablations upon learning, visual discrimination ability, problem solving, and delayed responding in the Rhesus monkey. Interestingly, he began the proseminar lectures with a description of the frontal lobe syndrome of Phineas Gage and the prediction that human neuropsychology would one day become a major component of the clinical enterprise. The pathfinding work of people like Brenda Milner, Hans-Lukas Teuber, D. O. Hebb, and Ward Halstead was appearing in the literature. Correspondingly, Harry Harlow and Clinton Woolsey organized a week-long symposium in 1953 that was attended by the entire graduate faculty and student body in the department. This symposium covered the essential body of knowledge on brain–behavior relationships at that time. The psychologists who participated, in addition to the above, included James Olds, Joseph Brady, and Karl Pribram. Ralph Reitan had just completed his work toward a Ph.D. with Ward Halstead and was beginning to publish extensively and to appear at Midwestern Psychological Association meetings where the annual program, beginning in about 1953 or 1954, included entire sections of both animal and human neuropsychology.

Harlow later offered me the opportunity to pursue a joint major in physiological and clinical psychology. I had married and was about to embark on a VA internship. Economic circumstances dictated the pursuit of more realistic career goals rather than further prolonging my studies. Harlow's offer probably would have led straight to an academic position in a department of psychology. This would not have been a wise direction for me to take since I would never have developed the necessary commitment to become a truly happy and productive animal psychology researcher. Instead I accepted a position offered by Starke Hathaway at the University of Minnesota. The position called for work in the outpatient psychiatry clinic where interpreting MMPIs was my primary responsibility, along with supervising medical students and doing outpatient supportive psychotherapy. I did manage to negotiate an agreement with Hathaway, however, to permit me to further my neuropsychological interests by attending conferences in neurology and neurosurgery.

I was overjoyed to be offered a position at Minnesota since I had been in correspondence with Meehl and had been mentored by Samuel H. Friedman, a Minnesota Ph.D., circa 1950. I came under Friedman's influence at the University of Wisconsin where he taught courses on the MMPI and on "brain damage testing." I also worked with Friedman as an intern at the Wood VA in Milwaukee, Wisconsin, where he was chief of psychology. Friedman had developed a Parietal–Frontal

Scale for the MMPI based on an empirical analysis that identified items that discriminated between patient groups with demonstrated lesions in one or the other of these brain regions. I performed a number of studies on a group of patients with partial complex seizures before and after removal of the anterior temporal lobe on one side of the brain. Accordingly, I was moving from a mass action–equipotentiality perspective with my Ph.D. dissertation to a regional localization orientation based on the identification of psychological test deficits following unilateral temporal lobectomy.

My dissertation was derived from Kretch's cortical conductivity hypothesis and demonstrated an empirical relationship between a measure of reminiscence in motor learning and the degree of kinesthetic, figural aftereffect, a sensory–perceptual illusion. My dissertation dealt primarily with various psychiatric populations (e.g., neurotics, schizophrenics, and depressives) and did not include a brain-damaged sample. The theory permitted predictions in functional psychiatric populations following some of the classifications (e.g., hysteric and dysthymic) being developed by Hans Eysenck in the 1950s. A major problem confronting clinical researchers in neuropsychology at that time, as well as currently, was the availability of well-defined, focal-lesioned samples. This circumstance raises doubts regarding the credibility of some of the larger scale studies that have been reported since access to such populations remains limited in most settings.

Ferment and Growth

After joining the medical school faculty at Minnesota in 1957, I spent about four years in the outpatient psychiatry unit but gradually appeared at functions of the Neurology and Neurosurgery Departments to make my neuropsychological interests known. These departments had received a joint grant from the (then) National Institute of Neurological Diseases and Blindness (NINDB) to examine the effects of removal of the anterior temporal lobe in individuals with psychomotor seizures, now called partial complex seizures. Such patients had been routinely administered the Wechsler Bellevue II, the MMPI, and the Bender Gestalt Test pre- and post-operatively for a period of about three years. However, the neurologists and neurosurgeons had virtually exhausted their populations of such patients, so there were very few new cases on the horizon when I joined their group in 1962.

My interests were recognized by some of the major players in that group including Lyle A. French, who was about to become the new head of Neurosurgery; Frank Morrell, a neurologist and neurophysiologist who was very much involved in Russian theories of higher cortical function; and A. B. Baker, head of the Division of Neurology of the Department of Psychiatry and Neurology, which subsequently became the Department of Neurology in the Medical School. French and the head of Psychiatry and Neurology, Donald Hastings, co-sponsored my application for a Research Career Development Award from the NINDB. The receipt of that award from 1962 to 1972 gave me the necessary time to expand my knowledge and skills by taking full advantage of the educational opportunities afforded by the clinical neurological–neurosurgical–psychiatric setting. It also gave me the opportunity to develop tests to assess further the behavioral correlates of temporal lobe lesions and ablations in a sample of psychomotor (complex partial) seizure patients.

The interdepartmental milieu was collegial, and friendships flourished. Minnesota was a haven for clinical psychologists and young neuropsychologists. Grants were readily available at the height of the Kennedy–Johnson years, before the impending Vietnam War. The senior faculty were highly effective and influential. These were academically exciting times, despite the troubles that were starting to ferment across the country. Psychiatry and neurology constituted a single department within which Starke Hathaway's Division of Clinical Psychology was an administrative entity. Neurosurgery was a division of the Department of Surgery but there was considerable interaction between neurosurgery and psychiatry and neurology by virtue of the collegial relationships among the senior people. French and Morell paved the way for my initial research activities. Baker facilitated expansion of these activities. Neurology and Neurosurgery subsequently became separate departments, though the functional links among these various operations remained relatively intact.

A separate chapter could be written on the social and psychological dynamics of the players and their respective roles in increasing the effectiveness of this milieu for teaching, research, and service. It is sufficient for present purposes to point out that the milieu always plays a large part in the direction and in the content of the activities of the participants. Such factors facilitate or impede movement, depending upon the personalities of the participants. The milieu provided ample opportunities for me to engage in research not only in seizure disorders but also in the areas of cerebrovascular disease and movement disorders in the 1960s and 1970s.

The term "neuropsychology" was coming into wider use at that time, and there were distinctly different emphases in orientation emerging among Midwestern and Eastern neuropsychologists. In the Midwest, Halstead's battery was being studied extensively by Ralph Reitan and his associates (e.g., Charles Matthews, Homer and James Reed, Hallgrim Kløve) whose work focused primarily on diagnostic issues and the localization of function. In the East, Brenda Milner was publishing extensively on the effects upon memory of temporal lobe ablations. Hans-Lukas Teuber was developing a team of researchers (e.g., Sid Weinstein and Josephine Semmes) at New York University's Bellevue Medical Center before moving to the Massachusetts Institute of Technology. The Eastern emphasis was largely cognitive–experimental in nature, with many of the people whose careers began in this region of the country later moving to other universities and into the National Institutes of Health to establish laboratories. The latter included such stalwarts as Karl Pribram, Mortimer Mishkin, and Allan Mirsky.

Other groups were becoming identified with laboratories in the United States and Europe that were unifying behavioral neurology and neuropsychology, most notably the Boston group including Harold Goodglass, Edith Kaplan, Nelson Butters, and Norman Geschwind. Arthur Benton at the University of Iowa was attracting many people to his laboratory to obtain further training on the design and construction of quantitative neuropsychological tests. Benton's activities added another dimension to Midwestern neuropsychology insofar as he attempted to relate the findings of his quantitative procedures to the characteristics of the various syndromes discussed in the nineteenth century neurological literature. Accordingly, his work bridged the traditional quantitative emphasis in the Midwest with the more cognitive–experimental emphasis in the East and the behavioral–neurological foundations that had been established earlier in Europe and elaborated in the United States by Norman Geschwind and his group (e.g., Ken Heilman, Frank Benson, and Alan Rubens).

As observer and participant in the 1960s and beyond, I had the privilege of meeting these already-senior contributors and their various protegés. Having minored in social psychology (within the Department of Psychology) and in philosophy of science (in the Department of Philosophy) as a graduate student, I was fascinated by the relationships among all these developments as well as by the content of the research. I began to appreciate the overarching sociological phenomenon of the emergence of clinical neuropsychology as a professional psychological specialty, an interest that became the major preoccupation of the latter segment of my career.

A Change in Course

Upon completion of the research career development award in 1972, I had enjoyed a productive research career and had acquired a considerable amount of new knowledge in the field of clinical neuroscience. My research interests had focused on prediction of outcome following cerebral vascular accident, longitudinal monitoring of alterations in higher cortical functions following temporal lobectomy, and the effects of neurosurgical and pharmacological treatment of movement disorders (especially Parkinson's disease). I also completed scattered studies on closed head injury and toxic encephalopathy.

A fortuitous event, however, changed the course of my career. Lyle French, the head of Neurosurgery, became the first Vice President for Health Sciences at the University of Minnesota in 1971. He asked me to serve as Coordinator for Allied Health Professions in his office in order to help launch an integrated and interdisciplinary effort across the health sciences. My first assignment was the organization and writing of an interdisciplinary educational grant request for the dozen or more allied health programs of the various collegiate units of the health sciences. The ultimate intent was to establish a school of allied health professions, a development that never occurred for internal political reasons. This coordinator role, however, provided extensive opportunity to acquire familiarity with national developments in what was then called "health manpower development."

To my surprise, we became one of the few recipients nationally of a very large education and training grant for the development of interdisciplinary team training activities and special courses in areas such as consumer health education and educational technology. The Vice President of the Health Sciences then established intercollegiate committees to guide various health science curricula. As chair of a number of committees, I gained knowledge and competence in educational administration at the planning level, working largely with deans, department heads, and program directors.

The shift in orientation from directing a small laboratory to becoming engaged in such broad activity areas seemed almost overwhelming. Were it not for the early interest in the sociological aspects of what was happening within neuropsychology, I would have felt entirely out of place in this new role, but it appears to have been earlier comments I had made about such directions that induced Dr. French to consider me for the role. Being in my early 40s—still young enough to be foolish—and having landed a large grant that provided funds for such activities, I decided to proceed. Subsequent experiences led to increased comfort in this arena and helped me develop the guiding concepts and leadership skills that would serve me well in later years when I pursued organizational work that ultimately led to recognition of clinical neuropsychology as a specialty.

The Formation of a Specialty

As neuropsychology began to take form as a professional field, regional and national meetings of the American Psychological Association (APA) provided the opportunity for neuropsychologists to convene and to present their research findings. Each participant often represented the only person interested in neuropsychology on a given university campus. These meetings, therefore, provided an opportunity to become acquainted with other (some isolated) individuals around the country. The Midwestern Psychological Association, for example, provided opportunities to meet Ralph Reitan, Charles Matthews, Hallgrim Kløve, and Paul Satz. APA meetings provided the arena for meeting people such as Aaron Smith, Louis Costa, Sidney Weinstein, and Mortimer Mishkin, as well as many others. Some neuropsychologists presented at medical–neurological meetings as well as at the APA. In my experience, the prime example was Arthur Benton who, in addition to his presentations to APA, presented frequently at meetings of the American Academy of Neurology and the American Neurological Association. Small groups formed to provide impetus for the development of new organizations. For example, Ray Dennerll and Aaron Smith fostered the development of the International Neuropsychological Society (INS) as did a steering committee that evolved out of informal meetings held at the APA. Unfortunately, the APA provided a major administrative obstacle to the formalization of new groups insofar as the formation of a division required a much larger number of individuals than we could muster in the 1960s and 1970s.

In the meantime, some initiatives were less conspicuous but certainly deserve mention as a part of our history. For example, at the University of Minnesota, Starke Hathaway, better known as the codeveloper of the MMPI, provided some funds to invite a group of neuropsychologists to the medical school to discuss their research as well as their educational and service activities. This brought together in 1965 a group of Midwestern and some Eastern neuropsychologists. We all reflected informally on where neuropsychology was going in the future. Ralph Reitan had begun to conduct formal workshops as he continues to do to this day. There was some early discussion of educational, particularly postdoctoral, activities and the outlook for credentialing competencies of individual neuropsychologists.

The subsequent decade saw the development of the INS, out of which grew the next major occurrence—the formation of the INS Task Force on Education, Accreditation, and Credentialing (TFEAC). Arthur Benton, as past president of the INS, suggested in 1976 at the APA meeting in Toronto that such a task force be established and that I serve as chair. The TFEAC was designed to fill a void by identifying realistic directions that the INS might take to generate professional standards for the practice of neuropsychology.

At the 1977 INS meeting in Santa Fe, New Mexico, the TFAEC held a symposium to address these issues. The Task Force published a report in the 1981 INS Bulletin to provide a foundation for guiding future educational initiatives. It was difficult, however, dealing with such professional issues as educational standards within INS, an organization that was both interdisciplinary and international in scope. An organization this broad was perhaps not the best place to address issues that were at least partly defined by professional and regional boundaries. Not surprisingly then, from TFEAC grew a steering committee made up of Task Force members to establish a new APA Division (Division 40) devoted to neuropsychology. As Division 40 became established, the activities of TFEAC gradually were transferred to it and, over time, they became the exclusive responsibility of this new division.

Because of my ongoing involvement with these issues, I was invited to present a statement on education and the practice of neuropsychology at the American Board of Professional Psychology (ABPP) Convocation at the Toronto APA meeting. ABPP did not pursue a formal relationship with us, however, until four more years elapsed. In this interim period, a group of us formed the American Board of Clinical Neuropsychology (ABCN) in Minneapolis. Included on the steering committee that formed ABCN were Paul Satz, Steve Mattis, Barbara C. Wilson, Charles Matthews, Edith Kaplan, Muriel Lezak, Linas Bieliauskas, and myself. Others were added as the ABCN formed. In 1981 to 1982 the ABCN negotiated an arrangement to become a new practice area under the aegis of ABPP with appropriate representation on the ABPP Board of Trustees. The ABCN demonstrated its proposed use of an examination before the board, and this began the profound effect that ABCN subsequently had on the ABPP organization as a whole. Other practice areas of the ABPP began to modify their examining procedures to incorporate aspects of ABCN's approach to assessing competence and knowledge. Thus the ABCN can be regarded as a fulfillment of credentialing goals set by the original INS Task Force on Education, Accreditation, and Credentialing and as a catalyst for organizational change within ABPP.

But let me again emphasize how neuropsychology has impacted other psychology practice areas and the organizational structure of ABPP. ABPP has adopted a cooperating member–board structure. This frees individual member boards to upgrade, coordinate, validate, and manage their individual examining procedures. The movement to a federation of member boards constitutes, in my opinion, the largest single advance professional psychology ever has taken in the credentialing arena. Clinical Neuropsychology became the first new professional specialty in 28 years following School, Industrial–Organizational, Counseling, and Clinical Psychology. In rapid succession have followed Forensic, Family, Health, Psychoanalytic, Rehabilitation, Behavioral, and (soon) Group Psychology. The second mission of the original INS Task Force (i.e., credentialing) has now been actualized on a wider scale than anyone ever envisioned!

With the formation of the Association of Postdoctoral Programs in Clinical Neuropsychology (APPCN) in the 1990s, the INS Task Force's original goals were advanced even further. The APPCN arose as a consequence of efforts of a group of Midwestern postdoctoral programs to develop their own accreditation "self-study evaluation" and "site visit evaluation" procedures. Although predoctoral programs continued to exist, clearly the major thrust for clinical neuropsychology training was at the postdoctoral level through some combination of internship and supervised postdoctoral activities. An informal "Midwestern Neuropsychology Group" had been meeting for years. Many members were located in large medical schools including some senior people (e.g., Arthur Benton, Charles Matthews, Paul Satz, and myself) but also a growing number of younger people (e.g., Linas Bieliauskas, Eileen Fennell, Tom Hammeke, Kerry deS. Hamsher, and Bob Ivnik). Many of these medical school programs supported a "resident" or "postdoctoral fellow." The directors of these programs formed the cadre that responded to a major new initiative from ABPP.

The ABPP Board of Directors, of which I was a member representing ABCN, heard me talk about the efforts of the Midwestern Neuropsychology Group and were inspired to fund a pathfinding conference on postdoctoral accreditation in neuropsychology to be held during a quiet early September week on the Minnesota campus in 1991. It was hoped that the conference would help the Midwestern Group formalize its procedures and ultimately expand into a national network of postdoctoral programs in neuropsychology. The conference did, in fact, facilitate the expansion of the Midwest group into the APPCN, but it opened new avenues of change by precipitating the formation of the Interorganizational Council for the Accreditation of Postdoctoral Programs in Professional Psychology (IOC). The conference was attended by representatives from many professional organizations including ABPP, APA, the National Register of Health Service Providers in Psychology, the Association of State and Provincial Boards of Psychology, the Association of Psychology Postdoctoral and Internship Centers

(APPIC), and the various specialties already recognized by ABPP. The IOC provided a mechanism for monitoring and evaluating specific accreditation initiatives, specialty by specialty, beginning with clinical neuropsychology. Our (new) specialty was again instrumental in affecting major changes within the field of psychology as a whole. The IOC has since been disbanded owing to the acceptance of the responsibility for accrediting postdoctoral programs by the APA.

Collectively, these developments made it possible to justify the claim of neuropsychology to specialty status within APA. Division 40 asked me to serve as chair of a planning committee in 1994 that wrote a mission statement and a set of goals for the Division and that responded to a request from APA to prepare a petition to the Commission on Recognition of Specialties and Proficiencies in Professional Psychology (CRSPPP). This commission was established by APA to review and approve claims to specialty or proficiency status. A subcommittee comprised of myself, Bruce Crosson, and Dan Eubanks, utilizing information from the various task force documents and developments, assembled the petition package for successful processing through the APA organizational structure. That document has been lauded for providing a definitive model for other specialties seeking recognition by the profession. Specialty recognition will be based on meeting evolving criteria as promulgated by CRSPPP. Of course, the socialization of a profession and its component specialties will evolve throughout its lifetime. (See Meier, 1997, for a more extensive account).

Clearly, clinical neuropsychology deserves to be recognized as a specialty, if for no other reason than its effective handling of credentialing and accreditation issues to date. Attainment of one set of goals, however, requires the development of future goals and demands a process for continuing this development. The continued development of our specialty and profession also depends upon a firm knowledge base for professional practice and the development of new roles (while modernizing or deleting older roles) for our professional repertoire. In this direction, the establishment of the Neuropsychology Synarchy—an interorganizational mechanism to bring Divison 40, The National Academy of Neuropsychology (NAN), APPCN, ABCN, and other interested organizations together—hopefully will yield a unified set of goals for the specialty in the future.

Accreditation should in the future become a more orderly and effective process, which is what the new specialty movement is really all about—standards of practice and education for competency assurance. If standards collapse under the weight of managed care, clinical neuropsychology will self-destruct. If standards prevail, neuropsychology should continue to grow in expertise and professional effectiveness.

Having been heavily involved in these developments over the past few decades, my inclination is to heave a sigh of relief and retire into relative obscurity. However, what I found most gratifying throughout an interesting career (really multiple careers) has been the opportunity not only to model upon more senior people (of which Arthur Benton has had the greatest influence on my professional and personal development) but also to form collegial relationships and friendships with contemporaries (of which Charles Matthews, Paul Satz, and Louis Costa have had a signal impact upon my development). As I reflect upon my career, I am impressed also with the qualities and the fervor demonstrated by the next generation of neuropsychologists (of which Ken Adams, Linas Bieliauskas, Bruce Crosson, Dan Eubanks, Eileen Fennell, Tom Hammeke, Kerry deS. Hamsher, Julia Hannay, Bob Ivnik, Ann Marcotte, and Byron Rourke, among many others, stand out). The future of our specialty is clearly in very capable hands!

REFERENCE

Meier, M. J. (1997). The establishment of clinical neuropsychology as a psychological specialty. In M. E. Maruish & J. A. Moses, Jr. (Eds.), *Clinical neuropsychology: Theoretical foundations for practitioners* (pp. 1–31). Mahway, NJ: Lawrence Erlbaum Associates.

12

Jersey to Oklahoma
A Neuropsychologist's Trajectory*

Oscar A. Parsons

*T*he trajectory and accomplishments of one's career are the result of factors such as familial influences, educational opportunities and choices, avocational interests, mentor(s)' influence, opportunities in a chosen career area, and chance (i.e., being at the right place at the right time). I will consider the role of these factors in my career, together with what I consider to be my contributions to clinical neuropsychology. Finally, I will share some thoughts concerning the future of neuropsychology.

Chance and Choice

I was born in Glendora, New Jersey, on March 19, 1920. My father was a salesman. My mother was a schoolteacher who taught primary grades off and on until she was 70 years of age. I had an older sister and a younger brother. Reading and education were emphasized in our home. In my sophomore year of high school, I took my first biology course and found it fascinating. At the same time, several of my friends and I formed a microscopy club. We each had our own cheap microscopes and spent hours looking at slides of all kinds of microscopic objects. These two experiences provided a foundation for my lifelong interest in biology. Also, in high school I had the opportunity to learn how to fence; fencing was to have a profound effect on my life and my career.

I graduated from high school in 1937 when our country was still in the Great Depression. My father had a heart attack and could not work, so I had to help support the family. From 1937 to 1944, I worked at a number of jobs. During those years, I read extensively. The book that was most interesting to me was Paul de Kruif's *The Microbe Hunters*. I decided that I would like to become a bacteriologist (now microbiologist). Fencing also interested me. I joined the Philadelphia Sword Club in 1938 and had lessons from the Club's professional maestro. In 1939, he began to have trouble controlling his right hand in giving lessons. Eventually he was diagnosed as having a brain tumor in the left hemisphere and died several months thereafter. His untimely death led me to read up on brain tumors at that time, a precursor of future interest!

183

In 1942, I was working as an expediter in a shipbuilding company and could afford to start my college education, albeit at night. I attended the College of South Jersey for two years, four nights a week. One of the courses was introductory psychology. I found it interesting and decided to take more courses in psychology when that became possible.

By 1944, my father had recovered enough that my mother could resume teaching and provide support for the family. I volunteered for the Navy and started boot camp in June of 1944 in Bainbridge, Maryland, and then attended Hospital Corps School for 12 weeks. During this period, I was also able to fence with the Bainbridge Naval Base Fencing Team under another fencing maestro. We fenced several university and city clubs, and I emerged as the only undefeated fencer on the team. After graduation from Hospital Corps School, my orders were to report to the fleet marines. (The Navy provided the hospital corpsmen for the Marines.) The fleet marines corpsmen were all sent at that time to the South Pacific, and casualty rates were very high. I went to the maestro to say "goodbye." In brief, he had my orders changed; I was to stay at Bainbridge and fence with the team. My avocation, fencing, probably saved my life or at least prevented me from suffering serious injury.

In the spring of 1945, I entered Sampson Naval Base in upper-state New York for medical laboratory technology training. My experiences there deepened my interest in microscopy, and the goal of becoming a bacteriologist became more salient in my thinking. This experience also gave me a lifelong appreciation of the importance of measurement with quantified procedures. I was discharged from the Navy in October of 1945, the result of a phlebitis condition, but I had completed my medical laboratory technology training.

As soon as I returned to our home, I applied to Rutgers University for spring admission to their program in bacteriology. To my dismay, the spring semester of 1946 was completely filled with returning veterans, and I could not enter until the following fall. My alternative choice, Temple University in Philadelphia, did admit for the spring semester, and I enrolled in the pre-med program. I attended all semester and summer school sessions, including several more courses in psychology, so by the summer of 1947 I had completed all requirements for the pre-med program and obtained a bachelor's degree in science. Meanwhile, the time had come to take the medical school aptitude test. I did not take it because I had become interested in a career in psychology. This decision also was related to my fencing. I was the amateur student coach of the Temple fencing club and team. There were two members of the team who were psychology majors and were going to attend graduate school in psychology. After talking extensively with them about career opportunities in psychology, I decided to apply to graduate school in psychology—a major career choice! Incidentally, our Temple fencing team entered the National Collegiate Athletic Association (NCAA) Fencing Championships held in the spring of 1947. We came in third place as a team. I won the saber championship, placed third in the foil championship, and was named an All-American in both weapons.

Influence and Opportunity

I enrolled in the master's degree program in psychology at Temple in the fall semester of 1947 (Temple did not have a Ph.D. program at the time). I found the clinically oriented courses to be most interesting. They were taught by Dr. James Page, who had co-authored a good text on abnormal psychology with Carney Landis, an influential psychologist at Columbia University. I became convinced that the new profession of clinical psychology was the career path for me. I received my M.A. in psychology at the end of the summer school session of 1948.

On the advice of Dr. Page, I applied to and was accepted by Worcester State Hospital in Worcester, Massachusetts. I chose Worcester State because of its recognized importance in the history of internship training programs in clinical psychology. In September of 1948, I started my training. The psychology section was headed by Dr. Eliot Rodnick, a Clark Hull Ph.D. from Yale University. My training at Worcester State included intensive experience in diagnostic testing of a variety of patients with mental illness, especially psychotic depressions, schizophrenia, and organic brain disorders. In the spring of the year, Rodnick accepted a position for the following fall at Duke University as director of their clinical psychology training program. Incidentally, several months after I arrived, I learned that one of the reasons I had been accepted was my NCAA championship in fencing that I had listed on my resume, another instance where my fencing had helped determine my future.

My most important life experience during the internship was that I met my future wife, Mildred Benson. She was a Tufts-trained occupational therapist and on the staff of Worcester State Hospital. We were married on September 10, 1949, in Worcester and left immediately for a honeymoon trip to Duke University in North Carolina where I had been accepted into the Ph.D. program in clinical psychology.

Duke proved to be an excellent choice for my Ph.D. The Duke faculty had a firm commitment to the scientist–practitioner model. Further, the Ph.D. program required a minor. Clinical psychology graduate students could take a special split minor of cultural anthropology and neuroanatomy. I selected that option. The neuroanatomy course was taught by Dr. Duncan Hetherington, who taught in the Duke Medical School. It was so interesting that I took a second course with him in brain modeling, using the Johns Hopkins model. This course consisted of 120 hours of working on brain specimens and slides to produce our own model of the brain from the spinal cord to the cortex. By the end of this course, I felt that I really had mastered the neuroanatomy of the brain. In addition to the graduate courses in psychology, I also took advanced clinical practicums at the Durham Child Guidance Clinic and Duke University Hospital, the latter under Dr. Louis Cohen.

I spent two years of intensive work at Duke and finished all requirements except the dissertation. In the spring of 1951, Dr. Berkeley from the research service of Worcester State Hospital contacted me and offered me a research position on a new project beginning in September of 1951. With the approval of my dissertation chair, Rodnick, I accepted the job offer from Worcester with the explicit understanding that I could do my dissertation on some aspect of the project that was not part of the original proposal.

After we arrived back in Worcester, I worked on a major research project on stress responses in schizophrenia. This was a joint project with the Worcester Foundation for Experimental Biology. The foundation was headed by Hudson Hoagland, known for his work on the importance of potassium in the brain. My part of the project included developing a psychological stress test (a success–failure experience) as well as data management and reduction. My first two published papers were from data collected on the project. My dissertation also was based on data collected with the normal controls of the project: I successfully tested the hypothesis that performance under failure stress could be predicted from perceptual and psychosocial variables.

During this period, I also participated in the training of clinical psychology interns. The national prominence of our internship training program was such that we had excellent students. For example, Raymond Fowler and Charles Spielberger, both of whom later became presidents of the American Psychological Association, were interns while I was on the research staff. We also had a constant stream of visiting lecturers, one of whom was Ward Halstead. Halstead was an impressive person. He was dapperly dressed, had a professorial air about him and a good delivery. In his talk he described how a battery of tests he had developed could be used to diagnose brain damage and also to lateralize and localize brain lesions. Our group, still heavily influenced by Kurt Goldstein's theory and tests, thought that his presentation sounded too good to be true. We also got the impression that he was trying to sell his battery: the rumor was that it would cost $5,000, a hefty sum in those days. Nevertheless, the quantification of his techniques impressed me, and I resolved at the time to learn more about them.

I defended my dissertation at Duke in April of 1954. A month afterward, I was invited to join the faculties of the Duke School of Medicine's Department of Psychiatry (two-thirds time) and the Duke University Department of Psychology (one-third time) as an assistant professor in both departments to begin July 1, 1954. I readily accepted. Our family of four, having added a girl and a boy during the three years at Worcester, moved back to Durham in the summer of 1954.

Duke University

My primary office was in the Department of Psychiatry housed in the Duke Hospital complex. Dr. Ewald Busse, a psychiatrist, was chair of our department. The psychology group was headed by Dr. Louis Cohen, an experienced clinical psychologist who had been teaching and supervising graduate students in clinical work for many years. He was a good tutor for someone like myself—a new Ph.D. who was not familiar with the politics and procedures of medical schools. I was in charge of inpatient psychological services. Cases were handled by interns and sometimes practicum students under my supervision. Dr. Charles Spielberger, whom we recruited at the end of his Worcester State Hospital internship, managed outpatient psychological services. I conducted the assessment seminar for our interns, and Charley conducted the therapy seminar. I was also the Assistant Director of Internship Training. Our internship was a joint one between the University and the Durham Veterans Administration Hospital located about one mile from our hospital.

My service had many referrals from the Neurology Department. One of the neurologists, Dr. Heyman, also headed the VA Neurology Service. I was a consultant to the VA psychology service and in that role had much contact with him. He proposed that we have a weekly joint case conference, one that would involve neurology, psychiatry, and clinical psychology. Each week a patient would be worked up and presented by a neurology resident, a psychiatry resident, and an intern in clinical psychology. This case conference was a great success. The neurology service at the VA was also part of a multi-site investigation of the possible therapeutic value of isoniazid in the treatment of multiple sclerosis (MS). My first research project at our VA was to investigate whether flicker detection could be used to measure the damage to the optic nerve in MS patients. It could. My second project was to investigate whether abstracting abilities were impaired in such patients, and indeed they were. The first study laid the groundwork for my first extra-mural grant—"Flicker–Fusion Visual Fields in the Brain-Damaged." This was a three-year grant from the National Institute of Neurological Diseases and Blindness (NINDB) awarded in 1958. This initial grant was followed by others from NINDB, over subsequent years.

In 1956, Cohen and I visited Dr. Ralph Reitan's laboratory in Indianapolis for a firsthand look at the Halstead battery. We were considering adopting it for a project on adolescents who had a history of neonatal asphyxia. Ralph graciously had the procedures demonstrated to us and spent much time discussing his current research on lateralization and localization of brain lesions. We were very impressed with his data and arranged for him to give a colloquium at Duke Hospital on his research. He did give the talk, and the reaction of the psychologists, psychiatrists, neurologists, and neurosurgeons who attended it was uniformly positive. Time constraints on the project, however, precluded inclusion of this battery.

In 1958, I was in charge of the Department of Psychiatry's colloquium series. Among other guest speakers, I was able to get the noted Duke parapsychologist, J. B. Rhine, to give a presentation on parapsychology. He did so in a very humble and scientific fashion, emphasizing the tentative nature of the findings. We all thought that we had misjudged the man; however, several weeks later, I happened to tune in on a radio program where he was addressing a lay group. No longer was he emphasizing the tentative nature of parapsychology; rather he sounded like a true believer who was continually searching for ways to prove something that he was sure existed.

In the summer of 1959, I was promoted to Associate Professor with tenure in both the Medical School and the Department of Psychology. My wife and I were also the proud parents of a third child and were settled members of the Duke University community. My future seemed to be assured. Then a phone call changed our lives.

Dr. Louis Jolyon (Jolly) West, from the University of Oklahoma College of Medicine, called to ask if I would be interested in a position as head of the Division of Behavioral Sciences in his Department of Psychiatry and Behavioral Sciences. I went to Oklahoma City, the site of the College of Medicine, as a candidate for the position. What I found surprised me. The position not only was one of heading up a Division of Behavioral Sciences but also involved the development of a program of psychological services for the University and Children's Hospitals. West had a firm commitment to the teaching of relevant material from the behavioral sciences to medical students and residents. The potentials of the programs, as set out by West, were so attractive that I had to give the position much more serious consideration than I had expected. After discussions with my wife, I accepted the position. I was appointed as Professor in the Department of Psychiatry and Behavioral Sciences at University of Oklahoma Health Sciences Center in Oklahoma City (OUHSC) and the Department of Psychology on the Norman Campus.

My Duke experience had come to an end. It was a productive, exciting, and professionally maturing five years. It had prepared me well for a leadership role, thanks especially to Cohen and Rodnick. Most of my older colleagues in the Medical School and the Department of Psychology were nationally or internationally known. My peer colleagues, the younger faculty members of the Department of Psychology, were all persons who eventually became top leaders in our profession and occupy or have retired from named chairs at other universities.

Oklahoma Health Sciences Center

We arrived in Oklahoma City in late October 1959. At OUHSC, I organized our teaching programs in the Behavioral Sciences for our first- and second-year medical students and taught most of the first-year students myself. I also developed and led a weekly seminar in behavioral sciences for our psychiatric residents covering language, communication, and symbols in myths and dreams. I recruited psychologists to develop psychological services for inpatient and outpatient diagnostic and treatment programs. In 1961, we started an internship training program in clinical psychology. It was approved by the American Psychological Association (APA) in 1962. In the mid-1960s, we expanded our internship to include the Oklahoma City Veterans Administration Hospital located on our OUHSC campus. This internship, modeled after the one we had at Duke, has had continuous APA approval up to the present and has trained 300 interns.

As a consultant to the VA, I was able to gain a laboratory setup in the VA Hospital for conducting research on brain-damaged patients. We broadened our research support by grants from NINDB to investigate the perceptual–cognitive and perceptual–motor functioning of patients with central nervous system (CNS) dysfunction. My colleague in this research was Arthur Vega. In 1961, we also estab-lished a psychological laboratory in the University Hospital to conduct psycholog-ical evaluations and research on psychiatric and CNS dysfunction patients. We both attended one of Ralph Reitan's early workshops on the Halstead Battery in 1961 and obtained the battery for our laboratory. It became an important compo-nent for our evaluation of known or suspected CNS patients.

By 1965, our teaching and research programs were well-established, and our faculty in psychology had grown considerably. West suggested that we should apply to the University of Oklahoma for permission to offer a master's degree in Behavioral Sciences, one that would be open to graduate students and to residents in psychiatry who had academic aspirations. I was asked to develop such a pro-gram. Working with my colleagues, Drs. Robert Edelberg, Frank Holloway, and Harold Williams, we developed two programs. The first was a well-formulated program leading to a master's degree in Behavioral Sciences, and the second was a much more tentative Ph.D. experimental psychology program in Biological Psy-chology. In 1966, we proposed our programs to the Academic Council. To our astonishment, the Ph.D. program in Biological Psychology was approved, but the master's degree in Behavioral Sciences was denied!

The Ph.D. program began in the fall of 1966 with a class of 10 graduate stu-dents. The program had three tracks: animal neuroscience and psychopharmacol-ogy, human neuropsychology, and psychophysiology–electrophysiology. The stu-dents took basic courses in all three areas and then went on to one of the more specialized tracks. I was away the first year of the program. In early 1965, I had applied for a Fulbright professorship to teach at the University of Copenhagen. My former colleague from Duke, Norman Garmezy, had a Fulbright and suggested that I should apply because the Psychology Department in Copenhagen was look-ing for someone to teach for a year in the brain–behavior area. The Fulbright awards are quite competitive; however, I was "at the right place at the right time" and received the award.

Our family moved to Copenhagen in early September of 1966. At the Univer-sity, I organized and led a seminar on the history of neuropsychology in the first semester and a seminar on neuropsychological findings in adult and child patients in the second semester. Two of the students came to our Center in Oklahoma for advanced training the year after taking my seminars. The year at Copenhagen Uni-versity was very productive. Not only did I have the time to organize two neu-ropsychological courses, but also I became much more familiar with British, Euro-pean, and Russian contributors to neuropsychology. The writings of the Russian neurologist–psychologist A. R. Luria made a deep impression on my thinking. I also prepared a renewal of my grant on brain-damaged patients and a new grant to study alcoholism's effects on cognitive–perceptual functioning. Both were funded in the following year. I gave invited Fulbright lectures in Oslo, Norway, the Univer-sity of Lund in Sweden, Maudsley Hospital in London, and universities in Milan and Catatonia, Italy. In Milan, I met Ennio DeRenzi, an outstanding neurologist and editor of *Cortex*, one of the few journals at that time that was devoted to brain–behavior research. Several years later, we had DeRenzi give a talk to our department in Oklahoma.

We returned to Oklahoma City in August of 1967. I learned that I had been recognized for my research achievements by the award of a George Lynn Cross Research Professorship. I began teaching my neuropsychology courses in our Ph.D. program in Biological Psychology and supervising graduate students who were working in my laboratories. In early 1968, we were notified by the National Institute of Mental Health that a proposal by West to establish a Center for Alcohol and Drug-Related Behaviors on our campus was to be funded. My project, to study alcoholism's effect on cognitive–perceptual functioning from a neuropsychological perspective, was one of the proposed projects approved for funding.

In 1969, West resigned as chair of our department to become the chair of the Department of Psychiatry at UCLA. He was an innovator in medical school curricula. His introduction of a teaching program in the behavioral sciences into our medical school curriculum was one of the first, if not the first, in the nation's medical schools. It was widely regarded as a model for such programs. He had a longstanding interest in brain–behavior relationships as well as dynamic psychiatry. He supported our psychology and social work training programs wholeheartedly. West had a profound effect on my career, probably more so than any other professional.

He was succeeded as chair in 1969 by Gordon Deckert, M.D., a talented teacher, therapist, and administrator. In 1970, our department was reorganized on a more functional basis. I was made vice-chair, and we had three councils that handled the three main functions of the department (i.e., education, research, and service). Under Deckert's leadership, the teaching and research programs of the department flourished despite occasional state funding problems. Vega and I were collaborating in productive research, and my Ph.D. students were doing dissertations on the neuropsychology of alcoholism. We had an active program of invited speakers in clinical neuropsychology, among them Arthur Benton, whose approach to research on clinical neuropsychological problems was one that I greatly admired; Anne-Lise Christensen, the Luria-trained neuropsychologist whose clinical work was impressive; and Ralph Reitan, whose work had influenced us for several decades.

In 1975, Vega resigned and was replaced by Dr. George Prigatano, who had just completed his internship in clinical psychology with us. Prigatano accepted another position in 1978. After a national search for a person who could direct our internship training program in clinical psychology and also head the neuropsychological laboratory, we selected Dr. Russell Adams, a talented and experienced clinical neuropsychologist and internship supervisor. With the presence of Adams in 1978, I started our postdoctoral training program in clinical neuropsychology, one of the four oldest of such training programs in the country. It has continued up until the present under the direction of Adams.

Between 1978 and 1991, my activities centered on our alcohol research program. (I became Executive Director of the Alcohol Center in 1985.) In addition, I was teaching in the Ph.D. Biological Psychology program and supervising clinical neuropsychology assessment experiences of clinical psychology interns and post-doctoral trainees. Activities with professional neuropsychological organizations, reviewing articles submitted for publication in a variety of psychological journals, and national research grant review committees consumed a lot of time. Much of my time also was involved in writing journal articles and book chapters and in editing a book on the neuropsychology of alcoholism (Parsons, Butters, & Nathan, 1987). In the course of preparing that book, I had intensive contact with the late Nelson Butters. We had numerous discussions by phone. I could always tell Nelson was calling. His pronounced New England accent when he said "Hello, Oscah Pah-sons" left no doubt as to the caller. Nelson was a stimulating colleague and friend. His theory-driven research provided a model that influenced my research efforts. I retired from the University in 1991 with the title of George Lynn Cross Research Professor Emeritus.

Professional and Scientific Contributions to the Field of Neuropsychology

I am fortunate to have been among the early contributors to the development of the present-day professional and scientific aspects of clinical neuropsychology. I have grouped professional contributions under three major headings: program development and teaching, organizational activities, and overviews of the field and awards. Scientific contributions are grouped under two main headings: studies of patients with brain dysfunction or damage and studies of the effects of alcohol and alcoholism on neuropsychological functions.

Program Development and Teaching

As noted earlier, I started a postdoctoral training program in clinical neuropsy-chology that is nationally recognized as one of the oldest and best. I was centrally involved in the development of our Ph.D. program in experimental biological psychology and was responsible for the human neuropsychology track up until the time I retired. My courses in neuropsychology were among the first to be listed by that specific name in a university catalog. Most of my Ph.D. students have had additional clinical training and are working as clinical neuropsychologists. Dr. Ralph Tarter, now Professor of Psychiatry and Neurology at the University of Pittsburgh, is probably the most eminent. I have had several postdoctoral students in the biological psychology program—most notable of these is Sara Jo Nixon, now Professor and Associate Director of our Center for Alcohol and Drug-Related Studies. I have taught neuropsychological assessment in seminars and case conferences to several hundred clinical psychology interns and postdoctoral fellows at Duke and OUHSC, and supervised the clinical work of those trainees until I retired. Among my former interns, George Prigatano has made outstanding contributions to the treatment of brain-injured patients.

Organizational Activities

I was an early member of the International Neuropsychological Society and served on the Board of Directors of that organization from 1980 to 1983. I was one of two persons nominated for president of the organization in 1984 but lost to Dr. Muriel Lezak. From 1983 to 1987, I was a member of the first American Board of Clinical Neuropsychology and helped develop the methods and procedures used in the diplomate examination. I participated as an examiner of candidates for several years. In 1991, I was elected to serve as president of the American Psychological Association Division 40, Clinical Neuropsychology, and served from 1992 to 1993. From 1994 to 1998, I served on the Levitt Early Career Award Committee.

I have served as a member and chair of four national grant review committees. For each of these committees, I was responsible for grants involving basic or clinical neuropsychology. The committees were VA National Merit Review Committee for Research in Psychiatry and Behavioral Sciences (1977–1980), NIMH Psychological Sciences Subcommittee on Research Training (1980–1984), NIAAA Alcohol Psychosocial Research Review Committee (1985–1989), and the Behavioral Science Advisory Council of the Alcoholic Beverage Medical Research Foundation (1990–1996).

I am an ABPP diplomate in Clinical Psychology and Clinical Neuropsychology and a diplomate in Assessment Psychology. I am a Fellow in APA Divisions 6 (Behavioral Neuroscience and Comparative Psychology), 12 (Clinical Psychology), 38 (Health Psychology), 40 (Clinical Neuropsychology), and 50 (Addiction).

Overviews and Awards in Clinical Neuropsychology

I have produced three overview papers on the status of the profession of clinical neuropsychology, two of which were associated with awards. The first paper was one that I consider to be one of my best. It was a chapter entitled "Clinical Neuropsychology" and was published in 1970 (Parsons, 1970). I reviewed the progress and current status of the "new subspeciality" of clinical neuropsychology and predicted a glowing future for this new discipline.

In 1990, I received the National Academy of Neuropsychology's Award, "Distinguished Clinical Neuropsychologist," and used that occasion to review the status of clinical neuropsychology at that time (Parsons, 1991). I concluded that there was every indication that clinical neuropsychology would continue to be a challenging, vital, and expanding profession. In 1997, I received the Benton Lectureship Award from the American Psychological Foundation. I used the lecture to again review the current status of the profession and the factors that contributed to its impressive growth; however, I pointed out that the unforeseen rapid shift to managed care business approaches to health care posed very real problems for the future of our profession (Parsons, 1997).

Scientific Contributions: Studies of Patients with Brain Damage or Brain Dysfunction

After my first study on flicker–fusion discrimination impairment in patients with multiple sclerosis, I was impressed with what deficits in speed of information processing might tell us about the functioning of the brain. Over the years, I have continued to pursue this interest in studies that can be grouped as flicker–fusion studies (Parsons & Huse, 1958; Vega, Parsons, & Chandler, 1966), reaction time studies (Bruhn & Parsons, 1971; Holloway & Parsons, 1972), and efficiency studies (Glenn & Parsons, 1990, 1992). I have cited several of the more important papers for each group. The first two groupings consistently point to reduced speed of information processing in the damaged or dysfunctional brain and indicate that such measures can lateralize lesions. The studies of efficiency indicate that more molar measures of time (e.g., time taken to perform untimed neuropsychological tests) also discriminate between patients with brain dysfunction (in this case alcoholics) and controls. Our overall conclusion was that time taken to perform any intellectual or cognitive–perceptual task is a useful measure in the assessment of brain-compromised persons.

I also have made a substantial contribution to clinical neuropsychology research methodology. In 1967, Vega and I published a cross-validation of the Halstead–Reitan Battery (Vega & Parsons, 1967). We also emphasized that age and education should be considered in impairment scores, suggested that T-scores should be used rather than cut-off scores, and noted that there might be regional differences in patients that should be considered in establishing norms.

We have published two papers on methodology in clinical neuropsychology research and have made suggestions for the improvement of that research. The first and most important of the papers was entitled "Methodological Considerations in Neuropsychological Research" (Parsons & Prigatano, 1978). In the first issue of the *Journal of Clinical Neuropsychology* (now the *Journal of Experimental and Clinical Neuropsychology*), the editors advised reading our article before conducting research or submitting research articles for publication. The second paper was invited by the journal *Psychological Assessment* (Prigatano, Parsons, & Bortz, 1995). In that paper, we extended the scope of our previous paper to include additional contemporary issues such as the need to use techniques developed in cognitive psychology. Other areas of contribution that have been recognized in the literature are studies of lateralization (Gaede, Parsons, & Bertera, 1978; Parsons, Vega, & Burn, 1969) and psychophysiological functioning (Holloway & Parsons, 1971, 1972) in brain-damaged patients. Largely on the basis of these contributions and those to be covered below, I was given an award—Distinguished Scientific Contribution to Clinical Psychology—by Division 12 of the American Psychological Association in 1987.

Scientific Contributions:
Effects of Alcoholism on Neuropsychological Functions

There is little doubt that the work for which I am best known currently stems from our extensive publications and presentations in this area. Although we conducted studies on the acute effects of alcohol, especially ascending and descending limb effects on cognitive functions (Chandler & Parsons, 1977; Jones & Parsons, 1975), our more important work is on the cognitive–perceptual deficits in sober alcoholics. Starting with our first publication (Jones & Parsons, 1971) and continuing to the present, we have contributed over 140 papers and chapters to the world literature on that topic. Our studies have made empirical and theoretical contributions.

At the empirical level, we have demonstrated in numerous studies that sober alcoholics manifest deficits on a variety of neuropsychological tests, including measures of learning, memory, abstracting, verbal problem-solving, perceptual analysis and synthesis, perceptual-motor speed, speed of information processing, and efficiency (Parsons, 1993, 1994, 1998). We also have demonstrated that male and female alcoholics have essentially the same pattern and degree of deficits on the neuropsychological tests. We have conducted a number of studies to determine whether the neuropsychological impairment might be due to variables other than alcoholism per se. For example, the impairment could result from drinking practices, severity of alcoholism, family history of alcoholism, altered motivation for test taking, pretest expectancies concerning performance, childhood conduct disorder, attention deficit disorder, antisocial personality behaviors, or depression and anxiety. On the biological side, we have investigated the possible effects or influences of aging, event-related potentials, male sex hormones, menstrual cycle, cortisol levels, blood pressure, and general medical status. We have found no consistent effects of these variables that would attenuate the neuropsychological differences between alcoholics and controls.

Another series of studies was designed to determine whether alcoholics' neuropsychological functioning would improve over time if they remained sober. Our three longitudinal studies suggested that some neuropsychological deficits persist up to 22 months. Our cross-sectional study suggested that after an interval of four years, considerable improvement may occur. We have demonstrated that resumption of drinking can be predicted by poor neuropsychological test performance, depressive symptoms, psychosocial adaptation and event-related potentials, consistent with the formulation of alcoholism as a biopsychosocial disorder. Theoretical contributions included testing four brain–behavior hypotheses that might explain neuropsychological deficits in alcoholism: (a) the "frontal lobe" hypothesis (i.e., alcohol primarily affects frontal lobe functions); (b) the "right hemisphere" hypothesis (i.e., alcohol affects the functions of the right hemisphere to a greater extent than the well-organized, language-dominant functions of the left hemisphere); (c) the "generalized–diffuse" hypothesis (i.e., alcohol affects all areas of the brain); and (d) the "premature aging" hypothesis (i.e., alcohol's effects on the brain are similar to the effects of aging). My overall conclusion is that the "generalized–diffuse" hypothesis best fits the extensive neuropsychological data obtained in our laboratories.

A second theoretical contribution has resulted from our studies of the possible causes of the individual differences in vulnerability to neuropsychological deficits in alcoholics. From these studies I have concluded that the most likely reason for these individual differences lies in a genetically determined variability in brain vulnerability to alcohol's effects.

A third theoretical contribution is our support of a hypothesized continuum of alcohol's effects ranging from the neuropsychological deficits found in most sober alcoholics to mild deficits and inefficiencies in neuropsychological performance in heavy-to-moderate, sober social drinkers. In our recent review of social drinking effects (Parsons & Nixon, 1998), we found sufficient evidence to propose the following: ingesting five or six U.S. Standard drinks (USSD), five to seven days per week, results in mild neuropsychological inefficiencies or deficits; ingesting more than that results in moderate neuropsychological deficits.

For these empirical and theoretical contributions, I have received the following awards: Distinguished Research Award, Research Society on Alcoholism, 1997; Tharp Foundation Award for Contributions to Research on Alcoholism, 1997 (Memphis, TN); and the Jellinek Award for Distinguished Contributions to the Neuropsychology of Alcoholism, 1998 (Jellinek Foundation, Toronto, Canada).

The Future of Neuropsychology

In my opinion, the future of the basic science aspects of neuropsychology is one of exciting expansion. The developments in genetics, computer science, cognitive science, and neuroscience will continue to fuel the experimental and theoretical activities of the basic science neuropsychologist much as they have for the last decade. To a somewhat lesser extent this will hold true also for the clinical neuropsychologist.

There is no doubt that clinical neuropsychology has had a spectacular growth during the latter half of the twentieth century (Parsons, 1991, 1997). In this decade, however, our profession, in common with other health professions, is currently facing severe challenges posed by Managed Care Organizations (MCOs). Payments for what MCOs judge to be unnecessary, prolonged or insufficiently validated services are likely to be greatly reduced or not approved. Frequently, clinician recommendations for treatment are not accepted. These practices have had deleterious effects on practice and income (Phelps, 1997).

I believe the solution, in part, lies in advocacy. Each of us must take an active leadership role in streamlining and validating our assessment techniques and establishing the efficacy of our treatment techniques. It means joining forces with our medical colleagues and other health professionals to reserve the clinical decision-making process for those who are best able to make such decisions—the trained professional clinicians. Finally, it means that we must actively support state and federal legislation that will prevent the excesses of MCOs.

I am optimistic about the outcome. Clinical neuropsychology has had and continues to have talented, forward-looking energetic leadership and a productive, well-trained, professionally oriented membership. We will surmount the current health profession challenges, but there is no doubt that future neuropsychologists will work under different conditions. Hopefully they will find the future to be as rewarding as the past.

196 PATHWAYS REMEMBERED

REFERENCES

Bruhn, P., & Parsons, O. A. (1971). Continuous reaction time in brain damage. *Cortex, 7,* 278–291.

Chandler, B. C. & Parsons. O. A. (1977). Altered hemispheric functioning under alcohol. *Journal of Studies on Alcohol, 38,* 389–391.

Gaede, S., Parsons, O. A. & Bertera, J. H. (1978). Hemispheric differences in music perception: Aptitude vs. experience. *Neuropsychologia, 16,* 379–374.

Glenn, S. W., & Parsons, O. A. (1990). The role of time in neuropsychological performance: Investigation and application in an alcoholic population. *The Clinical Neuropsychologist, 4,* 344–354.

Glenn, S. W., & Parsons, O. A. (1992). Neuropsychological efficiency measures in male and female alcoholics. *Journal of Studies on Alcohol, 53,* 546–552.

Holloway, F. A., & Parsons, O. A. (1971). Habituation of the orienting reflex in brain-damaged patients. *Psychophysiology, 8,* 623–634.

Holloway, F. A. & Parsons, O. A. (1972). Physiological concomitants of reaction time performance in normal and brain-damaged subjects. *Psychophysiology, 9,* 189–198.

Jones, B., & Parsons, O. A. (1971). Impairment of abstracting ability in chronic alcoholics. *Archives of General Psychiatry, 25,* 71–75.

Jones, B., & Parsons, O. A. (1975). Alcohol and consciousness: Getting high, coming down. *Psychology Today, 8,* 53–58.

Parsons, O. A. (1970). Clinical neuropsychology. In C. D. Spielberger (Ed.), *Current topics in clinical and community psychology, Vol. II* (pp. 1–60). New York: Academic Press.

Parsons, O. A. (1991). Clinical neuropsychology, 1970–1990: A personal view. *Archives of Clinical Neuropsychology, 6,* 105–111.

Parsons, O. A. (1993). Impaired neuropsychological cognitive functioning in sober alcoholics. In W. A. Hunt & S. J. Nixon (Eds.), *Alcohol-induced brain damage.* NIAAA Monograph. (pp. 173–194). Washington, DC: NIAAA.

Parsons, O. A. (1994). Determinants of cognitive deficits in alcoholics: The search continues. *The Clinical Neuropsychologist, 8,* 39–58.

Parsons, O. A. (1997). Clinical neuropsychology *in the decade of the brain.* Paper presented at the Annual Meeting of the American Psychological Association, Chicago, IL.

Parsons, O. A. (1998). Neurocognitive deficits in alcoholics and social drinkers: A continuum? *Alcoholism: Clinical and Experimental Research, 22,* 954–961.

Parsons, O. A., Butters, N., & Nathan, P. E. (1987). *Neuropsychology of alcoholism: Implications for diagnosis and treatment.* New York: Guilford Press.

Parsons, O. A., & Huse (1958). Impairment of flicker discrimination in brain-damaged patients. *Neurology, 8,* 750–755.

Parsons, O. A., & Nixon, S. J. (1998). Cognitive functioning in sober social drinkers: A review of the research since 1986. *Journal of Studies on Alcohol, 59,* 180–190.

Parsons, O. A., & Prigatano, G. P. (1978). Methodological considerations in clinical neuropsychological research. *Journal of Consulting and Clinical Psychology, 46,* 608–619.

Parsons, O. A., Vega, A., & Burn, J. (1969). Different psychological effects of lateralized brain damage. *Journal of Consulting and Clinical Psychology, 33,* 551–557.

Phelps, R. (1997). Profiling Division 40 members: The CAPP practitioner survey. *Division of Clinical Psychology Newsletter, 40* (15) 5–7.

Prigatano, G. P., Parsons, O. A., & Bortz, J. J. (1995). Methodological considerations in clinical neuropsychological research. *Psychological Assessment, 7,* 396–403.

Vega, A., & Parsons, O. A. (1967). Cross-validation of the Halstead–Reitan tests for brain damage. *Journal of Consulting Psychology, 31,* 619–625.

Vega, A., Parsons, O. A., & Chandler, P. (1966). Localization of brain lesions by flicker–fusion perimetry: A quantitative method. *Cortex, 2,* 213–221.

13

Autobiography in Anecdote
The Founding of Experimental Neuropsychology

Karl H. Pribram

*I*n these days of competitive grant writing and large-scale projects, it is difficult to remember that research can be fun. The founding of neuropsychology incorporated a good deal of horseplay despite the seriousness and dedication of the protagonists involved. In this paper I will relate some anecdotes that display the human side of the scientific process—the motivations and emotions that are hidden from view in the publications that result from research.

Antecedents in Physiological Behaviorism

The story begins at the Johns Hopkins University in the first decade of the twentieth century with John Watson, who had gathered a small group of young men that included Ivory Shepard Franz and Karl Lashley. Their gospel was that every psychological process is accompanied by a measurable behavioral manifestation. The target behavior consisted of a muscular contraction or an endocrine secretion. The brain acted as coordinator, and it is this coordination that is, on occasion, experienced as a psychological process. This physiological behaviorism differed considerably from the stimulus–response behaviorism and the operant behaviorism that followed. Stimulus–response behaviorism was primarily a study of measurable environmental input–output relations in which the role of the physiology of the organism was inferred in terms of constructs and intervening variables. Operant conditioning, that supplanted stimulus–response behaviorism, was again a totally environmental enterprise, this time a study of response–stimulus relations in which the response of the organism became the stimulus for modifying (reinforcing or deterring) subsequent behavior.

But at Hopkins, before all these developments in behavioral psychology, the young men interested in the *physiological* manifestations of psychological processes were naturally attracted to those of their girlfriends. So they set out to measure vaginal contractions and secretions under conditions of sexual arousal. As was the case many decades later in the experiments of William Masters and

197

Virginia Johnson, these young men had no difficulty in recruiting female participants into the experiments. Young women appeared to be curious about their
own sexual functions and welcomed scientific explorations of their sexuality.
Unfortunately, the administration of the University during these Edwardian times
was not as enlightened as the subjects, and Watson was relieved of his professorship, and the group disbanded. Over the long range, Lashley did not abandon this
interest in sexual behavior, whether of bees, birds, or humans. Shortly, he pro-
cured a set of pornographic movies, showed them in theaters around the country,
had the viewers answer a set of questions, and hastily beat it out of town. With
regard to reports of these early studies, Lashley used them as examples of instinc-
tual behavior.

At the end of one colloquium in which Lashley presented his fascinating
findings with birds, I asked him for his definition of instinct. He replied with
other examples, and I countered that he had, as yet, not provided a definition.
This went on through three more rounds of questions and answers. Finally,
Lashley said, "Dr. Pribram, in this life one has the option of being vague or
wrong. On this occasion I choose to remain vague." (We addressed each other as
Dr. Lashley and Dr. Pribram for years—until his wife died. At that time he
wrote me a treasured note, saying that it was time we called each other Karl and
that, as he was childless, he considered me to be the closest thing he had to a
son.)

Lashley had become head of the Sex Committee of the National Academy of
Sciences, and one of his accomplishments was to interest a fellow zoologist to con-
tinue assessing the sexuality of the American people. The result: the path-breaking
Kinsey reports.

After Lashley's departure from the committee in the 1950s Frank Beach took
over as chair, and I became a member. After a few years, it seemed to us that the
National Institutes of Health were providing adequate funding, and therefore our
committee was no longer needed. I argued long and hard that we could provide
funding for research on cognitive differences between men and women, but the
committee members were interested in sex, not cognition—this despite the fact
that Frank Beach had shown that female sexual behavior in the cat is seriously disrupted by brain resections restricted to the cerebral cortex. (I had done the
anatomical reconstructions for this experiment.) The committee disbanded, but I
was later able to pursue my interest in this topic in collaboration with Diane
McGuinness who joined my laboratory group during the 1970s.

When Watson's research team broke up, Lashley turned, for the most part, to
the politically safer pursuit of studying brain function. He joined Ivory Shepard
Franz at St. Elizabeth's Hospital, a government neuropsychiatric establishment
where Franz was performing a series of brain resection experiments on monkeys.
With their newly found behaviorism, Franz and Lashley tried to pin down the
behavioral manifestations of brain injury. What impressed Lashley most about the
results was that very few specific changes seemed to occur; rather, behavioral functions in general seemed to be blunted. Turning to rat experiments later, this

impression was fortified and ultimately led to Lashley's doctrines of mass action and equipotentiality of cortical function as enunciated in his monograph, *Brain Mechanisms and Intelligence* (Lashley, 1923).

The Name of the Game

I first met Lashley in 1946 when I began the practice of neurosurgery in Jacksonville, Florida. I had asked Lashley whether I might conduct some research at the Yerkes Laboratories for Primate Biology in Florida, which he was heading. He was delighted, since he was looking for a neurosurgeon to help him. I told him how happy I was to have the opportunity to work with him, as I thought he had died many years earlier. I had obtained a copy of his book, *Brain and Intelligence*, for ten cents, and I teased him, saying his ideas were of nineteenth-century vintage. We had a delightful interchange that came to fruition in a plan to perform experiments on monkeys and apes to help resolve the discrepancies between the results of his studies on rats and my knowledge derived from human clinical lesions (which Lashley knew of from his extensive reading of the literature). The issue between us was whether the brain was organized into systems, each of which served a separate psychological process. Lashley had no problem with localized systems serving sensory and motor functions—his point was that the brain functions involved in higher-order psychological process, which today we would label cognitive, were distributed over much of the cerebral cortex. My view stemmed from clinical observations of specific agnosias (cognitive deficits) from lesions in different parts of the human brain. The program of research we inaugurated resolved the issue, to my satisfaction at least. To a large extent we were both right: the resolution was published in "Localization and Distribution of Function in the Brain" (Pribram, 1982) and "The Deep and Surface Structure of Memory" (Pribram, 1997).

Some of the fun in research comes during discussions, at lunch, at colloquia, and so on. On one such occasion at the Yerkes Laboratories, Lashley and I posed the problem of finding a name for our type of research. Lashley, a zoologist, preferred the name "psychobiology"; I, as a neurosurgeon, opted for "neuropsychology." Our model for our choices was the term "biochemistry"—the use of chemical techniques to investigate biological problems. Thus Lashley, by this time no longer a behaviorist, wanted to use biological techniques including manipulations of brain function, to investigate psychological processes. I wanted to use behavioral techniques to investigate the organization of brain processes. The small luncheon group (we helped ourselves to the fruit and nuts meant for the laboratory animals) consisted of postdoctoral and graduate students: Bob Blum and Josephine Semmes-Blum-Evarts; Don Hebb; Austin Riesen; Roger Sperry; and Marjory Wade. We all were interested in brain (or at least sensory) function so, for the moment, the term "neuropsychology" won out.

"Sensory-Deprived," "Split," and "Lobectomized" Brains: Early Seminal Studies

Sensory development was of great interest to Riesen and Hebb. Lashley had found that sensory (visual) deprivation in infant cats resulted in only temporary (two to three week) impairment. When this was presented at colloquium, I pointed out that the situation was entirely different for humans: amblyopia-ex-anopsia, if not taken care of within the first two years of life, resulted in a severe and permanent deficit. When Hebb asked for references, I suggested any text-book of ophthalmology. Hebb found a monograph by von Zenden that described case histories of amblyopia-ex-anopsia patients who had been behav-iorally tested. Riesen wanted to know the effects of visual deprivation on chim-panzees, and Hebb wondered what would happen to human adults who were sensory deprived. Long lines of excellent research followed from these initial for-ays, culminating for brain science in the now classical findings of Torsten Wiesel and David Hubel on the degeneration of connectivity of developing cortical cells in the absence of sensory stimulation.

Our discussions of those days also led to other long lines of research. The sec-tioning of the corpus callosum to produce a "split brain" became a focus of interest for Roger Sperry. My findings of sensory-specific systems in the so-called "associa-tion" cortex of the parietal, temporal, and preoccipital regions of the brain, and methods to analyze the functions of the frontal "association" cortex, all stemmed from excited interchanges among us.

On the Taming of Spider Monkeys

One such interchange between Lashley and myself concerned the extent of the lesion that "tames" spider monkeys. Lashley was puzzled by the paradox of the very precise connectivity that bounded brain anatomical systems and the fact that psychological functions seemed to be distributed and "determined by masses of excitation, by form or relations or proportions of excitation within general fields of activity, without regard to particular nerve cells. It is the pattern, not the ele-ment that counts" (Lashley, 1942, p. 306). Thus, when I began to demonstrate localization within the "association" systems of the cortex or basal ganglia, he did not acknowledge the finding.

For instance, Lashley interpreted the dramatic taming of behavior following temporal lobectomy—observed first by Sanger-Brown and E. A. Schaefer and a half-century later by Paul Bucy and Heinrich Klüver—as due to an unintended extension of the lesion into the hypothalamic region. This would be more consis-tent with Lashley's anti-localizationist position. Having been Bucy's first neuro-surgical resident, I was confident of his surgical skills. I, therefore, decided to demonstrate that Lashley was incorrect about the extent of the lesion in these cases. Up to that point, no anatomical verification of the extent of the lesions had been documented, although both Lashley and I had tried to convince Klüver to sacrifice at least one of his animals to permit such verification. Klüver, however, was much more interested in the behavioral effects of the lesions Bucy had made, and in my visits to him, he proudly showed off a rather obese male rhesus monkey tamely sitting on his desk.

A few anecdotes regarding Lashley's views of the temporal lobe-lesioned monkeys are worth recounting. Having produced my first "tame" monkeys, I asked Lashley to come see them. He rather curtly told me he was too busy. So, a few weeks later, during a site visit from the Rockefeller Foundation, I took two of my tame spider monkeys by the hand and led them past Lashley and the site visitors who were looking at some chimpanzees. Lashley glanced up and saw me and the monkeys; he called out, "What do you have there Dr. Pribram?" I blandly replied, "Nothing you'd be interested in," and calmly walked on. Lashley came running after me, and we all laughed at the joke I had pulled on him.

Two things made this incident amusing: Lashley's beliefs about the effects of temporal lobe lesions and the fact that Lashley could not abide Spider monkeys— they always got the best of him. For example, on one occasion Lashley asked me to help clean the spiders' cages. I was to stand outside and shoo them out of their little huts while Lashley went into the enclosure to hose everything down. A few minutes after starting the process, I heard Lashley yelling, "Dr. Pribram, come here, come here, hurry." I went around to the front of the enclosure and saw Lashley cornered by several spider monkeys holding and accurately directing the hose onto Lashley. I howled with laughter, went in, and retrieved the hose. This was easy, as I had established a close and warm relationship with the spider monkeys.

Thus, Lashley's surprise when I paraded the two spider monkeys before him. Although he trusted my surgery to some extent, to see his mortal adversaries docile and led by the hand was a bit too much. I believe I succeeded in conveying my point about the effects of the focal surgical ablation. Among many other events, episodes such as these led to a deep and enduring friendship between us.

Experimental Neurosurgery and Early Neuropsychology

Lashley was a terrible brain surgeon. Good as his anatomical techniques were, his surgical technique was poor—to some extent, I believe, deliberately so. He would sew up wounds with a simple through-and-through stitch from dura (if there was any left intact) to skin. This was a perfect route for brain infection to take hold, especially since Lashley did not believe in aseptic technique (and sulfonamides and antibiotics were not as yet available). For making brain lesions in rats, Lashley had used his wife's curling iron and simply burned off the cortex to be removed. And for rats, sterile technique is unnecessary. But it must be remembered that brain research in general was crude in Lashley's day unless carried out by neurosurgeons. For instance, Ivan Pavlov complains in his 1924 volume on conditioning, that unfortunately none of his dogs survived brain surgery: they either succumbed to brain abscesses or to epilepsy. I succeeded only partly in "training" Lashley to sterile technique—and that only after the occurrence of an unfortunate brain abscess in a chimpanzee after he had insisted on drawing a ruler out of his hip pocket to measure the extent of a proposed resection.

But even in surgery it was not a one-way street as to who was learning. One Saturday I came to the laboratory with two of my nurses to perform a temporal lobectomy on a chimpanzee. One of the nurses was skilled in anesthesia, the other an excellent scrub nurse. We brought a flask of human blood along, which we had matched for blood type to that of the chimpanzee to be operated upon. I anticipated a rather difficult procedure due to the thickness and configuration of the chimpanzee skull and so wanted to have everything well prepared.

I walked into surgery and found instead a complete mess; nothing had been cleaned or readied for the task ahead. I was furious and let everyone know: opportunities to get a surgical staff together, even on weekends, were rare. I was calmed down by my nurse colleagues and left orders with Lashley and student helpers that the surgery be made ready. The nurses and I went out, sat on some benches (our luncheon spot), and thoroughly enjoyed some much needed fresh air and sunshine. In about an hour I went in to see how things were progressing with the cleanup: it was underway. Lashley was on his knees with a bucket of soapsuds and a cloth, scrubbing the floor!

Research at that time was not like medical or surgical practice: there was no backup team; you did it yourself, or it did not get done. The nurses and I pitched in, and within another hour and a half everything was ready. It turned out, as expected, a difficult access to the temporal lobe, but once the brain was properly exposed the rest of the procedure went smoothly. We finished around midnight, cleaned up, and went home around 2 a.m.

Neuropsychology was born of just such a mating between the traditions and practices of clinical neurology and neurosurgery with those of experimental psychology. Before that mating, the results of studies in both fields were flawed: human clinical studies by the difficulty in specifying the site and extent of a lesion, and the lack of sophistication in experimental design. I detailed these deficiencies in a 1954 paper entitled "Toward a Science of Neuropsychology" (Pribram, 1954).

Physiological psychologists fared no better; their lack of surgical skill and anatomical naïveté made it common knowledge that no two experimenters ever obtained the same results. Even the same experimenter could rarely replicate his or her own findings. As a result, Gary Boring (1950), in his *History of Experimental Psychology,* proclaimed that we know so little about how the brain operates in learning and remembering that it seems futile for psychologists to study brain science.

Combining the know-how of clinical neurology and neurosurgery with that of experimental psychology changed all that. Replicable results are now standard, and clinical neuropsychology, with the aid of new imaging techniques, continues to fuel the search for the relation between brain and conscious experiences. Neuropsychology has become a science.

My Transition to Yale

I had set my goal to teach as well as to do research, and teaching required a university appointment. Lashley wrote letters of recommendation to Harvard, Yale, and other universities (as he did for others, for example, Nico Tinbergen), often without receiving even the courtesy of a response. But fortunately Fred Mettler, with whom I had corresponded regarding his work on the basal ganglia, had initiated a project to study the effects of partial resections of the anterior frontal cortex in humans. Mettler (with Vernon Rowland) had shown that the site of entry for the standard Walter Freeman and J. W. Watts procedure for frontal lobotomy was Broca's area. My own experience with lesions of this area was that I had never seen a case of Broca's aphasia resulting from such damage. I had asked Percival Bailey, my mentor in neuropathology who had classified brain tumors, about his experience. He said that it was the same as mine, and furthermore it matched the experience of his teachers as well. It had been Pierre Janet who exposed the fallacy of Broca's localization, which had depended in part on the phrenological doctrine that speech, a special attribute of humans, was related to their uniquely high foreheads—ergo, speech must be localized in the frontal cortex.

Mettler's project included two resections of Broca's area in catatonic patients who had been mute for at least a decade. One of the patients began to speak fluently immediately after surgery; the other did so in about a week. I summarized these results and subsequent findings in my book *Languages of the Brain* (Pribram, 1971), to no avail. Imaging studies continue to assign the label Broca's area to a variety of precentral and midfrontal locations that become active during speech, areas that have little in common with the one signified by Paul Broca. The Mettler project was of great interest to me as I had been given a ward of psychiatric patients on whom I was to perform prefrontal lobotomies. I had asked Lashley's help in devising tests that I could administer both pre- and postoperatively to quantitatively assess the effects of the procedure. I also devised some tests of my own based on the hypothesis that the effect of the procedure was to shorten the duration of experiences such as pain and frustration. I had shown these effects to follow frontal resections in chimpanzees. But as I became acquainted with the patients and found them responsive to my psychotherapy, which consisted mainly of paying them heed, listening empathetically to their experiences, and training them on interpersonal skills, I became more and more reluctant to perform the surgery.

A similar situation arose later on when I was at Yale with patients scheduled for lobotomy who had been tested for six months with a bevy of biochemical procedures to assess their responsiveness to stress. The patients improved so much during the six months, that I questioned the need for surgery. The vote was to proceed anyway since we had put so much effort into the study. I resigned from the project and devoted myself to studies using monkeys. Animal rights agitators might question whether this decision was indeed as noble as I thought at the time.

The Mettler study provided me with the scientific knowledge I sought and thus made it easier for me to assess the necessity to perform lobotomies. The study was based not on crude lobotomies but on carefully performed resections limited to the cerebral cortex. I asked Mettler if I could visit, and he welcomed me enthusiastically, making me privy to all the preliminary results. None of the participants in the study had such access—surgeons, psychiatrists, psychologists, and biochemists were precluded from access to each other's data to assure a minimum of cross-biasing. The final result of this and the subsequent Columbia–Greystone study, aside from the Broca finding, was that the postoperative therapy, especially the charisma of the psychiatrist, was more important than the site of the frontal resection in assuring improvement.

Since I had traveled as far as New York to see Mettler, I decided to make an appointment with John Fulton at Yale as well. Bucy had advised me that the Yale laboratory was the "best place to do research." The Yale Library where Fulton agreed to meet me filled me with awe. The entrance was through a star-studded rotunda, and I was tempted to genuflect as I proceeded. Fulton's greeting was hearty, and he soon put me at ease. I told him of my findings with a patient who had localized seizures consisting of facial sweating as a result of a tumor localized to the precentral motor cortex and discussed how this fit with his own results showing cortical control over the autonomic nervous system. I also told him of my temporal lobe studies and my research with frontal lobectomized chimpanzees. The latter had shown results different from those Fulton published, and I wondered about the differences in procedure that could account for the disparate findings.

Fulton went to some shelves and picked out two volumes of protocols, gave them to me, showed me to a reading room and said, "These may have the answer. I'll pick you up for lunch at noon." At lunch (I don't recall where or what we ate—only our discussion), he asked whether I had found what I was looking for. I answered that I had. Fulton did not ask what I had found; he simply asked whether I would like to come to work at Yale. I was dumbfounded, told him how Lashley had written the Dean about me without receiving an answer, and how Bucy, during my residency, had so often spoken about the Fulton laboratory. I also told him about my experience with his *Physiology of the Nervous System* (Fulton, 1949) the weekend it was published. I had used it at the University of Chicago to answer Ralph Gerard's pithy final exam question: "Discuss the Organization of the Nervous System." I had received high praise for my writing—the best answer Gerard had ever received. Gerard became my mentor from then on.

Fulton told me that the Veterans Administration had informed him that if he could find a neurosurgeon, they would supply him with funds to study the functions of the frontal cortex of monkeys. Of course I accepted, and Fulton said he'd be in touch once he had definite word about the grant. Word came in a few months. I received a telegram asking me to start promptly, as Fulton was leaving for England. I gave a lecture to the Duval County Medical Society that I had committed myself to, performed my final surgical operations, and headed for Yale with a fever of 102 degrees Fahrenheit in the throes of a case of influenza. I had had a double virus pneumonia the winter before, but the excitement proved healing during my long drive, and by the time I arrived at Yale I was a bit weak but cured.

What I had learned from Fulton's meticulously detailed and honest protocols was that one of the two chimpanzees he had operated upon behaved postoperatively just as my Yerkes laboratory chimpanzees had done. One of the tasks used to assess the chimpanzees was the delayed response procedure. On this task, a reward is hidden within sight of the monkey, an opaque screen is lowered and then raised after a period of 5 to 15 (or more) seconds, and the monkey is then allowed to find the reward. Delayed response in one of Fulton's chimpanzees survived the lobectomy; she tested well on this task before and after the surgery. The other chimpanzee had been "neurotic" prior to surgery and had failed to test properly. After surgery, she was relieved of her neurosis but failed to learn to perform adequately on the test. The report of this finding stimulated Egaz Moniz to perform frontal leukotomies (lobotomies) on humans, an endeavor for which he received the Nobel Prize.

Unfortunately, the protocols revealed that Fulton's neurotic chimpanzee had suffered a brain abscess following the lobectomy. Fulton had had a gallery of visitors watching his surgery; the visitors included Harvey Cushing, the pioneer neurosurgeon who had trained Percival Bailey, and others who had trained me. The abscess became encapsulated after a few stormy weeks but was still present some years later at autopsy.

On the basis of this finding, one of my first tasks at Yale was to demonstrate that an irritating lesion of the brain such as an abscess or epileptic focus is much more devastating to a subject than a clean surgical removal. I published the results in a paper submitted to *Surgical Forum* (Pribram, 1951) and reviewed this and other findings related to the effects of frontal lobotomy in an editorial for the journal *Surgery, Gynecology and Obstetrics* in 1950.

The Frontolimbic Forebrain

Once at Yale, I studied hard and stood for my board examination in neurological surgery. The year before, some 40 candidates had tried, and all but two had failed to pass. Only a few intrepid souls volunteered at the time I did. My biggest hurdle, it turned out, was my Yale appointment; was I really going on in neurosurgery or was I going to devote myself wholly to research? My answer was sufficiently vague to get me by. What helped was that the exams were held in familiar territory—the Neuropsychiatric Institute of the University of Illinois where, as a neurosurgery resident, I had worked with Eric Oldberg, Percival Bailey, and others and had learned the techniques of chemical neuronography. Thus, I knew some of the trick questions Percival Bailey was wont to set up.

After passing my board examination, I quickly became involved in full-time teaching and research. John Fulton had left for England two days after I had arrived at Yale, leaving me in charge of the primate laboratory that was filled with a motley assortment of monkeys and apes. Fulton had bought up whatever was on the market with little thought about the necessity for homogeneity in research reports. I also found when I tested for tuberculosis that about a third of the colony showed positive reactions. Fortunately there were a sufficient number of rooms so that I could segregate the infected animals away from the rest of the colony. Then I had to negotiate with each experimenter as to how quickly we could dispose of each of the tuberculous monkeys. This was not a good way for a newcomer to become popular.

Meanwhile, I set up my own laboratory in the sub-basement of the building, renovating a space that had been occupied some years before by Warren McCulloch and Dusser de Barenne. I used grant funds for the renovation, making deals directly with outside contractors. Some six months later I received a notice that I was to always go through Yale University channels if I were to use these funds, but by that time I was already deep into the research and did not need any further renovations. There are times when the sluggishness of the administrative apparatus can be advantageous.

Two experiments were undertaken immediately: one was behavioral and the other electrophysiological. This dual research strategy was to become standard for me for the rest of my career.

For the behavioral experiments I set up a crude Yerkes testing apparatus (also known as the WGTA, the Wisconsin General Testing Apparatus, due to Harry Harlow). I made mine out of wood with a cardboard screen that I had to insert between the monkey and myself during the delay period in a delayed response task. Yerkes came to visit me to see how I was doing and in a most gentlemanly fashion indicated to me that perhaps a somewhat more elegant piece of equipment might be in order. This I made promptly.

The experiments I initiated were based on my previously mentioned work at the Neuropsychiatric Institute at the University of Illinois and at the Yerkes Laboratories in Florida. From the Illinois experiments, I had a thorough knowledge of what chemical (strychnine) neuronography had shown to date about cerebrocortical organization. The Yale grant support was to try to understand the effects of frontal lobotomy that was being performed on thousands of psychiatric patients at the time. My work with Bucy and subsequently at Yerkes was aimed at unraveling the temporal lobe syndrome. Neuronography had shown that the orbital surface of the frontal lobe, the anterior part of the insula (the Island of Ryle), and the pole of the temporal lobe formed a unit. Voila! I could study both the frontal and temporal lobes simultaneously.

One of the reasons for originally choosing Yale was that, at the time, Fulton's laboratory was one of the few, if not the only, physiology laboratory in the world to possess a square wave stimulator. Up to that time, everyone was using a Harvard inductorium for brain stimulation. The inductorium put out an unreliable facsimile of a sine wave whose frequency could not be accurately controlled. Bob Livingston and Arthur Ward had made good use of the square wave to stimulate the orbital surface of the frontal lobe and the anterior portion of the cingulate gyrus with the result that changes were observed in respiratory and cardiac rates and also in the blood pressure of the monkey. On the advice of Wilder Penfield, who occasionally had observed such results from manipulations of the insular cortex in humans, I had tried to obtain such visceral and autonomic nervous system changes by stimulating with the inductorium with only negative results. Yale offered the perfect opportunity to perform the required experiments. I enlisted a graduate student, Berger Kaada, who intended to follow up on some of Arthur Ward's experiments on the cingulate cortex, and J. A. Epstein, a fellow neurosurgeon who was doing a postdoctoral fellowship at Yale, to perform the experiments. Epstein and I soon worked out a technique to expose the entire medial and basal portions of the frontal and temporal lobes, and Kaada contributed his mastery of the square wave stimulator. The result was a thesis for Kaada and a publication on what I called the "mediobasal motor cortex" (Kaada, Pribram, & Epstein, 1949; Pribram, 1958, 1961).

The importance of the study is that it showed the frontal cortex to be intimately related to visceroautonomic functions that, according to the James–Lange and Cannon–Bard theories, were responsible for our experience and expression of emotions. Patrick Wall took off from these experiments and traced connections from the mediobasal motor cortex to the hypothalamus. A large step had been taken to understand the effects of lobotomy on emotions.

Sounds simple in retrospect; however, a Nobel laureate denounced our experimental results as being artifacts of stimulations of the dura mater. After all, didn't we know that the hypothalamus was the "head ganglion" of the autonomic nervous system, a portion of the brain this laureate had devoted to spending his life to study? Fortunately, Fulton was totally on our side and saw to it that the results of our studies were published in the *Journal of Neurophysiology* (Kaada et al., 1949). Within two years, most of the graduate students in physiology who were tackling the brain were pursuing this line of research.

Paul MacLean and a Gift for Naming

Paul MacLean, who had just obtained his M.D. and was taking a postdoctoral year at the Massachusetts General Hospital, asked to come to Yale because we were doing just the kind of work he was interested in. Paul's interests and mine were so compatible that I was sure it would be a joy to have him at Yale. Paul and I decided to collaborate on a series of animal strychninization experiments. He was a delightful companion, and it proved a joyous experience all around. We continued the chemical stimulation studies begun by Warren McCulloch, Gerhardt Bonin, and Percival Bailey—concentrating on the medial and basal cortex, which they had not been able to reach. We worked with monkeys and also with acallosal opossums (they really smelled awful), and found the cortical region (orbitofrontal and perirhinal) excited by electrical stimulation of the vagus nerve.

When it came to writing up our results, we encountered great difficulty. Paul's gift for naming, though often useful in promoting ideas, seemed to me to be applied rather rashly: The term "limbic" used by Broca (his Grande Lobe Limbique) was at this time more often restricted to the cortex of the cingulate gyrus in cytoarchitectonics. My friend and mentor, Jerzy Rose, was dead-set against extending the term to the entire mediobasal rim of the hemisphere. Paul MacLean's persuasion won the day, and I happily supported his enterprise since I had shown a commonality of physiological effects from electrical stimulation and a commonality of effects on behavior from resections of the variety of anatomical structures that comprised the Grande Lobe. My studies were reviewed in a paper published with one of my graduate students (Pribram & Kruger, 1954).

Another term that Paul coined was the "schizophysiology of cortical processing." This term was based on the finding that, although much of the neocortex has an input to the hippocampus, there is apparently no direct output from the hippocampus to the neocortex. This was an important finding, which I have used recently in trying to model the effect on learning of the hippocampal formation. The term "schizophysiology" never attained the recognition it deserved, partly because chemical stimulation of the cortex (i.e., strychnine neuronography) went out of fashion.

The Visceral Brain

On the basis of the work that Livingston, Ward, Kaada, Epstein, and I had done to show that electrical excitation of the mediobasal cortex produced changes in respiratory and heart rate, in blood pressure, and later in gastrointestinal activity, Paul termed the limbic forebrain the "visceral brain." This resonated with established views. James Papez had announced his famous circuit responsible for emotions. William James had popularized the James–Lange theory that emotions were due to feedback to the brain from the viscera when they were engaged by a stimulating event. Walter Cannon and P. Bard had critiqued James's theory and replaced it with a thalamic theory. Lashley had critiqued the Cannon–Bard theory as similarly flawed. Papez and MacLean came to the rescue: the limbic system, not the thalamus nor the viscera per se, is responsible for our emotions, though both (hypo)thalamus and viscera are critically involved because of their connections to the limbic brain.

I, however, had reservations about this conceptualization. My reservations stemmed from the patient I had described to Fulton who had localized seizures of sweating (a visceroautonomic response) induced by a localized tumor in the classical precentral motor cortex. I enlisted Patrick Wall to use the same stimulation technique that I had used to map the mediobasal motor cortex to map visceroautonomic responses from the lateral motor cortex. We aimed to discern whether the lateral and mediobasal responses could be distinguished as to which were more parasympathetic and which were more sympathetic. We were unable to make such a distinction. But the experiments did demonstrate that the mediobasal motor cortex is not the exclusive cortical regulator of the visceroautonomic system. In fact, our data supported Papez's view that emotions were attitudes that involved the entire body, including the somatic as well as the visceral musculature.

The lack of exclusivity of visceroautonomic control by the mediobasal cortex made it inappropriate to call the limbic forebrain a visceral brain. Nor could I go along with the uncritical acceptance of the James–Lange viscerally based theory of emotions. MacLean and I agreed to seriously disagree on this point and did so publicly on several occasions.

Some years later at Stanford University, my experiments uncovered the importance of the amygdala to the habituation of the orienting response. My colleague Muriel Bagshaw and I used visceral and autonomic indicators and showed that when visceroautonomic activity failed to be involved in generalized orienting, the response failed to become habituated. Orienting to novelty was, as the experiments of Eugene Sokolov had shown, due to a mismatch between an established representation of the familiar, a neuronal model, and the current sensory input. (Of note in this regard is that Sokolov and Aleksandr Luria had visited my new laboratories at Stanford University when I received an appointment there in 1959.) MacLean's intuition was not so far off, after all! However, visceroautonomic processing had more to do with the familiarization and valuation of episodes of experience, a kind of memory process, than it had to do with emotional feeling. By the end of the 1970s, I endorsed Nina Bull's attitude theory of emotions to which Lashley had alerted me. As noted, I found that James Papez also supported Bull's theory in a chapter of her book. The attitude theory's biological base included not only visceral manifestations but also endocrine and, importantly, somatic muscular responses to situations and therefore practically the entire brain.

The Penn State Symposium in 1950

Despite the seriousness of the work I was doing at Yale, I continued to find opportunities for fun—often in unexpected places. In 1948, at the time of my transition to Yale, Bob Blum, Josephine Semmes-Blum-Evarts, and I decided to present our frontal lobe research findings on chimpanzees at the meetings of the American Psychological Association (APA). We were pleased when the paper was accepted and especially so when we learned that Carlyle Jacobsen, the discoverer of the relationship between the delayed response task and the frontal cortex, was to chair the session. We arrived at the appointed time and location and had waited for about 10 minutes when Jacobsen arrived, apologizing for his lateness and the fact that he had to leave immediately for a committee meeting. We had hoped for an in-depth discussion of the meaning of the delayed response task with him, so we were seriously disappointed. Once he left, we wondered what to do: no one was there to listen to our paper! Interest in physiological psychology was at low ebb; its APA division had been absorbed into the Division of Experimental Psychology.

Two years later, at Pennsylvania State University, Luke Teuber, Joe Zubin, Harry Harlow, and I decided it was time for a change. We organized a symposium and asked Don Hebb to chair it. We decided that we would liven things up by vocally criticizing each other's work but with humor and good will. Much to our amazement, the auditorium, which seated 1,000, was filled to overflowing.

I made the first presentation. As I had severe hay fever and asthma, I had taken an antihistamine. My mouth went dry, and I therefore abbreviated my talk but nevertheless was able to make my point that the so-called association region covering the posterior convexity of the brain had within it areas that were sensory-specific. I also noted that the anterior part of the frontal cortex functioned in a non-sensory-specific fashion.

Harry Harlow followed, then Joe Zubin, the presentations ending with a long, long, hour and more talk by Luke Teuber. The audience was becoming restless; a few walked out. It was my turn to start the discussion. I was afraid that we were about to lose this golden opportunity to put the brain back into psychology. My adrenaline was flowing, taking care of the hay fever for the moment. I waded in with verbal fists flying. To Harlow: We at Yale had known for some decades that the front part of the brain did something different from the back part—it was gratifying to find out that the Wisconsin laboratories were catching on. To Zubin: Didn't we all know that factor analysis is useless unless we already know what we want to find out, or how would we know how to rotate the axes? To Teuber, who had quoted every German and English brain scientist of the past century or more: Isn't it sad that Professor Teuber doesn't know the literature; he failed to quote the seminal work on the motor cortex edited by Paul Bucy.

The audience was howling with laughter; more people came in to see what the noise was all about and sat in the aisles. Harlow proceeded to tear my work to shreds: Pribram bases his results on the use of one or two tests. It would be nice if he learned some psychology. I countered that at least I gave more that one or two trials per test. Zubin explained the intricacies of factor analysis to the uninitiated, including neurosurgeons such as Pribram. Teuber pointed to my charts that were still decorating the entire front of the hall: Typical of a neurosurgeon—occupying all the available space. (I could not afford to have slides made at that time, so I used colored crayons to draw brain maps on window shades. I had rolled open the shades and hung them all over the blackboards, the podium etc.) And as a final touch, Teuber stated that from the brain maps of Franz Gall to those of Pribram, we seemed to have made little progress in the century and a half that had elapsed since the phrenologists. Don Hebb remained quiet and dignified through all this, adding another dimension to the scene.

Of course the symposium was a huge success and accomplished what we had intended. Harry Harlow and I continued to use the confrontational technique for many years to enlighten and entertain.

The Politics of Academe

Besides being able to accomplish what, to my mind, was important research, I also was introduced to the politics of Academe while at Yale. Politics at Yale were serious. Yale is a prestigious university and therefore attracts ambitious individuals, including me. But I was totally unprepared for what I had to deal with. For instance, pressure had been put on Fulton and on me by the Veterans Administration to have a bona fide psychologist for our initial projects. Those of us doing the research were all neurosurgeons or neurophysiologists, neuroanatomists, neurochemists, or medical students. As a consequence of this pressure, Hal Rosvold, a recent Stanford Ph.D. in Psychology, was invited to join our research team as a postdoctoral fellow. Mortimer Mishkin, a graduate student who came to us from McGill, also joined the team.

My colleagues warned me that the newcomers might take over and that they would usurp our carefully initiated research. There was even a movement afoot, I was told, to have me out of Yale by the end of the year. They predicted that MacLean would be known for the physiological research on the limbic forebrain, and the psychologists would assert their territorial prerogative on the neurobehavioral studies of the frontal and temporal lobes. At one time I wrote Lashley for advice. His reply was simple: "You need to decide whether you want to do politics or do science." I chose to do science.

Unfortunately, the dire predictions proved all too accurate. For example, Mishkin received recognition by the American Psychological Association for the work on analyzing the temporal lobe syndrome. He also received the Lashley Prize from the American Philosophical Society for continuing Lashley's tradition of surgical procedures to investigate neuropsychological function. These honors were certainly deserved on the basis of Mishkin's work that related the "match from sample task" to human episodic memory. But Ernest Hilgard had put me up for the APA prize, and to my disappointment I did not share it.

Departures

Patrick Wall and I remained at Yale for a few years. All the rest of the early team went elsewhere to more permanent positions. John Fulton was maneuvered out of being chair of the Department of Physiology and into a chair in the History of Medicine. I remained at Yale as lecturer for a decade and maintained my laboratory, but meanwhile I built a much larger laboratory at a psychiatric hospital, The Institute of Living, in Hartford, Connecticut, some thirty miles north of Yale. (I was not the first to utilize research space in psychiatric hospitals: Don Lindsley and Herbert Jasper did their early research in a psychiatric hospital in Providence, Rhode Island.) Mort Mishkin came with me from Yale, and over the years several other graduate students were allowed to do their theses with me: Martha Helson (later Wilson) also from Yale; Lawrence Weiskrantz and Elaine Smulekoff from Harvard; William Wilson from University of California-Berkeley; and Jerry Schwartzbaum from Stanford.

Growing Up: Operants, Plans, and the Cognitive Revolution

The decade during which I taught at Yale and established a satellite laboratory at the Institute of Living in Hartford, Connecticut, was a seminal one for neuropsychology. David Rioch organized a parallel group at the Army Institute of Research. His research team included Bob Galambos, Joe Brady, L. Schreiner, A. Kling, and Walle Nauta. Rioch and I became close friends, and he saw to it that my laboratory was properly funded. The story of how this started is of interest even today. Paul Schiller, a Gestalt psychologist from Hungary, came to work with Lashley on the problem of motor gestalts. We had interacted at Yerkes; on one occasion we had gone swimming in St. Augustine and were on our way to an offshore island when a baby shark popped up between us. I reasoned that where there were babies there were likely to be mothers and beat a hasty retreat to the shore. Paul at first insisted on going on, but I managed to get him to return with me. A week later someone had a leg bitten off in that same channel.

Somehow, Paul Schiller had become interested in the work of B. F. Skinner. He decided to spend the summer at Harvard. On the way there he stopped for the weekend at my home in Connecticut. Two weeks later he was reported missing in Tuckerman's Ravine in the Green Mountains where he'd gone skiing. He was never found (and many years later Claire Schiller, his wife, became the second Mrs. Lashley after the first had died).

I decided that if a Gestalt psychologist were interested in operant conditioning, there must be more to it than my colleagues (especially Hal Rosvold) were telling me. I took off for Harvard and had many discussions with Skinner and his associate Charlie Ferster. They told me that there was a graduate student, Lawrence Weiskrantz, who was interested in physiological psychology and that I might recruit him to do his thesis with me in Hartford. With the substantial aid of Mortimer Mishkin, I persuaded Weiskrantz to come. Skinner and Ferster were enthusiastic about setting up an operant conditioning laboratory for monkeys, so we went to work to build such a set-up.

We used a Yerkes box and delivered peanuts through a tube by hand, according to either a variable ratio or variable interval schedule. Shaping the monkeys had been easy in this crude apparatus, but to do anything more precise we needed to automate—a problem that Lashley and I had discussed repeatedly with no insights as to how to accomplish it. The operant technique was automation personified. I went to Rioch with a grant application for $2,000. He laughed gently but heartily. He said in no way would we ever obtain such a grant; it would take more than that to process the application. He suggested $20,000. I applied, included a salary for Mishkin and Weiskrantz, and we were on our way. Lesson: When applying for support, ask for what you can profitably use (but not more), and don't be overly modest.

The meaning of the delayed response task continued to puzzle me through this period. Jacobsen (1936) had rightly stated in his original publication that the task was not just a test of short-term memory. What then might it be? Bob Malmo had shown that the "frontal lobe deficit" on this task would disappear if the task were presented under diminished illumination. The task might well be a test of distractibility, which would fit my experience with frontally lesioned patients whose duration of frustration and suffering had been shortened by the surgery. But what might distractibility be in physiological terms? Lashley had written a classic paper on serial ordering in behavior, and the problem of chaining of responses was of concern to operant conditioners. Duration of a response, distractibility, and chaining seemed somehow related to the kinesthetic–proprioceptive–physiological dimension. My experiments as well as those of others, however, had shown that tactile and kinesthetic afferents projected to the cortex surrounding the central fissure; resection of this cortical tissue did not impair performance on the delayed response (nor the delayed alternation task).[1]

While teaching at Harvard one summer, I presented the issue to B. F. Skinner. His immediate response was that kinesthetic cues must mediate between each of the successive responses in a chain to indicate the conclusion of one and the occasion for the onset of the next. I told Skinner of the above experiments and then added, tongue-in-cheek, that he, as a biologist (he had obtained his Ph.D. doing vision research), could postulate kinesthesia but that I, as a dedicated Skinnerian, had no such luxury since I must hew to the doctrine of the empty organism.

We had come to an impasse but continued the discussion at luncheons in the Psychology Department. One noon, George Miller overheard us and declared that he had a method of assuring the serial ordering of behavior. The method was called computer programming—specifically "lisp" programming. I spent the afternoon with George, he showed me how to program, we devised some experiments, and the rest became the history of the cognitive revolution in psychology.

In 1958 I obtained a Fulbright fellowship to spend the year at Cambridge University in England to refresh my clinical neuropsychology and, at the same time, was invited to the Center for Advanced Study in the Behavioral Sciences at Stanford. George Miller and Jerry Bruner also were invited. I talked to George and Jerry, and they agreed that it was a great opportunity to explore the relationship between the brain and behavioral sciences in terms of what we were learning about computers and computer programming. I decided to go forward in my explorations rather than back to my clinical roots; Jerry, at the last minute, opted for a trip around the world, but Gene Galanter filled in.

By January we had decided that computers and programming really didn't add much to the seemingly intractable non-trivial aspects of the relation between brain and behavior. George and Gene wanted to give up, but I insisted that at least

---

1. In the delayed alternation procedure rewards are hidden behind an opaque screen in two identical sites. The screen is raised, and the monkey is allowed to find the reward. The screen is lowered for 5 to 15 seconds and then raised, once more allowing the monkey to find the reward. The monkey must adopt a win-shift strategy; that is, he must shift his response to the site other than the one in which he found the reward on the previous trial. For subsequent trials, the reward is alternately hidden in the two locations while the screen is down.

we write up our disappointment and the reasons for it. In February, George came into my office and said, "It can't be done."

"Oh no," I exclaimed. "We have to."

George put me at ease immediately. "We can't do it in a paper; it will take a whole book." I was elated; we divided up the task and went to work. After a considerable amount of discussion, each final draft that Gene and I produced was rewritten by George to assure a uniform style. As George put it, he had to wipe off the starch from Gene's contribution (Gene had a propensity for spelling things out in symbolic logic) and the blood off mine (I tended to insert brain processes wherever I could). The book, *Plans and the Structure of Behavior* (Miller, Galanter, & Pribram, 1960), was finished by the end of June.

Gene's proclivities were gestalt and existential. George and I were behaviorists. But I had encountered clinical cases where verbal reports of subjective experience and the patient's behavior were at odds. George's focus was on language, and we were good friends with Noam Chomsky who had written a devastating attack on Skinner's behaviorism. Change was in the air, and my staunch behaviorism was beginning to give way. (Quite apropos, in an office next to ours, Thomas Kuhn was writing his famous book on revolutions in science.)

The central problem with behaviorism was that to explain behavior and experience one needed a "representation" construct. Lashley and I had discussed the issue at great length on the boardwalk of Atlantic City, circa 1956. In fact, I still identify representations with herringbone patterns as they stretched in front of me as we walked. On another occasion, when I was to take over the Yerkes Laboratories, I asked Lashley whether he was sure that he wanted a Skinnerian, operant conditioner, and purveyor of the notion of an empty, representation-less organism, to succeed him. His answer, as always, was penetrating: "That's all right, Dr. Pribram; I had my Watson period. You'll grow up some day." With *Plans and the Structure of Behavior*, with its emphasis on plans as neural representations of intended actions, I grew up.

Within six months, Aleksandr Luria and Eugene Sokolov visited my newly established laboratory at Stanford University, a visit I have already alluded to. Over the next week we planned experiments to discover the brain processes involved in establishing "neuronal models"—representations of sensory input using the psychophysiological techniques developed by Sokolov. Muriel Bagshaw, who had worked with me at Yale as a medical student, was now a full-fledged pediatrician, and we went to work focusing on the role of the amygdala. The results of these experiments led directly to tracing top-down brain influences as they organize sensory input. Using electrical stimulation techniques, Nico Spinnelli and I showed that such systems as the sensory specific association cortex, the frontal cortex, and the structures of the limbic forebrain had access to sensory processing as far peripheral as the receptors themselves.

All of these currents led me to modify the operant technique (by programming cues, responses, and reports of reinforcement into software) to allow recording of choices among twelve levers. The resulting computerized apparatus I called

DADTA, a Discrimination Apparatus for Discrete Trial Analysis. The dream Lashley and I had shared for automated testing had come to pass: all through the next three decades we tested as many as 100 monkeys per day with complete trial-by-trial behavioral and physiological recording.

The Temporal Lobe and the Valuation of Experience

Bob Douglas and I, in a series of neuro-behavioral experiments, showed that resections of the amygdala resulted in deficiencies in processing the reinforcing and deterrent aspects of learning and remembering—the valuation of episodes of experience. We did this by training monkeys on a proportional reinforcement discrimination task and then, in a subsequent procedure, matching a novel stimulus to the previously highly rewarded or the previously less-rewarded cues. The amygdalectomized monkeys behaved as did their normal controls when the match was to the less-rewarded cue, but they chose the novel cue over the previously more rewarded cue 100 percent of the time—as if they had never had any experience with the more rewarded cue.

By contrast, monkeys who had their hippocampal gyrus resected performed in just the opposite way: they chose the previously more rewarded cue as did their controls but chose the less rewarded cue and the novel cue almost equally. Some decades earlier, Nissen and Spence had shown that in a learning situation, chimpanzees' learning depended as much on attending to the non-rewarded cue as attending to the rewarded one. In our experiments we were able to separate these functions according to the parts of the brain involved.

The hippocampal finding was confirmed in a surprising result. Doug Crowne and I trained monkeys on a go/no-go discrimination task and recorded hippocampal electrical activity. We were able to reliably differentiate the electrical waveforms generated during the no-go trials from those generated during the go trials. We then trained the monkeys on a simultaneous discrimination task in which they had to respond on every trial. The surprising finding was that, despite going on every trial, the hippocampal electrical activity was identical to that found previously on the no-go trials. One interpretation of these results is that valuation (reinforcement and deterrence) takes place within (sets of) non-rewarded cues that form the context of an episode. Richard Hirsch, a doctoral student in the laboratory, developed this theme into a full-fledged model in his thesis.

In another set of experiments, Abe Spevack and I used a modified decision theory procedure. The response operator characteristics (ROC curves) showed that hippocampal resections influenced the bias of the decision process toward caution. (The opposite was found for resections of the inferotemporal cortex; those monkeys became biased toward risk.) The hippocampectomized monkeys failed to proceed efficiently toward problem solution; rather, they became "stuck" in more wasteful paths toward a goal. This finding was confirmed in a discrimination reversal task in which hippocampally lesioned monkeys became "stuck" for weeks at chance level of performance, despite the fact that the slopes of both the immediate reversal and ultimate reaching of criterion performance were indistinguishable from those of their unoperated controls. In terms of non-linear dynamics, the hippocampally lesioned monkeys became trapped in energy "wells" that did not lead to the most efficient performance.

The results of these experiments tell us something about the functions in behavior that are disrupted by the brain resections. The same type of analysis was pursued for the effects of resections of the amygdala and those of the inferotemporal cortex. In short, these results of the analysis of the "temporal lobe syndrome" (discovered, as noted, by Sanger-Brown and Schäffer and more recently rediscovered by Bucy and Klüver) lead to an understanding of temporal lobe functioning in behavior. The relationship between these results obtained with non-human primates and the human neuropsychological observations can be formulated best in terms of the familiarization of episodes of experience and the influence of the familiar on subsequent performance and experience. The full account of the results and the conclusions derived from these have been published in several readily accessible sources (47 of my own studies over a 30-year period from 1949 to 1980) and reviewed in *Brain and Perception* (Pribram, 1991). To my disappointment, these studies have been, for the most part, ignored by the establishment.

The Brain and Perception

During this period, Lashley visited several times. Kao Liang Chow (who as a graduate student had taken over my temporal lobe studies at Yerkes when I left for Yale) came to work a month each year, and I reciprocated by going to work with him at Orange Park for a month. We completed three anatomical studies tracing the differences between the organization of the thalamic projections to frontolimbic and posterior hemispheric cortex during these visits.

Wolfgang Köhler visited often. Weiskrantz had taken courses from him at Swarthmore, and I had met Köhler repeatedly with Lashley and Luke Teuber. We decided to see whether we could obtain evidence for the Direct Current (DC) theory of cortical encoding of perception. We used monkeys, and on one occasion, a human patient who had his occipital lobes exposed. We did indeed find a direct current change in the appropriate cortex when we held up a white stimulus in front of an anesthetized monkey's (or human's) eyes or when we produced a sound. Köhler would come to Hartford, and we would pack up a monkey and surgical equipment and proceed to MIT where we did the experiments.

When it came to publishing the results as indicating that we had obtained evidence for a neural correlate of perception, I balked. DC currents could not account for the fine grain, the texture that is such a prominent and important aspect of perception. I was to voice this same objection again to the feature detection theory of perception.

I had meanwhile undertaken other experiments to test the DC theory. I implanted discs filled with aluminum hydroxide cream onto the primary visual cortex of monkeys to produce electrical seizures that I recorded. I tested the monkeys on discrimination between fine vertical versus horizontal stripes and showed their performance to be intact. Interestingly, however, their learning was retarded some seven-fold. In subsequent experiments, John Stamm and I showed that a cathodal current imposed on the appropriate cortex would produce similar delays while an anodal current would boost the learning curve. Köhler's disappointment was palpable. He asked what I was going to do now that I had disproved not only his but every other neural theory of perception. I was moving to Stanford and said I'd keep my mouth shut—and refused to teach anything about sensation and perception.

Some five years later, the issue became resolved for me. Jack Hilgard asked what my views on perception might be. I recounted the above results of experiments and told him I hadn't a clue as to what to think. I expressed my doubts about the theory that visual percepts were constructed from line detectors, a theory that was becoming popular. A few weeks later while walking across the Stanford campus, Hilgard asked once more and expressed the hope that I would give the matter some thought. "You may have the luxury of not knowing, but I'm committed to producing another revision of my textbook. What'll I say?"

I took the matter up with my lab group. DC didn't work. Feature detection didn't fill the bill. What was left? Perhaps Lashley's interference pattern theory was the answer. It had the virtue of being totally untested, and perhaps untestable, so at least we couldn't say it was wrong. Lashley and I had discussed it repeatedly, and he had given it up because he could not envision how interference patterns would be generated in the cortex. Reverberating circuits, the basis for Hebb's cell assemblies and phase sequences, wouldn't do. I had asked Lashley on several occasions while Hebb was writing his book to hold a colloquium on it. Lashley's comment: "Hebb is right in every detail, but the proposal is just oh-so-wrong." Lashley could not articulate his intuition.

In a few days Nico Spinelli, the neurophysiologist in our group, came up with an article in *Scientific American* written in 1970 by John Eccles (see Pribram, 1971). Eccles pointed out that although he had been studying synapses all his life, it was always one at a time. Synapses had to be considered as ensembles. Most axons branch as they approach their termination (the branches are called teledendrons). Thus the presynaptic polarizations that are produced by nerve impulse in axons produce wave fronts! Neither Lashley nor I had had the wit to see this. Half of the puzzle of interference patterns in the brain was solved: pre- and post-synaptic polarizations could be viewed as wave fronts, and the fronts approaching the postsynaptic dendritic network from various axons would interfere.

The second part of the puzzle took only a few days to become resolved. I received in the mail my current *Scientific American* (fortunately before Spinelli received his; P comes before S alphabetically) with an article by Leith and Upatnicks on optical holography. Some years earlier, Dennis Gabor (a mathematician) had suggested that storing an image in terms of its complex conjugate (i.e., as interference patterns) would allow better resolution of its reconstruction than simply recording the point-to-point intensity. In short, Lashley's intuition (which as a zoologist he inherited from Jacques Loeb and A. Goldscheider, who had made similar though less sophisticated conjectures around the turn of the nineteenth century) was explicated and could be tested. I reported all this to Hilgard, but he thought holographic ideas too avant-garde to put into his text. I'm sad to say, even today, the research that stemmed from this approach to perception is barely acknowledged in texts of psychology, perception, or neuroscience.

Some years later, I had the opportunity to articulate these holographically-inspired ideas. I organized a Neuroscience Wine and Cheese Symposium on the subject and invited Russ and Karen DeValois, Horace Barlow, and David Hubel (who, with Torsten Wiesel, had by then received the Nobel Prize for the work on feature detectors). Russ and Karen had done critical experiments to show that the line sensitive elements in the visual cortex were actually tuned to the spatial frequency (the basis of holography) of a grating composed of equally spaced lines, a finding also obtained by Fergus Campbell at Cambridge University from whence Barlow came. Spinelli and I had confirmed these findings and those of Dan Pollen at the Massachusetts General Hospital and the University of Massachusetts. Finally, we had shown that each cell, each receptive field, in the primary visual cortex was selective of a variety of features, not just one such as an oriented line. Changes in luminance, direction, velocity, and acceleration of movement of a stimulus, as well as color in many instances, changed the response of this cell. These propensities were distributed over the cortical surface.

Hubel graciously accepted my invitation to the symposium, and I asked him to go last in the order of speakers. The symposium admitted only 300 registrants. Wine and cheese were served. Each speaker had a carafe of claret in front of him. By the time of Hubel's turn, we had all had a good deal to drink. I challenged Hubel with the DeValois's research findings and the fact that each cortical cell, much as each person, was characterized by attributes that were distributed over the population. For example, a person may be male, tall, blond, have blue eyes, and be required to wear glasses. Another may be female, short, also blond, have blue eyes, but is not required to wear glasses. Still another may be tall, brunette, have brown eyes, and be required to wear glasses, and so on. Each person is characterized by a more or less unique coterie of attributes.

I added that with a line detector type of theory, a composite face would necessarily have to be composed for each distance, each angle of view—a horrendous computational problem. (I also noted that although DeValois's work involved mathematics that David had been a math teacher before he went to medical school.) David was as gracious in his response as he was in accepting the invitation to participate. He said that he agreed with everything I had said but still believed that a cell's response was greater for the detected stimulus than for the others. As for DeValois's work, he said that he had never seen any such responses in his own laboratory. Russ immediately invited David to his laboratory. David retorted that even if he saw it, he wouldn't believe it. I remarked in feigned surprise that I didn't know David was a flatlander.

All in all it was fun, and I found out afterward that David had gotten the best of the argument as far as many if not most of the audience was concerned. In part this was due to Barlow's reasoned compromise between the feature (line) detector and the spatial frequency (gratings) views, in part due to David's charisma.

In my 1971 book, *Languages of the Brain*, and in my 1991 book, *Brain and Perception*, I distinguish between feature detection and feature filter (or feature analyzer) viewpoints. As is currently shown by the Independent Component Analysis technique, a visual (or auditory) scene can be analyzed into components such as lines (or tones). As is also shown by this technique, however, the analysis must involve high-order statistics, which with periodic stimulation, as with gratings, implicates their phase relations. In real life, sensory stimulation *is* periodic; if not, the stimulus fades through adaptation. Actuality is often simpler and more beautiful than the results we impose on it in our experiments.

Recognition

A good bit of the research performed by the graduate students and postdoctoral fellows (some 100 of them) working with me over the 1960s, 1970s, and 1980s has failed to become part of the usually quoted references in neuropsychology. I have wondered about the reasons for this. One might be the overwhelming publicity my holographic/holonomic (holonomy, also called quantum holography, deals with a phase space composed not only by frequency but by space–time constraints as well) theorizing has attained—publicity not, as yet, welcomed by establishment science. Thus, quoting any solid experimental achievements would be "tainted" by association with the theory—though the data had nothing at all to do with it. In fact, most of my laboratory work deals with neural systems and the localization of components of psychological processes, whereas the holographic/holonomic theory deals with distributed, holistic aspects of psychological processes that cannot be explained on a purely localistic basis.

Another possible reason for lack of recognition of the published papers is the fact that my name does not appear on all publications, thus continuity of purpose fails to be apparent. My policy was that my name would be on a paper only if I did a major portion of the work *aside* from setting up the equipment and doing the surgery. In this way I was able to keep the number of authors on a publication to between two and four, assuring prominence to the students who were at the beginning of their careers. Every action has its unforeseen consequences, and in this case I did not foresee that the individual papers would simply disappear from everyone's awareness once their authors either became inactive or, when successful, refused, for whatever reasons, to quote any neurobehavioral studies done in my laboratory after they left. My only recourse has been to write reviews and books, which integrate their work with that of my laboratory, and hope for the best.

The best has come in a surprising fashion in the guise of widespread acknowledgement of the influence of the published experimental results by word of mouth. Associated with this acknowledgement have been numerous awards and prizes—a number of them during the last decade.[2] More importantly, I have a laboratory in which I continue to work. I also have an endowed professorship and honorary professorships from the University of Montreal and the University of Bremen. Just recently, I received another distinguished research professorship. All of these professorships involve teaching and will doubtlessly provide sufficient challenge during my seventies and eighties.

I have enjoyed playing a significant role in the development of experimental neuropsychology, working with some of the field's most prominent contributors, mentors, and students for over half a century. I have just returned from a centennial celebration honoring John Fulton. What would he say to these ruminations? He was totally supportive of my aspirations when I told him that I hoped that our work would become a part of the flow of the history of brain science. A half-century later, at the end of a most rewarding decade of the brain, his faith in the then-younger generation appears to have been on the mark.

REFERENCES

Boring, E. G. (1950). *A history of experimental psychology* (2nd ed.). East Norwalk, CT: Appleton-Century-Crofts.

Fulton, J. F. (1949). *Psychology of the nervous system* (3rd ed.). New York: Oxford University Press.

Jacobsen, C. F. (1936). The functions of the frontal association areas in monkeys. *Comparative Psychology Monograph, 13*, 3–60.

Kaada, B. R., Pribram, K. H., & Epstein, J. A. (1949). Respiratory and vascular responses in monkeys from temporal pole, insula, orbital surface and cingulate gyrus. *Journal of Neurophysiology, 12*, 347–356.

Lashley, K. S. (1923). *Brain mechanisms and intelligence.* Chicago: University of Chicago Press.

Lashley, K. S. (1942). The problem of cerebral organization in vision. In *Biological symposia, Vol. VII, visual mechanisms* (pp. 301–322). Lancaster, PA: Jaques Cattell Press.

Miller, G. A., Galanter, E., & Pribram, K. H. (1960). *Plans and the structure of behavior.* New York: Henry Holt.

Pribram, K. H. (1950). Psychosurgery in mid-century. *Surgery, Gynecology and Obstetrics, 91*, 364–367.

Pribram, K. H. (1951). Some aspects of experimental psychosurgery: The effect of scarring frontal cortex on complex behavior. *Surgical Forum, 36*, 315–318.

Pribram, K. H. (1954). Toward a science of neuropsychology (method and data). In R. A. Patton (Ed.), *Current trends in psychology and the behavioral sciences* (pp. 115–142). Pittsburgh, PA: University of Pittsburgh Press.

Pribram, K. H. (1958). Comparative neurology and the evolution of behavior. In A. Roe & G. G. Simpson (Eds.), *Behavior and evolution* (pp. 140–164). New Haven: Yale University Press.

Pribram, K. H. (1961). Limbic system. In D. E.

2. Outstanding Contributions Award, American Board of Medical Psychotherapists, 1990; Honorary Ph.D., University of Montreal, Canada, 1992; Realia Laurate, Institute for Advanced Philosophic Research, 1993; International Neural Network Society First Neural Network Leadership Award, 1994; Honorary Ph.D., University of Bremen, Germany; Computing Anticipatory Systems Award, Liege, Belgium, 1999; Dagmar and Václav Havel Vize 97 Foundation Prize, 1999; IEEE, Information Sciences Award, 2000; and Culver Man of the Year Award, Culver Military Academy, Indiana, 2000.

Sheer (Ed.), *Electrical stimulation of the brain* (pp. 311–320). Austin, TX: University of Texas Press.

Pribram, K. H. (1971). *Languages of the brain: Experimental paradoxes and principles in neuropsychology.* Englewood Cliffs, NJ: Prentice-Hall. (Monterey, CA: Brooks/Cole, 1977; New York: Brandon House, 1982)

Pribram, K. H. (1982). Localization and distribution of function in the brain. In J. Orbach (Ed.), *Neuropsychology after Lashley* (pp. 273–296). New York: Erlbaum.

Pribram, K. H. (1991). *Brain and perception: Holonomy and structure in figural processing.* Hillsdale, NJ: Lawrence Erlbaum Associates.

Pribram, K. H. (1997). The deep and surface structure of memory and conscious learning: Toward a 21st century model. In R. L. Solso (Ed.), *Mind and brain sciences* (pp. 127–156). Cambridge, MA: MIT Press.

Pribram, K. H., & Kruger, L. (1954). Function of the "olfactory" brain. *Annals of the New York Academy of Science, 54,* 109–138.

14

The Best-Laid Plans— and the Vagaries of Circumstantial Events

Ralph M. Reitan

I was fortunate to be born into a close, caring, and loving family consisting of my mother, father, one sister, and three brothers. In age, I was the middle of the five siblings.

Both of my parents had strong ties to Norway. My father emigrated from Norway when he was 16 years of age, and my mother's parents were Norwegian immigrants. As a child, I learned to speak Norwegian, and this language was essentially my only language until I began school. We continued to speak Norwegian exclusively in my home until I was about 14 years old.

My mother completed her education at the Valley City Teacher's College in North Dakota, and my father completed his training as a clergyman at the Augsburg Seminary in Minneapolis. My early training was grounded in the importance of maintaining high ethical and moral standards and a sense of social responsibility. Religious values were also deeply inculcated; two of my brothers became clergymen, and my sister, a nurse, married a clergyman. My youngest brother and I earned doctoral degrees and spent most of our lives in university settings. The early influences on my value system have had both good and bad effects; I have been pleased to have developed a sense of personal responsibility that supports my self-respect, but on the other hand, I am apparently somewhat naïve in my expectations of others. When encountering disappointments with regard to such expectations, it is not uncommon for my close and valued associates to offer the following advice, "Grow up, Ralph!"

The early years, during the Depression, were difficult for my family. My older brother and I worked both before and after school in order to contribute to the financial resources of the family. Although these circumstances brought the family members closer together and helped us to develop a sense of responsibility and contribution, the amount of time required essentially precluded any extra-curricular activities through grade school and high school. One of my jobs was delivering newspapers, and when I was about 12 years old I developed a habit of buying two malted milk balls, which cost one penny, before beginning my afternoon paper route. Scarcely ever having had candy before this time, this practice quickly led to my developing dental cavities, which actually may have been of critical significance with respect to my later career. I had an appointment with the dentist on Monday evenings. Unfortunately, my dentist suffered a heart attack and died between my appointments. The dentist's wife was quite resourceful and quickly located another dentist to take over the practice, and I did not miss a single appointment. However, I continued to have a considerable amount of pain from the tooth that was repaired. I went to another dentist, who determined that the tooth was dead and needed to be extracted. Apparently, the replacement dentist had not performed adequately and had actually killed the tooth, and it was necessary that this tooth, a molar, be removed.

It was some years later that the consequences of this extraction became apparent, when I was facing the prospect of military duty during World War II. I had finished two years of college and I decided to enlist in the Marine Corps since I would be eligible for Officer Candidate School. All applicants were required to have a physical examination. I was generally in excellent health and in fine physical condition. The last part of the physical was a dental examination. The dentist inspected my teeth and immediately pronounced that I would be rejected because I was missing a molar. My plan to become a Second Lieutenant in the Marine Corps suddenly disintegrated.

I sought other opportunities, and I discovered that I could enlist in the Army. As a full-time college student, I was assigned to the Army Specialized Training Corps and could continue my education until I was called. This allowed me to complete a third year of college. During that time, while playing football with some colleagues, I suffered a severe dislocation of my left shoulder. After being called to military service, it was necessary to go through Army basic training, and I discovered that my shoulder injury had resulted in chronic and permanent damage. I dislocated my shoulder repeatedly during basic training, and after about three months, I received a disability discharge from the Army. Thus, I had fulfilled my military obligation during World War II during a single summer, and I came back to school in the fall for my final year of college.

The significance of my dentist's death lay in its influence in keeping me from joining the Marine Corps. After a short training period, I would have become a Second Lieutenant, and in all probability I would have been assigned to lead troops invading the South Seas islands. My understanding is that the mortality rate among Second Lieutenants leading these invasions was the highest of any group in the military service. Retrospectively, it would seem that my dentist's death very probably kept me from dying on the South Pacific beaches.

It was a struggle for both my older brother and me to achieve a college education. The financial circumstances of the family required that we continue to work. My brother discovered that he could work full-time while taking courses at the Central YMCA College in downtown Chicago, thus making considerable progress toward earning his college degree. I followed in my brother's footsteps and adopted this same plan. We both worked full-time, contributing to the family's support, and managed to earn our college degrees in about four and one-half years.

My decision to major in psychology in college was due entirely to a chance circumstance. I did much of my studying in the college library, and one day while studying before class I picked up a book that happened to have been left on the table. The book was concerned with clinical contributions to psychology and contained case studies that illustrated the value of psychological counseling. I had intended to major in chemistry, having developed a considerable degree of admiration for a high school chemistry teacher, but I was so intrigued with the book on psychological counseling that I decided to take a course in psychology. My instructor was George Speer (who later became heavily involved in organizing and managing meetings of the American Psychological Association), and his enthusiasm for psychology led me to take additional courses and eventually to major in psychology. Unfortunately, the demands of full-time work and full-time academics led to many instances in which I was poorly prepared when it came time to take examinations. My grade point average was only about B-, hardly a good basis for admission to graduate school.

In any case, I did not have the financial resources to attend graduate school. With a B.A. in psychology, however, I found that I qualified for a position at the Armed Forces Induction Station in Chicago. My responsibility was to determine whether illiterate inductees had the basic abilities to learn to read and write. The Army did not want to induct draftees who were unable to read and write well enough to stay in touch with their families and friends through correspondence. Thus, the purpose and responsibility of our group at the Induction Station was to administer several tests and conduct interviews to determine whether draftees should be accepted into the Army. In the evenings I worked in a war plant as a drill press operator. This job required constant movement and extension of my arms, which caused a great deal of irritation and pain in my injured shoulder. Eventually I was unable to continue with this job, but I did obtain a statement from the personnel office stating that my injured shoulder was the reason that I had to quit. This letter turned out to have major significance in permitting me to pursue graduate studies in psychology.

Of more immediate significance, however, was the fact that one of the Army officers that I had replaced at the Armed Forces Induction Station had mentioned my name and given me a good recommendation for a position at the Mayo General Hospital in Galesburg, Illinois. The Mayo General Hospital had a section for soldiers who had received head and brain injuries, and was apparently in rather desperate need for professional assessment of psychological impairment in these patients. One bachelor's-level person was attempting to do this work, but at least one more person was needed; considering the shortage of trained psychologists, I was hired. Thus, at the beginning of 1945, I received my introduction into the area of neuropsychology (long before the term was commonly used) at the Mayo General Hospital, working with one other essentially untrained person and three neurologists.

Based on my personal observations and formal testing of brain-injured soldiers, I was tremendously impressed with the significance of the brain as the organ of adaptive behavior. I particularly remember one man who had sustained an extensive shrapnel wound involving the posterior part of the left side of his head and brain. When I first saw him, he was grossly aphasic and very much impaired in verbal communication. He was hospitalized in our unit for about three months, and during that time I saw him daily. By the time he was discharged, he was able to communicate verbally so well that no one would have suspected his prior impairment. I was totally fascinated by the impairment I observed as well as the recovery possibilities. This led me to a search for any information that I could find on the psychological effects of brain injury. The work of Piotrowski on the Rorschach Test, the writings of Kurt Goldstein and Martin Scherer, the publications of Rapaport and Schafer of the Menninger Clinic, and the publication by Howard Hunt on the Hunt Minnesota Test for Organic Brain Damage influenced me greatly as I put together a battery of tests that we later used routinely. It was also clear to me, however, that there were very few publications in this area, and I was eager to perform some formal studies of the patients whom I was examining. I enlisted the help of our section chief, a neurologist named John Aita (who has since gone on to a very impressive career in neurology), and we organized a number of studies. Together with other colleagues, we published four papers in 1947 and 1948 on the psychological consequences of brain injury in national journals, based on data collection over 12 months during 1948.

Another chance event had major significance for my future and me. Dr. Aita heard Ward Halstead give a lecture and later told me that Halstead was at the University of Chicago and that he appeared to have developed impressive knowledge of the effects of brain injuries. Aita suggested that I go to Chicago to see Halstead, and I arranged an appointment. My visit with Halstead turned out to be extremely stimulating to me and apparently a pleasure to him as well. At that time, Halstead was a professional researcher and associate professor in the Department of Psychiatry of the Medical School at the University of Chicago. He was not doing any formal teaching and had no administrative relationship with the Psychology Department; however, he was very encouraging with respect to my desire to attend graduate school, suggested that I apply to the Psychology Department at the University of Chicago, and asked me to come back on a return visit and take the tests that he had developed in order to see what they were like. I returned a few weeks later to take the tests and earned an Impairment Index of 0.0, a score that fell in the normal range on all of the tests. At that point, Halstead said that if I were accepted by the Psychology Department, he would be most pleased to have me join his laboratory as a research assistant. I immediately applied for admission as a graduate student, but my chances of acceptance appeared to be relatively poor because of my B- average at a college that did not have a very high status or reputation. Halstead, however, said that he would give me a strong recommendation.

I received notification that I also would need to be interviewed by a member of the Psychology Department faculty and was instructed to arrange an appointment with Louis Thurstone. Of course, I had never heard of Professor Thurstone and had no idea that he was one of the most outstanding mathematical psychologists in the world. My ignorance about Thurstone was a great advantage for me, inasmuch as I had totally renounced arithmetic and mathematics since the sixth grade. I had had a serious altercation with my teacher over an arithmetic problem, which led to her striking me a rather powerful blow. While I continued working in other classes, I did no further arithmetic or mathematics, never turned in any homework, never went to the blackboard to work out problems, and quietly sat through classes without paying attention. I took mathematics courses through high school because I was taking a college preparatory program. Fortunately, no one raised a question about my attitude or behavior (probably because my older brother had gone through the same courses with the same teachers and had done very well), and I was routinely given a G for Good in every course. Fortunately, there were no school psychologists to refer me to, and this saved me a good deal of additional trouble. The requirement in college was that every student take at least one mathematics course. I never did this, and I do not know how I managed to elude the requirement.

Thus, being entirely uninformed about Thurstone's background or area of expertise, I happily went for the interview. As it turned out, there was no discussion of mathematics or even of psychology. I did have an opportunity to tell Thurstone briefly about my experience in examining brain-injured soldiers. Then he asked about the derivation of my last name. When he learned that I was Norwegian, he began telling me about his childhood in Sweden. I mentioned that my native language was Norwegian, and he said that his was Swedish. The languages are in many ways quite similar, and we continued the interview using the two languages. The situation turned out to be an unexpected pleasure for each of us, and it seemed to me that we were good friends when we said good-bye. I never have seen Thurstone's evaluation of me, but I was admitted to graduate school and began my course work in January 1945. Thus began my troubled career as a graduate student at the University of Chicago.

During my first term as a graduate student, I had the misfortune of taking a class from a relatively young assistant professor who spent a considerable amount of time during the course discussing the effects of brain injury and disease in human beings. I had just completed a year in which I had tested, observed at length, and personally associated with a large number of brain-injured soldiers. I also had read the literature in this area at considerable length. Perhaps it was not surprising that I found the instructor's lectures on this subject to be selective, superficial, pedantic, and essentially unrealistic. Unfortunately, I felt some obligation to make the limitations of the instructor's presentation clear not only to the instructor himself but also to the rest of the class. I offended and quickly lost rapport with this particular professor.

Before the beginning of my third quarter, Halstead advised me to enroll in first-year medical school courses because I needed a biological background for the work I intended to pursue, and no such courses were available in the Psychology Department. This advice led to two significant and serious problems: (1) the assistant professor that I had offended proposed to the Psychology Department that I be dismissed as a graduate student because I was not taking courses in the Psychology Department, and (2) my miserably deficient undergraduate background in biology left me very poorly prepared to compete with the medical students. For example, I recall obtaining a copy of the textbook for my histology course and realizing immediately that the words might as well have been in a foreign language. My histology professor, who was co-author of the textbook, distributed a box of slides to each student. I quickly learned that many of the medical students were already familiar with the histological characteristics of tissues from various organs in the body, while I did not even know what a cell, of any type, actually looked like. I had never even looked through a microscope. The situation was indeed stressful, but with a great deal of study and effort I was able to pass the medical school courses. During this time, strong forces were at work to expel me from graduate school, and the young professor who had initiated this action told me personally that he was going to do everything he could to see me dismissed. In fact, he suggested that I did not have the personality characteristics to become a psychologist. I did not help my situation by asking just what those characteristics might be. I was later told that it took personal appeals by both Halstead and Thurstone to keep me in graduate school. I apparently came within inches of never entering the field of psychology.

There was an unbelievable difference in the pleasure and satisfaction I derived from working as Halstead's assistant as compared to my role as a graduate student in the Psychology Department. In Halstead's laboratory I learned to test patients using the interesting tests that he had developed; to expand my knowledge of impairment in patients with brain lesions by observing their test performance, deficiencies, and frustrations as they took the tests; to assist in various special projects; to be involved in data analysis; and to obtain experience in real-life activities. In my academic work, however, I had a feeling that my activities were far from the real world; that students tended by be very self-satisfied and smug, if not actually snobbish; and that my course work, at least to a large extent, amounted mainly to memorizing what someone had written in a book. In time I began to realize that my courses were providing me with a range of knowledge that would be significant for future professional work, and as I got to know my professors and fellow students, I began gradually to accept the Psychology Department and to feel the Department's acceptance of me. My major interest, without question, was focused on the experience and training I was receiving in Halstead's laboratory, even though it was entirely separate from my academic program and I received no academic credit for this work.

My plan for the future was to start my own laboratory in a medical school. I was well aware of the fact that essentially the only psychologists in medical schools were in Departments of Psychiatry, where they worked with people who had emotional and psychiatric disorders. Thus, my role on a medical school faculty would be quite unusual. I also realized that an initial appointment would require that I publish to survive, especially when I was not in a position to offer any significant clinical services. These considerations led me to ask Halstead's permission to administer some tests of my own after patients had completed his test battery, and he kindly permitted me to do this. Thus, I was able to collect some additional data, part of which I used for my doctoral dissertation and part of which was reserved for analysis and publication after I started my own laboratory. I realized that it would take a considerable amount of time to collect my own research data in a new setting, that some years would probably go by before I was able to produce research findings of my own, but that it was imperative that I publish promptly after starting my own laboratory. Because I was able to get such an early start in the collection of data for my doctoral dissertation, I was able to complete my doctorate in less time than most students, and I received my Ph.D. in 1950.

In July 1951, I had completed my work in Chicago and accepted an appointment as an assistant professor of surgery at the Indiana University Medical Center (IUMC). I was told that this was the only title that could be conferred upon me because I was planning to work with neurosurgeons and they were in the Department of Surgery. There had never been a prior appointment of a psychologist to the faculty of the Indiana University Medical School.

The beginning of my own laboratory was carefully considered and planned, by myself and by Halstead, being aware of the absolute necessity of obtaining research–quality information about the condition of each patient's brain as a basis for correlation with psychological test measurements. One of the most fortunate circumstances in my entire career was provided by the support and encouragement offered by two young assistant professors of surgery (neurological surgery), who welcomed me to the IUMC and offered their help. These two men, Robert F. Heimburger and Leslie Willard (Bill) Freeman, both had earlier connections with the University of Chicago, and I had known them at that time. They both had been trained by the eminent neurosurgeon Paul Bucy, who not incidentally and very importantly was a close friend, supporter, and research collaborator in earlier days with Ward Halstead.

Heimburger and Freeman were of inestimable help in promoting the grand experiment that we were undertaking—that of trying to learn how the brain subserved intelligence, cognition, and behavior in a more general sense. Their cooperation set the tone for a remarkable period of assistance and facilitation of my research efforts, spreading to faculty and residents in Neurology and Neuropathology as well. Heimburger, Freeman, William DeMyer, Mark Dyken, John Kalsbeck, Robert Campbell, and Wolfgang Zeman contributed hundreds of hours individually (and thousands of hours collectively), providing detailed summaries of clinical histories, medical and surgical findings, diagrammatic representations of brain lesions observed at surgery, graphic reconstructions of lesions based upon autopsy findings, and so on, all of which were prepared specifically for my research files (and which I still have). I could not have hoped for a more complete contribution to the critically needed definition of the independent variables in my research plan, namely, the status of the brain and characteristics of the damage. Without this cooperation, and the professional expertise that it represented, I never could have made progress in understanding the neuropsychological effects of brain lesions. My gratitude for this gift will never die.

While working in Halstead's laboratory, I had become acutely aware that "brain damage" was such a broad term that it was nearly meaningless, considering the great range of variations that it subsumed. Thus, I recognized the importance of, and my need for, the help that neurologists, neurological surgeons, and neuropathologists could provide. The task, as I saw it, was to relate objective neuropsychological test findings to the host of variables that characterized brain pathology.

Even though I realized that I had a fantastic opportunity, the early years of my research at IUMC were, nevertheless, very lonely in a professional sense. Except for my close colleagues, no one seemed to comprehend what I was attempting to do. For example, other faculty members, whom I had known for months or even years, when introducing me to others would say, "What is it that you do again? Is it something to do with EEG?" It apparently was essentially incomprehensible that a psychologist would be attempting to learn about the behavioral correlates of the brain through studying deficits in persons with brain lesions. In fact, at that time, most textbooks included very little information of this type. So little was known that I myself did not feel that I was able to make a significant clinical contribution through my evaluation of individual patients but that my role instead must be oriented toward gaining new knowledge. I wondered how I ever would be accepted at the medical school, or how I ever might qualify for a promotion in rank, when my colleagues did not even know why I was there or what kind of work I did. It was clear to me that if I did not produce new knowledge I would fall flat on my face, with no pillows to cushion the fall.

During these years I received a great deal of support and encouragement from Halstead. He knew exactly what I was experiencing since he had faced, even more acutely than I, the same challenges and stresses. He had been trained as a physiological psychologist and had experience only with the brains of pigeons (based on his doctoral research) before being faced with evaluating the effects of brain lesions in human beings. Considering the strides he made and the respect he engendered for a neuropsychological approach from neurologists, neurosurgeons, and others, there is no doubt that he laid the seeds for the development of our field and truly deserves to be called the father of modern clinical neuropsychology (Reitan, 1994). I was fortunate in being able to visit him in 1968 a few weeks before he died. The ravages of amyotrophic lateral sclerosis had made it almost impossible for him to move, and his speech was barely intelligible. Despite this, in preparation for my visit he asked his wife to assemble a mass of printout sheets of the data and findings from his latest study, and his bed was covered with these data sheets when I came to see him. By chance, and quite fortunately, the study he was doing was actually very similar to one that I had just recently completed, and his results were essentially similar to my own findings. This made it easy for me to understand the words that he was struggling with to explain his results. As I commented on his findings, and pointed out their significance, his attention was rapt and his eyes danced with pleasure. We had a most enjoyable and satisfying visit, even if I did most of the talking! It was the last time I saw Halstead, and I was once again reminded of what a true scientist he was and how devoted he was to our field, all the way to the end.

The Secret to Any Success I May Have Achieved

One of the things that distressed me greatly as a student was the gap between research findings and clinical applications. This gap was not due to a failure to promptly apply research findings nor to any tendency for research to be basic rather than applied. Halstead and I discussed this matter many times and agreed that research is aimed toward producing generalizations, whereas clinical application focuses on the individual person. In order to produce generalizations, research findings are based upon groups of subjects that reflect data produced by a number of individual persons. Variability is a given and occurs not only within individuals but especially between individuals. On the one hand, such considerations have led to the conclusion that there can be no science of the individual person, although everyone would agree that scientific findings are of great significance in application to the individual person. Nevertheless, as a student, I regularly read research reports that seemed to be important and to provide significant generalizations, and just as regularly I puzzled over how to use the reported information in clinical application.

Before I left Halstead's laboratory to begin my own work at the IUMC, he gave me some very important advice with respect to this problem. I was definitely planning to do research that involved group comparisons and that produced generalizations, but at the same time, I was equally eager to reach a point at which I could draw valid conclusions about brain–behavior relationships in individual cases. Halstead's advice to me was to make it a standard practice to separate data collection (administration of neuropsychological tests) and the initial interpretation of these data from criterion information gathered from the history, the physical neurological examination, specialized neurological diagnostic procedures, findings at surgery, and autopsy findings. The procedure, in practice, would be to test the subject without even knowing whether he or she was a brain-damaged patient or a control subject, and to write an evaluation of the test results with conclusions about the subject being as detailed as possible based only on the test results. After these conclusions were committed to writing, the next step would be to obtain from my medical and surgical colleagues as much definitive information as possible about the person's diagnosis and the specific points of information about the pathology of the individual's brain. The comparison and correlation of conclusions based on the test results alone and the conclusions based upon the entire array of neurological findings would clearly indicate what I knew and what I did not know about interpretation of brain–behavior relationships for each individual subject. This plan was obviously directed toward learning from one's mistakes.

Halstead pointed out to me that if I followed this procedure it could lead to a very profitable interaction between formal research and clinical application. Once

I began to understand clearly what I did not know with respect to clinical application, I would begin to generate hypotheses that needed further investigation. Secondly, when I discerned a degree of consistency in test findings that permitted accurate inferences about the individual patient, I would be in a position to formulate research hypotheses that then could be tested through group comparisons. Confirmation of such hypotheses through formal research would, in turn, provide information about those generalizations that could be applied regularly to the individual subject and identify those generalizations that, because of excessive variability among subjects (or perhaps for other reasons), were not sufficiently reliable for individual application.

I took this advice from Halstead very seriously and followed it rigorously through many hundreds of patients, having first discussed it thoroughly with my neurological and neurosurgical colleagues. Following this procedure, particularly at the beginning, was truly a humbling experience. Even though I was routinely fairly successful in differentiating between patients with brain damage and control subjects, I found that I could not go a great deal further than this with respect to inferences about brain pathology. It became quite clear to me that I needed a much more extensive battery of tests than Halstead's ten measures provided. (In fact, our initial research indicated that only seven of Halstead's ten tests yielded valid differentiations between groups with and without cerebral damage.) The procedure recommended by Halstead turned out to be extremely valuable, both in enlarging the battery to the point that it produced valid results and in drawing conclusions for individual subjects. It also was a wonderful procedure for generating research hypotheses. We were able to conduct and publish a large number of individual studies quite efficiently, mainly because our hypotheses for investigation had already been strongly supported by our findings on individual subjects. Thus, we did not have to pick hypotheses for research either out of the blue sky or from some type of theoretical formulation. Instead, our research hypotheses were based on observations of natural phenomena. We dug very few dry holes, with nearly every research study producing publishable findings. In fact, our "blind" interpretations of test scores for individual subjects, compared and correlated with independently gained definitive neurological information, did much more for our research efforts than our research efforts did for our clinical applications.

Dependent Variables

The dependent variables constituted the tests that made up our battery. It was clear in the initial phases of our program that we needed a much more extensive battery than was initially available. Halstead had never used the Wechsler Scales, but I felt that it would be important to document carefully the general intelligence of every subject in addition to evaluating findings on a range of neuropsychological tests. My first investigation (Reitan, 1955) indicated that three of Halstead's ten tests, on which the Impairment Index was based, did not differentiate between a group of hospitalized control subjects and a group of brain-damaged subjects. Two of these tests were derived from determination of critical flicker frequencies and a third test, which required the subject to engage in time estimations, showed an unacceptable degree of variability both among brain-damaged subjects and controls. Thus, we were left with seven measures. We quickly learned that these seven measures were not sufficient to permit great accuracy, even in identifying the damaged hemisphere in patients with unilateral cerebral lesions. It became clear to me that we were going to have to add a number of tests to the battery that were correlated with the "hard wiring" of the nervous system.

We proceeded to devise tests that were dependent upon sensory input and motor output. Halstead had never measured finger-tapping speed with the non-preferred hand, and we quickly learned that intraindividual comparison of finger-tapping speed was a very useful measure for determining lateralization of a lesion. The work of the neurologists Morris Bender and McDonald Critchley, on sensory imperception, prompted us to develop standardized procedures for evaluating and comparing unilateral and bilateral simultaneous stimulation involving the tactile, auditory, and visual systems. I had experimented with tactile finger recognition and fingertip number-writing perception while in Halstead's laboratory, and I quickly developed standardized procedures for administration and scoring of these tests. We were soon not only in a position of being able to identify accurately all persons with lateralized lesions, but also gained the tremendous additional advantage of correlating these lower-level neuropsychological manifestations with higher-level deficits such as differences in verbal and performance intelligence, the presence of even a mild degree of dysphasia and/or constructional dyspraxia, and so on. I still recall the tremendous excitement I experienced when I first realized that verbal intelligence was consistently impaired with left cerebral lesions, and performance intelligence was even more consistently impaired with right lesions. In fact, in my initial group of subjects, 13 of 14 patients with left cerebral lesions had lower Verbal than Performance IQ values, whereas 15 of 17 subjects with right cerebral lesions had lower Performance than Verbal IQs.

There is also an amusing aside to this study. I submitted this paper for publication to Harry Harlow, who was editor of the *Journal of Comparative and Physiological Psychology*. Harlow wrote back to me, saying that he appreciated receiving the paper and wanted me to understand that he had nothing against studies of brain lesions in human beings (his journal published almost entirely animal studies), but he had one critical question. While I had groups of patients who had undergone operations for brain lesions of the right and left cerebral hemispheres, I had failed to include results on *operated* control subjects. I responded by saying that at our hospital the surgeons did not operate on the brains of control subjects. I heard nothing from Harlow for several weeks, then finally received a letter in which he thanked me for the submitted paper and said that he would accept it for publication. No mention was ever made about his previous inquiry. Many years later, Harry Harlow moved to the University of Arizona after retiring from the University of Wisconsin and had an office across the hall from me. Although we had many interesting discussions, he was never able to remember our correspondence about my study of differential IQ values with relation to lateralization of cerebral lesions.

A tremendously important factor in the development of my research program stemmed from success in competing for research grants, and I wish to acknowledge my gratitude to the National Institutes of Health (from whom I received most of my grant support), the United Cerebral Palsy Foundation, and the James Whitcomb Riley Memorial Association. My first grant, which enabled me to get started, came from this latter organization and represented the funding that permitted us to begin our research on the development of neuropsychological tests for children. This research eventually culminated in development and validation of the Halstead–Reitan Neuropsychological Test Battery for Older Children (ages 9 through 14 years) and the Reitan–Indiana Neuropsychological Test Battery (for children aged 5 through 8 years).

The Halstead–Reitan Neuropsychological Test Batteries have a number of advantages and meet a number of criteria that are not met by individual neuropsychological tests, casually composed test batteries, or even other standard batteries. First, the batteries were developed on a case-by-case basis, in which an experiment was conducted for each individual who was tested. This experiment followed the procedure described above, in which the subject was tested, conclusions recorded in writing with regard to interpretation of the test results, and the adequacy or inadequacy of the conclusions checked out against all of the additional history material and neurological findings. Our early experiences, of course, consisted of many cases in which our conclusions, based on the test results alone, were far from adequate.

As I have noted, it became necessary to add testing procedures as we went along in order to reach the point where we could draw valid conclusions from the test data. In addition, we tried many tests that are not presently included in the battery, omitting them because we found that those tests did not add new information about either the neuropathological findings or neuropsychological deficits. In this sense, we kept the battery as short as possible, trying to achieve a bare-bones testing process. Nevertheless, because of the complexity of brain–behavior relationships, the broad range of pathological conditions that occur, and the variability that must be expected to exist among human beings, the battery (including the Wechsler Scale and the MMPI) does require about six hours for administration.

The case-by-case approach in developing the battery, as described above, was of critical importance in developing a set of tests that had clinical applicability in assessing the individual subject. At the beginning, we wondered about the range and organization of abilities that brain functions would represent and concluded that it was next to impossible to answer this question because brain functions subserve essentially all human behavior. The question of measuring the effects of brain pathology could be answered on an empirical basis, however, by accruing a sufficient number of cases to represent essentially the entire range of brain pathology, supported by evidence that the test battery was differentially relevant to patients with brain-related disorders and control subjects. No other test battery has been developed using this procedure, essentially because of its very time-consuming nature and the necessity of involving neurologists, neurosurgeons, and neuropathologists in the case-by-case validation process.

Over and beyond the case-by-case procedure, we felt that it was necessary to evaluate each individual test included in each of the batteries (adults, older children, younger children) in order to be sure that every test was contributing to the identification of brain involvement. This required a considerable amount of research effort, but our publications now indicate that every test included in the battery serves a purpose with respect to interpretation of individual results. Some tests that are not particularly sensitive to brain damage were included in order to provide a contrast in the individual case with tests that are especially sensitive to brain damage. In addition, the entire battery for each of the age ranges was developed to permit the use of four basic methods of inference that are necessary to describe the uniqueness of neuropsychological impairment in the individual case: (1) level of performance, (2) the occurrence of pathognomonic signs, (3) evaluation of differential scores and patterns of test results, and (4) comparison of similar performances for the individual on the two sides of the body.

The final step in testing the validity of the test batteries concerned the accuracy of classification of individual subjects on the basis of the full range of test results. We have performed and published such studies in considerable detail, and the results support the validity of the test batteries not only in terms of differentiating brain-damaged from control subjects but also in terms of many other characteristics of brain involvement. For example, diffuse versus focal lesions are classified with a high degree of accuracy, lateralized lesions are correctly identified in the great majority of cases, chronic and static brain involvement versus acutely destructive brain involvement can be differentiated, and the type of brain disease or damage can be inferred from the test results alone with considerable accuracy. This latter advantage is extremely important in cases of litigation, inasmuch as there are a great number of brain disorders that can occur and may be present in individual cases. If the lawsuit is based upon traumatic brain injury, and the expert neuropsychologist cannot differentiate between traumatic brain injury and other types of brain disorders on the basis of the litigant's test results, specificity of conclusions is lost.

After having spent 19 years at the Indiana University Medical Center, and having achieved the results described above, I was eager to move to a location that would permit me to continue working at a medical center but also would give me an opportunity for teaching psychology graduate students. The University of Washington offered this type of situation under the caption of two professorships: professor of neurological surgery in the medical school and professor of psychology in the school of arts and sciences. Being housed in the Child Development and Mental Retardation Center at the University of Washington, much of my research at that institution focused on children. Nevertheless, the time required for the combination of clinical work and teaching, preparation of grant applications, research studies, and publication of individual papers. made it quite impossible to accomplish the next step that was necessary, which was to publish books. Although it had been possible to complete one edited book (Reitan & Davison, 1974), it was clear that our research studies and clinical procedures required much more detailed publication in book form.

Finally, in 1977, I decided to leave the medical environment entirely and moved to the Psychology Department of the University of Arizona, particularly hoping that I would find time to write books summarizing my work. I had not realized that every position, whether in a psychology department or in a medical school, had the potential for consuming all of one's time, and by 1985, I had scarcely even begun the first book. At that time, I applied for and received a sabbatical year, planning to sequester myself in my office and devote my time to writing a book. Fortunately, I received a critically important piece of advice from a seasoned member of the department. He advised me not to come into my office at all, because if I did, I would find myself still involved in Psychology Department business and my book-writing attempts would suffer. I took this advice, and in less than a year I had completed my first book. This experience made it clear to me that I should not return to the University but instead should resign and go without a paycheck in order to complete my obligations to the profession. I did return half-time for another year, largely because of responsibilities to several graduate students, but decided that the only way to get my work done was to leave the University. Deborah Wolfson, who had become thoroughly experienced and expert in the Halstead–Reitan methodology, joined me in preparation of books that described the test batteries, reviewed and summarized the many research studies that had been published, and illustrated in detail the interpretation of the test results. An extensive series of books ensued, not only on the test batteries themselves but also on specific topics and categories of brain damage (e.g., aphasia in both children and adults, mild and severe traumatic brain injuries, spontaneous recovery from brain injury, and methods for facilitating further recovery). In fact, these recent years have been spent in the preparation of nine or ten major books, many chapters for books edited by others, and a continuing series of individual studies covering a broad range of topics in clinical neuropsychology.

The most recent chapter, being completed as this writing is in process, concerns the use of the Halstead–Reitan batteries with children who have learning disabilities. Our approach has been to study children with clear limitations in making academic progress but who have no significant neurological findings, and compare them with children who are able to make normal progress and with children who have brain damage and corresponding neurological evidence of brain pathology. With respect to level of performance, these three groups routinely fall in sequence on nearly all of the tests in our battery. The controls perform best, the learning-disabled children occupy an intermediate position, and brain-damaged children generally perform most poorly. However, level of performance obviously is not a sufficient basis for understanding the neuropsychology of any particular child. As described above, our test batteries include a broad range of measures, and intraindividual variations provide tremendously important information about the uniqueness of neuropsychological functioning of the individual child. In brief, the test results alone permit more than 80% accuracy in assignment of each child into his or her correct group. This finding makes it quite clear that neuropsychological impairment, at least to a degree, is a highly significant factor in the characterization of learning-disabled children as well as brain-damaged children, even though neurological (medical) findings are within normal limits in both the learning-disabled and normal groups.

The implications of these findings have tremendous significance for appropriate remediation of children with learning disabilities. Neuropsychological testing using the Halstead–Reitan batteries identifies the deficits of the child with learning disabilities, which in turn identifies the fundamental abilities in need of remediation. Following this procedure, we have had remarkable success in individual cases in remediation of fundamental neuropsychological deficits that have served to block normal acquisition of academic skills. Interestingly, the deficits most commonly seen that require remediation involve (1) attention and concentration abilities, and (2) abilities in the area of reasoning, abstraction, and logical analysis. In a number of instances, when we have had the opportunity to remediate deficits in these areas, progress in development of academic competencies has come along very well, almost as if the gate that had barred progress had been opened (Reitan & Wolfson, in press).

Grateful acknowledgment must be given to the many students, fellows, and colleagues who have played a role in my work and who have attended the training workshops that I have given over more than a 30-year period with the participation of Hallgrim Kløve, James C. Reed, Homer B. C. Reed, Deborah Wolfson, Jim Hom, and Janice Nici. This list is made up of thousands of neuropsychologists, many of whom have gone on to become leaders in the field, including Kenneth Adams, Sureyya Dikmen, Carl Dodrill, Donald Doehring, Alan Finlayson, Francis (Joe) Fishburne, Kathleen Fitzhugh-Bell, William Gaddes, Gerald Goldstein, Igor Grant, Robert Heaton, Lawrence Hartlage, Robert Knights, Joseph Matarazzo, Ruth Matarazzo, Charles Matthews, Manfred Meier, Oscar Parsons, Byron Rourke, Elbert Russell, and Paul Satz.

Final Conclusions

Development of the Halstead–Reitan Neuropsychological Test Batteries had a strong influence on development of clinical applications, as well as further research, regarding the effects of brain lesions. Dean (1985), in his review of the Halstead–Reitan Neuropsychological Test Battery for Adults, commented that

> neuropsychological assessment in North America has focused on the development of test batteries that would predict the presence of brain damage while offering a comprehensive view of a patient's individual functions.

Numerous batteries have been offered as wide-band measures of the integrity and functioning of the brain. However, the Halstead–Reitan Neuropsychological Test Battery (HRB) remains the most researched and widely utilized measure in the United States." (p. 644)

Meier (1985) also reviewed the HRB for Adults, and commented as follows:

This comprehensive neuropsychological test battery has a long and illustrious history of clinical research and application in American clinical neuropsychology. Following its inaugural presentation to the psychological community (Halstead, 1947), the careful nurturance of concept and application by Reitan (Reitan & Davison, 1974), the battery has had perhaps the most widespread impact of any approach in clinical neuropsychology. It seems reasonable to state that in the first half of the period since World War II, during which neuropsychology expanded so remarkably, this approach was the primary force in stimulating clinical research and application in this country. (p. 646)

It is indeed gratifying to have been a participant in the rapid growth and development of this field, despite all the vagaries and circumstantial events.

REFERENCES

Dean, R. S. (1985). Review of the Halstead-Reitan Neuropsychological Test Battery. In J. V. Mitchell (Ed.), *The ninth mental measurements yearbook* (pp. 642–646). Highland Park, NJ: Gryphon.

Halstead, W. C. (1947). *Brain and intelligence: A quantitative study of the frontal lobes.* Chicago: University of Chicago Press.

Meier, M. J. (1985). Review of the Halstead-Reitan Neuropsychological Test Battery. In J.V. Mitchell (Ed.), *The ninth mental measurements yearbook* (pp. 646–649). Highland Park, NJ: Gryphon.

Reitan, R. M. (1955). An investigation of the validity of Halstead's measures of biological intelligence. *Archives of Neurology and Psychiatry, 73,* 28–35.

Reitan, R. M. (1994). Ward Halstead's contributions to neuropsychology and the Halstead-Reitan Neuropsychological Test Battery. *Journal of Clinical Psychology, 50,* 47–70.

Reitan, R. M., & Davison, L. A. (Eds.). (1974). *Clinical neuropsychology; Current status and applications.* Washington, DC: Hemisphere Publishing.

Reitan, R. M. & Wolfson, D. (in press). The Halstead–Reitan Neuropsychological Test Battery: Research findings and clinical application. In A. S. Kaufman & N. L. Kaufman (Eds.), *Specific learning disabilities: Psychological assessment and evaluation.* Cambridge, UK: Cambridge University Press.

15

My Odyssey in Child–Clinical Neuropsychology

Byron P. Rourke

*T*he editors of this volume have asked for an explanation of the principal influences that have been formative vis-à-vis my work as a scientist–practitioner. Although this may seem a formidable task, it is, for me, fairly simple and straightforward. These influences are tangible and obvious to me and are quite easy to recount. I trust that they will shed light on the odyssey that I have experienced.

Early Influences

I learned to read on the lap of my Aunt Eileen. She was a good teacher. She led initially, and then followed what I was doing, and gently corrected the mistakes I made. From her, I learned how to teach.

When I went to kindergarten, I knew how to read single words, and I had some appreciation for the context in which they contributed to meaning. My trek through elementary school, however, was not pleasant. It was marked by almost persistent boredom, punctuated only by my trips to and from the public library, where I immersed myself in the pleasures of everything from *Tom Sawyer* to *The Great Escape*. Nothing that transpired outside of this bookish atmosphere seemed relevant. I gleaned from these experiences that learning proceeds best when the learner is allowed to develop along paths of his or her own choosing.

Around age seven, I recovered from a chronic illness that has yet to be explained. What I remember most about this time is that I was finally able to run. The exhilaration that ensued was unprecedented—I ran all over the place. Never content with sashaying along, I jumped hedges quickly and, in my mind, overwhelmingly—whether or not the hedges were there. When enthusiasm and capacity coalesce, much development can clearly transpire.

Around the age of 12, I discovered that I could play basketball. That marked a very significant departure from just running and jumping. It constituted a focus for energies that had, theretofore, run in more directions than Carter had little liver pills. Thus I found from playing basketball the value of focused energy and learning.

What I liked about basketball was that you could practice it by yourself. You could launch jump shots (which I thought I invented) from any angle—with your back to the basket, under the basket, several feet from the basket, facing straight on. Once learned through agonizing repetitions, potting these shots during a game was a piece of cake. I believe all those jump shots taught me that there is no substitute for practice and that you can do much of that on your own.

High school followed, bringing boring, vapid lectures on everything from the evils of virtually all forms of sexual behavior to the glories of the faded Roman Empire. High school was about as interesting as finding out that water in the toilets in the Southern Hemisphere flush backward. Fortunately, there was basketball. I learned from high school that a low threshold for boredom, although advantageous for any number of reasons, can have a very negative side.

University of Windsor I

Then came university. For reasons that I won't go into here, I did not play competitive basketball. This turned out to be a good move. Instead of wrecking my elbows on thick glass backboards, I got back to what Aunt Eileen and I used to do—reading.

I read—please pardon the overused term—voraciously. Particularly fascinated by the pre-Elizabethan period, I foraged for and downed everything I could find on Thomas More, Henry VIII, and Archbishop Cranmer. I was fascinated with Anne Boleyn. Slowly, my interest in the chronology of events turned to a quest for understanding the principal players; this served as the foundation for my desire to study psychology. I should note that my interest in history is abiding and is reflected in two publications dealing with the history of neuropsychology in Canada (Fuerst & Rourke, 1995a; Rourke, Fisk, Strang, & Gates, 1981) and one that deals, in a rather person-centered manner, with the early years of the history of the International Neuropsychological Society (Rourke & Murji, 2000).

Getting back to the skein of this story, I should point to the very good teachers I had in philosophy, especially one who was an expert on Plato and Aristotle. I also was—actually, still am—fascinated by the existentialists of the late nineteenth and early-to middle-twentieth centuries. Albert Camus was and is my hero. All of these interests arose because of excellent pedagogues and avid reading.

I also had the good fortune to have several excellent teachers in psychology. Two of these were quite psychoanalytically inclined, and both were excellent lecturers. Toward the end of my undergraduate years, I took only psychology courses. When applying to graduate school, I was convinced that I wanted to apply experimental techniques with children for the elucidation of psychoanalytic hypotheses. Naturally, I applied to Yale in hopes of working with Neal Miller and John Dollard. Unfortunately, my application arrived too late to be considered. About that time, I was awarded a Woodrow Wilson Fellowship, and I decided to apply to Fordham. I entered that hallowed institution in September 1962.

Fordham University

My first encounters with professors at Fordham were most uplifting. I was especially impressed by Anne Anastasi and John Walsh. I also was captivated by Joseph Kubis. Perhaps the following paragraphs from my unfinished memoirs will convey just how exciting this period was for me.

It was the early 1960s. I was in graduate school at Fordham University in "da Bronx," and two JFKs were part of my everyday life. One was a president; the other, a professor—Joseph Francis Kubis.

The son of Polish immigrants, Kubis worked his way through secondary school and St. John's University by lugging blocks of ice up the stairs of tenements in the boroughs of Brooklyn and Queens. He was also an excellent football player.

An abiding interest in mathematics led him to choose graduate school rather than a career as a professional football player. Once embarked on this academic path, however, his interests turned to psychology, especially its biostatistical dimensions. This led him to Fordham where he obtained a doctoral degree in psychology.

When I arrived at Fordham, JFK had been teaching there for some 20 years. By this time, his interests were decidedly eclectic in nature. As would be expected, he taught a course in biostatistics. But he also conducted seminars in stress and anxiety, in the psychology of emotion, and in some dimensions of psychological intervention. His intense activity as a scholar was reflected in his multifaceted studies of lie detection, stressful interrogation, and the impact of conflict on adaptive functioning. His abiding interest in emotional development, stress, and anxiety was reflected in the supervisory role that he played in the psychology section of a large public institution devoted to assisting people in adapting to their psychosocial conflicts. His deep curiosity about space exploration led him to direct the psychophysiological dimensions of experiments carried out with the astronauts in the very first years of the U.S. space program.

There was no difference between his teaching styles and his approach to life. His formal lectures were lively, engaging, far-ranging, and marked by a degree of incisiveness and eloquence that all but precluded inattention on the part of his students. His seminars were conducted on a quite different note, marked by a constant pressure on his students to ask the right questions and to follow through with their resolution. Both styles were appropriate to the subject matter and proved to be models for those of us who later embarked upon academic careers.

His research always was conducted with the active participation of students. Every step of the project was discussed and evaluated in the context of small group discussions. Although he was quite clearly in charge of the final "product," he made us feel that we had made important contributions to, and had a clear stake in, the experiments.

But all of the foregoing is only the rather public side of Kubis. The very important dimensions of my relationship with him included the long hours of discussion over lunch and at the end of the day, the walks before classes in the late afternoon, the spontaneous bursts of enthusiasm that marked the achievement of an insight; these were the dimensions of "teacher" that were most inspirational to me and that changed my life in an irrevocable manner.

Kubis did not have clearly delineated slots into which he fit the intellectual life. He flowed easily between and among physiology, philosophy, physics, chemistry, literature, mathematics, history, and psychology. He knew how to lead his students to insight and how to keep them questioning their conclusions. He was relentless in his pursuit of truth and humble in its presence. In all of this, he never hesitated to encourage me to develop the combination of open-mindedness and tough-headedness that he so clearly exemplified and so clearly wanted me to emulate.

This marvelous man never had to apologize. He was never out of touch or out of place. His unerring and uncompromising pursuit of excellence in pure and applied science was palpable and inspirational. He lived his academic life fully and without compromise. The pursuit of truth permeated his being. He could not be understood without an appreciation of these dimensions of his personality.

I have had the honor of encountering, and being influenced by, several excellent teachers. Some of what I do today stems from their influence. But *what* I am today—that I presume to call my essence—is very much the product of my interactions with JFK. There is no dimension of my academic and personal life that is not influenced by him.

In line with my initial aims for research, my doctoral dissertation was entitled "Effect of Anxiety on Causal Thinking and Performance on a Cognitive–Perceptual Task." Convinced that anxiety was the fundamental cause of faulty perception, learning, and thinking, it seemed logical to compose groups of school-aged children on the basis of level of anxiety and then measure aspects of their perception, learning, and thinking. I was not disappointed by the statistically significant relationships that emerged, but I was struck by the rather meager amounts of variance explained thereby. In other words, this no longer struck me as a fruitful area of inquiry.

At the urging of Joe Kubis, I began to read the work of Ralph Reitan. Kubis and Reitan (or one of Ralph's associates) had collaborated on a number of projects related to the NASA astronaut program. (As stated above, Kubis was the director of the program relating to psychological and psychophysiological dimensions of astronaut selection and monitoring.) I came away from these readings with an entirely different, though complementary, slant with respect to problems in perception, learning, and thinking—that is, that problems in these areas could be due to limitations in some neurodevelopmental dimensions, including neurological disease, disorder, and dysfunction.

University of Windsor II

In the midst of all of this, I accepted an offer of a tenure-track position from my alma mater. There were several reasons for taking this offer over others: my wife and I wanted to raise our children in Windsor, the University very much valued teaching, and there would be little pressure to produce a lot of research early in my career. This pretty well coincided with my view that a stable developing family is the bedrock upon which to build anything worthwhile. I also love teaching, and I needed time to develop a research program.

While a professor at Windsor, my reading in neuropsychology, especially of the child/developmental variety, intensified. I took any course I could find that would lead to an understanding of neuroanatomy and neurophysiology. I went to visit Ralph Reitan in Indianapolis and then in Seattle, took all of his workshops, and kept in touch with him as my research plans progressed. I remember him as being very open and friendly with me and enormously generous with respect to clarifying my research aims and methods. I never asked him a question that he did not answer, and his answers were far more than I bargained for. I was especially impressed by his scientific approach to clinical problems and his clinically inspired approach to scientific issues. My attempt to characterize this sort of approach appeared much later (Rourke, 1995b). At the same time, I was studying the methods used by Robert Knights in London, Ontario. He too was very generous with his time and advice.

Although barely aware of it then, I was "becoming" a child–clinical neuropsychologist. I acquired a license (actually, "registration" where I live) to practice psychology and was fortunate enough to establish a center for the study of brain–behavior relationships at a local hospital that specialized in neurosurgery. That was in 1967, and I shuffled my activities between there and the University of Windsor until 1986.

During that time period, I met George Carbonin, who has become a lifelong friend. George and his wife were born in Venezia. They emigrated to Canada after World War II so that George could begin his six-year neurosurgical residency at the Montreal Neurological Institute. Following a brief sojourn in New Brunswick, he came to Windsor to practice neurosurgery. We struck up an immediate friendship, and he offered me access to his operating room and his patients for study.

By 1970, our research center was turning into an assessment center as well. We now felt confident not only in studying our patients but also in offering assessment results and recommendations for their habilitation/rehabilitation. We were inundated with referrals.

Also at this time, the neuropsychology program at the University of Windsor was in the throes of development. Students in the program did their practica and internships with me at the research center that now had clinical responsibilities. Although this sort of "inbreeding" procedure is now frowned upon, it should be remembered that, in the late-1960s and early-1970s, there were precious few places in North America where a student could go to get organized practica and internships in clinical neuropsychology.

Our first studies of children were published in the early 1970s: Rourke and Telegdy (1971); Czudner and Rourke (1972); Rourke, Young, and Flewelling (1971); Rourke and Czudner (1972); Rourke, Dietrich, and Young (1973); Rourke, Yanni, MacDonald, and Young (1973); Rourke and Finlayson (1975). I am especially pleased that these investigations have stood the test of time, in that their results and conclusions have, to my knowledge, never been disputed. More important, all of these studies were quite instrumental in the models that we subsequently developed. In addition, they were all done in collaboration with my students.

Notice that Gerald Young looms large in these early studies. His clinical insights inspired many of them. And these insights do not stop there. We have continued our collaboration (e.g., Rourke, Young, & Leenaars, 1989; Rourke, Young, Strang, & Russell, 1986) and friendship over 'lo these many years.

Things were going well. The graduate students were exposed to quite appropriate educational experiences: for example, they were being taught neuroanatomy, neurophysiology, and neuropathology by George Carbonin. They were dressing up in their "greens" to watch him and other neurological and vascular surgeons perform their work. The students came away from these experiences with a wealth of information that, I am sure, remains with them to this day.

By the mid-1970s, we had become much more interested in complex problems relating to the neuropsychology of learning disabilities (LD). Investigations in these areas have proven to be the foundation upon which we have developed models of the syndrome of Nonverbal Learning Disabilities (NLD) and Basic Phonological Processing Disabilities (BPPD) (Rourke & Finlayson, 1978; Rourke & Strang, 1978; Strang & Rourke, 1983. Among other things, we have been able to demonstrate that these two subtypes can be reliably differentiated from each other and that the psychosocial consequences of each are also quite different (Rourke & Fisk, 1988; Rourke & Fuerst, 1991, 1995).

In parallel with this research program, we generated some principles and models of assessment and intervention for children with frank brain damage and the more subtle patterns of neuropsychological assets and deficits that characterize LD (Rourke, 1976, 1994; Rourke & Adams, 1984; Rourke, Bakker, Fisk, & Strang, 1983; Rourke, Fisk, & Strang, 1986).

In the midst of these efforts, I was energized by the "international" figures that I met and befriended during this period. Harry van der Vlugt was the most influential among these. He obtained doctoral degrees from the University of Florida (under the mentorship of Paul Satz) and the University of Leiden in The Netherlands. The latter degree was in medicine (neurology). I first met Harry in conjunction with two meetings in the United States (the first International Neuropsychological Society [INS] meeting in New Orleans in 1973 and another meeting at American Psychological Association [APA] in New Orleans in 1974). We became fast friends during a NATO conference in Korsor, Denmark, in 1975. Our collaboration in research and the refining of clinical neuropsychological practice since that time has been especially important to me (e.g., Rourke, van der Vlugt, &

Rourke, in press). Also, my longtime friendship with Robert Stelmack inspired my interest in evoked potential studies (Dool, Stelmack, & Rourke, 1993; Stelmack, Rourke, & van der Vlugt, 1995). It is especially gratifying that his testing of our models of LD (e.g., Miles & Stelmack, 1993; Stelmack & Miles, 1990) continues to extend our knowledge of brain–behavior relationships in this area.

With respect to content and methodology, it is important to note that my work with my students has been particularly productive. For example, we helped to pioneer the application of subtyping methodology to learning disabilities (e.g., Fisk & Rourke, 1979; Petrauskas & Rourke, 1979). This line of research (Rourke, 1975) led to a concentration on the reliability of such subtypes (e.g., Rourke, 1985) and their validity (e.g., Rourke, 1991). Our research effort reached a kind of culmination in our work on subtypes of psychosocial functioning in children with LD (Fuerst, Fisk, & Rourke, 1989, 1990; Fuerst & Rourke, 1993, 1995; Rourke, 1988a, 2000; Rourke & Fuerst, 1991, 1995). My collaboration with John Fisk and Darren Fuerst has been very fruitful and has arisen out of our ease of communication with and respect for each other.

Throughout this period, our interest in the syndrome of NLD rose to a kind of fever pitch (Rourke, 1982, 1987, 1988b, 1989). This theoretical development resulted largely from my collaboration with Louis Costa. His landmark paper with Elkhonon Goldberg (Goldberg & Costa, 1981) changed the entire course of my views with respect to hemisphericity and, especially, the importance of the distinctions between inter- and intramodal integration (Rourke, 1982; Rourke & Fisk, 1988). The salience of accommodation to novel material and the development of descriptive systems to deal with such material looms large in the neurodevelopmental model of NLD and the "white matter" theory that we have developed to account for its complex manifestations (Rourke, 1989, 1995a). As would be predicted on the basis of deductions from this theory, several forms of pediatric neurological disease, disorder, and dysfunction in which the NLD phenotype is paramount (e.g., Asperger syndrome, early shunted hydrocephalus) have been shown to involve perturbations in white matter development and/or function (e.g., Ellis & Gunter, 1999; Fletcher et al. 1992). (The interested reader may wish to consult Rourke et al. [in press] for a recent update of some of this evidence.)

A little historical vignette may help illustrate this interaction. While traveling together from Copenhagen, Denmark, to Helsinki, Finland, and eventually to Bergen, Norway, I was attempting to write the INS presidential address that I was to deliver in Bergen (Rourke, 1982). The address was my first attempt to extend the Goldberg and Costa model to the realm of LD. Having the great fortune to have Louis sitting across from me during this particular odyssey allowed me the opportunity to ask him crucial questions that arose when attempting to do this. Had he not been there throughout those several days leading up to the final address, I am sure that the final product would have been considerably less than illuminating.

Although I must take credit for the view that the NLD syndrome is a phenotype for a wide variety of types of pediatric neurological disease, disorder, and dysfunction, this notion rests on the pioneering work of several neuropsychologists with whom I have had a very cordial relationship. Principal among these is Jack M. Fletcher, whose groundbreaking work in traumatic brain injury (e.g., Fletcher & Levin, 1988) and early shunted hydrocephalus (e.g., Fletcher et al., 1992; Fletcher, Brookshire, Bohan, Brandt, & Davidson, 1995) has been pivotal in the development of this theory.

The Journals

I played a role in founding three neuropsychology journals. I must sound a similar refrain in recounting how each of these journals came to be. For example, the founding of the *Journal of Clinical Neuropsychology* (eventually transformed into the *Journal of Clinical and Experimental Neuropsychology*) has a history that relates to friendship. I could put this no better than Louis Costa (1998) did:

> At the Santa Fe (INS meeting) Byron Rourke suggested to me that I start a journal of clinical neuropsychology. The idea of starting such a journal had never occurred to me. I had first met Byron in Toronto where he had played a major role in setting up the 1976 (INS) meeting. I was quite impressed with his verbal skills and his organizational ability. I thought about the journal for a few minutes and then asked him to join me in the project. He rapidly accepted and somehow I got the impression that that was what he had had in mind at the outset. It was the beginning of a warm friendship. (p. 5)

So too, *The Clinical Neuropsychologist* evolved out of several conversations in Italy with my good friend Kenneth Adams. And *Child Neuropsychology* was born one evening in Madeira during a dinner attended by Sara Sparrow and Harry van der Vlugt. We retired to a quiet place and, with great enthusiasm, decided to collaborate in developing this journal. The rest, as they say, is history.

Recent History

As for recent history, I would pay tribute to three former students with whom I have worked and whose research exemplifies the type of collaborative efforts that members of our group have been able to mount. Katy Butler (Fuerst) passed away two years ago. This was a tragedy on a variety of levels, one of these being the snuffing out of a very bright future in pediatric neuropsychology. Her contributions to the explications of white matter theory and related considerations (e.g., Fuerst & Rourke, 1995b; Fuerst, Dool, & Rourke, 1995) and her groundbreaking work in the delineation of subtypes of psychosocial functioning in pediatric traumatic brain injury (e.g., Butler, Rourke, Fuerst, & Fisk, 1997) stand as an impressive legacy that we intend to continue and develop. Also, the work of Nancy Fisher in the area of the subtyping of Alzheimer's disease (e.g., Fisher, Rourke, & Bieliauskas, 1999; Fisher et al., 1996, 1997), carried out in conjunction with my good friend and colleague Linas Bieliauskas, will, in my opinion, continue to leaven this field. Finally, Katherine Tsatsanis and I have collaborated on a number of projects to which she brought her considerable insight and scholarship (e.g., Rourke & Tsatsanis, 1995, 1996, 2000; Tsatasanis, Fuerst, & Rourke, 1997; Tsatsanis & Rourke, 1995a, 1995b). My work with Nancy and Katherine will proceed. They continue to inspire me, and I continue to learn from them.

Yale University

The university to which I applied too late for graduate study invited me to take up a faculty appointment in the Child Study Center, School of Medicine, in 1993. I readily accepted and found myself once again inspired by the work of persons who, before that time and since, have been marvels of dedication and cooperation. The projects that we have worked on together are ones about which I am particularly pleased (e.g., Cicchetti, Showalter, Rourke, & Fuerst, 1992; Cicchetti et al., 1992; Klin, Volkmar, Sparrow, Cicchetti, & Rourke, 1995). As the studies of persons with autism, Asperger syndrome, and other developmental disabilities evolve at Yale, it is certain that much will be learned. As one might expect, I am particularly concerned about the light that the results of these investigations and others (e.g., Ellis & Gunter, 1999) will shed upon the white matter model.

Concluding Remarks

If all of this above sounds like friendship and mentorship have played major roles in my progress in neuropsychology, I make no apologies. Without the bonds that friendship fosters and cements, not much would have been accomplished. Without such alliances, my efforts in neuropsychology—and, especially, clinical neuropsychology—would languish. This is my experience. I suppose I would consider contrary opinions, but they had best be very compelling.

In closing, let me return to my relationship with Joseph Kubis. My graduation from Fordham, and even his death some years ago, did not bring our relationship to an end. His abiding presence is apparent to me when I talk with my students, when I pursue a scientific project, when I ponder a particularly difficult clinical problem, and when I write.

Especially when the going gets tough in these arenas, I can hear him say: "Are you sure, Byron?" "Is that all there is to it?" "Have you overlooked something?" "Have you asked the right question yet?"

My invariable replies to these resonating queries: "Joe, I'm still working on it." "I am pretty sure that something will come of this." "But, then, . . . ?"

Science—and, indeed, any form of serious intellectual inquiry—is about questions, not answers. Once you pose the right question, the answer is a piece of cake.

JFK taught me that. If I have a message, it is this one. Actually, it is the only thing that I ever really try to teach—to my students and to anyone else who would care to listen.

So continues my odyssey.

REFERENCES

Butler, K., Rourke, B. P., Fuerst, D. R., & Fisk, J. L. (1997). A typology of psychosocial functioning in pediatric closed-head injury. *Child Neuropsychology, 3*, 98–133.

Cicchetti, D. B., Showalter, D., Rourke, B. P., & Fuerst, D. R. (1992). A computer program for analyzing ordinal trends with dichotomous outcomes: Application toneuropsychological research. *The Clinical Neuropsychologist, 6*, 458–463.

Cicchetti, D. V., Volkmar, F., Sparrow, S. S., Cohen, D., Fermanian, J., & Rourke, B. P. (1992). Assessing the reliability of clinical scales when data have both nominal and ordinal features: Proposed guidelines for neuropsychological assessments. *Journal of Clinical and Experimental Neuropsychology, 14*, 662–675.

Costa, L. (1998). Professionalism in neuropsychology: The early years. *The Clinical Neuropsychologist, 12*, 1–7.

Czudner, G., & Rourke, B. P. (1972). Age differences in visual reaction time of "brain-damaged" and normal children under regular and irregular preparatory interval conditions. *Journal of Experimental Child Psychology, 13*, 516–526.

Dool, C. B., Stelmack, R. M., & Rourke, B. P. (1993). Event-related potentials in children with learning disabilities. *Journal of Clinical Child Psychology, 22*, 387–398.

Ellis, H. D., & Gunter, H. L. (1999). Asperger syndrome: A simple matter of white matter? *Trends in Cognitive Sciences, 3*, 192–200.

Fisher, N. J., Rourke, B. P., & Bieliauskas, L. A. (1999). Neuropsychological subgroups of patients with Alzheimer's disease: An examination of the first 10 years of the CERAD data. *Journal of Clinical and Experimental Neuropsychology, 21*, 488–518.

Fisher, N. J., Rourke, B. P., Bieliauskas, L.,

Giordani, B., Berent, S., & Foster, N. L. (1996). Neuropsychological subgroups of patients with Alzheimer's disease. *Journal of Clinical and Experimental Neuropsychology, 18*, 349–370.

Fisher, N. J., Rourke, B. P., Bieliauskas, L. A., Giordani, B., Berent, S., & Foster, N. L. (1997). Unmasking the heterogeneity of Alzheimer's disease: Case studies of individuals from distinct neuropsychological subgroups. *Journal of Clinical and Experimental Neuropsychology, 19*, 713–754.

Fisk, J. L., & Rourke, B. P. (1979). Identification of subtypes of learning-disabled children at three age levels: A neuropsychological, multivariate approach. *Journal of Clinical Neuropsychology, 1*, 289–310.

Fletcher, J. M., Bohan, T. P., Brandt, M. E., Brookshire, B. L., Beaver, S. R., Francis, D. J., Davidson, K. C., Thompson, N. M., & Miner, M. E. (1992). Cerebral white matter and cognition in hydrocephalic children. *Archives of Neurology, 49*, 818–825.

Fletcher, J. M., Brookshire, B. L., Bohan, T. P., Brandt, M., & Davidson, K. (1995). Early hydrocephalus. In B. P. Rourke (Ed.), *Syndrome of nonverbal learning disabilities: Neurodevelopmental manifestations* (pp. 206–238). New York: Guilford Press.

Fletcher, J. M., & Levin, H. (1988). Neurobehavioral effects of brain injury in children. In D. K. Routh (Ed.), *Handbook of pediatric psychology* (pp. 258–295). New York: Guilford Press.

Fuerst, D. R., Fisk, J. L., & Rourke, B. P. (1989). Psychosocial functioning of learning-disabled children: Replicability of statistically derived subtypes. *Journal of Consulting and Clinical Psychology, 57*, 275–280.

Fuerst, D. R., Fisk, J. L., & Rourke, B. P. (1990). Psychosocial functioning of learning-disabled children: Relations between WISC Verbal IQ-Performance IQ discrepancies and personality subtypes. *Journal of Consulting and Clinical Psychology*, 58, 657–660.

Fuerst, D. R., & Rourke, B. P. (1993). Psychosocial functioning of children: Relations between personality subtypes and academic achievement. *Journal of Abnormal Child Psychology*, 21, 597–607.

Fuerst, D. R., & Rourke, B. P. (1995). Psychosocial functioning of children with learning disabilities at three age levels. *Child Neuropsychology*, 1, 38–55.

Fuerst, K. B., Dool, C. B., & Rourke, B. P. (1995). Velocardiofacial syndrome. In B. P. Rourke (Ed.), *Syndrome of nonverbal learning disabilities: Neurodevelopmental manifestations* (pp. 119–137). New York: Guilford Press.

Fuerst, K. B., & Rourke, B. P. (1995a). Human neuropsychology in Canada: The 1980s. *Canadian Psychology*, 36, 12–45.

Fuerst, K. B., & Rourke, B. P. (1995b). White matter physiology and pathology. In B. P. Rourke (Ed.), *Syndrome of nonverbal learning disabilities: Neurodevelopmental manifestations* (pp. 27–44). New York: Guilford Press.

Goldberg, E., & Costa, L. D. (1981). Hemisphere differences in the acquisition and use of descriptive systems. *Brain and Language*, 14, 144–173.

Klin, A., Volkmar, F. R., Sparrow, S. S., Cicchetti, D. V., & Rourke, B. P. (1995). Validity and neuropsychological characterization of Asperger syndrome: Convergence with Nonverbal Learning Disabilities syndrome. *Journal of Child Psychology and Psychiatry*, 36, 1127–1140.

Miles, J. E., & Stelmack, R. M. (1993). Reading disability subtypes and the effects of auditory and visual priming on event-related potentials. *Journal of Clinical and Experimental Neuropsychology*, 15, 43–64.

Petrauskas, R. J., & Rourke, B. P. (1979). Identification of subtypes of retarded readers: A neuropsychological, multivariate approach. *Journal of Clinical Neuropsychology*, 1, 17–37.

Rourke, B. P. (1975). Brain–behavior relationships in children with learning disabilities: A research program. *American Psychologist*, 30, 911-920.

Rourke, B. P. (1976). Issues in the neuropsychological assessment of children with learning disabilities. *Canadian Psychological Review*, 17, 89–102.

Rourke, B. P. (1982). Central processing deficiencies in children: Toward a developmental neuropsychological model. *Journal of Clinical Neuropsychology*, 4, 1–18.

Rourke, B. P. (Ed.). (1985). *Neuropsychology of learning disabilities: Essentials of subtype analysis.* New York: Guilford Press.

Rourke, B. P. (1987). Syndrome of nonverbal learning disabilities: The final common pathway of white-matter disease/dysfunction? *The Clinical Neuropsychologist*, 1, 209–234.

Rourke, B. P. (1988a). Socio-emotional disturbances of learning-disabled children. *Journal of Consulting and Clinical Psychology*, 56, 801–810.

Rourke, B. P. (1988b). The syndrome of nonverbal learning disabilities: Developmental manifestations in neurological disease, disorder, and dysfunction. *The Clinical Neuropsychologist*, 2, 293–330.

Rourke, B. P. (1989). *Nonverbal learning disabilities: The syndrome and the model.* New York: Guilford Press.

Rourke, B. P. (Ed.). (1991). *Neuropsychological validation of learning disability subtypes.* New York: Guilford Press.

Rourke, B. P. (1994). Neuropsychological assessment of children with learning disabilities: Measurement issues. In G. R. Lyon (Ed.), *Frames of reference for the assessment of learning disabilities: New views on measurement issues* (pp. 475–514). Baltimore: Paul H. Brookes.

Rourke, B. P. (Ed.). (1995a). *Syndrome of nonverbal learning disabilities: Neurodevelopmental manifestations.* New York: Guilford Press.

Rourke, B. P. (1995b). The science of practice and the practice of science: The scientist–practitioner model in clinical neuropsychology. *Canadian Psychology*, 36, 259–287.

Rourke, B. P. (2000). Neuropsychological and

psychosocial subtyping: A review of investigations within the University of Windsor laboratory. *Canadian Psychology*, 40, 34–37.

Rourke, B. P., & Adams, K. M. (1984). Quantitative approaches to the neuropsychological assessment of children. In R. E. Tarter & G. Goldstein (Eds.), *Advances in clinical neuropsychology* (Vol. 2, pp. 79–108). New York: Plenum.

Rourke, B. P., Bakker, D. J., Fisk, J. L., & Strang, J. D. (1983). *Child neuropsychology: An introduction to theory, research, and clinical practice.* New York: Guilford Press.

Rourke, B. P., & Czudner, G. (1972). Age differences in auditory reaction time of "brain-damaged" and normal children under regular and irregular preparatory interval conditions. *Journal of Experimental Child Psychology*, 14, 372–378.

Rourke, B. P., Dietrich, D. M., & Young, G. C. (1973). Significance of WISC verbal–performance discrepancies for younger children with learning disabilities. *Perceptual and Motor Skills*, 36, 275–282.

Rourke, B. P., & Finlayson, M. A. J. (1975). Neuropsychological significance of variations in patterns of performance on the Trail Making Test for older children with learning disabilities. *Journal of Abnormal Psychology*, 84, 412–421.

Rourke, B. P., & Finlayson, M. A. J. (1978). Neuropsychological significance of variations in patterns of academic performance: Verbal and visual–spatial abilities. *Journal of Abnormal Child Psychology*, 6, 121–133.

Rourke, B. P., & Fisk, J. L. (1988). Subtypes of learning-disabled children: Implications for a neurodevelopmental model of differential hemispheric processing. In D. L. Molfese & S. J. Segalowitz (Eds.), *Brain lateralization in children: Developmental implications* (pp. 547–565). New York: Guilford Press.

Rourke, B. P., Fisk, J. L., & Strang, J. D. (1986). *Neuropsychological assessment of children: A treatment-oriented approach.* New York: Guilford.

Rourke, B. P., Fisk, J. L., Strang, J. D., & Gates, R. D. (1981). Human neuropsychology in

Canada: The 1970s. *Canadian Psychology*, 22, 85–99.

Rourke, B. P., & Fuerst, D. R. (1991). *Learning disabilities and psychosocial functioning: A neuropsychological perspective.* New York: Guilford Press.

Rourke, B. P., & Fuerst, D. R. (1995). Cognitive processing, academic achievement, and socioemotional functioning: A neuropsychological perspective. In D. Cicchetti & D. Cohen (Eds.), *Manual of developmental psychopathology* (Vol. 1, pp. 391–423). New York: Wiley.

Rourke, B. P., & Murji, S. (2000). A history of the International Neuropsychological Society: The early years (1965–1985). *Journal of the International Neuropsychological Society*, 6, 491–509.

Rourke, B. P., & Strang, J. D. (1978). Neuropsychological significance of variations in patterns of academic performance: Motor, psychomotor, and tactile–perceptual abilities. *Journal of Pediatric Psychology*, 3, 62–66.

Rourke, B. P., & Telegdy, G. A. (1971). Lateralizing significance of WISC verbal–performance discrepancies for older children with learning disabilities. *Perceptual and Motor Skills*, 33, 875–883.

Rourke, B. P., & Tsatsanis, K. D. (1995). Memory disturbances of children with learning disabilities: A neuropsychological analysis of two academic achievement subtypes. In A. D. Baddeley, B. A. Wilson, & F. N. Watts (Eds.), *Handbook of memory disorders* (pp. 501–531). London: Wiley & Sons.

Rourke, B. P., & Tsatsanis, K. D. (1996). Syndrome of nonverbal learning disabilities: Psycholinguistic assets and deficits. *Topics in Language Disorders*, 16, 30–44.

Rourke, B. P., & Tsatsanis, K. D. (2000). Syndrome of Nonverbal Learning Disabilities and Asperger syndrome. In A. Klin, F. Volkmar, & S. S. Sparrow (Eds.), *Asperger syndrome* (pp. 231–253). New York: Guilford Press.

Rourke, B. P., van der Vlugt, H., & Rourke, S. B. (in press). *The practice of child–clinical neuropsychology: An introduction.* New York: Guilford Press.

Rourke, B. P., Yanni, D. W., MacDonald, G. W., & Young, G. C. (1973).Neuropsychological significance of lateralized deficits on the Grooved Pegboard Test for older children with learning disabilities. *Journal of Consulting and Clinical Psychology, 41,* 128–134.

Rourke, B. P., Young, G. C., & Flewelling, R. W. (1971). The relationships between WISC verbal–performance discrepancies and selected verbal, auditory–perceptual, visual–perceptual, and problem-solving abilities in children with learning disabilities. *Journal of Clinical Psychology, 27,* 475–479.

Rourke, B. P., Young, G. C., & Leenaars, A. (1989). A childhood learning disability that predisposes those afflicted to adolescent and adult depression and suicide risk. *Journal of Learning Disabilities, 21,* 169–175.

Rourke, B. P., Young, G. C., Strang, J. D., & Russell, D. L. (1986). Adult outcomes of childhood central processing deficiencies. In I. Grant & K. M. Adams (Eds.), *Neuropsychological assessment of neuropsychiatric disorders* (pp. 244–267). New York: Oxford University Press.

Stelmack, R. M., & Miles, J. (1990). The effect of picture priming on event-related potentials of normal and disabled readers during a word recognition memory task. *Journal of Clinical and Experimental Neuropsychology, 12,* 887–903.

Stelmack, R. M., Rourke, B. P., & van der Vlugt, H. (1995). Intelligence, learning disabiliites, and event-related potentials. *Developmental Neuropsychology, 11,* 445–465.

Strang, J. D., & Rourke, B. P. (1983). Concept-formation/non-verbal reasoning abilities of children who exhibit specific academic problems with arithmetic. *Journal of Clinical Child Psychology, 12,* 33–39.

Tsatsanis, K. D., Fuerst, D. R., & Rourke, B. P. (1997). Psychosocial dimensions of learning disabilities: External validation and relationship with age and academic functioning. *Journal of Learning Disabilities, 30,* 490–502.

Tsatsanis, K. D., & Rourke, B. P. (1995a). Conclusions and future directions. In B. P. Rourke (Ed.), *Syndrome of nonverbal learning disabilities: Neurodevelopmental manifestations* (pp. 476–496). New York: Guilford Press.

Tsatsanis, K. D., & Rourke, B. P. (1995b). de Lange syndrome. In B. P. Rourke (Ed.), *Syndrome of nonverbal learning disabilities: Neurodevelopmental manifestations* (pp. 171–205). New York: Guilford Press.

16

Pathways and Reflections

Otfried Spreen

Pathways

Neuropsychology today is a well-established discipline with a firm program of training, often including graduate as well as post-graduate steps, frequently accredited by the American Psychological Association (APA) or the Canadian Psychological Association (CPA), and often including further specialization in child, adult, or geriatric neuropsychology. It may be of interest to take a look back at the "training" available at the time when,I began my academic life.

In the Germany of 1946 when I began my training, there were no such guidelines. The training offered depended on the "chair" of the university one chose to attend. Cologne, my first university, offered general experimental psychology by Maria Krudewig, a student of the Jesuit psychologist Johannes Lindworski of the Wuerzburg school. Changing to Bonn University, I was fascinated by comparative psychology as taught by Erich Rothacker, although we were expected to study other areas as well in order to pass the Pre-Diploma in Psychology (the equivalent of a Bachelor of Science, but restricted to basic areas of psychology); this included physiology taught at the medical school. Among others, Bonn also offered a series of demonstration–lectures by Martha Moers, a psychologist at the Bonn neuro-rehabilitation institute. When I finally transferred to Freiburg University (switching universities was quite common in those days), I was intrigued by the interests of Robert Heiss, who taught personality theory (including a course in analytic or "depth" psychology), clinical psychology, and logics: the "chair" had combined psychology with philosophy.

Freiburg, a lovely town at the foot of the Black Forest and near both the French and the Swiss borders in Southwest Germany, had a university-owned lodge on the nearest mountain—the Schauinsland, both for skiing in winter and for meetings of visitors, staff, and students. Hildegard Hiltmann and Martha Muchow acted as teaching assistants for courses in the Rorschach Test and graphology for advanced students. We met with guest lecturers from nearby Switzerland such as Szondi, author of the Szondi-Test; Hans Luescher, who had developed a new Color Pyramid Test; Hans Zulliger, who had created a parallel form of the Rorschach Test; and Hans Boehm, whose book on the Rorschach Test was our constant guide. A young American visited and introduced us to the Thematic Apperception Test.

Hans Bender, the only associate professor at Freiburg, invited us to attend his interviews with visiting telepathic media and offered a course in parapsychology. Physiological psychology was taught by Richard Jung, the chair of physiology at the medical school who was very much involved with the potential of the relatively new EEG recordings. We traveled across the border to Basel, Switzerland, to hear lectures by Karl Jasper whose *Psychopathology* was then the best recognized text in clinical psychology and psychiatry, and to Rome, Bonn, and Stockholm to attend international conventions. It was at Bonn's International Convention of Applied Psychology where I first heard a lecture by Hans-Lukas Teuber who, to our surprise, quickly arranged for an extracurricular two-hour seminar in fluent German, reporting on his studies of patients with frontal lobe damage.

Having passed the main Diploma in psychology (the equivalent of a Master's degree in applied psychology which, under German rules, provides the licence to practice psychology), I became a doctoral student of Robert Heiss's, and a member of the "inner circle"—a handful of students who worked with him studying child and adult "cases" with numerous tests and discussing at length the implications of these tests for an evaluation of the client's personality.

I wish I could say that I always wanted to be a neuropsychologist, but it was by serendipity rather than design: just as I passed my doctoral orals, Robert Heiss received a request from a German veterans hospital for the position of a clinical psychologist. I went to Bad Pyrmont, a small resort town near Hannover, and got my first job: for lack of an appropriate position, it carried the title of "speech therapist" at first although it was soon converted into a psychologist's position.

Gerhard Kloos, the head of neurology, was also a clinical professor at Kiel University and author of the then most popular German compendium of neurology and psychiatry. He loved to teach and quickly introduced me to all phases of the neurological examination, including cysternal puncture, and to brain surgery through Dr. Vogt who invited me to regularly observe surgery, primarily shrapnel removal, on patients I had seen for a neuropsychological examination. But as far as neuropsychology was concerned, I was on my own: I was expected to write reports on the mental impairments of veterans with head injury. My basic equipment from Freiburg included the Rorschach, graphology, the Color–Pyramid Test, a tachistoscope (Spreen, 1957), various measures of motor skills and motor steadiness, the German Binet–Bobertag, and the newly introduced Hamburg–Wechsler intelligence test. I searched around and discovered the many tests of André Rey, available from Geneva; Arthur Benton's Visual Retention Test; the Bender Gestalt Test; and the writings of Poppelreuter, Kleist, Goldstein, Ward Halstead, and Klaus Conrad. We saw many frontal lobe injury patients, and so it is perhaps no surprise that my first two publications dealt with the Rorschach test in 100 frontal lobe injury patients (Spreen, 1955, 1956). I also translated the Benton Visual Retention Test (Spreen, 1958, 1961b) for a German audience (now in its seventh edition) (Sivan & Spreen, 1996).

Neuropsychology as a discipline did not exist in Germany at that time. For reasons of professional politics, psychologists had not worked in medical settings during World War II. A few of us worked in situations similar to mine. We asked for time during the annual convention of the Professional Association of German Psychologists (Berufsverband Deutscher Psychologen) and were allotted two hours, during which a dozen of us presented case descriptions and exchanged information on assessment. (Today, the German Neuropsychological Society [Deutsche Gesellschaft fuer Neuropsychologie] has 1,500 members.) I remember Walter Kerschbaum from Bonn, Hans Szewczyk from Berlin, and Hans Boettcher from Leipzig. In the following year, we invited the Countess von Kuenburg, a psychologist who had worked with Isserlin in the 1920s, as an honored guest. She was probably the first neuropsychologist in Germany.

After three years in neurology, I felt that I should broaden my horizon in the clinical field to include psychiatric patients. I moved to a position at the mental hospital in the city of Bremen where, in addition to half-time work in neurology, I could spend time in adult and child psychiatry. Bremen also offered a training institute for psychotherapy, affiliated with the hospital, complete with teaching analysis (mostly Jungian) and supervised work experience. I might have become a psychotherapist had I not, on a whim, applied for and won a Fulbright postdoctoral fellowship in the United States. So, after three years in Bremen, in 1957 I set out for Washington University medical psychology at St. Louis where I worked for a year with other interns under the guidance of Ivan Mensh, rotating through adult out- and inpatient psychiatry and child guidance. Occasionally, we saw cases for a workup of "organicity," and I was amused to see that the state of the art for such a workup in American clinical psychology at the time consisted mainly of the Wechsler–Bellevue, the Bender Gestalt, and the Minnesota Multiphasic Personality Inventory (MMPI), not too dissimilar from what I had done in Germany.

During my year at St. Louis, Arthur Benton invited me for a visit, and so I went by train to Iowa City and was cordially welcomed into his family, introduced to his friend and statistical genius, Harold Bechtoldt, and other members of the staff of Iowa neurology. We quickly designed plans for two experimental studies on simulation of mental impairment on the Benton Visual Retention Test, which I had encountered in patients at the VA hospital in Germany (Spreen & Benton, 1960, 1961, 1963). Arthur generously bought a ticket for me so I could fly back to St. Louis—my first flight ever (on a DC–3 plane). At the Midwestern Psychological Association meeting in St. Louis I also heard a lecture by Ward Halstead, whose book I had reviewed in a German journal, and, at another time, a lecture by his collaborator, Ralph Reitan, who was then preparing the foundations of his major contribution to neuropsychological assessment in Indianapolis.

After a year in St. Louis, I was due to return to Bremen, but on a honeymoon with my wife Georgia (a fellow intern at Washington University) we visited my old mentor, Robert Heiss, in Freiburg. He directed us to the newly established Saarbruecken University for a job interview. At the time, 1959, the Saar area was under post-war French administration, although a plebiscite had already decided its return to Germany. The concept of the new university was international and multilingual with teachers from Belgium, Poland, and many other countries (although, to my regret, this concept disappeared soon after the Saar's integration with Germany). The chair in psychology was held by a Swiss student of Piaget's, Ernst Boesch, who offered me a teaching position. I did not have to give up clinical work altogether, because I was to direct a child guidance clinic and teach mostly clinical courses including neuropsychology. In addition, I prepared a first translation of the MMPI (Spreen, 1960) and the Taylor Manifest Anxiety Scale (Spreen, 1961a) and began to appreciate the complex problems of cross-cultural research (Spreen, 1961c; Spreen & Spreen, 1963). We completed, supported by U.S. Air Force grant funds, a psychological and physiological study of anxiety (Spreen, 1963, 1964); our subjects were volunteers from the nearby Koblenz German army base. I invited Warner Schaie, a fellow intern from St. Louis with fluent German, as guest lecturer during the summer; Warner taught me the basics of factor analysis, and we tried our first analysis of my anxiety study data on the old IBM 360; it required hand-wiring and babysitting the machine for a whole night to get the results. Warner also opened up my interest in geriatric neuropsychology, a field in which he and one of our Saarbruecken students, Paul Baltes, are well-recognized today.

After three years in Saarbruecken, Arthur Benton offered me a position as assistant professor of neurology at the University of Iowa Medical School, and we made the big jump to the American continent. The psychology part of the "Neurosensory Center" at Iowa consisted of five rooms in a half-basement and included one or two psychometrists, a fellow, David Jones from England, Arthur, and myself. It was supported by a generous grant, had free access to patients, and contributed to special cases presented at the Saturday morning "grand rounds" of neurology and related departments, directed by Adolph Sahs and his lieutenant, Maurice Van Allen. I also participated in teaching neuropsychology for neurology interns and courses offered in the psychology department. However, the main purpose of the center was research in neuropsychology, with Arthur constantly generating new ideas (ranging from a new aphasia test called the Neurosensory Center Comprehensive Examination of Aphasia [Spreen & Benton, 1967], the popular FAS word fluency test [Borkowski, Benton, & Spreen, 1967], and a first adaptation of the Token Test [Spellacy & Spreen, 1969]). He also introduced me to the excellent Iowa school of speech therapy and audiology and to the work with mentally handicapped patients at the Woodward Institution and with learning disabled children in a special school at Davenport, Iowa.

The four years in Iowa provided continuous stimulation. All, even obscure, ideas were discussed and often developed immediately into experimentation. We started a series of experiments on lateralization of the phi–phenomenon (Spreen, Miller, & Benton, 1966) and on dichotic listening (Crockett, Clark, Klonoff, & Spreen, 1983; Higenbottam & Spreen, 1971; Jones & Spreen, 1967; Spellacy, Reid, & Spreen, 1970; Borkowski, Spreen, & Stutz, 1965; Spreen & Boucher, 1970), and exchanged ideas with Doreen Kimura at the Chicago Midwestern Psychological Association meeting. We encountered problems of stimulus selection for the aphasia battery. I found answers in a psycholinguistics course and in collaboration with

Rudolph Schulz (Spreen & Schulz, 1966). This work also resulted in a series of new tests, now referred to as tests of the "Benton group" (Benton, Hamsher, Varney, & Spreen, 1983). Every patient referred to the laboratory provided new questions to be explored experimentally. This included a patient with sound agnosia but minimal aphasia (Spreen, Benton, & Fincham, 1965) and one with what appeared to be a modality-specific naming problem (Spreen, Benton, & van Allen, 1966). The basement of the medical library building housed a collection of historical neurology literature that can rarely be found even in European libraries and which provided the basis for many of Arthur's excursions into the history of neuropsychology (Benton, 2000) and for my own study of Arnold Pick (Spreen, 1973), a neurologist and early pioneer of psycholinguistic studies of aphasia. Visitors for short or extended stays were constantly introduced as old friends. I often learned later that they had worked with Arthur in circumstances similar to mine. In fact, we joked that anybody working in neuropsychology would be seen at Iowa sometime or other, if one stayed there long enough.

Arthur's gentle and cordial manner minimized divisiveness. "Schools" of neuropsychology were meaningless to him; he could absorb such a variety of interests and personalities as those of Jaques Barbizet, Herbert Birch, Amiran Carmon, Norman Geschwind, Henry Hécaen, Mariusz Maruszewski, Ennio de Renzi, and Luigi Vignolo. A Midwestern roundtable conference rotated from Iowa to Madison (Hal Kløve, Chuck Matthews) to Minneapolis (Manfred Meier) and attracted guests from other parts of the country and the world. At such meetings I first met Louis Costa and Paul Satz who were later to join us as faculty at the University of Victoria. Even Arthur's most critical paper ("The Fiction of the Gerstmann Syndrome," Benton, 1961) did not create enmity but stimulated numerous and ultimately useful discussions about the meaning of a syndrome. A widely quoted paper on cutoff scores and hit-rates (Spreen & Benton, 1965) perhaps gradually convinced many in the profession that much effort was wasted "diagnosing" brain damage with psychological tests when other aspects of clinical research deserved more of our efforts. I have written about working with Arthur Benton elsewhere (Spreen & Costa, 1985).

At Iowa, I also was introduced to former students such as Alick Elithorn, Max Fogel, and Donald Shankweiler. During later visits I met new students of Arthur's such as Julia Hannay, Kerry Hamsher, and Harvey Levin. At the annual meetings of the Academy of Aphasia I met the Boston group including Norman Geschwind, Harold Goodglass, Edith Kaplan, Sheila Blumstein, and Peter Rosenberger. Gradually, another nucleus formed around the International Neuropsychological Society (INS) with Paul Satz, Manfred Meier, Ken Heilman, and Aaron Smith as well as the Boston group. I remember fondly one of the first meetings at Tampa, Florida, where we all fit into a medium-sized lecture room.

Through my interest in psycholinguistics, I met Robert Wachal at Iowa—a meeting that led to a longtime collaboration in the study of a large number of free-speech samples of aphasic patients (Spreen & Wachal, 1973; Wachal & Spreen, 1973). Bob joined us later at Victoria for two summers of busy work and discussion.

A visit by William Gaddes from the University of Victoria led to the jump to another country, Canada. Bill, a former teacher, had almost single-handedly built up a small psychology faculty at the Victoria College which took a leap to university status as one of three provincial universities in British Columbia in 1958. I joined the faculty in 1966, just after a new building with ample clinic space had been completed. Graduate studies at the university had been approved a year before my arrival, and I was fortunate to graduate the university's first doctoral student, Frank Spellacy, in 1970. Bill had introduced neuropsychology as a formal undergraduate course, and he, Stuart Meikle, and I offered graduate seminars with small groups of three to five students. Bill also had started the "neuropsychology clinic" that saw mostly learning disabled children, one of his major interests (Gaddes, 1985; Gaddes & Edgell, 1994), and I soon added adult patients to the clinic population. We also provided unpaid neuropsychology consultation to patients in newly equipped laboratories at the Royal Jubilee Hospital and at the Gorge Road Rehabilitation Hospital.

A good program in neuropsychology can continue only through frequent exchange of ideas with other researchers. Bill Gaddes had started a "Neuropsychology Workshop" in 1965, which brought Arthur Benton (for one of his many visits) and Ralph Reitan to Victoria after the Canadian Psychological Association meeting in Vancouver. We continued these annual workshops with growing success for many years, and we were able to attract people such as Norman Geschwind, Ken Heilman, Harvey Levin, Steven Mattis, Manfred Meier, Brenda Milner, Byron Rourke, Hans-Lukas Teuber, and many others. We were also fortunate to host the Academy of Aphasia in Victoria in 1977. Our neuropsychology faculty was rounded out by new faculty members: Louis Costa, Roger Graves, Paul Satz, Frank Spellacy, and Esther Strauss.

Initially, my own work focused on studies of aphasia, both with tests and with psycholinguistic studies, but then encompassed many other forms of brain damage. My continuing interest in aphasia led to further contributions to aphasia assessment (Spreen & Risser, 1982, 1998).

I often had felt that many neuropsychologists avoided the area of mental retardation either because it did not seem to generate fruitful research or because, by long-standing tradition, the group of psychologists working with the mentally handicapped was well-entrenched in state hospitals and schools with limited interest in neuropsychological issues. Stimulated by Arthur Benton, who was one of the few who disregarded this gap, and by my experience at the Woodward State Hospital in Iowa, I compiled a review of language studies in mental retardation (Spreen, 1965a, 1965b). I started a study of changing attitudes toward mental retardation over the years (Spreen, 1977; Rees, Spreen, & Harnadek, 1991) and a new undergraduate course in mental retardation and learning disabilities in 1968. (A grant from the Canadian Mental Retardation Institute freed me from other teaching duties that year.) I worked actively with the local and provincial mental retardation societies (now called the "Society for Community Living") and started a book on mental retardation in German (Spreen, 1978). We were honored by guest speakers like Wolf Wolfensberger, Herbert Birch, and Nancy Robinson who were at the forefront of research and of re-thinking the care of the mentally handicapped. This eventually led to the closure of the many traditional state hospitals across North America that were often, in spite of good intentions, no more than warehouses of human misery far removed from the sight of the public.

We started a computer data bank of cases seen at our laboratory in 1970, and this provided the basis for a long-term follow-up study of learning-disabled children (Spreen, 1982, 1983, 1987) who had by then grown up to the age of 19 (Phase I) and then to the age of 25 (Phase II). The study also provided insights into the prognosis of learning disabilities in early adulthood (Spreen, 1984, 1988, 1989c). My interest in children broadened into a seminar in child neuropsychology, which eventually stimulated four of our former students to collaborate with me on a book on *Developmental Neuropsychology* (Spreen, Tupper, Risser, Tuokko, & Edgell, 1984; Spreen, Risser, & Edgell, 1995), a first in the field. The development and use of the many tests in our clinic also led to the development of normative data (Blair & Spreen, 1989; Gaddes & Spreen, 1969; Seyfort, Spreen, & Lahmer, 1980; Strauss & Spreen, 1990; Strauss, Spreen, & Hunter, 2000) and to the writing of a clinic manual that eventually became the *A Compendium of Neuropsychological Tests* (Spreen & Strauss, 1991, 1998).

Eventually, mostly through the initiative of members of the INS, and particularly through the driving force of Manfred Meier, neuropsychology became accepted as a branch of clinical psychology, recognized by the American Board of Professional Psychology through the American Board of Clinical Neuropsychology of which I became a founding member. The INS grew from a group of 120 to 4,500 members worldwide. I remember fondly my years on the Board when we debated what journal should become our official society journal and whether or not we should have summer meetings in Europe, Mexico, and Australia. I was honored by being elected president of INS and introduced by Nelson Butters at the 1989 meeting in Lahti, Finland; the North American meeting that year was held close to my home in Vancouver, British Columbia. Speaking of British Columbia, I also recall my years on the governing board of the British Columbia Psychological Association, which honored me with their "Excellence in Teaching" award in 1989. I cherished late honors in 1999 when the American Psychological Foundation gave me the Arthur Benton Lectureship Award, and the German Neuropsychological Society made me one of their first honorary members.

In Victoria, we had provided our students with integrated clinical training by clinical faculty members like Edward Tryk and Pam Duncan, in addition to training in neuropsychology. This was finally formalized: the "neuropsychology laboratory" became a "psychology clinic," including therapy rooms, and our program was fully accredited by both CPA and APA in 1993. I left active teaching duties that year in the hands of its new director, Catherine Mateer, who with new faculty members Dan Bub and Kim Kearns, as well as Roger Graves and Esther Strauss, carried it through re-accreditation in 1998.

Reflections

I look back with fondness to my association with so many distinguished colleagues who helped me formulate problems and research questions in neuropsychology, and with many of my 30 doctoral students who collaborated with me and did the necessary probing into the soundness of my own research. I had the good fortune to work in the field at a time when it expanded rapidly and became a formal discipline, and when *Cortex* and *Neuropsychologia* were the first ventures into a field that now has countless new journals.

In some ways I regret that during the second half of the twentieth century neuropsychology became such a highly specialized discipline—even subspecialities like pediatric, forensic, and geriatric neuropsychology appeared. The drawback of specialization is that we become more isolated, sometimes even antagonistic to neighboring disciplines like occupational therapy, speech therapy, audiology, social work, and educational psychology. We even battle with neurology, psychiatry, and radiology. In some settings, we become isolated even from clinical psychology.

Neuropsychology probably has made its most unique contribution in the field of assessment: its greatest strength is the sophisticated description and quantification of mental and emotional deficits in patients with damage to or diseases of the brain. More recently, a related focus has been on malingering and symptom validity testing. The price of this development, however, is the danger of losing touch with therapy, with ways of helping the client. For the future, a better integration with neighboring disciplines and more focus on therapy will be of primary importance.

In addition, the focus has been on neurological diagnostics, a battle we can't win considering the great strides made in developing new neuroradiological procedures. Just because the Rorschach Test shows poverty of associations, which is found often in some patients with dorsal frontal lobe damage, does not make the Rorschach Test a "frontal lobe test"; nor does the psycho-diagnostic concept of "executive functions" translate automatically into "frontal lobe function." We develop psychological concepts and theories that may reflect typical neurodiagnostic syndromes but that are not diagnostic in the same way as the results of a Magnetic Resonance Imaging scan or the findings of a pathologist. Only in a few areas does neuropsychology contribute to diagnosis (e.g., in borderline cases of dementia). In some instances, however, we have gone beyond neurological diagnosis and offered subtyping of complex disorders such as learning disabilities or pervasive developmental disorders. These efforts lead to theories of subtyping of a unique neuropsychological nature, which may stimulate future neurological confirmation research (Spreen, 1989a, 1989b). Unfortunately, these typologies differ considerably, as do the neurological deficits proposed for them. There is as yet scant neurological evidence for the proposed underlying defects (Spreen, 2000; Spreen & Haaf, 1985). For the time being, it is probably better to consider them as psychological rather than neurological subtypes. As Benton (1982) already noted,

"Much of the research. . . that we categorize as neuropsychological is, in fact, purely behavioral in nature" (p. 57).

In contrast to other colleagues who were fortunate to remain in a research program focused on a major area of neuropsychology, I have worked in many areas, ranging from head injuries to the aphasias, to a variety of problems of childhood and adolescence, as well as from strictly clinical to experimental work. I do not regret this, because it opened for me the full range of neuropsychology.

REFERENCES

Benton, A. L. (1961). The fiction of the "Gerstmann syndrome." *Journal of Neurology, Neurosurgery and Psychiatry, 24,* 176–181.

Benton, A. L. (1982). Child neuropsychology: Retrospect and prospect. In J. de Wit & A. L. Benton (Eds.), *Perspectives in child study* (pp. 41–61). Lisse, Netherlands: Swets & Zeitlinger.

Benton, A. L. (2000). *Exploring the history of neuropsychology. Selected papers.* New York: Oxford University Press.

Benton, A. L., Fangman, M. W., Carr, D. L., & Spreen, O. (1967). Visual Retention Test, Administration C: Norms for children. *Journal of Special Education, 1,* 151–156.

Benton, A. L., Hamsher, deS. K., Varney, N. R., & Spreen, O. (1983). *Contributions to neuropsychological assessment: A clinical manual.* New York: Oxford University Press.

Blair, J., & Spreen, O. (1989). Predicting premorbid IQ: A revision of the National Adult Reading Test. *The Clinical Neuropsychologist, 3,* 129–136.

Borkowski, J. G., Spreen, O., & Stutz, J. Z. (1965). Ear preference and abstractness in dichotic listening. *Psychonomic Science, 3,* 547–548.

Borkowski, J. G., Benton, A. L., & Spreen, O. (1967). Word fluency and brain damage. *Neuropsychologia, 4,* 135–140.

Crockett, D., Clark, C., Klonoff, H., & Spreen, O. (1983). Psychometric properties of dichotic word tests. *Journal of Clinical Neuropsychology, 5,* 169–179.

Gaddes, W. H. (1985). *Learning disabilities and brain function.* New York: Springer.

Gaddes, W. H., & Edgell, D. (1994). *Learning disabilities and brain function.* New York: Springer.

Gaddes, W. H., & Spreen, O. (1969). Develop-

mental norms for 15 neuro-psychological tests, age 6 to 15. *Cortex, 5,* 171–201.

Higenbottam, J., & Spreen, O. (1971). Perceptual asymmetry with dichotically presented click–sentence stimuli. *Journal of Auditory Research, 10,* 164–175.

Jones, D., & Spreen, O. (1967) Dichotic listening by retarded children: The effects of ear order and abstractness. *Child Development, 38,* 101–105.

Rees, L., Spreen, O., & Harnadek, M. (1991). Do attitudes towards persons with handicaps really shift over time? Comparison between 1975 and 1988. *Mental Retardation, 29,* 65–72.

Seyfort, B., Spreen, O., & Lahmer, V. (1980). A critical look at the WISC–R with Native Indian children. *Alberta Journal of Educational Research, 26,* 14–24.

Sivan, A. B., & Spreen, O. (1996). *Der Benton–Test* (7th German ed.) Bern, Germany: Huber Verlag.

Spellacy, F. J., Reid, J., & Spreen, O. (1970). Effect of interstimulus interval and intensity on ear asymmetry for nonverbal stimuli. *Neuropsychologia, 7,* 141–148.

Spellacy, F. J., & Spreen, O. (1969). A short form of the Token Test. *Cortex, 5,* 390–397.

Spreen, O. (1955). Stirnhirnverletzte im Rorschach–Versuch. *Zeitschrift für Diagnostische Psychologie und Persönlichkeitsforschung, 3,* 3–23.

Spreen, O. (1956). Stirnhirnverletzte im Rorschach–Versuch II. *Zeitschrift für Diagnostische Psychologie und Persönlichkeitsforschung, 4,* 146–173.

Spreen, O. (1957). Über Tachistoskopversuche bei Normalen, Hirnverletzten und Neurotikern. *Psychologische Beiträge, 3,* 80–93.

Spreen, O. (1958). Der Benton–Test Anwendungen und klinische Ergebnisse. *Zeitschrift für Experimentelle und Angewandte Psychologie, 5*, 347–393.

Spreen, O. (1960). *MMPI–Saarbrücken. Handbuch und testheft.* Bern, Germany: Hans Huber. (2nd ed., 1972; 3rd ed., 1977)

Spreen, O. (1961a). Konstruktion einer Skala zur Messung der Manifesten Angst in experimentellen untersuchungen. *Psychologische Forschung, 26*, 205–223.

Spreen, O. (1961b). *Der Benton–Test.* Handbuch. Bern, Germany: Hans Huber Verlag.

Spreen, O. (1961c). The translation of personality scales and their adaptation for cross-cultural and clinical use. *Acta Psychologica, 18*, 337–341.

Spreen, O. (1963). The position of time estimation in a factor analysis and its relations to some personality variables. *Psychological Record, 13*, 455–464.

Spreen, O. (1964). Die Stellung von vier motorischen Variablen in einer Faktorenanalyse und ihre Beziehungen zu Angst und Stress. *Psychologische Forschung, 27*, 403–418.

Spreen, O. (1965a). Language functions in mental retardation: a review. I. Language development, types of retardation, and intelligence level. *American Journal of Mental Deficiency, 69*, 482–494.

Spreen, O. (1965b). Language functions in mental retardation: a review. II. Language in higher level performance. *American Journal of Mental Deficiency, 70*, 351–362.

Spreen, O. (1973). Arnold Pick's contribution to psycholinguistics. In H. Goodglass & S. Blumstein (Eds.), *Psycholinguistics and aphasia.* Baltimore: Johns Hopkins University Press.

Spreen, O. (1977). Attitude towards mental retardation and attitude change: An experimental study. *Zeitschrift für Experimentelle und Angewandte Psychologie, 24*, 303–323.

Spreen, O. (1978). *Geistige behinderung.* Heidelberg, Germany: Springer Publishers.

Spreen, O. (1982). Adult outcome of learning disorders. In R. H. Malatesha & P. G. Aaron (Eds.), *Reading disorders: Varieties and treatments.* New York: Academic Press.

Spreen, O. (1983). Learning disabled children growing up. In G. Schwartz (Ed.), *Advances in research and services for children with special needs.* Vancouver, British Columbia: University of B.C. Press.

Spreen, O. (1984). A prognostic view from middle childhood. In M. D. Levine & P. Satz (Eds.), *Middle childhood: Development and dysfunction* (pp. 405–432). Baltimore: University Park Press.

Spreen, O. (1987). *Learning disabled children growing up.* Lisse, Netherlands: Swets & Zeitlinger, and New York: Oxford University Press.

Spreen, O. (1988). Prognosis of learning disability. *Journal of Consulting and Clinical Psychology, 56*, 836–842.

Spreen, O. (1989a). The relationship between learning disability, emotional disorders, and neuropsychology: Some results and observations. *Journal of Clinical and Experimental Neuropsychology, 11*, 117–140.

Spreen, O. (1989b). Learning disability, neurology, and long-term outcome: Some implications for the individual and the society. *Journal of Clinical and Experimental Neuropsychology, 11*, 389–408.

Spreen, O. (1989c). Long-term sequelae of learning disabilities: A review of outcome studies. In D. J. Bakker & H. van der Vlugt (Eds.), *Learning disabilities: Vol. 1: Neuropsychological correlates and treatment.* Lisse, Netherlands: Swets & Zeitlinger.

Spreen, O. (2000). The neuropsychology of learning disabilities: The search for neurological substitutes, and the search for subtypes. *Zeitschrift Fuer Neuropsychologie, 11*, 168–193.

Spreen, O., & Benton, A. L. (1960). Visual Memory Test: The simulation of mental incompetence. *AMA Archives of General Psychiatry, 4*, 79–83.

Spreen, O., & Benton, A. L. (1961). Zur simulation intellektueller leistungsdefekte im Benton–Test. *Psychologische Beiträge, 7*, 147–150.

Spreen, O., & Benton, A. L. (1963). The simulation of mental deficiency on a visual memory test. *American Journal of Mental Deficiency, 67*, 147–150.

Spreen, O., & Benton, A. L. (1965). Comparative study of some psychological tests for cerebral damage. *Journal of Nervous and Mental Disease, 140,* 323–333.

Spreen, O., & Benton, A. L. (1967). *Neurosensory Center Comprehensive Examination for Aphasia.* Victoria, British Columbia: Neuropsychology Clinic.

Spreen, O., Benton, A. L., & Fincham, R. W. (1965). Sound agnosia without aphasia. *Archives of Neurology, 13,* 86–92.

Spreen, O., Benton, A. L., & van Allen, M. (1966). Dissociation of visual and tactile naming in amnestic aphasia. *Neurology, 16,* 807–814.

Spreen, O., & Boucher, A. R. (1970). Effects of low-pass filtering on ear asymmetry in dichotic listening and some uncontrolled error sources. *Journal of Auditory Research, 10,* 45–51.

Spreen, O., & Costa, L. (Eds.). (1985). *Studies in neuropsychology: Selected writings of Arthur Benton.* New York: Oxford University Press.

Spreen, O., & Haaf, R. (1985). An attempt to replicate empirically derived subtypes of learning disability and their relationship to neurological status. *Journal of Clinical and Experimental Neuropsychology, 7,* 159–160.

Spreen, O., Miller, C. G., & Benton, A. L. (1966). The phi-test and measures of laterality in children and young adults. *Cortex, 2,* 308–321.

Spreen, O., & Risser, A. H. (1982). Assessment of aphasia. In M.T. Sarno (Ed.), *Acquired aphasi* (pp. 67–128). New York: Academic Press.

Spreen, O., & Risser, A. H. (1998). Assessment of aphasia. In: M. T.Sarno (Ed.) *Acquired aphasia* (3rd ed.) (pp. 71–156). San Diego, CA: Academic Press..

Spreen, O., Risser. A. H., & Edgell, D. (1995). *Developmental neuropsychology* (2nd ed.). New York: Oxford University Press

Spreen, O., & Schulz, R. W. (1966). Parameters of abstraction, meaningfulness, and pronunciability for 329 nouns. *Journal of Verbal Learning and Verbal Behavior, 5,* 459–468.

Spreen, O., & Spreen, G. W. (1963). The MMPI in a German speaking population. Standardization report and methodological problems of cross-cultural interpretation. *Acta Psychologica, 21,* 265–273

Spreen, O., & Strauss, E. (1991, 1998). *A compendium of neuropsychological tests: Administration, norms, and commentary.* New York: Oxford University Press.

Spreen, O., Tupper, D., Risser, A. H., Tuokko, H., & Edgell, D. (1984). *Human developmental neuropsychology.* New York: Oxford University Press.

Spreen, O., & Wachal, R. S. (1973). Psycholinguistic analysis of aphasic language: Theoretical formulations and procedure. *Language and Speech, 16,* 130–146.

Strauss, E., & Spreen, O. (1990). A comparison of the Rey and Taylor figures. *Archives of Clinical Neuropsychology, 5,* 417–420.

Strauss, E., Spreen, O., & Hunter, M. (2000). Implications of test revisions for research. *Psychological Assessment, 12,* 237–244.

Wachal, R. S., & Spreen, O. (1973). Some measures of lexical diversity in aphasic and normal language performance. *Language and Speech, 16,* 169–181.

PART III
PATHWAYS IMAGINED

17

To Infinity and Beyond
Clinical Neuropsychology in the Twenty-First Century

Russell M. Bauer

*I*t's New Year's Eve; name your year. Amid the tumultuous joy, the loud music, the revelers packed tightly on the dance floor, you sit back just for a moment and take stock. This is the stuff of which New Year's resolutions are made. It is natural, almost in the genes, to simultaneously look back and look ahead at important moments in our lives. So it is as clinical neuropsychology enters the twenty-first century. What have we accomplished? Where are we going? What are the challenges and threats from outside and from within our profession? This chapter represents one set of answers to these questions. In preparing to write this chapter, I consulted several existing reviews of the status of clinical neuropsychology (Benton, 1987, 1992; Bigler, 1991; Costa, 1998; Parsons, 1991; Puente, 1992; Rourke, 1991, 1995). My esteemed predecessors have already mentioned some of what I will discuss. I do not intend to comprehensively cover all our noteworthy achievements, and I do not present an exhaustive list of the challenges that face us. Instead, my goal is to highlight some of the important issues that face clinical neuropsychology now and tomorrow.

Definition and Scope of Clinical Neuropsychology

Recent surveys of the practice of neuropsychology (Putnam & DeLuca, 1990, 1991) suggest that neuropsychologists act in diverse clinical settings, from independent practice to private and university-affiliated tertiary care hospitals, and that they devote significant portions of their time to clinical assessment and consultation. The diverse activities and placements of neuropsychologists in the health care market have sometimes made it difficult to understand and define the core activities and roles performed by members of the field. One of the most remarkable things about our field is that, despite the significant recent attention devoted to standards for education and training of new neuropsychologists, we are still quite unclear about defining and enforcing standards of neuropsychological practice for existing practitioners. Unfortunately, there is still no clear way to determine whether a practicing psychologist is a neuropsychologist or not. We have been successful in providing a reasonable operational definition of neuropsychological practice (American Psychological Association, 1989; Hannay, Bieli-auskas, Crosson, Hammeke, Hamsher, & Koffler, 1998) and in obtaining recognition by the American Psychological Association (APA) of the specialty status of neuropsychology. Still, the fact remains that any licensed psychologist can hold himself or herself out as qualified to provide neuropsychological assessment, consultation, or intervention services.

One of the most significant advancements in recent years is the formalization of standards of education and training in neuropsychology. These standards specify that appropriate preparation for neuropsychological practice involves broad grounding in the science and practice of psychology, acquisition of core concepts from neuroscience, and direct training in the application of psychological procedures to clinically significant problems. This stage of training should be followed by extensive and intensive practical experience at the internship and postdoctoral levels. The complexity of the knowledge base has led to the idea that specialization should take place during the latter stages of training (Hannay et al., 1998).

At present, however, there is somewhat of a "disconnect" between our clear-headed notions regarding criteria for entry into the field, and our muddle-headed notions about the methods by which current practitioners can, and should, demonstrate ongoing competence to render neuropsychological services. Most states, in administering their statutes related to psychological practice, caution psychologists that they must operate only within their areas of competency. The major problem, of course, is that such cautions ultimately allow a self-assessment of competency, and we all know about the strengths and weaknesses of self-report as a measure of actual behavior. This method leaves room for a variety of interpretations, and it is clear that any random sampling of the products of neuropsychological services would reveal something representing the good, the bad, and the ugly. Many neuropsychologists have at least a small collection of horror stories regarding the practice of clinical "neuropsychologists" in hospital, private practice, and medicolegal settings (Bauer, 1997). Such instances are decidedly bad for the profession, since they reveal practices that are damaging to patients and that distort the image of the neuropsychological profession in the eyes of other disciplines and of the public. The prevalence of such examples is a symptom of a much larger problem. In my view, neuropsychologists have not done enough to regulate themselves, to educate the public and other professions about appropriate standards of neuropsychological conduct, or to make known the empirical basis of our profession. As I will note later, we may have been too busy with our own internal affairs to devote sufficient time to reasoned enforcement of appropriate standards of conduct within the profession.

Opportunities and Challenges in the Age of Managed Care

As the control of U.S. health care dollars has moved from practitioners to consumers (Frank & VandenBos, 1994; Johnstone, Frank, Belar, Berk et al., 1995), neuropsychologists have had to adjust in significant ways. For the first time in their professional lives, neuropsychologists have had to compete with other professions for patients and reimbursement levels, and have faced significant pressures to make changes in the very way they do assessment and intervention. Most neuropsychologists feel that managed care will have (or has had) a negative impact on practice, will decrease patient evaluation time, will decrease clinical income, and will increase administrative paperwork (Sweet, Westergaard, & Moberg, 1995). In addition, most neuropsychologists report spending more time in clinical activity to compensate for reductions in reimbursement. While this is understandable in terms of simple reinforcement principles, the potential impact on the profession is far-reaching. Given that many neuropsychologists engage in both clinical practice and empirical research, the most obvious implication is that the time devoted to building the empirical basis of neuropsychology will dwindle, thus retarding needed empirical developments. At the same time, however, the evolving managed care environment has, in no uncertain terms, defined a new research agenda for the field of neuropsychology (see below). How neuropsychologists will meet these seemingly conflicting challenges will be a critical next step in our history.

While experiences with managed care may leave neuropsychologists feeling besieged, oppressed, or misunderstood, the situation is moving so swiftly that we cannot afford the kind of downtime necessary to really indulge ourselves in good, cleansing self-pity. Instead, we need to move quickly to learn the managed care language and to adjust to a rapidly evolving marketplace. In my view, neuropsychologists must respond swiftly and effectively to three major demands that flow from the currents in contemporary health care: (1) be brief, or at least cost-effective; (2) be relevant; and (3) demonstrate economic and functional outcomes that prove our worth. I will briefly consider each of these demands in turn.

Be Cost-effective

As reimbursement and authorization for clinical services become more modest and restrictive, neuropsychologists will increasingly face the demand to perform customary services at lower cost. The most obvious way of reducing the costs of assessment is to shorten the amount of time it takes to collect the data. Many "baby boom" neuropsychologists were trained within an assessment tradition that emphasizes comprehensive testing of neurocognitive skills and that values an approach in which important neuropsychological functions (e.g., psychomotor speed, verbal memory) are tested at least twice to allow the assessment of deficit stability or consistency. Recent reviews of neuropsychological assessments within the medicolegal context have likewise stressed the importance of using multiple memory measures so that the clinician can search for patterns of consistency and inconsistency and can evaluate them in regard to whether they make neuropsychological sense (Larrabee, 1990). The use of multiple redundant measures of specific functions is so central to the way we collect and interpret data in neuropsychological assessment that it is hard to imagine doing assessments any other way.

In the last 20 years, there have been major advancements in neurodiagnostic technology such as Computerized Tomography/Magnetic Resonance Imaging and functional neuroimaging (e.g., Positron Emission Tomography, Single Photon Emission Computed Tomography, and now Functional Magnetic Resonance Imaging). Biological treatments for neurological and psychiatric disorders (e.g., electroconvulsive therapy, transcranial magnetic stimulation, and, in the future, transplant and gene knockout approaches) have been developed. These developments have had exciting implications for the role of neuropsychology in clinical trials research (Ryan & Hendrickson, 1998) and will provide great opportunities for broadening the role neuropsychologists play in treatment evaluation research. In the clinic, the goals of neuropsychological assessment have shifted from an exclusive focus on lesion localization to a focus on a functional analysis of the patient's neurocognitive strengths and weaknesses. This often requires detailed, time-consuming analysis of a variety of cognitive, sociocultural, affective, and health-related variables. Such exquisite behavioral analysis takes time, time is money, and money is short. As a result, the time-honored tradition of using a large number of items, graded in difficulty, to assess a broad range of neuropsychological functions may have to be forsaken in favor of a screening approach that starts with broadly sensitive items and works toward increasing specificity (Bauer, 1994; Mitrushina & Fuld, 1996; Tarter & Edwards, 1988). I predict that, during the next decade, we will radically redefine the process of neuropsychological assessment. In many settings, the comprehensive assessment will be abandoned in favor of a series of short, modular, problem-focused or screening batteries. This will, of course, require a new generation of validity studies and perhaps new thinking about the nature of test validity. Let the research begin.

Be Relevant

Although neuropsychologists generally tend to have a high degree of confidence that the results of their assessments yield relevant and important information, recent trends in managed care demand more than a "trust me" kind of product. Having been a practicing neuropsychologist for nearly 20 years, and having been primarily situated in a training and educational setting, it is my view that many neuropsychologists continue to struggle when, in a feedback session, the patient or a family member says, "So, what does this have to do with everyday life?" Answers to this question frequently utilize a pound of clinical experience along with an ounce of empirical data. Despite recent attempts to demonstrate real-life applicability of neuropsychological services (Franzen & Wilhelm, 1996; Guilmette & Kastner, 1996; Larrabee & Crook, 1996; Sbordone & Long, 1996), the ecological validity of many, if not most, neuropsychological instruments has not been established or developed to the point that such information can be used directly when making prescriptions for patients. For example, little, if anything, is known about the in-vivo behavior of a patient with a California Verbal Learning Test (CVLT) Long Delayed Free Recall standard score of -2. Similarly, the failure to shift from one sorting principle to the next on the Wisconsin Card Sort has not yet been shown to relate meaningfully to mental flexibility in real life. To respond to the demand to be relevant, a whole new generation of research will need to be conducted in which neuropsychological test results are forced to predict real-life behaviors such as instrumental activities of daily living, performance on real-life memory tasks (e.g., Crook & Larrabee, 1988; Larrabee & Crook, 1989; Youngjohn, Larrabee, & Crook, 1992), affective competence, job-worthiness, and everyday decision-making capacity.

Demonstrate Outcomes

In the very near future, neuropsychologists will be regularly asked to demonstrate that the techniques of neuropsychological assessment and intervention have measurable health outcomes. Although the importance of outcomes assessment has long been recognized within health psychology (Kaplan, 1994), the notion that practices need to be defined by their behavioral outcomes is only recently gaining acceptance within neuropsychology (Bieliauskas, Fastenau, Lacy, & Roper, 1997; Kane, 1997; Kerner, Patterson, Grant, & Kaplan, 1998). A good sign is that a recent issue of *Applied Neuropsychology* (Vol. 5, No. 4, 1998) was devoted entirely to the topic of neuropsychological outcomes research (Farmer & Brazeal, 1998; Kalechstein & van Gorp, 1998; Miller & Mittenberg, 1998; Ricker, 1998; Ryan & Hendrickson, 1998; Vanderploeg, 1998).

Outcomes research is an evolving methodology, designed to assess the effect of health-care interventions using measures such as health improvement, adaptive behavior changes, patient satisfaction, level of functioning/symptom severity, self-reported quality of life, or costs related to health-care utilization (Vanderploeg, 1998). As applied to neuropsychology, a focus on health outcomes means that the patient's behavioral adaptation to his or her natural environment is a key criterion by which neuropsychological services (assessment and intervention) should be measured. It has been convincingly argued that behavior is the major criterion by which the effectiveness of a health-care assessment or intervention should be judged (Kaplan, 1990). In the future, the effectiveness of a neuropsychological evaluation or intervention (e.g., cognitive rehabilitation) may well be indexed not just by patient satisfaction (Bennett-Levy, Klein-Moonschate, Batchelor, McCarter, & Walton, 1994) but also by the impact it has on behaviorally relevant dimensions of health.

The concept of behavioral outcomes measurement (Kaplan, 1994; Kaplan & Anderson, 1990) should be better understood by practicing neuropsychologists and should receive considerably more emphasis in neuropsychological training than it currently does. Kaplan's General Health Policy Model separates aspects of health status into the following components: life expectancy (mortality), functioning and symptoms (morbidity), the degree to which people value being in particular functional states (utility), and duration of stay in health states (prognosis). Measures such as the Quality of Well-Being Scale (QWB) (Kaplan & Anderson, 1988) measure functioning and symptoms, while other components of the model are derived from other data sources, including value assessments and health-care utilization statistics (Kaplan & Anderson, 1990). Using observable behavioral levels of functioning, individuals are placed on a scale of wellness derived from pre-existing human value studies. Then, taking into account the level and duration of wellness, the *well life expectancy* (i.e., the current life expectancy adjusted for the diminished quality of life associated with dysfunctional states and the duration of each state) can be calculated and expressed in terms of "quality adjusted life years" (QALY) (Kaplan, 1994). Statistics like the QALY can then be used to quantify a health-care activity or treatment program in terms of its impact on life quality. The overall blueprint for public health in the United States (Healthy People 2000) uses the concept of a "healthy life," which is quite similar to the QALY, so it can be said that this overall approach is quite in keeping with emerging federal public health policy.

For neuropsychology, the major question concerns our impact on the current and future quality of life of our patients. Considering these issues is important, not only because it focuses us on accountability, but also because it can help us begin to think about what the health outcome goals of neuropsychological assessment and intervention should be in the coming decades. Given that most neuropsychologists spend the majority of their practice time in assessment activities (Sweet, Moberg, & Westergaard, 1996), we must begin to ask about the impact such assessments have, in QALY terms, on people's lives. This, at first, seems daunting since, strictly speaking, assessments do not change lives. For example, assessments do not treat neurocognitive impairment *per se* or slow the progression of degenerative brain disease. Well-conducted assessments, however, can help justify needed therapeutic and rehabilitative services; can serve to educate patients, families, employers, and the general public about the patient's neurocognitive status; and can lead to practical alterations in the environment that may improve the patient's functional level. While we all know these benefits of assessment exist, we must now provide proof of their importance with clinically relevant, in-vivo behavioral outcome measures.

Within neuropsychology, some strides have already been made in developing disease-specific quality of life measures. For example, the Quality of Life in Epilepsy (QUOLIE), in both short and long versions, has been used to measure health outcomes in patients undergoing surgical or pharmacological treatment for chronic seizures (Devinsky et al., 1995; Hermann, 1995; Meador, 1993; Perrine, 1993; Vickrey et al., 1992). The specific contribution made by clinical neuropsychological services (assessment or intervention), however, has not been firmly established in these patients through the use of a broad health outcomes approach.

While the new focus on health outcomes assessment is daunting enough, let us go one step further in hopes of alerting the reader to steeper trends that are only beginning to be realized. It has been proposed recently that the traditional fee-for-service model should be replaced by a fee-for-benefit model, whereby payment would be based on measured outcomes rather than on time spent with the patient and preparing the report (Diamond, Denton, & Matloff, 1993). In a health-care market that adheres to this kind of model, neuropsychologists will need to have in place an empirical database relating practice to outcome if we are to effectively survive and flourish. Now is the time to begin building this foundation.

When we begin to develop relevant measures of outcome, a number of methodological issues will have to be considered. While numerous measures of health outcome already exist, many are based on self-report of symptoms, affective states, activities, and life achievements. While the use of self-report methodology has been successful in the evaluation of behavior relevant to many health psychology conditions (e.g., arthritis), its application to the neuropsychological arena is complicated by the presence of neurocognitive deficits that might threaten the accuracy or validity of the data thus derived. For example, the retrospective reporting of daily activities might be threatened by memory or language impairment, and the reporting of symptom levels might be rendered inaccurate by deficits in self-awareness (Prigatano & Schacter, 1991). Even in the absence of severe neurocognitive deficit, self-report is subject to a number of motivational and attributional biases. The patients' reports may be subject to their expectations regarding the symptoms they should be experiencing or to distorted notions about the degree to which they experienced such symptoms prior to being injured (Mittenberg, DiGiulio, Perrin, & Bass, 1992). These issues will complicate the way in which such data actually relate to objective health status.

Thus, while it is generally agreed that patient-oriented outcomes measurements are critical to the evaluation of health-care interventions, methodologies developed in other areas of psychology may not be directly imported into neuropsychological practice. This means that neuropsychologists must develop outcomes measures based on their unique understanding of how brain injury affects the real-life behavior of the patient in social, familial, and vocational settings. I contend that this is something that the vast majority of practicing neuropsychologists are not trained to do. It has been suggested that training programs should devote increasing attention to these issues (Johnstone & Farmer, 1997), and it is clear that we will have to prepare students to more effectively respond to these trends if we are to have a meaningful impact on our patients' lives.

Up to this point, I have focused the discussion on the development of behavioral outcomes relevant to the process of neuropsychological assessment. Similar issues confront the expanding practice of cognitive rehabilitation (Ben-Yishay & Diller, 1993; Boake, 1991; Bontke, 1998; Ricker, 1998), which refers to a broad array of restorative or compensatory interventions designed to help patients with brain injury to achieve maximal post-injury function. It is difficult to clearly assess the efficacy of cognitive rehabilitation as it specifically relates to neuropsychological practice, since such services are offered in a wide variety of settings to a bewildering array of patients, by a broad range of clinical practitioners, most of whom are not professional neuropsychologists. Currently, the domain of cognitive rehabilitation (CR) is undergoing an important developmental phase in which questions regarding efficacy and cost effectiveness are being systematically raised on a large scale. Are CR interventions efficacious when compared to other treatment or no-treatment controls? What are the active ingredients in CR, and what are the mechanisms of change underlying CR interventions? Is CR cost-effective? All three of these questions demand the development of functionally relevant outcome measures on which to evaluate the clinical effects of rehabilitative interventions. The focus on functional outcomes in rehabilitation has already begun to bear fruit (Adamovich, 1998; Mills, Nesbeda, Katz, & Alexander, 1992), though much more work and methodological development are needed. While other allied health professionals (e.g., occupational therapists, speech/language pathologists) are active in the delivery of CR services (Joint Committee, 1995; Poole, Dunn, Schell, Tiernan, & Barnhart, 1991; Radomski, 1994; Wheatley, 1994), the expertise that neuropsychologists have in research design and methodology clearly positions members of our field to be leaders in the design and analysis of treatment efficacy research. It seems fair to say that a clear demonstration of the efficacy of CR has yet to emerge due to a lack of well-controlled research, though early data returns are optimistic (Heinemann, Hamilton, Linacre, Wright, & Granger, 1995; Prigatano & Wong, 1999; Robertson, 1993; Ruff & Niemann, 1990; Wilson, 1997). Ricker's (1998) assessment of the cognitive rehabilitation literature is that "overall, many studies of cognitive rehabilitation are confounded by natural recovery, poor ecological validity of outcome measures (e.g., neuropsychological tests), and failure to demonstrate a relation between interventions and psychometric outcome measures" (p. 189). Currently, broad federally supported evaluations of the state of the outcome literature in cognitive rehabilitation are underway.

Some Needed Developments in Neuropsychological Assessment

I have already considered two future characteristics of neuropsychological assessment that will likely change compared to current practices: assessments will be briefer, and they will be tied more directly to behavioral health outcomes. While significant, these developments are only part of the picture. Even if we commit a fatal error and respond to none of the challenges described above, we still need to make some internal changes in neuropsychological practice in order to make progress on solving some persistent, thorny issues. In this section, I discuss my armchair views on needed developments in the internal practice of neuropsychological assessments.

Let me begin by stating the obvious: we have made remarkable progress in assessing a vast array of neurocognitive functions in the past two decades. A formidable array of testing procedures is available for a vast number of cognitive functions, thanks to the interplay between clinical neuropsychology, cognitive psychology, and neuroscience (Lezak, 1995). Yet nagging questions remain about the meaning of test indicators, the relevance of available norms for particular patients, and the degree to which non-neuropsychological factors influence assessment results. We still suffer, as does the broader field of clinical psychology, from the "disconnect" inherent in applying group studies of psychological function to individual cases. To borrow terminology used in reviewing federal grants, my view is that we are "very good" to "excellent" at performing many assessment tasks, but not "outstanding." Neuropsychologists will have to do better in four major areas.

First, we need to better address the needs of minority populations by developing culturally sensitive assessment instruments that reflect more than just a well-intentioned, but ill-conceived attempt to translate existing methods to different languages (Artiola i Fortuny & Mullaney, 1998; Demsky, Mittenberg, Quintar, Katell, & Golden, 1998; Rees, 1991). Problems and complexities abound in developing an effective cross-cultural neuropsychology, some of which relate to broader issues that have made difficult a truly international professional collaboration (Mathews, 1992). Many neuropsychologists seem ill-equipped to interact effectively with patients from minority populations who do not share either their language or worldview. For example, a recent survey (Echemendia, Harris, Congett, Diaz, & Puente, 1997) suggested that many neuropsychologists in the United States provide both assessment and treatment services to Hispanics, yet those who do so report that they are inadequately prepared to work with this population. The general belief voiced by respondents in this study was that clinical neuropsychology has paid little attention to cultural factors. In her 1026-page treatise, Lezak (Lezak, 1995) devoted two paragraphs (pp. 310–311) to a discussion of social and cultural variables.[1]

Although many neuropsychology courses or workshops deal *generally* with the effects of culture and race on neuropsychological test performance, such discussions typically lead only to the simple-minded conclusion that different test norms are needed. Dealing with cultural differences goes far deeper than developing different population-specific metrics, and instead will involve organized training in how such differences affect the patient–examiner relationship and the manner in which qualitative aspects of behavior are to be understood and interpreted in their cultural context. We need to understand that minority populations possess different sociocultural mores, backgrounds, and worldviews that might significantly influence the manifestation and reporting of symptoms, the qualitative aspects of neuropsychological test performance, and the response to feedback and intervention (Puente, Sol Mora, & Munoz-Cespedes, 1997). At the present time, many neuropsychologists are not appropriately trained in minority issues, perhaps because training in diversity is not yet well-integrated into the graduate curriculum.

Second, we need to develop a more consistent approach to the treatment of age- and education-related variables in terms of how they affect neuropsychological test scores. Although many neuropsychological test procedures contain age/education corrections (Heaton, Grant, & Matthews, 1986, 1991), and much good work has been done to provide normative information for older populations (Ivnik, Malec, Smith, Tangalos, et al., 1992a, 1992b, 1996; Lucas et al., 1998; Malec, Ivnik, Smith, Tangalos, et al., 1992), such improvements are inconsistently applied in

1. This statement is not meant to find fault, only to illustrate the scope of the problem.

everyday practice. The availability of large-scale normative studies (e.g., Heaton et al., 1991) is, in fact, extremely limited. Instead, when reporting neuropsychological assessment results, neuropsychologists routinely compare raw scores from separate tests to normative tables in which age and education ranges may vary. For example, bias and potential inaccuracy are introduced when, on Test A, a 62-year-old patient scores at the 50th percentile of a >50-year-old group, and on Test B, is at the 72nd percentile of a sample of 60- to 65-year-olds. This is a particular problem when the neuropsychologist attempts to perform pattern analysis using the patient's relative standing on norm-referenced scores. It is known that the application of "cutting scores" developed on one population can lead to significant diagnostic errors when applied to a population of different age or education (Adams, Boake, & Crain, 1982; Bornstein, 1986; Marcopulos, McLain, & Giuliano, 1997). There are many barriers to the development of adequate normative standards, not the least of which is the fact that large-scale normative studies are exceedingly difficult to conduct and are not of high priority among those who determine policy for federal or foundation support. Still, we need to somehow rectify this situation empirically.

Third, we need to develop more effective means of evaluating executive and problem-solving skills (i.e., "frontal" functions). Impairments in frontal/executive skills may affect performance on a broad range of tests, even those that are not labeled as "executive" in nature (Lezak, 1995). A large number of qualitative indicators of executive deficits have been described (Luria, 1966) and are in routine use. However, because of the amount of inherent structure available in the neuropsychological examination, subtle impairments in problem-solving, organization, and behavioral activation may not readily emerge unless specifically elicited by the examiner (Shallice & Burgess, 1991). For example, the patient who has difficulty initiating complex behavior in an unstructured environment may do relatively well on a neuropsychological examination in which the examiner takes the lead in introducing test items and eliciting responses. Furthermore, recent data suggest that some "tried and true" tests of frontal ability (e.g., the Wisconsin Card Sort) (Heaton, Chelune, & Talley, 1993) may, in fact, be neither specific nor sensitive to frontal pathology per se (Anderson, Damasio, & Tranel, 1990). This is an area where we critically need more ecologically valid tests and clinical validation of experimental tests shown to be sensitive to frontal pathology. Clinical neuropsychologists would do well to develop or modify more "process pure" measures of: working memory (Baddeley, 1998; D'Esposito et al., 1995; Goldman-Rakic & Friedman, 1991; Ungerleider, Courtney, & Haxby, 1998), memory for temporal order (Meudell et al., 1985; Shimamura, Janowsky, & Squire, 1990; Shuren, Jacobs, & Heilman, 1997), delayed response (Oscar-Berman, McNamara, & Freedman, 1991), memory for self-generated responses (Petrides & Milner, 1982), cognitive estimation (Shallice, 1978; Smith & Milner, 1984), or interference susceptibility (Moskovitch, 1981; Squire, 1982).

Fourth, we need to develop more effective methods for assessing the impact of motivation, emotional disturbance, and effort on neuropsychological performance. It is widely recognized that neuropsychological test performance can be affected by a variety of such factors, though there are few clear (or consensually accepted) methods for eliciting them on neuropsychological examination. Clinicians often infer the presence of such factors by noting inconsistencies in test performance, inconsistencies between the clinical history and the presentation, and emotional reactions to the testing situation or materials (Larrabee, 1990, 1992; Lezak, 1995). At the present time, however, the process by which this task is accomplished is as much art as science. For example, in what may be the most comprehensive treatment of relevant measures, Lezak (1995) stated, "some of the recommendations for testing or evaluating test performances for functional complaints are based on studies, and others come from clinical experience" (p. 792). We need to do better than this.

One particularly controversial area, for example, is the neuropsychological detection of malingering (Beal, 1989; Faust, 1991; Faust, Hart, Guilmette, & Arkes, 1988; Guilmette & Giuliano, 1991; Heubrock & Petermann, 1998). Several useful testing procedures have evolved to assist the practitioner in determining whether malingering may have occurred during an examination (Binder, 1993; Lee, Loring, & Martin, 1992; Pankratz, 1979, 1983; Rey, 1964). While many of these tests are quite helpful, some may, at least in some populations, correlate with patient ability level (Hays, Emmons, & Lawson, 1993) and may yield normal results in cases where the rest of the neuropsychological profile suggests malingering or exaggeration (Trueblood & Schmidt, 1993). Furthermore, the accuracy and utility of tests of malingering may improve when the tests are given early in the examination to avoid contrast effects (Guilmette, Whelihan, Hart, Sparadeo, & Buongiorno, 1996). Malingering tests may be affected by the knowledge and sophistication of the examinee (Martin, Bolter, Todd, Gouvier, & Niccolls, 1993) and may be rendered insensitive if the patient is coached on how to perform (Coleman, Rapport, Millis, Ricker, & Farchione, 1998; Rapport, Farchione, Coleman, & Axelrod, 1998).[2]

Thus, though the use of these measures has greatly improved the neuropsychologist's ability to detect malingering and symptom exaggeration, interpretation of the meaning of such test performances is subject to the same sorts of qualifications that face interpretation of any neuropsychological test. Further development of techniques designed to evaluate functional complaints is desirable. This should incorporate paradigms from cognitive psychology and cognitive neuroscience in an effort to evaluate non-conscious forms of memory (Cochrane, Baker, & Meudell, 1998; Horton, Smith, Barghout, & Connolly, 1992) or other types of automatic behavior not subject to deliberate strategies.

---

2. Incidentally, this fact raises the general question of whether, like soft-drink manufacturers and software vendors, neuropsychology should have trade secrets. Our practice of publishing results of malingering studies in the public domain may make such results available to those who may attempt to malinger. Since these methods are designed to evaluate "volitional" or "strategic" processes, placing such results in the public domain is problematic.

Promises and Threats of Emergent Technologies

As computerized tomography (CT) and now magnetic resonance imaging (MRI) became routinely applied in the clinical evaluation of patients with suspected central nervous system damage, the goals and procedures of neuropsychological assessment shifted from a focus on lesion localization to a focus on deficit analysis. In the past ten years, exciting new developments in functional neuroimaging have made it possible to visualize and analyze patterns of activation that are, to a greater or lesser extent, time-locked to the performance of cognitive tasks (Liddle, 1997; Nadeau & Crosson, 1995). For example, Functional Magnetic Resonance Imaging (fMRI) allows visualization of the hemodynamic response to a single stimulus event, thus expanding the utility of the technique dramatically (Buckner et al., 1998; D'Esposito, Zarahn, & Aguirre, 1999; Friston et al., 1998).

The rapid developments in the field of functional neuroimaging may, in the not-too-distant future, have implications for the practice of neuropsychology. It is possible that certain questions for which neurocognitive assessments are currently indicated will be addressed with functional imaging. The beginning signs of this already are being seen in the epilepsy literature, where recent studies of language lateralization in surgical candidates have shown that lateralized hemodynamic changes measured with fMRI correlate impressively with results from the more invasive Wada test (Binder et al., 1996; Desmond et al., 1995). It may not be too long before fMRI is used in place of the Wada test, at least for the purposes of lateralizing language function in epilepsy surgery candidates. Functional neuroimaging measures may, in the future, be utilized to predict outcome from stroke or traumatic brain injury (Levin et al., 1997), to better understand the process by which neurocognitive interventions effect change in individual patients (Small, Flores, & Noll, 1998), or to identify those patients whose residual or reorganized function would make them good candidates for cognitive rehabilitation. These are tasks currently performed primarily by neuropsychologists who purportedly specialize in identifying and measuring behavioral predictors of such outcomes.

The dramatic advances in functional neuroimaging will not, however, put clinical neuropsychologists on the unemployment line, since the descriptive and prescriptive evaluation of the cognitive, behavioral, affective, and psychosocial outcome of neurological and psychiatric illness is not something that such techniques are designed to address. In my view, the practice of clinical neuropsychology actually stands to benefit from advances in functional neuroimaging. Results from neuroimaging studies have the capacity to validate or qualify results from the ablation paradigm so central to the history of clinical neuropsychological investigation. More importantly, neuropsychologists will continue to play critical roles in the development of the functional imaging field, since well-informed and well-designed cognitive paradigms are the rate-limiting step in all functional imaging investigations. That is to say, the relevance of technological advancements in functional neuroimaging depends upon the degree to which such technology can be brought to bear on neuropsychologically relevant phenomena. Thus far, functional imaging research has clearly focused on the regional architecture of basic neuropsychological processes such as memory, visual perception, motor perform-ance, and language. The next generation of functional imaging studies will rely more heavily on input from clinical neuropsychologists as we move toward apply-ing this technology to solving clinically relevant problems. Neuropsychologists need to be ready to meet this challenge by becoming more knowledgeable about this technology and more aware of its promises and limitations.

A second technological issue for the future concerns advancements in com-puter-assisted neuropsychological assessment. Reviewers have documented the increasing availability of both computer-administered tests and computer-assisted scoring and interpretation programs (Kane & Kay, 1997; Kane & Reeves, 1997). Some of these tests involve broad assessment of neuropsychological skills (Kane, 1995; Letz, Green, & Woodard, 1996), while others focus on specific domains of functioning such as memory assessment (Larrabee & Crook, 1991; Larrabee, Pathy, Bayer, & Crook, 1990). A detailed discussion of the many computerized test-ing programs, batteries, and scoring systems in use today is beyond the scope of this chapter, but a few comments regarding the practice implications of such devices will be offered. In my opinion, we need to exercise caution before imple-menting computerized approaches to neuropsychological assessment in willy-nilly fashion, since automating neuropsychological assessment instruments is more complicated than it seems. Although many studies comparing standard versus computerized versions of neuropsychological tests have shown good transfer to the digital environment (Berger, Chibnall, & Gfeller, 1997; Larrabee & Crook, 1989), we cannot assume uncritically that all tests will show such flexibility. Patient familiarity and comfort with the computer interface may have significant effects on performance and motivation. Certain populations of patients (e.g., the elderly, the physically or perceptually impaired, or those with limited computer experi-ence) might be less amenable to computer-assisted evaluation. Also, the interactive process between patient and examiner, which traditionally has been the richest and most direct source of qualitative performance observations, is lacking within computerized assessment procedures.

Despite these complications, the use of computers to collect behavioral per-formance data has certain distinct advantages. Highly accurate stimulus control (timing, presentation rate, orientation, size, etc.) is possible, as is the automatic recording of reaction times and other quantitative or qualitative features of behav-ior (Poizner, Mack, Verfaellie, Rothi, & Heilman, 1990). For example, exciting new possibilities in assessment and treatment of memory and visuospatial/visuomotor skills have arisen through the use of virtual reality technology (Christiansen et al., 1998; Rizzo & Buckwalter, 1997; Rose, Attree, & Brooks, 1997). In these applica-tions, the patient can actually navigate through a virtual environment or can manipulate a three-dimensional stimulus for purposes of assessing visual mem-ory, topographical orientation, or visuospatial skill. This type of application may provide at least a degree of ecological validity in both assessment and training pro-grams. The use of computers to administer and score neuropsychological tests also makes possible the development of the kind of large-scale, archival database that is needed to construct a more effective empirical foundation for contemporary clinical neuropsychology. For example, through the use of readily available Internet access, it should be possible for practitioners to perform online submission of patient and normal data (stripped of uniquely identifying information) to a centralized location for entry into a database that would be both comprehensive and continually updated. If a sufficient number of practitioners participated in a project such as this, a detailed database containing information on a broad range of patients and normals could quickly be assembled and accessed for use in the clinical assessment enterprise. Although the technical issues may be daunting, the technology for this kind of industry-wide sharing of data is currently at our disposal, but currently underutilized. This kind of service could be supported by nominal user fees and could be sponsored with the combined efforts of software vendors and professional societies. A website with some of these characteristics is currently under construction in conjunction with a compendium of normative data for use in neuropsychological assessment (Mitrushina, Boone, & D'Elia, 1999).[3]

Such technological advancements can be, and have been applied to intervention services. Computerized cognitive training programs have also been developed in recent years and have been claimed to produce gains in attention, memory, or logical thinking skills (Batt & Lounsbury, 1990; Chen, Thomas, Glueckauf, & Bracy, 1997; Middleton, Lambert, & Seggar, 1991; Niemann, Ruff, & Baser, 1990; Robertson, Gray, Pentland, & Waite, 1990). The use of computers in cognitive training programs also has certain advantages, including the ability to control and alter aspects of the learning or perceptual environment based on patient performance, and the automatic collection of performance data for purposes of plotting treatment gains. These advantages will need to be weighed against potential drawbacks (ethical issues concerning "therapist-less" training and appropriate professional charges, and practical issues related to customizing the human–machine interface to accommodate physical and perceptual defects) as we continue to incorporate advances in computer technology into the assessment and treatment enterprise.

Intra- and Inter-Professional Relationships

Psychologists know by training and experience that much can be learned about people by examining their relationships. As neuropsychology enters the twenty-first century, we can learn important lessons about the status of clinical neuropsychology by evaluating the way in which neuropsychologists relate to each other and by examining the way they interact with members of other professions. In this concluding section, I offer some of my views about these issues.

Let me begin with some comments on inter-professional relationships. In general, it can be said that neuropsychology has done remarkably well as a psycholog-

3. The URL for this website is http://www.normativedata.com

ical specialty. If recent practice statistics are any indication, most of us are very busy, and most of us interact on a regular basis with a wide variety of outside professionals within the interdisciplinary health-care team. Neuropsychologists are employed in diverse settings, and the clinical literature on neuropsychological manifestations of literally hundreds of medical conditions has exploded exponentially (Lezak, 1995; Tarter, Edwards, & Van Thiel, 1988), indicating that we are hard at work at understanding many disorders and problems. In addition to their ubiquitous collaboration with medical colleagues, neuropsychologists are active in legal and educational settings and have made significant contributions to industry (Hartman, 1995), to collegiate and professional athletics (Kelly & Rosenberg, 1997; McCrea et al., 1997; Ruchinskas, Francis, & Barth, 1997), and to veterans affairs (Goldstein et al., 1996; Haley et al., 1997; Hom, Haley, & Kurt, 1997; Kotler-Cope et al., 1996; Sillanpaa et al., 1997). By these criteria, we are a vibrant, expanding, and valued profession, and we should be proud of all we have accomplished. Despite all of the concerns I have raised, I must say that if one of my children decided to aim his or her professional crosshairs toward neuropsychology, I would lend vocal support (though based on my earlier comments I would probably also suggest a double major in Business Administration).

Despite these obvious signs of health, there are troublesome lab results we need to recognize. The first has to do with our overall public image as a profession. Although data describing consumer satisfaction of patients who have consumed neuropsychological services are favorable (Bennett-Levy et al., 1994), I am continually amazed at how little people outside our profession seem to know about neuropsychology. The majority of what the lay public knows about neuropsychology seems to come from cameo appearances on television or in movies (most of which depict neuropsychologists as sniveling, neurotic fools who have anything but professional excellence on their minds), or from the input that neuropsychologists have provided to media stories about rare forms of neurological disease such as agnosia, reduplication, or multiple personality. Among our medical colleagues, the value of neuropsychological assessment and consultation is, in my opinion, appreciated, but generally underestimated. My experience tells me that many medical practitioners do not understand the distinctive nature of neuropsychology as a psychological specialty and have not learned to utilize our skills effectively. We need to be more active in educating others about what we can do.

I say this having spent my entire career at a university-based health science center that boasts one of the most prominent behavioral neurology programs in North America. Even in this setting, many otherwise sophisticated medical practitioners seem to feel that the five-minute mental status examination sufficiently captures the complex cognitive status of the patients they care for. I have long felt that we need to engage in a more aggressive marketing campaign among the medical community, and we need to more effectively communicate the results of our assessments in ways that other professionals can understand. We need to target not only neurologists, neurosurgeons, and psychiatrists (who comprise our most frequent referrals; Sweet et al., 1996) but also internal medicine specialists, oncologists, primary care physicians, and geriatricians who care for large numbers of patients with illnesses affecting the brain.

Two recent articles in the medical literature are relevant to this discussion. In 1996 the Therapeutics and Technology Subcommittee of the American Academy of Neurology published an assessment of the role that neuropsychological testing plays in the care of adult patients with neurological disorders (Therapeutics and Technology Subcommittee, 1996). This assessment sparked spirited responses from a number of neuropsychologists (Bieliauskas, Adams, Fennell, Hammeke, & Rourke, 1997; Bigler & Dodrill, 1997; Binder, 1997; Bowen, 1996; Goldstein, 1997; Reitan, 1997; Van de Voorde, 1997; Vega, 1997; Wade, 1997), most of whom felt that the report reflected a misunderstanding and underestimation of the independent professional contribution that neuropsychologists could make to neurological health care. A second article (Mendez, Van Gorp, & Cummings, 1995) illustrated major practical and conceptual differences between the allied fields of neuropsychiatry, neuropsychology, and behavioral neurology, and suggested how "interdisciplinary knowledge and interactions can lead to a greater understanding of the neurobiologic basis of behavior" (p. 297). Taken together, these two articles should focus our attention on the need to sharpen points of agreement and to identify and work on points of disagreement and misunderstanding with our medical colleagues.

Among our allied health colleagues, the relationships enabled by the interdisciplinary team concept have done much to foster cooperation and communication. Despite these advances, however, there is sometimes a competitive feeling, particularly in rehabilitation settings, that neuropsychologists perform the same functions as our allied health colleagues, but at a much higher cost, both to the patient and to the employer. The occupational therapy literature reflects strong concern with assessing cognitive aspects of illness and disability (Batt & Lounsbury, 1990; Baum, 1991; Mann & Svorai, 1994; Poole et al., 1991; Radomski, 1994; Warren, 1993), and the profession of speech pathology is primarily concerned with assessing the effects of neurological disease on speech and communication performance, though only a minority of speech pathologists practice from a neuropsychological/mechanistic perspective. The primary difference between neuropsychology and these other professions is that (though there are clear exceptions) neuropsychologists generally are more concerned with cognitive and neural mechanisms underlying performance, while practitioners in these other disciplines are more clearly focused on performance and outcome per se. There are also differences in research emphasis and training. These represent differences in philosophical viewpoint that should not impair the development of strong interdisciplinary relationships if such differences are recognized and respected. In fact, neuropsychologists have much to gain by learning from our allied health colleagues, particularly if we are to develop a more effective approach to fostering and measuring ecologically relevant health outcomes.

Neuropsychologists also are challenged by remarkable new developments within the parent field of psychology. There has recently been a dramatic explosion in cognitive science, and the last decade has witnessed the birth of a new field known as "cognitive neuroscience" (Churchland & Sejnowski, 1991). What is the difference between cognitive neuroscience and neuropsychology? Aside from the obvious difference that clinical neuropsychology has a long history as an applied psychological field while cognitive neuroscience is populated primarily by non-applied professionals, the major differences between the fields concern methodological approach and conceptual heritage. Cognitive neuroscientific investigations have made much stronger use of experimental paradigms borrowed from cognitive psychology and neuroscience, and have tended to utilize more technologically intensive, cross-platform measurement systems such as combined functional neuroimaging and electrophysiology (Rugg, 1998).

Many "cognitive neuroscientists" owe their conceptual allegiances to cognitive psychology or neuroscience, while the majority of "clinical neuropsychologists" were trained primarily within a clinical discipline such as clinical or counseling psychology. There is significant overlap, however, such that many individuals would deserve to be called both a clinical neuropsychologist and a cognitive neuroscientist. It cannot be said that neuropsychologists study "patients" while cognitive neuroscientists study "normals," nor can it be asserted that either field is more focused than the other on elucidating the neurocognitive mechanisms underlying normal and abnormal behavior. There have been numerous examples of fruitful collaboration between neuropsychologists and cognitive neuroscientists, but there are also undercurrents of tension between the two disciplines. In my experience, some cognitive neuroscientists feel that clinical neuropsychologists are not concerned with the critical issues concerning the "functional architecture" of cognition and that we lack a certain scientific rigor in our methods (Kosslyn & Andersen, 1992).

Many cognitive neuroscience colleagues do research involving patient populations, and in these settings there is, at times, little appreciation for the clinical skills that distinguish "us" from "them." Some neuropsychologists feel that the majority of cognitive neuroscience research has rediscovered what clinical and experimental neuropsychologists have already known. A detailed cataloguing of all of the issues is beyond the scope of this chapter. Nonetheless, we must critically evaluate our relationships with our clinical and experimental colleagues so that we can continue to grow as an active and vibrant profession, can benefit maximally from advances in cognitive psychology and neuroscience, and can maintain our position as valued, central players in the clinical and experimental arenas.

Although our relationships with adjacent disciplines will require focused attention and effort, perhaps the most significant challenge to professional neuropsychology comes from internal tensions. Neuropsychologists tend to fight amongst themselves about a variety of fundamental conceptual and definitional issues. There are disagreements about how best to conceptualize our past, present, and future (Hartman, 1991; Loring, 1991; Reitan, 1989) and about how we should represent ourselves to the health-care community. Are these debates a sign of health, or are they the early signs of cancerous demise? How we handle and resolve these debates in the next few years will help decide whether we flourish and grow, or live out the next decades with promise unfulfilled.

The philosophical diversity that characterizes neuropsychological training and practice has challenged the development of standard practices in assessment and has made it difficult to agree upon minimal standards of training and preparation necessary for entry into the field. There have been several attempts at defining the necessary and sufficient preparation, culminating in the recent document from the Houston Conference (Hannay et al., 1998). Perhaps we are on the threshold of achieving broad, consensual agreement about what new entrants into the field will have to know before they call themselves neuropsychologists.

The diversity in training and experience that characterizes current practitioners of neuropsychology has, however, had a retardant effect on the development of universal credentialing standards. Currently, neuropsychologists can formally demonstrate competency in the field by successfully completing a regionally accredited doctoral program, by obtaining additional supervised training at the internship and residency levels, and by seeking board certification after obtaining licensure in their state of residence. Historically, two separate boards—the American Board of Clinical Neuropsychology (ABCN), affiliated with the American Board of Professional Psychology (ABPP), and the American Board of Professional Neuropsychology (ABPN)—have granted such certification. While both boards have, as a primary goal, the formal assessment of competence to practice clinical neuropsychology, they have differed in their philosophical approach to such assessment and in the examination procedures. Recent attempts to merge the boards under the auspices of the ABPP have been unsuccessful, and the field is left to cope with a sometimes bitter lack of unity regarding the meaning of, and the path to, board certification. At times, the debate has focused on substantive issues regarding training, examination procedures, and methodological validity; at other times, it has degenerated into a useless and self-defeating argument about the relative height of the evaluative bar used by the two boards. Regardless of one's position in the debate, all agree that the resulting impasse is detrimental to the health of clinical neuropsychology as a professional specialty.

Although we must appreciate diversity in the paths by which neuropsychological competence is achieved, such diversity often begets disagreement. In some cases, the resulting arguments have been fruitful and have yielded essential resolution. For example, the long debate between fixed versus flexible battery approaches to neuropsychological assessment has yielded a sort of compromise within the profession, and the best answer now appears to involve decisions about "when" rather then "whether" to choose a fixed or flexible approach (Bauer, 1994). The debate between quantitative versus qualitative approaches, as another example, has yielded a richer understanding of the value of both numerical and process-oriented data. No contemporary neuropsychologist would favor either type of data to the exclusion of the other.

The more malignant, irreconcilable debates that are currently ongoing (e.g., the pseudo-debates between "academicians" and "practitioners" and between "my board" and "your board") have no apparent purpose other than to reify and secure a particular position in a competitive marketplace. Although infighting within the ranks is understandable from a developmental perspective, my opinion is that it is decidedly damaging to the profession. Current disagreement concerning appropriate training and credentialing of neuropsychologists seems to be more of a malignant problem because it appears to involve a willingness by some to accept lower standards of expertise, training, and experience. Regarding the existing board disagreement, I believe that we should strive to adopt the most stringent, and most consensually validated approach to board certification (which, in all existing psychological specialties occurs through the American Board of Professional Psychology). To continue to proliferate multiple boards essentially supports the idea that specialty certification has no real meaning. In my view, if we fail to agree on such matters, then we should not whine and cry when someone outside our profession (e.g., an insurance adjuster or a managed care specialist) decides for us by authorizing neuropsychological services to be performed by psychologists with no appropriate specialty training, or worse, by practitioners with no psychological background at all (see below).

Up to now, this has been mostly an internal, family matter;. however, the dysfunction within the neuropsychological family already has begun to boil over into the streets. We now are faced with the reality that many health-care practitioners, with no visible training or expertise in neuropsychology, are being authorized to perform neurocognitive tests. Almost daily, we are confronted with reports, testimony, and interventions rendered by "neuropsychologists" with no neuropsychological training whose only real understanding of the issues comes from "personal experience," weekend workshops, or a vague, pop understanding that the brain has two sides. In addition, we must deal regularly with federal and private health-care organizations that do not appreciate the difference between professional and technical activity, as evident in the Medicare/Health Care Financing Administration notion that neuropsychological testing does not entail any significant "work effort."

In my view, one of the most damaging effects of our internal (domestic) angst is that it may have distracted us somewhat from spending time on "foreign" relations. We need to spend more time lobbying for the importance and distinctiveness of neuropsychology at the state and national level and less time on subjecting each other to "friendly fire." At the state level, we could be doing much more to help legislators understand how neuropsychological practice differs from the general practice of psychology. It is in our best interest to see that psychological practice laws are reformed in such a way that professional psychologists would have to demonstrate competence in the neuropsychology specialty before they are given the right to practice it. In this regard, we need to become more involved in judicial (law enforcement) affairs rather than focus exclusively on legislative (law-making) matters, since one of the core domains of specialty practice in neuropsychology concerns consumer protection.

At the national level, we need to keep up our efforts to protect and enhance the view that neuropsychologists provide work-intensive "professional" and not just "technical" services. One obvious, direct goal of these efforts, of course, will be to continue work with the American Psychological Association (APA) and other organizations in providing input to the Health Care Financing Administration regarding the methodology by which Medicare reimbursement of psychological and neuropsychological testing services is calculated. These efforts have been somewhat successful already due to concerted political activity by neuropsychologists working with the APA Practice Directorate. These efforts have helped lead to an increase in Relative Value Reimbursement Unit (RVRU) values for psychological and neuropsychological testing codes (96117) (Federal Register, 1998), but there is still no value attached to the "work effort" involved in administering, scoring, and interpreting test results. These issues are important since many other payors generally follow such federal guidelines.

As we move into the twenty-first century, it is time to get busy insuring that the future of neuropsychology, from without and from within, is afforded the kind of security it deserves. This will require efforts by every professional neuropsychologist (from private practitioners to administrators and everyone in between) to become more educated and active in political, economic, and social issues—all of this, of course, in our spare time.

To Infinity and Beyond

In the movie *Toy Story*, Buzz Lightyear—that noble, proud, futuristic leader of the ragtag bunch of animated toys—attempted to marshal enthusiasm for the troops (and to muster up some self-confidence of his own) by uttering, in his commanding voice, "To infinity and beyond!" Clinical neuropsychology would do well to generate such enthusiasm as we enter our first new century as an organized professional specialty. At this point in our history, it is time to reflect on, and be thankful for, what great things we have accomplished, but it is also time to take a hard look at where we are going. We all have concerns about our trajectory, and it is now time for each of us to alter our course in a positive, constructive way.

In this chapter, I have taken a soapbox view, sometimes restricted only by my nerve but sometimes cognizant of data, to tell it like I see it. If my naïveté shows through on occasion, I'm sure that the more learned members of my neuropsychological family will set me straight. In this regard, I look forward to the next chapter in my own education. The suds I have generated from bouncing up and down on my soapbox are intended to provide a cleansing influence, but I know that some soaps can irritate and chafe. If so, then I hope that what will ensue is a dialogue of healing, regrowth, and renewed commitment to working together to advance the science and profession of neuropsychology both for those who practice the profession and for those we serve.

REFERENCES

Adamovich, B. B. (1998). Functional outcome assessment of adults with traumatic brain injury. *Seminars in Speech and Language*, 19(3), 281–290.

Adams, R., Boake, C., & Crain, C. (1982). Bias in a neuropsychological test classification related to education, age, and ethnicity. *Journal of Consulting and Clinical Psychology*, 50, 143–145.

American Psychological Association, Division 40. (1989). Definition of a clinical neuropsychologist. *The Clinical Neuropsychologist*, 3, 22.

Anderson, S., Damasio, H., & Tranel, D. (1990). Wisconsin Card Sorting Test performance as a measure of frontal lobe damage. *Journal of Clinical and Experimental Neuropsychology*, 13, 909–922.

Artiola i Fortuny, L., & Mullaney, H. A. (1998). Assessing patients whose language you do not know: Can the absurd be ethical? *The Clinical Neuropsychologist*, 12, 113–126.

Baddeley, A. (1998). Recent developments in working memory. *Current Opinion in Neurobiology*, 8(2), 234–238.

Batt, R. C., & Lounsbury, P. A. (1990). Teaching the patient with cognitive deficits to use a computer. *American Journal of Occupational Therapy*, 44(4), 364–367.

Bauer, R. (1994). The flexible battery approach to neuropsychological assessment. In R. Vanderploeg (Ed.), *Clinician's guide to neuropsychological assessment* (pp. 259–290). Hillsdale, NJ: Lawrence Erlbaum.

Bauer, R. (1997, February). *Brain damage incurred by collision with forensic neuropsychologists*. Paper presented at the annual meeting of the International Neuropsychological Society, Orlando, FL.

Baum, C. M. (1991). Addressing the needs of the cognitively impaired elderly from a family policy perspective. *American Journal of Occupational Therapy*, 45(7), 594–606.

Beal, D. (1989). Assessment of malingering in personal injury cases. *American Journal of Forensic Psychology*, 7, 59–65.

Bennett-Levy, J., Klein-Moonschate, M. A.,

Batchelor, J., McCarter, R., & Walton, N. (1994). Encounters with Anna Thompson: The consumer's experience of neuropsychological assessment. *The Clinical Neuropsychologist*, 8, 219–238.

Benton, A. (1992). Clinical neuropsychology: 1960–1990. *Journal of Clinical and Experimental Neuropsychology*, 14(3), 407–417.

Benton, A. L. (1987). Evolution of a clinical specialty. *The Clinical Neuropsychologist*, 1(1), 5–8.

Ben-Yishay, Y., & Diller, L. (1993). Cognitive remediation in traumatic brain injury: Update and issues. *Archives of Physical Medicine and Rehabilitation*, 74, 204–213.

Berger, S. G., Chibnall, J. T., & Gfeller, J. D. (1997). Construct validity of the computerized version of the Category Test. *Journal of Clinical Psychology*, 53, 723–726.

Bieliauskas, L., Adams, K., Fennell, E., Hammeke, T., & Rourke, B. (1997). Assessment of neuropsychological testing: Comment. *Neurology*, 49, 1182–1183.

Bieliauskas, L. A., Fastenau, P. S., Lacy, M. A., & Roper, B. L. (1997). Use of the odds ratio to translate neuropsychological test scores into real-world outcomes: From statistical significance to clinical significance. *Journal of Clinical and Experimental Neuropsychology*, 19(6), 889–896.

Bigler, E. (1991). Neuropsychological assessment, neuroimaging, and clinical neuropsychology: A synthesis. *Archives of Clinical Neuropsychology*, 6(3), 113–132.

Bigler, E., & Dodrill, C. (1997). Assessment of neuropsychological testing: Comment. *Neurology*, 49, 1180–1182.

Binder, J. R., Swanson, S. J., Hammeke, T. A., Morris, G. L., Mueller, W. M., Fischer, M., Benbadis, S., Frost, J. A., Rao, S. M., & Haughton, V. M. (1996). Determination of language dominance using functional MRI: A comparison with the Wada test. *Neurology*, 46(4), 978–984.

Binder, L. (1993). Assessment of malingering after mild head trauma with the Portland Digit Recognition Test. *Journal of Clinical and Experimental Neuropsychology*, 15, 170–182.

Binder, L. (1997). Assessment of neuropsychological testing: Comment. *Neurology, 49*, 1179.

Boake, C. (1991). History of cognitive rehabilitation following head injury. In J. S. Kreutzer & P. H. Wehman (Eds.), *Rehabilitation for persons with traumatic brain injury* (pp. 1–12). Baltimore: Brooks.

Bontke, C. F. (1998). Managed care in traumatic brain injury rehabilitation: Physiatrists' concerns and ethical dilemmas. *Journal of Head Trauma Rehabilitation, 12*, 37–43.

Bornstein, R. (1986). Classification rates obtained with "standard" cut-off scores on selected neuropsychological measures. *Journal of Clinical and Experimental Neuropsychology, 8*, 413–420.

Bowen, M. (1996). Assessment of neuropsychological testing: Comment. *Neurology, 49*, 1178.

Buckner, R. L., Goodman, J., Burock, M., Rotte, M., Koutstaal, W., Schacter, D., Rosen, B., & Dale, A. M. (1998). Functional–anatomic correlates of object priming in humans revealed by rapid presentation event-related fMRI. *Neuron, 20*(2), 285–296.

Chen, S. H., Thomas, J. D., Glueckauf, R. L., & Bracy, O. L. (1997). The effectiveness of computer-assisted cognitive rehabilitation for persons with traumatic brain injury. *Brain Injury, 11*, 197–209.

Christiansen, C., Abreu, B., Ottenbacher, K., Huffman, K., Masel, B., & Culpepper, R. (1998). Task performance in virtual environments used for cognitive rehabilitation after traumatic brain injury. *Archives of Physical Medicine and Rehabilitation, 79*, 888–892.

Churchland, P. S., & Sejnowski, T. J. (1991). Perspectives on cognitive neuroscience. In R. G. Lister & H. J. Weingartner (Eds.), *Perspectives on cognitive neuroscience* (pp. 3–23). New York: Oxford University Press.

Cochrane, H. J., Baker, G. A., & Meudell, P. R. (1998). Simulating a memory impairment: Can amnesics implicitly outperform simulators? *British Journal of Clinical Psychology, 37*(Pt. 1), 31–48.

Coleman, R. D., Rapport, L. J., Millis, S. R., Ricker, J. H., & Farchione, T. J. (1998). Effects of coaching on detection of malingering on the California Verbal Learning Test. *Journal of Clinical and Experimental Neuropsychology, 20*(2), 201–210.

Costa, L. (1998). Professionalization in neuropsychology: The early years. *The Clinical Neuropsychologist, 12*(1), 1–7.

Crook, T. H., & Larrabee, G. J. (1988). Interrelationships among everyday memory tests: Stability of factor structure with age. *Neuropsychology, 2*, 1–12.

Demsky, Y. I., Mittenberg, W., Quintar, B., Katell, A. D., & Golden, C. J. (1998). Bias in the use of standard American norms with Spanish translations of the Wechsler Memory Scale–Revised. *Assessment, 5*(2), 115–121.

Desmond, J. E., Sum, J. M., Wagner, A. D., Demb, J. B., Shear, P. K., Glover, G. H., et al. (1995). Functional MRI measurement of language lateralization in Wada-tested patients. *Brain, 118*, 1411–1419.

D'Esposito, M., Detre, J. A., Alsop, D. C., Shin, R. K., Atlas, S., & Grossman, M. (1995). The neural basis of the central executive system of working memory. *Nature, 378*, 279–281.

D'Esposito, M., Zarahn, E., & Aguirre, G. K. (1999). Event-related functional MRI: Implications for cognitive psychology. *Psychological Bulletin, 125*, 155–164.

Devinsky, O., Vickrey, B. G., Cramer, J., Perrine, K., Hermann, B., Meador, K., & Hays, R. D. (1995). Development of the quality of life in epilepsy inventory. *Epilepsia, 36*, 1089–1104.

Diamond, G., Denton, T., & Matloff, J. (1993). Fee-for-benefit: A strategy to improve the quality of health care and control costs through reimbursement incentives. *Journal of the American College of Cardiology, 22*, 343–352.

Echemendia, R., Harris, J., Congett, S., Diaz, M., & Puente, A. (1997). Neuropsychological training and practices with Hispanics: A national survey. *The Clinical Neuropsychologist, 11*, 229–243.

Farmer, J. E., & Brazeal, T. J. (1998). Parent

perceptions about the process and outcomes of child neuropsychological assessment. *Applied Neuropsychology,* 5, 194–201.

Faust, D. (1991). Forensic neuropsychology: The art of practicing a science that does not yet exist. *Neuropsychology Review,* 2, 205–231.

Faust, D., Hart, K. J., Guilmette, T. J., & Arkes, H. R. (1988). Neuropsychologists' capacity to detect adolescent malingerers. *Professional Psychology: Research and Practice,* 19, 508–515.

Federal Register (1998, November 2). Medicare program: Revisions to payment policies and adjustments to the relative units under the physician fee schedule for calendar year 1999; final rule and notice. *Federal Register,* 63, 58863–58912.

Frank, R., & VandenBos, G. (1994). Health care reform: The 1993–1994 evolution. *American Psychologist,* 49, 851–854.

Franzen, M. D., & Wilhelm, K. L. (1996). Conceptual foundations of ecological validity in neuropsychological assessment. In R. J. Sbordone & C. J. Long (Eds.), *Ecological Validity of Neuropsychological Testing* (pp. 91–112). Delray Beach, FL: GR/St. Lucie Press.

Friston, K. J., Fletcher, P., Josephs, O., Holmes, A., Rugg, M. D., & Turner, R. (1998). Event-related fMRI: Characterizing differential responses. *Neuroimage,* 7, 30–40.

Goldman-Rakic, P., & Friedman, H. (1991). The circuitry of working memory revealed by anatomy and metabolic imaging. In H. Levin, H. Eisenberg, & A. Benton (Eds.), *Frontal Lobe Function and Dysfunction* (pp. 72–91). New York: Oxford University Press.

Goldstein, G. (1997). Assessment of neuropsychological testing: Comment. *Neurology,* 49, 1179–1180.

Goldstein, G., Beers, S. R., Morrow, L. A., Shemansky, W. J., et al. (1996). A preliminary neuropsychological study of Persian Gulf veterans. *Journal of the International Neuropsychological Society,* 2, 368–371.

Guilmette, T. J., & Giuliano, A. J. (1991). Taking the stand: Issues and strategies in forensic neuropsychology. *The Clinical Neuropsychologist,* 5, 197–219.

Guilmette, T. J., & Kastner, M. P. (1996). The prediction of vocational functioning from neuropsychological data. In R. J. Sbordone & C. J. Long (Eds.), *Ecological Validity of Neuropsychological Testing* (pp. 387–411). Delray Beach, FL: GR/St. Lucie Press.

Guilmette, T. J., Whelihan, W. M., Hart, K. J., Sparadeo, F. R., & Buongiorno, G. (1996). Order effects in the administration of a forced-choice procedure for detection of malingering in disability claimants' evaluations. *Perceptual and Motor Skills,* 83(3 Pt. 1), 1007–1016.

Haley, R. W., Hom, J., Roland, P. S., Bryan, W. W., Van Ness, P. C., Bonte, F. J., Devous, M. D., Mathews, D., Fleckenstein, J. L., Wians, F. H., Wolfe, G. I., & Kurt, T. L. (1997). Evaluation of neurologic function in Gulf War veterans: A blinded case-control study. *Journal of the American Medical Association,* 277, 223–230.

Hannay, H. J., Bieliauskas, L. A., Crosson, B. A., Hammeke, T. A., Hamsher, K. D., & Koffler, S. P. (1998). Proceedings of the Houston Conference on Specialty Education and Training in Clinical Neuropsychology. *Archives of Clinical Neuropsychology,* 13, 157–250.

Hartman, D. E. (1991). Reply to Reitan: Unexamined premises and the evolution of clinical neuropsychology. *Archives of Clinical Neuropsychology,* 6, 147–165.

Hartman, D. E. (1995). *Neuropsychological Toxicology: Identification and Assessment of Human Neurotoxic Syndromes* (2nd ed.). New York: Plenum Press.

Hays, J. R., Emmons, J., & Lawson, K. A. (1993). Psychiatric norms for the Rey 15-item Visual Memory Test. *Perceptual and Motor Skills,* 76, 1331–1334.

Heaton, R., Chelune, G., & Talley, J. (1993). *Wisconsin Card Sorting Test. Manual.* Odessa, FL: Psychological Assessment Resources.

Heaton, R., Grant, I., & Matthews, C. (1986). Differences in neuropsychological test performance associated with age, education, and sex. In I. Grant & K. Adams (Eds.),

Neuropsychological Assessment of Neuropsychiatric Disorders (pp. 100–120). New York: Oxford University Press.

Heaton, R., Grant, I., & Matthews, C. (1991). *Comprehensive norms for an expanded Halstead–Reitan Battery: Demographic corrections, research findings, and clinical applications.* Odessa, FL: Psychological Assessment Resources.

Heinemann, A. W., Hamilton, B., Linacre, J. M., Wright, B. D., & Granger, C. (1995). Functional status and therapeutic intensity during inpatient rehabilitation. *American Journal of Physical Medicine and Rehabilitation, 74,* 315–326.

Hermann, B. P. (1995). The evolution of health-related quality of life assessment in epilepsy. *Quality of Life Research, 4,* 87–100.

Heubrock, D., & Petermann, F. (1998). Neuropsychological assessment of suspected malingering: Research results, evaluation techniques, and further directions of research and application. *European Journal of Psychological Assessment, 14,* 211–225.

Hom, J., Haley, R. W., & Kurt, T. L. (1997). Neuropsychological correlates of Gulf War Syndrome. *Archives of Clinical Neuropsychology, 12,* 531–544.

Horton, K. D., Smith, S. A., Barghout, N. K., & Connolly, D. A. (1992). The use of indirect memory tests to assess malingered amnesia: A study of metamemory. *Journal of Experimental Psychology: General, 121,* 326–351.

Ivnik, R. J., Malec, J. F., Smith, G. E., Tangalos, E. G., et al. (1992a). Mayo's Older Americans Normative Studies: WAIS–R norms for ages 56 to 97. *The Clinical Neuropsychologist, 6,* 1–30.

Ivnik, R. J., Malec, J. F., Smith, G. E., Tangalos, E. G., et al. (1992b). Mayo's Older Americans Normative Studies: WMS–R norms for ages 56 to 94. *The Clinical Neuropsychologist, 6,* 49–82.

Ivnik, R. J., Malec, J. F., Smith, G. E., Tangalos, E. G., et al. (1996). Neuropsychological tests' norms above age 55: COWAT, BNT, MAE Token, WRAT–R Reading, AMNART, STROOP, TMT, and JLO. *The Clinical Neuropsychologist, 10,* 262–278.

Johnstone, B., & Farmer, J. E. (1997). Preparing neuropsychologists for the future: The need for additional training guidelines. *Archives of Clinical Neuropsychology, 12,* 523–530.

Johnstone, B., Frank, R. G., Belar, C., Berk, S., et al. (1995). Psychology in health care: Future directions. *Professional Psychology: Research and Practice, 26,* 341–365.

Joint Committee on Interprofessional Relations Between Division 40 (Clinical Neuropsychology) of the American Psychological Association and the American Speech-Language–Hearing Association. (1995). Guidelines for the structure and function of an interdisciplinary team for persons with brain injury. *ASHA, 37*(3 Suppl. 14), 23–25.

Kalechstein, A. D., & van Gorp, W. G. (1998). Outcomes assessment for forensic neuropsychology: Recommendations and considerations. *Applied Neuropsychology, 5,* 202–208.

Kane, R. L. (1995). MicroCog: A review. *Bulletin of the National Academy of Neuropsychology, 11,* 13–16.

Kane, R. L. (1997). What outcomes matter in Alzheimer disease and who should define them? *Alzheimer Disease and Associated Disorders, 11*(Suppl. 6), 12–17.

Kane, R. L., & Kay, G. G. (1997). Computer applications in neuropsychological assessment. In G. Goldstein & T. Incagnoli (Eds.), *Contemporary Approaches to Neuropsychological Assessment* (pp. 359–392). New York: Plenum Press.

Kane, R. L., & Reeves, D. L. (1997). Computerized test batteries. In A. M. Horton & D. Wedding (Eds.), *The Neuropsychology Handbook (Vol 1: Foundations and assessment)* (pp. 423–467). New York: Springer Publishing.

Kaplan, R. (1990). Behavior as the central outcome in health care. *American Psychologist, 45,* 1211–1220.

Kaplan, R. (1994). The Ziggy theorem: Toward an outcomes-focused health psychology. *Health Psychology, 13,* 451–460.

Kaplan, R., & Anderson, J. (1988). The Quality of Well-Being Scale: Rationale for a single quality of life index. In S. Walker & R. Rosser (Eds.), *Quality of Life: Assessment and Application* (pp. 51–77). London: MTP Press.

Kaplan, R., & Anderson, J. (1990). An integrated approach to quality of life assessment: The general health policy model. In B. Spilker (Ed.), *Quality of Life in Clinical Studies* (pp. 131–149). New York: Raven Press.

Kelly, J. P., & Rosenberg, J. H. (1997). Diagnosis and management of concussion in sports. *Neurology, 48,* 575–580.

Kerner, D. N., Patterson, T. L., Grant, I., & Kaplan, R. M. (1998). Validity of the Quality of Well-Being Scale for patients with Alzheimer's disease. *Journal of Aging and Health, 10,* 44–61.

Kosslyn, S. M., & Andersen, R. A. (1992). General introduction. In S. M. Kosslyn & R. A. Andersen (Eds.), *Frontiers in cognitive neuroscience* (pp. xv–xxix). Cambridge, MA: MIT Press.

Kotler-Cope, S., Milby, J. B., Roswell, R., Boll, T., LaMarche, J., Marson, D., Novack, T., & Plasay, M. (1996). Neuropsychological deficits in Persian Gulf War veterans: A preliminary report. *Journal of the International Neuropsychological Society, 2,* 63.

Larrabee, G. J. (1990). Cautions in the use of neuropsychological evaluation in legal settings. *Neuropsychology, 4,* 239–247.

Larrabee, G. J. (1992). Interpretive strategies for evaluation of neuropsychological data in legal settings. *Forensic Reports, 5,* 257–264.

Larrabee, G. J., & Crook, T. H. (1989). Dimensions of everyday memory in age-associated memory impairment. *Psychological Assessment, 1,* 92–97.

Larrabee, G. J., & Crook, T. H., III. (1991). Computerized memory testing in clinical trials. In E. Mohr & P. Brouwers (Eds.), *Handbook of clinical trials: The neurobehavioral approach.* (pp. 293–306). Amsterdam: Swets & Zeitlinger.

Larrabee, G. J., & Crook, T. H., III. (1996). The ecological validity of memory testing procedures: Developments in the assessment of everyday memory. In R. J. Sbordone &

C. J. Long (Eds.), *Ecological validity of neuropsychological testing* (pp. 225–242). Delray Beach, FL: GR/St. Lucie Press.

Larrabee, G. J., Pathy, M. S. J., Bayer, A. J., & Crook, T. H. (1990). Memory assessment clinics: State of development and future prospects. In M. Bergener & S. I. Finkel (Ed.), *Clinical and Scientific Geriatrics (Vol. 1)* (pp. 83–97). New York: Springer Publishing.

Lee, G., Loring, D., & Martin, R. (1992). Rey's 15 item visual memory test for the detection of malingering: Normative observations on patients with neurological disorders. *Psychological Assessment, 4,* 43–46.

Letz, R., Green, R. C., & Woodard, J. L. (1996). Development of a computer-based battery designed to screen adults for neuropsychological impairment. *Neurotoxicology and Teratology, 18,* 365–370.

Levin, H. S., Scheller, J., Rickard, T., Grafman, J., Martinkowski, K., Winslow, M., & Mirvis, S. (1997). Dyscalculia and dyslexia after right hemisphere injury in infancy. *Archives of Neurology, 53*(1), 88–96.

Lezak, M. D. (1995). *Neuropsychological assessment* (3rd ed.). New York: Oxford University Press.

Liddle, P. F. (1997). Dynamic neuroimaging with PET, SPET, or fMRI. *International Review of Psychiatry, 9,* 331–337.

Loring, D. W. (1991). A counterpoint to Reitan's note on the history of clinical neuropsychology. *Archives of Clinical Neuropsychology, 6,* 167–171.

Lucas, J. A., Ivnik, R. J., Smith, G. E., Bohac, D. L., Tangalos, E. G., Graff Radford, N. R., & Petersen, R. C. (1998). Mayo's Older Americans Normative Studies: Category fluency norms. *Journal of Clinical and Experimental Neuropsychology, 20,* 194–200.

Luria, A. (1966). *Higher cortical functions in man.* New York: Basic Books.

Malec, J. F., Ivnik, R. J., Smith, G. E., Tangalos, E. G., et al. (1992). Mayo's Older Americans Normative Studies: Utility of corrections for age and education for the WAIS–R. *The Clinical Neuropsychologist, 6*(Suppl.), 31–47.

Mann, W. C., & Svorai, S. B. (1994). COMPETE: a model for vocational evaluation, training, employment, and community for integration for persons with cognitive impairments. *American Journal of Occupational Therapy, 48,* 446–451.

Marcopulos, B. A., McLain, C. A., & Giuliano, A. J. (1997). Cognitive impairment or inadequate norms: A study of healthy, rural, older adults with limited education. *The Clinical Neuropsychologist, 11,* 111–131.

Martin, R. C., Bolter, J. F., Todd, M. E., Gouvier, W. D., & Niccolls, R. (1993). Effects of sophistication and motivation on the detection of malingered memory performance using a computerized forced-choice task. *Journal of Clinical and Experimental Neuropsychology, 15,* 867–880.

Mathews, C. G. (1992). Truth in labeling: Are we really an International Society? *Journal of Clinical and Experimental Neuropsychology, 14,* 418–426.

McCrea, M., Kelly, J. P., Kluge, J., Ackley, B., & Randolph, C. (1997). Standardized assessment of concussion in football players. *Neurology, 48(3, Pt. 2),* 586–588.

Meador, K. J. (1993). Research use of the new quality-of-life in epilepsy inventory. *Epilepsia, 34 (Suppl 4),* S34–38.

Mendez, M., Van Gorp, W., & Cummings, J. (1995). Neuropsychiatry, neuropsychology, and behavioral neurology: A critical comparison. *Neuropsychiatry, Neuropsychology, and Behavioral Neurology, 8,* 297–302.

Meudell, P., Mayer, A., Ostergaard, A., & Pickering, A. (1985). Recency and frequency judgments in alcoholic amnesics and normal people with poor memory. *Cortex, 21,* 487–511.

Middleton, D. K., Lambert, M. J., & Seggar, L. B. (1991). Neuropsychological rehabilitation: Microcomputer-assisted treatment of brain-injured adults. *Perceptual and Motor Skills, 72,* 527–530.

Miller, L. J., & Mittenberg, W. (1998). Brief cognitive behavioral interventions in mild traumatic brain injury. *Applied Neuropsychology, 5,* 172–183.

Mills, V. M., Nesbeda, T., Katz, D. I., & Alexander, M. P. (1992). Outcomes for traumatically brain-injured patients following post-acute rehabilitation programmes. *Brain Injury, 6,* 219–228.

Mitrushina, M., & Fuld, P. A. (1996). Cognitive screening methods: Structured mental status measures—Validity and reliability. In I. Grant & K. M. Adams (Eds.), *Neuropsychological assessment of neuropsychiatric disorders (2nd. ed.).* New York: Oxford University Press.

Mitrushina, M. N., Boone, K. B., & D'Elia, L. F. (1999). *Handbook of normative data for neuropsychological assessment.* New York: Oxford University Press.

Mittenberg, W., DiGiulio, D. V., Perrin, S., & Bass, A. E. (1992). Symptoms following mild head injury: Expectation as aetiology. *Journal of Neurology, Neurosurgery and Psychiatry, 55,* 200–204.

Moskovitch, M. (1981). Multiple dissociations of function in the amnesic syndrome. In L. Cermak (Ed.), *Human memory and amnesia* (pp. 337–370). Hillsdale, NJ: Lawrence Erlbaum.

Nadeau, S. E., & Crosson, B. (1995). A guide to the functional imaging of cognitive processes. *Neuropsychiatry, Neuropsychology, and Behavioral Neurology, 8,* 143–162.

Niemann, H., Ruff, R. M., & Baser, C. A. (1990). Computer-assisted attention retraining in head-injured individuals: A controlled efficacy study of an outpatient program. *Journal of Consulting and Clinical Psychology, 58(6),* 811–817.

Oscar-Berman, M., McNamara, P., & Freedman, M. (1991). Delayed response tasks: Parallels between experimental ablation studies and findings in patients with frontal lesions. In H. Levin, H. Eisenberg, & A. Benton (Eds.), *Frontal lobe function and dysfunction* (pp. 230–255). New York: Oxford University Press.

Pankratz, L. (1979). Symptom validity testing and symptom retraining: Procedures for the assessment and treatment of functional sensory deficits. *Journal of Consulting and Clinical Psychology, 47,* 409–410.

Pankratz, L. (1983). A new technique for the

assessment and modification of feigned memory deficit. *Perceptual and Motor Skills, 57,* 367–372.

Parsons, O. (1991). Clinical neuropsychology 1970–1990: A personal view. *Archives of Clinical Neuropsychology, 6,* 105–111.

Perrine, K. R. (1993). A new quality-of-life inventory for epilepsy patients: Interim results. *Epilepsia, 34 (Suppl 4),* S28–33.

Petrides, M., & Milner, B. (1982). Deficits on subject-ordered tasks after frontal- and temporal-lobe lesions in man. *Neuropsychologia, 20,* 249–262.

Poizner, H., Mack, L., Verfaellie, M., Rothi, L. J., & Heilman, K. M. (1990). Three-dimensional computergraphic analysis of apraxia. Neural representations of learned movement. *Brain, 113* (Pt. 1), 85–101.

Poole, J., Dunn, W., Schell, B., Tiernan, K., & Barnhart, J. M. (1991). Statement: Occupational therapy services management of persons with cognitive impairments. *American Journal of Occupational Therapy, 45,* 1067–1068.

Prigatano, G. P., & Schacter, D. L. (1991). *Awareness of deficit after brain injury: Clinical and theoretical issues.* New York: Oxford University Press.

Prigatano, G. P., & Wong, J. L. (1999). Cognitive and affective improvement in brain dysfunctional patients who achieve inpatient rehabilitation goals. *Archives of Physical Medicine and Rehabilitation, 80*(1), 77–84.

Puente, A. (1992). The status of clinical neuropsychology. *Archives of Clinical Neuropsychology, 7*(4), 297–312.

Puente, A. E., Sol Mora, M., & Munoz-Cespedes, J. M. (1997). Neuropsychological assessment of Spanish-speaking children and youth. In C. R. Reynolds & E. Fletcher-Janzen (Eds.), *Handbook of clinical child neuropsychology (2nd. Ed.),* pp. 371–383. New York: Plenum Press.

Putnam, S., & DeLuca, J. (1990). The TCN professional practice survey: I. General practices of neuropsychologists in primary employment and private practice settings. *The Clinical Neuropsychologist, 4*(3), 199–243.

Putnam, S., & DeLuca, J. (1991). The TCN Professional Practice Survey: II. An analysis of the fees of neuropsychologists by practice demographics. *The Clinical Neuropsychologist, 5*(2), 103–124.

Radomski, M. V. (1994). Cognitive rehabilitation: Advancing the stature of occupational therapy. *American Journal of Occupational Therapy, 48*(3), 271–273.

Rapport, L. J., Farchione, T. J., Coleman, R. D., & Axelrod, B. N. (1998). Effects of coaching on malingered motor function profiles. *Journal of Clinical and Experimental Neuropsychology, 20*(1), 89–97.

Rees, E. L. (1991). ¡Que problema! How accurate is that translation? *Criminal Justice, 6,* 18–22.

Reitan, R. M. (1989). A note regarding some aspects of the history of clinical neuropsychology. *Archives of Clinical Neuropsychology, 4,* 385–391.

Reitan, R. M. (1997). Assessment of neuropsychological testing: Comment. *Neurology, 49*(4), 1179.

Rey, A. (1964). *L'examen clinique en psychologie.* Paris: Presses Universitaires de France.

Ricker, J. H. (1998). Traumatic brain injury rehabilitation: Is it worth the cost? *Applied Neuropsychology, 5,* 184–193.

Rizzo, A. A., & Buckwalter, J. G. (1997). Virtual reality and cognitive assessment and rehabilitation: The state of the art. In G. Riva (Ed.), *Virtual reality in neuro-psycho-physiology: Cognitive, clinical, and methodological issues in assessment and rehabilitation* (pp. 123–145). Amsterdam: IOS Press.

Robertson, I. H. (1993). Cognitive rehabilitation in neurologic disease. *Current Opinion in Neurology, 6*(5), 756–760.

Robertson, I. H., Gray, J. M., Pentland, B., & Waite, L. J. (1990). Microcomputer-based rehabilitation for unilateral left visual neglect: A randomized controlled trial. *Archives of Physical Medicine and Rehabilitation, 71,* 663–668.

Rose, F. D., Attree, E. A., & Brooks, B. M. (1997). Virtual environments in neuropsychological assessment and rehabilitation. In G. Riva (Ed.), *Virtual reality in neuro-psycho-physiology: Cognitive, clinical, and methodological issues in assessment and rehabilitation* (pp. 147–155). Amsterdam: IOS Press.

Rourke, B. (1991). Human neuropsychology in the 1990s. *Archives of Clinical Neuropsychology, 6,* 1–14.

Rourke, B. P. (1995). The science of practice and the practice of science: The scientist–practitioner model in clinical neuropsychology. *Canadian Psychology, 36*(4), 259–277.

Ruchinskas, R. A., Francis, J. P., & Barth, J. T. (1997). Mild head injury in sports. *Applied Neuropsychology, 4,* 43–49.

Ruff, R., & Niemann, H. (1990). Cognitive rehabilitation versus day treatment in head-injured adults: Is there an impact on emotional and psychosocial adjustment? *Brain Injury, 4,* 339–347.

Rugg, M. D. (1998). Convergent approaches to electrophysiological and hemodynamic investigations of memory. *Human Brain Mapping, 6,* 394–398.

Ryan, C. M., & Hendrickson, R. (1998). Evaluating the effects of treatment for medical disorders: Has the value of neuropsychological assessment been fully realized? *Applied Neuropsychology, 5,* 209–219.

Sbordone, R. J., & Long, C. J. (Eds.). (1996). *Ecological validity of neuropsychological testing.* Delray Beach, FL: GR/St. Lucie Press.

Shallice, T. (1978). The involvement of the frontal lobes in cognitive estimation. *Cortex, 14,* 294–303.

Shallice, T., & Burgess, P. (1991). Higher-order cognitive impairments and frontal lobe lesions in man. In H. Levin, H. Eisenberg, & A. Benton (Eds.), *Frontal lobe function and dysfunction* (pp. 125–138). New York: Oxford University Press.

Shimamura, A., Janowsky, J., & Squire, L. (1990). Memory for the temporal order of events in patients with frontal lobe lesions and amnesic patients. *Neuropsychologia, 28,* 803–814.

Shuren, J. E., Jacobs, D. H., & Heilman, K. M. (1997). Diencephalic temporal order amnesia. *Journal of Neurology, Neurosurgery, and Psychiatry, 62,* 163–168.

Sillanpaa, M. C., Agar, L. M., Milner, I. B., Podany, E. C., Axelrod, B. N., & Brown, G. (1997). Gulf War veterans: A neuropsychological examination. *Journal of Clinical and Experimental Neuropsychology, 19,* 211–219.

Small, S. L., Flores, D. K., & Noll, D. C. (1998). Different neural circuits subserve reading before and after therapy for acquired dyslexia. *Brain and Language, 62*(2), 298–308.

Smith, M., & Milner, B. (1984). Differential effects of frontal-lobe lesions on cognitive estimation and spatial memory. *Neuropsychologia, 22,* 697–705.

Squire, L. (1982). Comparisons between forms of amnesia: Some deficits are unique to Korsakoff's syndrome. *Journal of Experimental Psychology: Learning, Memory, and Cognition, 8,* 560–571.

Sweet, J., Moberg, P., & Westergaard, C. (1996). Five-year follow-up survey of practices and beliefs of clinical neuropsychologists. *The Clinical Neuropsychologist, 10,* 202–221.

Sweet, J. J., Westergaard, C. K., & Moberg, P. J. (1995). Managed care experiences of clinical neuropsychologists. *The Clinical Neuropsychologist, 9,* 214–218.

Tarter, R. E., & Edwards, K. L. (1988). Neuropsychological batteries. In T. Incagnoli, G. Goldstein, & C. J. Golden (Eds.), *Clinical application of neuropsychological test batteries* (pp. 135–153). New York: Plenum Press.

Tarter, R. E., Edwards, K. L., & Van Thiel, D. H. (1988). *Medical neuropsychology: The impact of disease on behavior.* New York: Plenum Press.

Therapeutics and Technology Assessment Subcommittee of the American Academy of Neurology. (1996). Assessment: Neuropsychological testing of adults. *Neurology, 47,* 592–599.

Trueblood, W., & Schmidt, M. (1993). Malingering and other validity considerations in the neuropsychological evaluation of mild head injury. *Journal of Clinical and Experimental Neuropsychology, 15*(4), 578–590.

Ungerleider, L. G., Courtney, S. M., & Haxby,

J. V. (1998). A neural system for human visual working memory. *Proceedings of the National Academy of Sciences USA, 95,* 883–890.

Van de Voorde, J. (1997). Assessment of neuropsychological testing: Comment. *Neurology, 49,* 1180.

Vanderploeg, R. D. (1998). Neuropsychological outcomes research: A necessity and an opportunity. *Applied Neuropsychology, 5,* 169–171.

Vega, J. G. (1997). Assessment of neuropsychological testing: Comment. *Neurology, 49,* 1178.

Vickrey, B. G., Hays, R. D., Graber, J., Rausch, R., Engel, J., Jr., & Brook, R. H. (1992). A health-related quality of life instrument for patients evaluated for epilepsy surgery. *Medical Care, 30,* 299–319.

Wade, J. B. (1997). Assessment of neuropsychological testing: Comment. *Neurology, 49,* 1178.

Warren, M. (1993). A hierarchical model for evaluation and treatment of visual perceptual dysfunction in adult acquired brain injury, Part 2. *American Journal of Occupational Therapy, 47,* 55–66.

Wheatley, C. J. (1994). Cognitive rehabilitation service provision: Results of a survey of practitioners. *American Journal of Occupational Therapy, 48,* 163–166.

Wilson, B. A. (1997). Cognitive rehabilitation: How it is and how it might be. *Journal of the International Neuropsychological Society, 3,* 487–496.

Youngjohn, J. R., Larrabee, G. J., & Crook, T. H. (1992). Test-retest reliability of computerized, everyday memory measures and traditional memory tests. *The Clinical Neuropsychologist, 6,* 276–286.

18

Amnesia for the Past Causes Deficits in Prospective Planning*

Laird S. Cermak

*H*aving spent most of my professional life living and working with individuals suffering from amnesia, I have become overly sensitized to the parallel that exists between my own discipline and these unfortunate individuals. An inability to remember the past creates a situation where each day is a blank page without notations to help guide future action. Like amnesic patients, researchers in psychology (including neuropsychology) seem capable of operating without recourse to the past but also, unfortunately, without a clue as to what the future may bring. As one of my amnesic patients would repeatedly say, "It's as if I'm just coming to." Or, as one of Elizabeth Warrington's patients used to write in his log every ten minutes, "I'm just waking up and becoming aware of where I am."

This inability to use the past to anticipate the future seems to produce far more forecasts of doom than of hope. This is true of my patients; because they cannot remember the past, they are convinced things will not get much better. The same is true of the profession of psychology. My professional life has been spent in the Department of Veterans Affairs (VA) where I have heard far more than my deserved share of speeches about the imminent destruction of psychology services in the VA system. My first chief of service would gather us together weekly to deliver a monologue that matched the "hell and damnation" sermons of the Midwest tent preachers. The worst was always just around the corner and just about to come down upon us. The problem, as he saw it, was that if we were challenged we would have nothing to justify our existence as a clinical service. "Document, docu-

*For the last two and one-half decades, my research has been supported by the National Institute of Alcohol and Alcohol Abuse Grant AA 00187 and by the Medical Research Service of the Department of Veterans Affairs. Over the last decade, my research has also been supported by the National Institute of Neurological Disorders and Stroke Program Project Grant NS 26985. For that support I am grateful. However, for the philosophy that guides my research and provides the basis for my prospectus on the future of psychological research, I am indebted to the mentorship of Delos D. Wickens, my advisor in graduate school, and to Harry P. Bahrick, my teacher as an undergraduate. It is to these two gentlemen that I dedicate this chapter and hope that I have not or would not have embarrassed them by my less-than-professional demeanor.

ment, document," he would beseech in the hope that we would end up with some data to validate what it was that psychologists did anyway.

Today, the overwhelming and highly depressing message I have harvested from professional meetings, informal gatherings, and texts is that researchers and clinicians cannot foresee how psychology can exist as an independent entity in the twenty-first century. Message upon message of doom and destruction is piled one upon the other to the point where I feel myself cringing much as I did before that "sorcerer of destruction" at our staff meetings two decades ago. The message is still that psychology is not going to make it into the twenty-first century because it has not produced a compendium of knowledge upon which to base such a transfer. But the reality of my situation (and that of other psychologists in the VA system) is that I still have a position here at the VA Medical Center, and I have not been struck down as the weekly predictions had foretold.

I believe that the same will hold true for our existence as research psychologists in the next century. There will still be a discipline called psychology, research will continue to be performed, and forecasters will still be predicting the field's imminent demise. The primary reason, however, for predicting the death of scientific psychology in the next century, and as a consequence the death of neuropsychology, is the projected proliferation of disciplines that overlap with psychology. Thus, we may be threatened by a brain drain from psychology to these competing fields. Many of us, trained during the last three decades in psychology, will have joined these other disciplines and will have ceased to call ourselves psychologists, preferring instead new titles such as cognitive neuroscientists, psychopharmacologists, psychoneuroimmunologists, cryogenic manipulators, virtual simulators, or neuropharmacognobiotechnologists.

It is not very difficult to make this prediction because it was happening already at the close of the twentieth century. Many individuals who previously aligned themselves with psychology, and who were trained in psychology departments, have pledged their allegiance to other, overlapping disciplines. For example, some universities have dropped their departments of psychology in favor of brain and cognitive science departments. Yet, the American Psychological Association (APA) and the American Psychological Society (APS) continue to grow by huge numbers; the number of universities with APA-accredited graduate programs continues to grow; and new liberal arts universities, colleges, junior colleges, and community colleges continue to include psychology curriculums. The number of professional psychology programs also continues to grow, though I am not at all certain that this is to the benefit of the discipline. Nevertheless, despite the notable escapees, runaways, and absentees from the discipline, the community of psychology is still growing unabated.

The number of people trained as psychologists, and especially as neuropsychologists, will continue to grow exponentially during at least the first quarter of the twenty-first century and probably far beyond that. The scientific study of mind and cognition also is going to continue to advance and enlarge its scope and domain. The question is: will psychology research, and by implication neuropsychology research, continue to play a significant role in the cognitive sciences? In order for it to do so, we are clearly going to have to adapt to the realization that we are no longer the sole, nor even the major, examiners of the mind, brain, and behavior. We must accept the reality that science will continue to explore mind and brain with or without psychologists. You may have noticed that I left behavior out of the last sentence. That was done quite purposefully, for I feel that where science will suffer without psychology is in the investigation of behavior. The study of mind and brain through measurable behavior will remain the area in which psychology research must retain its identity and heritage in order to interact significantly with the rest of the scientific world.

The major adhesive binding psychology together in the twenty-first century must be the same substance that provided the bond during the twentieth century—namely, the scientific study of behavior. The core agenda for psychology that we continually "rediscover," following the amnesia caused by each successive revolution in our discipline, is the study of behavior. Every time a new paradigm in psychological research takes over, it makes us forget that the prior paradigm also sought to explore behavior and developed ways to do this that could be adopted easily by the new regime. Unfortunately, like the little flash pen in the movie *Men in Black* that used a light force to erase the recent memory of encounters with extraterrestrial aliens, the brilliance of each new generation wipes clean the slate of prior research on behavior. To the surprise of no one who has straddled two or more revolutions, the same questions about behavior re-emerge and eventually have to be addressed. Why no one cites the previous regimes' solutions to these dilemmas is obvious: the group mentality is totally amnesic. That shouldn't mean that psychology is totally doomed—just that it is doomed to constantly replay the same scenario as Bill Murray did in the movie *Groundhog Day*. But enough references to the movie industry. The fact that we've already seen this plot is irrelevant. The question is what are we going to do about it and where do we go from here.

First, foremost, and undoubtedly the most difficult thing for us as psychologists to accept is that our subject matter is, and always has been, behavior. One reason this is hard to acknowledge is because of the many negative connotations that have come to be associated with the term "behaviorism." In the general public's view, the term invokes thoughts of manipulation and control. For many psychologists, the term evokes even stronger negative feelings because of the heavy-handed treatment afforded mid-twentieth century investigators who desired to study aspects of behavior other than those that are overt and observable. It is time for us to make a conscious decision to rid ourselves of these prejudices and recommit to the study (not control) of all indices of behavior (not just overt) using whatever means of investigation or proof we can harness.

I use the word "harness" instead of "control," because I had already used "control" as a negative referent earlier in the sentence. What I really mean by "harness" *is* control in the old experimental psychology definition of the term: the isolation of a behavioral variable and the study of the effects of change induced by the introduction of a well-controlled factor into the environment of that variable. This can continue to be done in the neuropsychology laboratory, in the clinical laboratory, under the microscope of the imaging system, or in the world at large.

What has to be emphasized is that the variable under investigation is the behavior of the organism or behavioral change of the organism: not the blood flow, not the sugar uptake, not the electrical activity, not the computer simulation, not the transportation in time or space (if it comes to that), but the behavior. If we lose that as the focus, then we lose psychology. I'm enlarging the concept of behavior to include cognition, feelings, intelligence, motives, and whatever else anyone wants to define as mentation. I also am stating that behavior is not amenable to reductionism, because observation on a level below behavior is not the province of psychology. Many neuropsychologists may choose to look for explanations below the level of behavior, but until, and unless, the study of behavior is unequivocally demonstrated to reside on one of these reductionist levels, the study of macroforms of behavior must continue. The description of new, emergent behaviors must always occur prior to attempts at a reductionist analysis.

While scientists who conduct reductionistic, micro-level research focus on questions of "how" a behavior occurs, behaviorally focused scientists conducting macro-level research ask "why" a particular behavior occurs. In fact, micro-levels of analysis are restricted to the "how" of behavior even when scientists imagine they are investigating the "why." For example, investigators using neural imaging sometimes write that the reason "why" implicit and explicit memory are independent is because different areas of the brain "light up" when implicit and explicit memory tasks are being performed. This is not at all an explanation of "why" the two memory systems are independent. Brain anatomy and the associated behaviors do not evolve outside of the environmental context of the organism.

Thus, I believe that any understanding of "why" implicit and explicit memory systems are independent requires an understanding of humankind's behavior (i.e., humankind's interactions with the environment and the need to survive in that environment). Neuronal migration to separate regions of the brain must have occurred as an adaptation to an environmental demand for separation. I am arguing here for the primacy of behavior in understanding the organism and its evolution. The study of behavior separate from the neuroanatomy of the brain depends on this belief. The continued evolution of our species probably depends on this belief as well. The continuation of psychology as an independent discipline in the study of mind and brain surely depends on this belief in the primacy of behavior as a unit of study.

As previously mentioned, we need to accept that psychologists are not the only scientists studying the mind and brain. We have to let go of the desire to incorporate each new advance in science and technology into our armament and let other disciplines have those technologies to themselves. Some individual psychologists may leave the nest and go live with these other scientific disciplines (e.g., biochemistry, neuroanatomy, mathematics); some may be lured by technology (e.g., Magnetic Resonance Imaging, virtual reality, genetic cloning). Let them go! They have been trained to study behavior scientifically. Let them use whatever instrumentation they desire to continue this investigation, but, don't let them make the discipline of psychology feel guilty about not including their specialty in the textbooks of future generations. One could scarcely imagine that engineers working with imaging are going to have a chapter on behavior in their textbooks.

Psychology as a discipline does not have to use imaging technology to advance its study of behavior. If imaging studies add to our understanding of the way people behave, that will be fantastic. Based on our own, already acquired knowledge of behavior and research paradigms, it is more likely that psychology will aid the engineer in developing paradigms to study artificial intelligence and machine "behaviors" than that engineering will provide the models for understanding human beings. This alignment will be true throughout the twenty-first century and, hopefully, well beyond. Psychologists have to become convinced that we exist independently of other scientific endeavors and that we can survive alongside these other fields in the investigation of mind and brain.

The final change that must occur to ensure the survival of psychological research in the twenty-first century is one of attitude. We have to become more attuned and responsive to the needs and desires of society. Psychology, as a discipline, is already quite sensitive to these ever-evolving demands, so some reading this paragraph will bristle at my statement that we must become even more aware. The fact remains, however, that research psychologists generally shy away from study of these essentially uncontrolled and uncontrollable environments. Large global descriptive studies and lengthy outcome studies are performed by some psychologists in response to issues in the "real world," but the controlled investigations of isolated single variables or concepts are, at best, still just "simulations" in the university laboratory.

Ulric Neisser has often encouraged psychologists to do naturalistic, ecologically relevant studies, but what I am advocating is that psychology begin to consciously reward these attempts with bona fide endorsements for those who attempt them. In today's academic marketplace, we are all extremely aware that the ultimate reward of tenure is based largely on quantity of accomplishment. This demands that mini-experiments be performed in settings where success is guaranteed. Thus, investigators feel compelled to have several small lines of investigation occurring simultaneously in their controlled laboratory environment, each designed with some guarantee of success, eliminating any wasted effort that does not culminate in a publication.

Psychology departments need to declare that an individual's research is important and relevant. They must reward that individual with time off from teaching and support for tenure, even when the research is unfunded and the results modest. The probability of acquiring funding from a public or private granting agency, especially for the very young investigator, is very low. A commitment to support a particular line of research needs to be made by the department and tenure committee at the start of a young investigator's career. In this way, young investigators would feel the support required to make these commitments to tenure-risky, but professionally-sound and societally-relevant research.

Academic psychologists also need to adopt specific agendas of applied research or training that will come to characterize their departments as distinct entities. I am definitely an intruder when it comes to giving advice to psychology departments since I have worked outside academia most of my career. But, as one who looks in frequently, as a sort of "peeping Laird," I have always wondered why psychology departments seem to have no other apparent mission than simply teaching students. It seems logical that psychology departments ought to have specific areas of focus. I realize that several do have such agendas, but far too few have any focus at all. What I am suggesting is that each psychology department ought to have a distinct role in the academic and/or non-academic community. If the college is enmeshed in an environment where alcoholism is a problem, this behavior ought to be researched by as many members of the department in as many ways as possible—neuropsychologically, developmentally, statistically, through attitudes, learning styles, family values, and expectations—and, if possible, clinical interventions should be introduced. Departments of psychology in the twenty-first century need to be relevant, focused, and committed.

Just as a fanciful aside, the department to which I want to be attached during my reincarnation in the year 2050 is one that studies all aspects of the effects of playing soccer on late child and adult development: level of academic skills as a function of number of successful "first touches," adjustment to marriage as a function of the number of "assists," level of accomplishment in the workplace as a function of number of goals scored, cognitive skills correlated with number of "headers," risk-taking as a function of position played, creative ability as a function of successful "breakaways," leadership potential as a function of number of "shutouts as goalie," criminal involvement as a function of the number of steals, and so on.

I realize that I am sounding like the aging hippie that I am when preaching a mandate for relevance; it was easier to have this feeling as a research psychologist during the 1960s. This was a time of great awakening, a time of questioning authority, and a time of creating new systems. We knew we were relevant because we were among similar voices for change. We were the ones to bring the principle of empiricism in philosophy and science to bear on the issues of cognition, and the whole world waited for our findings. The standards of those days were largely dictated by what we felt was moral, and justification for any research was sufficient if it favored freethinking and creativity. Psychological research just fit right into the zeitgeist.

But now, at the turn of the twenty-first century, all research has to be justified against standards of profitability and risk–benefit ratios. Against those challenges, we have no possible platform upon which to stand. We need to be measured against some other greater good, and until society returns to the values espoused soon after the midpoint of the century, psychology is going to appear to be irrelevant. But, as I always tell my students and kids, the pendulum will swing, and what goes around comes around. We have to be ready to play when our turn comes up, and it will come up. Will we be ready, or will we have conformed so entirely to the economic exigencies of the times that we are unprepared? We can build our bridge to the century on a foundation determined by the economic situation, or we can build it from materials that have proven valuable in the past. Either way, we need to start building before reaching the abyss.

None of this bothers me very much because I know I won't exist far into the twenty-first century or, if I do, I won't be able to remember any of my own personal past by then. Many of my younger colleagues and students will still be here, however, and I would hate for them to discover that the principles originally established by psychologists were no longer *within* a discipline called psychology. Clearly, this is going to happen unless those of us working at the cusp of the field begin constructing our own bridge into the twenty-first century (we can't use President Clinton's bridge—too crowded with bandwagons). This bridge has to be constructed using materials and methods forged during this century.

Maybe I feel this necessity more strongly than others because the sub-discipline I represent within psychology began during my professional lifetime, has a journal that will begin the new century under my tutelage, and because the discipline is already so strongly aligned with the study of brain function. Neuropsychology as a sub-discipline probably characterizes the schizophrenic character of psychology, containing both the drive to morph into a more basic neuroscience field and the drive to retain its individuality as a sub-discipline of psychology. I fully realize that the very nature of neuropsychology is to move in the direction of ever-increasing collaborative efforts with other members of the neuroscience community. In our quest to answer questions concerning the relationship of behavior to brain structure and function, we all feel a need to collaborate with experts in other fields. This is surely a prerequisite to continued progress in the frontiers of neuroscience. In these interactions, neuropsychologists have not played a secondary or purely supportive role. Instead, in most instances, they have been the prime movers of the research.

We have to realize, however, that the one treasure we bring to this endeavor is our history of developing and utilizing careful, rational, methodologicallyprecise research paradigms for the study of *behavior*. We cannot lose sight of the fact that we play a significant role in formulating the important questions and providing the correct methods for answering these questions. This is our legacy, and we should retain it. Technologies that utilize direct exploration of brain activity should not be dismissed from the pages of our journals; however, they must be scrutinized and judged on the basis of the extent to which the question that is asked concerns *behavior* and that question is the focus of the report. In the absence of a focus on behavior, technological advances will be of secondary importance in twenty-first-century neuropsychological research.

To reiterate the primary message of this small essay, neuropsychologists must ensure that their hypotheses about brain–behavior relationships go beyond neuroanatomical descriptions and, instead, are based on sound psychological principles and methodology. Behaviors, already painstakingly defined through psychological methodology, can gain further credibility by their association with neuroimaging insights. However, neuroanatomical corroboration should be viewed only as further evidence in support of what has already been discovered through psychological methods. The absence of neuroanatomical confirmation should not be taken as an indication that our methods and conclusions are faulty; rather, this may simply indicate technological delay or imprecision.

In short, we must continue to support the elevated status of behavioral research based on our time-honored ability to construct experimental paradigms. Technology must serve our discipline; we do not serve technology.

19

From a Decade of the Brain to a Century of the Brain
Neuropsychology and the Alleviation of Disability

Anthony Y. Stringer

The Decade of the Brain

*I*n a joint resolution of its two chambers, the U.S. Congress declared the decade beginning January 1, 1990, to be the "Decade of the Brain." Implicit in this declaration was recognition of both the great need of persons with brain-based disabilities and of the incredible potential for new discoveries in the neurosciences—discoveries that were thought to have the potential to transform the lives of the neurologically impaired.

In signing his own Decade of the Brain Proclamation, then-President George H. Bush asserted America's "determination to conquer brain disease." Americans love that word "determination." We think we can do anything, as long as we are determined. As a nation, we never seem to learn the contrary lessons that history tries to teach us.

How have we actually done with all this American determination during the Decade of the Brain? If we look at the basic neuroscience research conducted in the 1990s, we did not do too badly. For example, research in the 1990s showed us that learning and memory in mice can be enhanced through altering the NMDA receptor gene (Tang et al., 1999), and that the adult nervous system in both monkeys (Gould, Reeves, Graziano, & Gross, 1999) and humans (Eriksson et al., 1998) continues to manufacture new neural cells.

Advancement in the science of neurorehabilitation, however, has not been as evident as the advances in the basic neurosciences. If we take a serious look at the reports prepared by Randall Chesnut and others (Chesnut et al., 1999) on the efficacy of rehabilitation, we have reason to be worried about how rehabilitation has fared in the Decade of the Brain. The evidence for the efficacy of rehabilitation is not overwhelming. Although most neuropsychologists would assert, based on personal experience, that rehabilitation does improve patient functioning, demonstrating this efficacy under the dispassionate and scrupulous eye of the scientist is a daunting task.

One conclusion you can take from Chesnut's work is that we need to methodically investigate the efficacy of our rehabilitation techniques; however, we should be worried about the efficacy question. If our rehabilitation techniques were as potent as we might like to believe, it would not be so hard to find a clear and scientifically valid demonstration of their efficacy. We should be worried just a bit, because even when the evidence favors the efficacy of rehabilitation, the outcomes are still "underwhelming."

While our treatments are almost always better than nothing, many of them are only slightly better than nothing. Therefore, in addition to our efforts to demonstrate the efficacy of the rehabilitation techniques of today, we need to put as much or more energy into developing and studying the efficacy of the rehabilitation techniques of tomorrow. I am heartened by the findings coming out of the neuroscience laboratories in the United States (where we had the audacity to declare a Decade of the Brain) and around the world that suggest we are on the verge of something quite significant.

Anne-Lise Christensen has observed that brain injury is the preeminent health problem of the twentieth century. The case for this claim is easy to make. Two world wars, the advent of the automobile, and the explosion of urban violence in Western countries, especially in the cities of the United States, have thrust this health problem upon us. Thus, it is perhaps fitting that the United States closed out the twentieth century by declaring a Decade of the Brain.

But if the 1990s were, in fact, a Decade of the Brain, they were only a prelude to what is to come. I invite you to join me in the even more audacious proposal that this, the twenty-first century, will be a Century of the Brain. In this century, the neurosciences will eclipse even the physical sciences in their propensity for adding to the collective knowledge and wisdom of human beings. I invite you to join me on a speculative tour of what "might be" in the coming decades.

Prevention of Disability

A fairly obvious place to look for advancement in the new century is in the prevention of brain injuries. Most work on prevention has been done from a social and automotive engineering framework. By social engineering, I mean such steps as lowering the maximum speed limit on the expressways, requiring a driving safety course for teenagers prior to issuing their driving permits, teaching about the consequences of drunk driving in our schools, and so on. All of these steps are important in reducing fatality and injury, and they should be pursued. All of these things help, but only up to a point. Young males who are old enough to drive and to drink most likely will continue to have car accidents no matter how much effort we put into these preventative social policies. While social engineering is important in preventing brain injury, we will not find any major breakthroughs in this arena in the new century.

Automotive engineers will continue to make cars safer, but also only up to a point. Using today's materials and technology, I suspect that any automotive engineer could sit down at the computer and design a car that would keep us safe from injury in most of the crash scenarios that are likely to occur on our streets and highways. What limits the safety of cars is not the engineering but rather the cost of manufacturing. A car manufacturer does not want the engineers to just design safe cars; a manufacturer wants the engineers to design cars that are safe and that the average customer can afford. There is a tradeoff between safety and affordability, and this tradeoff limits the extent to which our cars can protect us from ourselves. This is not to say that advances in car safety will not continue to be made. I assert, however, that the major advances in brain injury prevention are not going to come through automotive engineering because of the price of such advances. In the new century, the significant advances in brain injury prevention, or more accurately stated, in the prevention of brain injury disability, will come in the form of neuroprotection.

Brain injuries do not occur in a vacuum. They happen to a brain that has a history and a context. Research is identifying a number of pre-injury factors that are neuroprotective. Education, age, sex, and overall health play a role in how an individual brain responds to neurotrauma. Youthfulness, healthiness, higher educational attainment, whether one is male or female, and whether the brain has suffered previous insult all affect the brain's response to an injury. The neuropsychologist Paul Satz (1993) has proposed that the brain has a reserve capacity based on these factors. This reserve capacity moderates the brain's ability to respond to and recover from trauma. Trauma eats away at this reserve capacity, but if we are high in reserve capacity to begin with, we are to some degree protected from the trauma. Understanding how neuroprotective factors work is the key to making progress in the prevention of many of the deleterious consequences of brain injury.

Researchers have made the most progress in understanding how sex and age can be neuroprotective factors. Groswasser, Cohen, and Keren (1998) examined the effect of sex on outcome in 334 consecutive admissions for brain injury to the Lowenstein Rehabilitation Hospital in Israel. Males outnumbered females 3 to 1 in their sample, but there were no differences in age or severity of injury (based on duration of unconsciousness) for their male and female groups. Their data showed that, after injury, females were more likely to return to work or school at their previous level while males were more likely to be working at a lower level. Males were also more likely than females to be unemployable subsequent to brain injury.

There are many problems with these data. It is possible, given the realities of Israeli society, that prior to injury, the males were in more intellectually or physically demanding occupations and consequently may have faced a greater challenge when attempting to return to work. Duration of unconsciousness may not do an adequate job of capturing the severity of brain injury, and it certainly does not take into account other injuries such as long-bone fractures that may have played a role in determining outcome. Hence, we do not know for sure that the males and females were matched in the severity of their injury. But even with its methodological limitations, the Israeli study still provides a strong suggestion that females may have a post-injury advantage.

We see the same female advantage in rats as they recover from experimentally induced brain injuries, and the advantage of studying this phenomenon in rats is that we can tease out what accounts for the female advantage. Donald Stein and his colleagues at Rutgers University (Roof, Duvdevani, & Stein, 1993) investigated the development of post-injury edema in rat brain tissue. Male rats have the most edema post-injury. Proestrus female rats have less edema, and pseudopregnant females have virtually no edema. These groups line up in terms of how much edema develops after brain damage. They also line up in terms of how much of the sex hormone progesterone circulates through their blood. Male rats, like male humans, have little to no progesterone, proestrus rats have more circulating progesterone, and pseudopregnant rats have the highest level of progesterone.

What happens when you remove the ovaries from female rats and then induce a brain lesion? They develop edema. Giving them estrogen does not alleviate the edema, but giving them either progesterone alone or in combination with estrogen greatly decreases brain edema. Progesterone appears to be neuroprotective and it may account for why female rats and female humans recover better from brain injuries.

Roof, Duvdevani, Heyburn, and Stein (1996) studied the effects of injecting brain-damaged rats with either progesterone or an inert substance (in this case oil). Progesterone injections reduced the amount of edema in both male and female rats, and the effect was evident as early as six hours after brain damage. A difference in amount of edema was still visible three days after the onset of brain damage. This is even stronger evidence of a neuroprotective effect of progesterone and, even more importantly, the effect occurs in both female and male rats.

Finally, to make the necessary link to behavior, Roof, Duvdevani, Braswell, and Stein (1994) showed that brain-injured male rats given an injection of oil had difficulty learning to reach a platform in a water maze. In contrast, brain injured male rats administered an injection of progesterone learned as well as control rats that received sham surgery (i.e., surgery that did not actually result in brain damage). Taken together, these studies suggest that progesterone prevents or decreases edema and this, in turn, has a demonstrable effect on the outcome of brain damage. The next logical step is to replicate these results in humans. Stein has moved his lab from Rutgers to Emory University where he will conduct the first human clinical trial in which progesterone will be compared to the standard use of steroidal agents to treat brain-swelling following injury.

Let us briefly consider the second neuroprotective factor that has been explored in some detail, namely age. Neurotrophic factors or neurotrophins are naturally occurring substances in the central nervous system that stimulate nerve growth.

There are high quantities of neurotrophins in the developing central nervous system, and the levels of these substances drop off as the nervous system ages.

In animal studies (Nieto-Sampedro, Lewis, & Cotman, 1982), brain lesions stimulate the natural release of neurotrophins. Neurotrophins promote the repair and regeneration of nerve cells, and the amount of regeneration correlates with the amount of neurotrophin that is released. There also is a clear age effect. The younger the animal, the more neurotrophin will be released and hence the more neural regeneration after a brain lesion. This is why age may be neuroprotective. A more youthful brain will respond to injury by releasing more naturally occurring, endogenous neurotrophins that promote repair and regeneration of nerve cells, and thus, recovery will be enhanced. An older nervous system will release less neurotrophin and thus needs to be helped along by the injection of exogenous neurotrophin.

Injecting a brain-lesioned animal with exogenous neurotrophins also promotes repair and regeneration of nerve cells (Varon & Conner, 1994). We encounter a problem, however, because neurotrophins do not cross the blood–brain barrier. They must be injected directly into the brain itself. This can be done in animal models of brain injury but cannot ethically be done in human research. Thus, this approach is not yet ready for human clinical trials; however, gene therapy provides a means by which we may move this line of investigation toward a human clinical trial.

Placing a gene that codes for the manufacture of neurotrophins in a harmless viral coating that can cross the blood–brain barrier and infect neuronal cells may increase neurotrophin levels in brain tissue (Hayes & Yang, 1997). This technique has been successful in promoting repair of nerve cells grown in culture. This technique has not been used in vivo, and we are a long way from using it in human clinical trials. In the future, it is highly probable that harmless viruses will be used to inject useful genes into human brain cells to treat a variety of diseases and pathologic conditions. In the decades to come, this technology doubtlessly will be used to induce the human brain to increase production of neurotrophic factors in response to brain injury.

To summarize, what we have seen are two lines of investigation that began with the observation of a difference in recovery in subgroups of brain-damage survivors. This observation led to the identification of neuroprotective factors in animal studies, namely progesterone and neurotrophins. Once these neuroprotective factors are identified, it is just a short step to the design of human clinical trials in which we apply these protective factors to enhance recovery. My prediction is that neuroprotective strategies in the acute care setting will be the major pharmacologic means of preventing brain injury–related disability in the new century.

Neural Implantation

Neural implantation also will become an important technology in the prevention of disability in the future. Studies have been conducted in which fetal brain cells culled from aborted fetuses are implanted in target areas in the brains of Parkinson's disease patients. Anders Björklund (Bjorklund & Lindvall, 1999) at Lund University has shown that such implants survive as long as ten years, continue to produce dopamine, and provide considerable, although variable, symptom relief for some Parkinson's patients.

This research, however, faces serious barriers. First, Björklund noted that it takes tissue from as many as six fetuses to provide an implant for one adult Parkinson's patient. There will never be enough fetal tissue to treat more than a small number of the world's Parkinson's patients. Second, voluntary abortion as a means of birth control continues to be controversial, and using fetal cells obtained in this or any other way poses an ethical quagmire. Consequently, investigators are looking at the possibility of using stem cell implants.

Stem cells are the forerunners of the cells that make up our tissues and organs. They are in abundance in fetuses, but recently they have been found in adult tissues where they become active when an organ is damaged and there is a need for replacement cells. This raises the possibility that stem cells could be obtained from adult donors or perhaps even grown in culture and implanted in organs in order to replace damaged cells.

This line of research will have a tremendous impact on neurodegenerative conditions, particularly conditions such as Parkinson's disease where a specific area of the brain is implicated. Neural implants require stereotactic surgery, and these procedures are inherently invasive and consequently will be used only in severe neurological conditions. The number of such cases, however, is far from trivial. Within the United States alone, there are 4 million cases of Alzheimer's disease, 1.5 million cases of Parkinson's disease, and 0.25 million cases of spinal cord injury that may be helped by advances in stem cell research (Perry, 2000). Results recently were reported from the first human clinical trial of embryonic stem cell transplants funded by the National Institutes of Health since the ban on use of fetal tissue in research was lifted in 1993 (Freed et al., 2001). While only mixed results were found in patients with Parkinson's disease, this situation will change with advances in stem cell technology in the coming decades.

Neuroprosthetics

Let me go on to an area that will be even less familiar to most readers. The word "prosthesis" usually conjures up an image of an artificial limb. In the Century of the Brain, however, we will have to expand our definition of prosthetics to encompass the neuroprosthesis. A neuroprosthesis is an artificial device or system designed to augment or replace a damaged neuronal function. One type of neuroprosthesis, the wearable computer, is already available and will, in the coming decades, grow to be a powerful tool for aiding persons who have cognitive disability.

In the 1980s, two Massachusetts Institute of Technology (MIT) students connected themselves to their computers 24 hours per day, turning into self-proclaimed "cyborgs." Steve Mann, one of these MIT students, is now a professor at the University of Toronto. In 1980, Mann looked like a cyborg. He wore a heavy battery pack on his back to power his computer. His head was encased in a helmet that sprouted antennae, a camera, and a computer screen that obscured much of his face. I suspect (and Mann admits) that he did not date much in those years. Mann evolved, however, as computers became smaller and lighter.

Today, Mann is still a cyborg, but the only outward sign of this is his perpetual pair of sunglasses. They actually are not sunglasses at all; the glasses are tinted not just to screen out excessive light rays but to blot out all of Mann's vision. He cannot see through them. Tiny cameras mounted on the sides of the glasses provide a continuous video stream of what is going on around him. The wearable computer system sends this video image through a wireless connection to the Internet. From there, it is again downloaded to Mann's wearable computer and projected onto the inside lens of the sunglasses. The inside of the pair of glasses is actually a computer monitor screen with a clarity and resolution as good as that of a desktop monitor. Mann views not the real world, but a video image of the world downloaded from the Internet.

Why do such a bizarre thing? Partly, Mann is making a political statement. He wants control of his own visual environment and resents the commercials that litter the urban landscape. When Mann finds something offensive, he can blot it out using a tiny one-handed keyboard that fits in the palm of his hand. He can eliminate an offensive image, leaving that part of his visual environment blank or replacing the offensive image with something more pleasant, such as a waterfall. In addition, once his wearable computer notes that there are certain images Mann does not want to see, it automatically blocks and replaces those images the next time they happen to appear in the world around him. Repression and denial may have just risen to a whole new level.

On the positive side, Mann's wearable computer system augments his natural human abilities. There are many potential uses of these wearable computers. They can give a patient instant access to the personal information he or she needs to remember during the course of a day as well as the wealth of information available over the Internet. They also can provide information about how to perform various tasks such as changing a flat tire or operating a fax machine. Having instant access to information about how to perform such tasks can potentially enhance the employability of a brain injury survivor whose memory impairment makes it difficult for him or her to learn new procedures.

Wearable computers also can provide information in a variety of sensory modalities, projecting words or pictures onto a computer screen or providing the information orally through a speech synthesizer. A three-pound wearable computer with a speech synthesizer can provide vocal commands to guide patients in performing various tasks. These systems become even more powerful when they are paired with cameras. A computer will one day view the environment, recognize the situation in which the patient is in, and prompt the patient with information even before he or she requests it. Future generations of these computers will have face recognition systems and will prompt patients with the name and background of the person standing in front of him or her.

The current generation of wearable computers can receive signals from the Global Positioning Satellite System to determine a person's current position and to map out directions to the person's destination. The computer can then guide the person to the destination. On a less ambitious scale, systems can be designed that receive signals from transponders scattered throughout a building. The system then uses these signals to guide a person from one location to another within a building itself. Systems such as these can obviously enhance a neurological patient's ability to travel independently from one location to another.

In the past, it has been difficult to nearly impossible for brain-injured patients to learn to use such computer aids. What will work with one patient will not work with another, and flexibility in the system is crucial. The current generation of wearable computers is much more flexible compared to the aids that have been available in the past. They can take input from a keyboard or a touch screen. Systems can be designed that are voice activated—they respond to verbal queries made by the patient. Through the use of artificial intelligence programs, systems can learn the cues that are most effective with a given patient and tailor cueing accordingly.

Let me go on to another, even more dramatic type of neuroprosthetic device by describing an experiment conducted at Hahnemann University in Philadelphia by John Chapin, a neurobiologist who is currently at the Downstate Health Science Center in Brooklyn, New York. In this study (Chapin, Moxon, Markowitz, & Nicolelis, 1999), a thirsty rat learned to depress a lever that moved a robotic arm into position to deliver a drop of water to the rat. A computer monitored brain electrical activity in the rat via 24 electrodes implanted in its frontal cortex. The computer eventually discerned a pattern of brain activity that reliably occurred just prior to the rat reaching for the lever. Once this pattern of activity was identified, the lever was disconnected so that it no longer moved the robotic arm. Now the computer controlled the robotic arm. The computer monitored the brain for the occurrence of the target activity pattern, and as soon as it was detected, the computer moved the robotic arm just as if the lever had been pressed, delivering water to the thirsty rat. The rat's brain activity was now driving the lever.

Several of the rats in the experiment seemed to have the equivalent of an "ah-ha" experience. Their eyes suddenly became wide, they looked startled, and then they stopped lever-pressing and learned to move the robotic arm by making the target brain activity. A team led by Miguel A. L. Nicolelis (Wessberg et al., 2000) at Duke University has obtained similar results with a different research paradigm using owl monkeys. This is more than just good news for lazy rats and monkeys that cannot be bothered with having to press levers for their food and water. This has implications for the rehabilitation of human beings.

Let me move again to Emory University in Atlanta to describe the work of bio-engineer Phillip Kennedy and the neurosurgeon Roy Bakay (Kennedy & Bakay, 1998). Kennedy has designed an electrode that can be implanted chronically in the human frontal cortex. The electrode has a hollow tip that contains a neurotrophic factor or, in other words, a chemical that encourages local neurons to sprout axonal extensions and grow into the tube where they make an electrical contact. These electrodes have been implanted in three patients diagnosed with locked-in syndrome. This syndrome results from damage to the descending corticospinal tract at the level of the pons. It leaves patients totally paralyzed with respect to voluntary movements, although some will have reliable control over some basic facial movements such as eyeblinks. These patients are alert, able to take in visual and auditory information, and may be cognitively intact, but are locked-in by their paralysis. Their only means of communicating with the outside world is often through a series of coded eyeblinks.

All three patients at Emory survived the implantation of the electrodes. The first patient died after 76 days due to complications of her underlying disease. The surgery itself was successful, however, and stable electrical signals could be recorded from the electrode implanted in her motor cortex. Even more importantly, this patient was able to turn the signal from the electrode on and off voluntarily. In other words, when presented with visual or auditory feedback that told her whether or not the electrode was recording activity, this patient learned to control the firing of the neurons that had grown into the electrode. Through essentially a biofeedback paradigm, she learned to turn the activity of those neurons on and off. The third patient has only recently had the surgery and results have not yet been reported. I will concentrate on the published results of the second patient that underwent this procedure.

The second patient developed the locked-in syndrome after a brainstem stroke in December 1997. He has some facial movement but cannot speak. His eye movements are dysconjugate. He is alert and is judged to be intact cognitively. About 20 days after implantation, neural signals could be recorded from the electrode indicating that neurons had grown into the tip. These signals became reliable and stable at about three-months post-surgery, and they remain so to this day with more than a year having passed since the surgery. At first the signals appeared in association with movements—mouth and tongue movements and later eye and eyebrow movements. After the fifth post-surgical month, the signals were no longer accompanied by any movements under the patient's voluntary control.

In the experiments done with this patient, visual and auditory feedback is provided to let the patient know the rate at which the neurons that have grown into the electrode are firing. This same biofeedback signal also lets the patient know the amplitude of the signal coming from the neurons. The computer monitors the activity of the electrode in a manner that allows increases in neuronal firing rate to move the computer cursor. The cursor stops moving when the firing rate decreases. A low amplitude signal from the electrode moves the cursor from left to right, and a high amplitude signal moves the cursor from top to down on the screen. The monitor screen displays a virtual keyboard so that the patient can type words that then are converted into speech by a speech synthesizer. Virtual buttons also can appear on the screen so that if the cursor is moved to a button and remains there for two seconds, the speech synthesizer will utter a phrase for the patient.

Using this feedback procedure, the patient reported by Kennedy and Bakay (1998) learned to move to the target buttons relatively quickly in order to get the computer to speak a phrase. Thus, Kennedy and Bakay succeeded in giving this locked-in syndrome patient a reliable means of communicating with the external world. The patient can make his needs known through computer-synthesized speech and can operate environmental controls for the air conditioning, the room lights, and so on. There is even hope that someday this patient will be able to send an e-mail message. This is still a very crude technology, but it is a first step in the direction of creating a neuroprosthesis—a device under direct neural control that can perform an activity that the brain and body can no longer perform.

Neuropsychological Assessment in the Century of the Brain

From the foregoing, it should be clear that the next few decades will see a leap in our ability to alleviate suffering and lessen disability in persons who have neurological diseases or disorders. The leap in technology will necessitate a change in the practice of neuropsychology. The traditional functions served by neuropsychological testing have included lesion detection, lateralization, and localization. These have become less important as neuroradiologic procedures have advanced from the now archaic pneumoencephalography to modern Magnetic Resonance Imaging.

Functional neuroimaging is a fairly recent technology that requires a close connection with neuropsychology. An image of the brain at rest is not that exciting. Resting Positron Emission Tomography or Magnetic Resonance Imaging scans certainly have their uses, but the really promising work combines functional neuroimaging with an activity. Getting a picture of the brain as it carries out various tasks promises to revolutionize our understanding of brain–behavior relationships and to extend our diagnostic capabilities. There is a need for a battery of neuropsychological tasks designed specifically for use during functional neuroimaging. There are many such tasks in the literature already, but to my awareness, no one has taken on the challenge of standardizing, norming, and validating these tasks. When someone does accomplish this, in effect creating a neuropsychological neuroimaging battery, we will have taken a big step into the future.

The new technologies for alleviating suffering and disability will at first be scarce and hard to access. As with all scarce resources, we will have to use them where they can do the most good. Thus, we must be prepared to identify the patients most likely to benefit from these procedures. Neuropsychological testing, with its sensitivity to human function, will be a powerful tool in the fair and sensible matching of patients to procedures.

Costly or risky new technologies must be justified in terms of their benefit to individuals and society. We must closely document and examine outcomes, not only to get insurance reimbursement for what we do today, but even more importantly, to justify what we hope to be able to do tomorrow. We have instruments that allow us to measure the impact of disease on quality of life, and some of those instruments contain sections on cognition, but we have no instrument in common use that specifically focuses on the impact of cognitive impairment on quality of life. We can conduct a literature search to find the impact of renal disease on quality of life but would search in vain for an article that can tell us, in quality-adjusted life years, the impact of having an executive function disorder. We need instruments that allow us to determine not just health-related, but also cognition-related, quality of life. Neuropsychologists, in partnership with health economists, must address this need as new technologies emerge.

Even before we can measure outcome and quality of life, there is much we must learn about the epidemiology of cognitive disorders. We know the incidence of brain injury and stroke both within and across national boundaries, but we have little knowledge of the epidemiology of so-called secondary conditions—that is, conditions that follow or are secondary to a primary disease process. This lack of information is particularly apparent when those conditions are cognitive disorders. We do not know, for example, how many patients exhibit agnosia, disinhibition, perseveration, and so on.

Part of the reason we lack this information is that neuropsychologists, at least in the United States, tend to think in numerical distributions rather than in terms of diagnostic categories. Epidemiology deals with diagnostic categories, and we need to think in those terms if we are to collect information on the incidence and prevalence of cognitive disorder. It is difficult to get insurance reimbursement in the United States for cognitive rehabilitation not just because of the limited data on its efficacy but also because society is unaware of just how many cognitively impaired people exist and struggle with "invisible" disabilities. I would make a strong argument for descriptive classificatory approaches to neuropsychological assessment and diagnosis in the future.

The Future of Neuropsychology: The Revolution That Must Be

Let me close with this final thought. This book opened by reviewing the history of neuropsychology and finding evidence for an evolution of the field to its present state. We found little evidence for anything that could unambiguously be called a revolution. Revolutions are taking place, however, in the neurosciences, and they will drive revolutions in neurorehabilitation as well. The developing technologies of the new century also will "revolutionize" the care of persons with disabilities. They even may banish the word "disability" from our vocabulary. For this reason alone, I think it not too audacious to dub the twenty-first century the Century of the Brain.

To stay vital in the new century, neuropsychological assessment also needs a revolution. What that revolution will be is difficult to say, but I suspect it will be a fundamental change in the way we assess human functioning. For example, it is not enough to just keep re-norming our intelligence tests. Nor is it enough to churn out new personality tests that find new ways of asking patients and relatives to tell us about behaviors that we cannot directly measure. We must face the fact that there is nothing particularly exciting about the prospect of a Wechsler Adult Intelligence Scale IV or a Minnesota Multiphasic Personality Inventory III. We must find a better way of characterizing and assessing what it means to be intelligent, and we must find a direct way of measuring behavioral tendencies and personality traits at a physiological level. This could lead to a true revolution in the science and practice of neuropsychology.

Our field may need an Einstein for this revolution to occur. I hope not, because as much as I respect my contemporaries in neuropsychology, I confess that I do not know any that measure up to this standard. But like it or not, and ready or not, the Century of the Brain will demand revolutions from us if neuropsychology as a science and a profession is not to go the way of the dinosaurs. While we lack an Albert Einstein in neuropsychology, perhaps we will find in our collective wisdom and effort the means to remain a part of this exciting century to come.

REFERENCES

Bjorklund, A., & Lindvall, O. (1999). Transplanted nerve cells survive and are functional for many years. *Lakartidningen, 96,* 3407–3412.

Chapin, J. K., Moxon, K. A., Markowitz, R. S., & Nicolelis, M. A. (1999). Real-time control of a robot arm using simultaneously recorded neurons in the motor cortex. *Nature Neuroscience 2,* 664–670.

Chesnut, R. M., Carney, N. C., Maynard, H., Mann, N. C., Patterson, P., & Helfand, M. (1999). Summary report: Evidence for the effectiveness of rehabilitation for persons with traumatic brain injury. *Journal of Head Trauma Rehabilitation, 14,* 176–188.

Eriksson, P. S., Perfilieva, E., Bjork-Eriksson, T., Alborn, A. M., Nordborg, C., Peterson, D. A., & Gage, F. H. (1998). Neurogenesis in the adult human hippocampus. *Nature Medicine, 4,* 1313–1317.

Freed, C. R., Greene, P. E., Breeze, R. E., Tsai, W.-Y., DuMouchel, W., Kao, R., Dillon, S., Windfield, W., Culver, S., Trojanowski, J. Q., Eidelberg, D., & Fahn, S. (2001). Transplantation of embryonic dopamine neurons for severe Parkinson's disease. *The New England Journal of Medicine, 344,* 710–719.

Groswasser, Z., Cohen, M., & Keren, O. (1998). Female TBI patients recover better than males. *Brain Injury, 12,* 805–808.

Gould, E., Reeves, A. J., Graziano, M. S., & Gross, C. G. (1999). Neurogenesis in the neocortex of adult primates. *Science, 286,* 548–552.

Hayes, R. L., & Yang, K. (1997). Gene therapy strategies for treatment of post-acute impairment following injury to the central nervous system. In J. León-Carrión (Ed.), *Neuropsychological rehabilitation* (pp. 173–190). Delray Beach, FL: St. Lucie Press.

Kennedy, P. R., & Bakay, R. A. (1998). Restoration of neural output from a paralyzed patient by a direct brain connection. *Neuroreport, 9,* 1707–1711.

Nieto-Sampedro, M., Lewis, E. R., & Cotman, C. W. (1982). Brain injury causes a time-dependent increase in neuronotrophic activity at the lesion site. *Science, 217,* 860–861.

Perry, D. (2000). Patients' voices: The powerful sound in the stem cell debate. *Science, 287,* 1423.

Roof, R. L., Duvdevani, R., Braswell, L., & Stein, D. G. (1994). Progesterone facilitates cognitive recovery and reduces secondary neuronal loss caused by cortical contusion injury in male rats. *Experimental Neurology, 129,* 64–69.

Roof, R. L., Duvdevani, R., Heyburn J. W., & Stein, D. G. (1996). Progesterone rapidly decreases brain edema: Treatment delayed up to 24 hours is still effective. *Experimental Neurology, 138,* 246–251.

Roof, R. L., Duvdevani, R., & Stein, D. G. (1993). Gender influences outcome of brain injury: Progesterone plays a protective role. *Brain Research, 607,* 333–336.

Satz, P. (1993). Brain reserve capacity on symptom onset after brain injury: A formulation and review of evidence for threshold theory. *Neuropsychology, 7,* 273–295.

Tang, Y. P., Shimizu, E., Dube, G. R., Rampon, C., Kerchner, G. A., Zhuo, M., Liu, G., & Tsien, J. Z. (1999). Genetic enhancement of learning and memory in mice. *Nature, 401,* 63–69.

Varon, S., & Conner, J. M. (1994). Nerve growth factor in CNS repair. *Journal of Neurotrauma, 11,* 473–486.

Wessberg, J., Stambaugh, C. R., Kralik, J. D., Beck, P.D., Laubach, M., Chapin J. K., Kim, J., Biggs, S. J., Srinivasan, M. A., & Nicolelis, M. A. (2000). Real-time prediction of hand trajectory by ensembles of cortical neurons in primates. *Nature, 408,* 361–365.

Biographical Index

For Product Safety Concerns and Information please contact our EU
representative GPSR@taylorandfrancis.com
Taylor & Francis Verlag GmbH, Kaufingerstraße 24, 80331 München, Germany